AF607985

PIERS PLOWMAN AND THE REINVENTION OF CHURCH LAW IN THE LATE MIDDLE AGES

Piers Plowman and the Reinvention of Church Law in the Late Middle Ages

ARVIND THOMAS

UNIVERSITY OF TORONTO PRESS
Toronto Buffalo London

Toronto Buffalo London
utorontopress.com

ISBN 978-1-4875-0246-1

Library and Archives Canada Cataloguing in Publication

Title: Piers Plowman and the reinvention of church law in the late Middle Ages / Arvind Thomas.
Names: Thomas, Arvind, 1972– author.
Description: Includes bibliographical references and index.
Identifiers: Canadiana 20189069384 | ISBN 9781487502461 (hardcover)
Subjects: LCSH: Langland, William, 1330?–1400? Piers Plowman (B-text) | LCSH: Langland, William, 1330?–1400? Piers Plowman (C-text) | LCSH: Canon law in literature. | LCSH: Law, Medieval, in literature. | LCSH: Christian poetry, English (Middle) – History and criticism.
Classification: LCC PR2017.L38 T56 2019 | DDC 821/.1—dc23

This book was published with the generous assistance of a Book Subvention Award from the Medieval Academy of America.

University of Toronto Press acknowledges the financial assistance to its publishing program of the Canada Council for the Arts and the Ontario Arts Council, an agency of the Government of Ontario.

Canada Council for the Arts   Conseil des Arts du Canada

Funded by the Government of Canada   Financé par le gouvernement du Canada   Canada

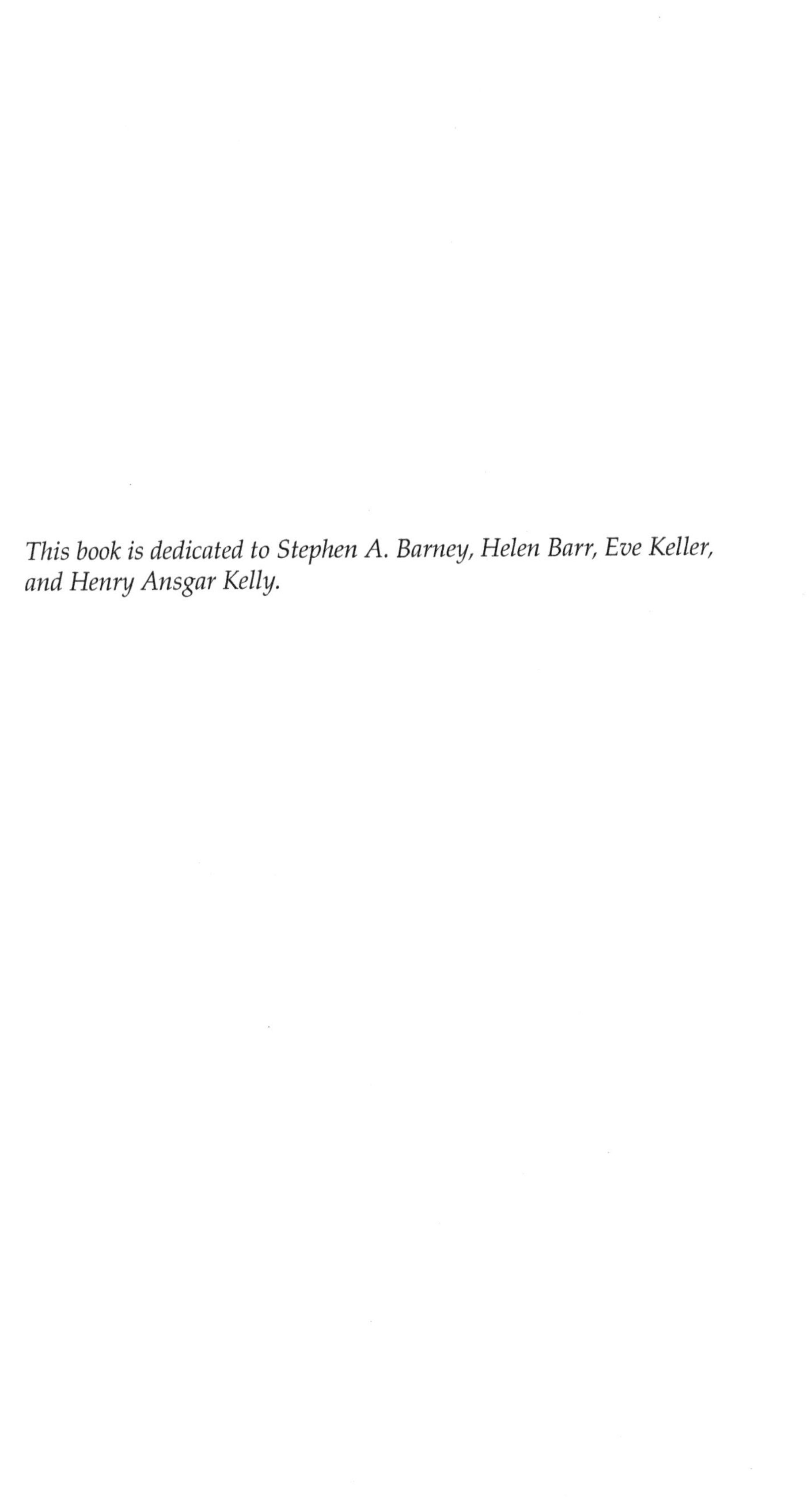

This book is dedicated to Stephen A. Barney, Helen Barr, Eve Keller, and Henry Ansgar Kelly.

Contents

Acknowledgments

This book has been long in the making and I owe much to individuals and institutions in several lands. First among them are the many who had to "swinken with hire handes and laboure" so that I could and can continue to undertake studies such as this. At the schools where I worked on the book, they include not just librarians but also security guards and custodial staff who went out of their way – and often far into the night – to ensure that I always enjoyed a clean office, could access rare books, and would even be transported home. Their tireless and invisible labour enabled the leisure I enjoyed in the making of this book, and to each of them I owe the privilege of writing and owning what should belong to them as well. They include George O. Adams, David Bedford, Richard Cunningham, Charlotte Labbe, Stuart Slutzky, Edward Tuck, David Poepoe, Ligia Alverado, and Marta and her family.

The genesis of this book began in another land at once foreign to and familiar with *Piers Plowman*: India. There I owe much to the poet Arvind Joshi for first introducing me to *Piers Plowman* B in Delhi one summer evening when he read aloud parts of it and discussed its alliterative form. At the University of Delhi, where I read English as an undergraduate, the late Professor H.N. Sanyal taught me much about medieval poetry and prosody, and inspired me to learn Latin and the modern languages that I later found indispensable for writing this book. I offer thanks and gratitude to Professor Ashley Tellis, who trained me to read literary texts both for their aesthetic features and for their socio-political functions. But for Ashley's own form-attentive historicist research and his insistence that *Piers* was a poem, I could not have paid close attention to Langland's poetics and the legal work it did. Also in Delhi, I owe much to Dr Shirshendu Chakrabarty for sharing his deep understanding of the intellectual traditions of premodern literature, and to Dr Tanya Roy for offering feedback on the project in its nascent stages, and assisting me with secondary sources in Italian. Thanks are also due to Tara Devi Roy for feedback on what was to become chapter 3.

The core of this book began during a seminar on *Piers Plowman* that Helen Barr gave at Columbia University, and without her patient and critical commentary long afterwards on early versions of this study, the book would not have taken the form it has. I thank her for being unflagging in her readiness to support the project.

I owe an immense debt to Paul Strohm, whose own writing and teaching radically shaped the book's treatment of the reciprocal relations between law and literature. Paul's influence can be seen in every chapter of the book. Indeed, over the past six years, Paul has contributed more to my writing and thinking process than I can possibly express in words. He has always found the time to lend his great acumen and kindness to the book's many versions. Not only that, Paul went out of his way to ensure that the book found the right publisher.

At Fordham University, I owe Wolfgang P. Mueller a deep debt of gratitude for encouraging me to compare the versions of the poem from the perspective of canonist thought. Wolfgang has consistently been a critical reader of this project, prompting me to engage the original canonical sources closely and to write in a language that historians would understand. I thank him also for always finding the time to discuss the project as it evolved.

I am deeply grateful to Eve Keller, who served as a mentor, and helped me shape the book's conceptual methodology, clarify it in terms of the project's "big picture," and shape an appropriate style. Her practice of form-attentive reading of premodern literature (both in her own scholarly work and in her feedback on individual chapters) has served as a model for the book.

I owe a great debt to Lenny Cassuto, whose graduate mentorship enabled me to stay in academia to work on the book. Although an Americanist, Lenny took a lively interest in the project from the very beginning and advised me throughout the process from book's composition to its final publication. His detailed feedback on the introduction has left a lasting mark on its prose. I have been most fortunate to have in Lenny not just an exemplary writer-friend but also the book's first non-medievalist reader.

My thanks also go to John Bugg, who shared with me both his own book proposals and book manuscripts. John's feedback on the readers' reports on the book manuscript was central to its revision process.

Without the intellectual support from Fordham's CMRS and its former director, Maryanne Kowaleski, I doubt if I could have made much progress in the early stages of my research into law and literature. From the very first day I broached the topic of my book, Maryanne enabled me to present my early research on *Piers* and canon law at conferences and helped me network with medievalists outside of Fordham. I owe her a profound debt of gratitude. Thanks are also due to Jocelyn Wogan-Browne, Mary Erler, Katie Little, and Maria Farland. A special thanks to Susanne Hafner for serving as an early critical reader of the book.

At Oxford, I incurred several debts: they include the staff and librarians in the Bodleian Library but also two non-medievalists interested in *Piers Plowman*: Robert Lemkin and Bridget Anderson. Both Rob and Bridget hosted me more times at Oxford than I can recall, offered enthusiastic encouragement and, above all, always asked sharp questions about Langland and law.

At the University of Toronto, I owe Joseph Goering an immense debt. Joe invited me to present early research for the book at a symposium on rule makers and rule breakers. Joe also hosted me several times, introduced me to late medieval *pastoralia*, offered insightful feedback on early versions of the first three chapters, and responded to innumerable email inquiries about penitential procedure. I thank also John A. Lorenc for permission to use his unpublished edition of John of Freiburg's title *De usuris*.

At Yale University, where amidst teaching I began working on the book in earnest, I had the good fortune of receiving intellectual support from colleagues and friends – many of whom always seemed to find the time for intense conversations about the book's initial evolution. They include John Burden, Ian Cornelius, Alastair Minnis, John Rogers, Heather Klemann, Traugott Lawler, Joseph Stadolnik, and Eric Weiscott. Special thanks are due to Joseph, Traugott, and Alastair for commenting respectively on the introduction, chapter 3, and chapter 5.

As a former colleague and friend, Briallen Hopper served as a timely and thoughtful interlocutor about the project in terms of its big picture. Not only that, she helped me to talk about the project to non-medievalists by both hosting me for several summers in New Haven and arranging meetings with scholars in other fields. I offer her my thanks and gratitude.

My thinking about the conceptual basis of the book was enriched by conversations with Prashant Keshavmurthy. I thank him for his intellectual generosity.

For access to Nicholas Gray's PhD dissertation "A Study of *Piers Plowman* in relation to the Medieval Penitential Tradition," and permission to cite from it, I thank both Dr Gray and the Cambridge University Library. For access to Michael Haren's PhD dissertation "A Study of the *Memoriale presbiterorum,* a Fourteenth Century Confessional Manual for Parish Priests," and to Leonard E. Boyle's PhD dissertation "A Study of the Works attributed to William of Pagula," I thank the Bodleian Library. I am grateful to the Österreichische Nationalbibliothek for supplying manuscripts of John of Freiburg's *Summa confessorum* (Codex 2135) and several copies of the *Liber Sextus*. I offer Penn Szittya my gratitude for sending microfilm reels of the *Omne bonum* (*MS Royal* 6 E. VI and *Royal* 6 E. VII), sharing his latest work on it, and offering encouragement. I am especially indebted to Andrew Galloway for his insightful comments on my treatment of usury in chapter 2 and for his advice on the scope of the book.

No classmate has shaped my intellectual and ethical trajectory more fundamentally than the brilliant medievalist historian Jay Gundacker. I owe him much not just for his critical feedback on chapters one and five but also for suggesting the book's conceptual argument about the co-production of law and literature. I have greatly benefited from his own approach, as a historian, to literary texts, and am grateful for the stimulating conversations on law and literature over vegan meals that he meticulously prepared.

Allen Strouse has generously read several versions of the book manuscript and hosted me more times than I can recall to discuss its gradual evolution, especially Langland's treatment of usury. Allen's perceptive and often challenging comments helped me to clarify the argument of chapter 2, and enliven the introduction. Above all, his commitment to questions of poetics and our numerous conversations on the aesthetics of poetry served as foundation for chapter 5.

At UCLA I have been fortunate to have shared book chapters with, among others, Joseph Falaky Nagy (Józsi), Chris Chism, Matthew Fisher, Eric Jager, and Henry A. Kelly. Józsi generously funded a research assistant to help copyedit an early draft of the book. He and Martha hosted me several times to ensure that the book was completed. Special thanks are due to Chris Chism and Matthew Fisher for offering both crucial advice on and models for responding to readers' reports. The introduction and chapter 4 have benefited from Matthew's detailed feedback. Eric Jager's feedback on the introduction as well as his own recent writing served as models when I revised the style of the introduction. I offer my thanks to him for anticipating and addressing problems faced by a first-time author. I also wish to thank the former Chair of UCLA's English Department, Ali Behdad, for intellectual and departmental support that extended long after he ceased to be Chair. Thanks are due to Carrie Hyde for commenting on the introduction, and to Mead Bowen for editing the introduction and the first two chapters. Others who served as discussants include Arthur Little, Donka Minkova, Chris Baswell, and Debora Shuger. I must thank the current Chair of the English Department, Lowell Gallagher, for his timely and enthusiastic support. I wish to record my thanks to UCLA's Friends of English, the Dean of Humanities, and the Medieval Academy of America for their contributions toward the book-subvention.

Thanks are due to Rick Fagin, Feng Huang, and Jeanette Gilkinson, who, along with Bronson Tran, never tired of printing out drafts of the book at short notice. Thanks are due to Lynda Tolly for offering advice and enabling me to take full advantage of the library resources of the English Reading Room. I will remain indebted to Janet Bishop, without whose timely intervention I might not have survived to write the book in the first place.

I wish particularly to mention my partner Dharmada Kerstin Knuepfer's patience, love, and moral support that I received at every stage of the revision process: helping with the German translations, and, above all, tirelessly prompting me to get the book done for the press.

I must thank my parents for their unstinting support of my literary wanderings all these years. Thanks are also due to my brothers – Vivek and Arun – for their affectionate support. I owe a profound debt to Anthony Sorge as well as to Caitlin, and Ben in my extended family of fellow activists for human and non-human animals for inviting me to share my research for the book on several occasions.

The labour of revising the book for copy editing was tremendously lightened by Hillary Gordon. I could not have finished the project within the scheduled deadline but for her generous and tireless feedback on innumerable drafts and for also copy editing the book. Special thanks are due to her for chapter 3, which was substantially rewritten and expanded in its scope in light of her excellent advice.

I thank the two external readers for the University of Toronto Press for their engaged and exhaustive feedback. Special thanks are due to

Suzanne Rancourt for her patience, encouragement, and, above all, for ensuring that the process from submission to publication was smooth and transparent. Although Miriam Skey arrived last on the scene, she has indeed been the book's first fresh reader: her feedback and quiet patience, and the indefatigable energy with which she has had to handle substantial last-minute revisions, have made this book better than it otherwise would have been. I am grateful to her and her team at UTP.

There are finally the book's four dedicatees – Stephen A. Barney, Helen Barr, Eve Keller, and Henry Ansgar Kelly – to whose "kynde knowying" I am most profoundly indebted. They have generously commented on several versions of the book and accompanied it from its earliest iterations to its final articulation. In many ways, the final version of the book emerged in the light or shadow of Professor Kelly's deep knowledge of the *Corpus iuris canonici* and its surrounding apparatus and, if the book succeeds in its argument, the credit should go to him and to the legacy of his own scholarship. I am also particularly grateful to Professors Kelly and Barney for promptly and painstakingly going over the Latin transcriptions and translations in the book.

PIERS PLOWMAN AND THE REINVENTION OF CHURCH LAW IN THE LATE MIDDLE AGES

Introduction

One day near the end of September 1396, a certain "cleric and canon," Walter de Brugge, drew up his will.[1] Among the items he recorded was "a book called *Pers Plewman*."[2] Within days he was dead, but that prosaic entry alone has immortalized him for being "the first historically recorded *owner* [and, presumably,] *reader*" of a version of the poem.[3] Walter's other and less memorable holdings that stood with *Piers Plowman* included tomes on canon law (church law) by the canonists Raymond of Peñafort, Hostiensis (Henry of Susa), and William of Pagula.[4] These were, as Walter itemized them, "a book called *Pars oculi*," "a *Summa* of Hostiensis," "a book called the *Summa praelatorum*," "a book called the *Summa summarum*,"[5] and "one pair of the *Decretales* with the

---

1 I adapt Rees Davies's account of the will in "The Life, Travels, and Library," 49. Published in its entirety in the *Testamenta Eboracensia* 1: 207–10, the will describes Walter as "clericus et canonicus" at 207.

2 The copy of *Piers Plowman* is described as "unum librum vocatum Pers Plewman" in *Testamenta Eboracensia* 1: 209. Unless otherwise noted, all translations from the Latin, German, and Italian are my own. In the interests of legibility, transcriptions of the Latin have been slightly modernized.

3 Davies, "The Life, Travels, and Library," 50; emphasis in original.

4 "Church law" or "canon law" (lex canonica) is a complex system that, as the canonist Huguccio explains, "contains a multiplicity of canons in itself or a variety of decisions/decretals, not adverse or contrary but consonant and decorous" (multiplicem in se canonum siue decretorum continens uarietatem; non aduersam uel contrariam, set consonam et decoram), *Summa decretorum*, 3; all quotations from Huguccio's *Summa* are taken from Oldrich Prerovsky's edition.

5 Attributed to William of Pagula, the *Summa summarum*, according to Leonard E. Boyle, "is in fact the only Summa of canon law which the two centuries before the Reformation produced in England ... [and] deserves to take its place with Acton's gloss to the Legatine Constitutions and the Provinciale of Lyndwood," section VII of the prefatory summary to Boyle's unpublished dissertation "A Study of the Works Attributed to William of Pagula."

Liber Sextus."[6] Walter's copy of *Piers Plowman* was to remain in the company of canon law for at least another generation. Bequeathed to the priest John Wormyngton, the poem accompanied William of Pagula's *Pars oculi*, which embodies the canon law on confessional practice as well as general and provincial legislation.[7]

Whether Walter de Brugge and John Wormyngton knew William Langland remains a matter of speculation.[8] What we do know for sure is that poem and canon law joined, or, if you prefer, jostled against, each other beyond Walter's or John's personal libraries. Take, for instance, another near-contemporary copy of *Piers Plowman*: MS 733B. Housed now in the National Library of Wales, this early fifteenth-century manuscript conjoins the A and C versions of *Piers Plowman*: "it was rebound in blind-tooled calf in the first half of the eighteenth century, but retains as flyleaves two cropped leaves from a fourteenth-century manuscript containing a Latin text on canon law, which

---

6 Here are the relevant excerpts from the *Testamenta Eboracensia* 1: 209–10: "Item lego Domino Johanni Wormyngton … unum librum vocatum Pers Plewman, et unum alium librum vocatum Pars Oculi, cum aliis tractatibus in uno volumine … Item lego Magistro Johanni Gorwell consanguineo meo utriusque juris Doctori, unam Summam Hostien'… Item lego Domino Thomae Chaunterell consanguineo meo … unum librum vocatum Speculum Praelatorum … Item lego Roberto Burgeys clerico meo … unum librum vocatum Summa Summarum … Item lego domino Thomae Overton … j par Decretalium cum sexto libro." [Also, I bequeath to Lord John Wormyngton … a book called *Pers Plewman*, and another book called *Pars Oculi*, with other treatises in one volume. Likewise, I bequeath to Master John Gorwell, my cousin and doctor of both laws (canon and civil), a *Summa* of Hostiensis … Also, I bequeath to Lord Thomas Chaunterell, my cousin, a book called *Speculum praelatorum* … Also, I bequeath to Robert Burgeys, my fellow cleric … a book called *Summa summarum* … Also, I bequeath to Lord Thomas Overton … one pair of *Decretals* with the *Sext*].

7 *Testamenta Eboracensia* 1: 209: "Item lego Domino Johanni Wormyngton … unum librum vocatum Pers Plewman, et unum alium librum vocatum Pars Oculi." In his unpublished dissertation "A Study of the Works Attributed to William of Pagula," Boyle notes that the *Pars oculi* is "the first part of the *Oculus sacerdotis*" and that it "was written to enable confessors to examine their penitents thoroughly, to suggest to them appropriate remedies for their moral weaknesses, and to assign salutary penances" (288); Boyle adds that William of Pagula "draws up a fine list of penitential canons and the great catalogue of censures which occupy the central chapters of the *Pars oculi*," and adds that the catalogue is "[b]ased on the general legislation of the church, on the constitutions of the legates Otto and Ottobono for the church of England and on statutes made for the province of Canterbury" (295–6).

8 Scholars such as Oscar Cargill have speculated that "the mansed prest" of "þe march of Ireland" in *Piers Plowman* C 22.221 and in *Piers Plowman* B 20.221 is modelled after Walter de Brugge; see Cargill's "The Langland Myth."

may well be part of the original binding structure."[9] The proximity between poetic and canonistic texts is reflected in an image found in yet another early fifteenth-century copy of *Piers Plowman*: MS Douce 104 that exemplifies the C version of the poem. The verso of folio 109 of this manuscript depicts a priestly figure that, as Katheryn Kerby-Fulton has brilliantly demonstrated, is iconographically analogous to one found in a manuscript version of the canonistic treatise on penance, the *Oculus sacerdotis*, whose first part (*Pars oculi*), we may recall, John inherited from Walter.[10]

We should consider it no coincidence that clerics like Walter de Brugge and John Wormyngton carried and circulated a copy of *Piers Plowman* together with digests of canon law. Nor should we find it unusual that the physical production of another copy of the poem included canonistic materials. Likewise, we need not dismiss as accidental that an anonymous "professional reader" of the poem's C version drew an illustration that resembled one found in a Latin handbook on the canon law of penance intended for parish priests.[11] In this study, I shall argue that poetic and canonistic compositions have everything to do with each other – not just materially but also conceptually.

This book draws from Walter de Brugge's bequest, MS 733B's binding, and MS Douce 104's illustration an interpretive principle: namely, that *Piers Plowman* was composed with such canonistic treatises on penance in mind as those that circulated with some of the poem's earliest copies. Such a hermeneutic view reconceptualizes the art of poetry as sharing in the craft of law-making and acknowledges the poet as a penitential

9 These words are cited from the description of the manuscript found on the National Library of Wales' website: https://www.llgc.org.uk/en/discover/digital-gallery/manuscripts/the-middle-ages/piers-plowman/, accessed 31 October 2017. No scholar – not even Lawrence Warner, who is currently editing MS 733B – has as yet been able to identify the canonistic text. Warner argues that MS 733B attests in part to "the first edition of the C version of the poem" (6); see his "The Ur-B *Piers Plowman.*"

10 Kerby-Fulton and Despres, *Iconography and the Professional Reader*, 19–20. Kerby-Fulton identifies the copy of the *Oculus sacerdotis* as MS 290, Hatfield House, Cecil Papers.

11 The expression "professional reader" is Kerby-Fulton's; she defines such readers as "those whose job it was to make decisions on behalf of the medieval reader about how the text should go down on the page – *conscious* decisions, that is, about editing, annotating, correcting, rubricating, or illustrating a text"; see "Professional Readers of Langland at Home and Abroad," 103.

legislator in a world shaped by both poetry and law.[12] Unravelling lateral rather than hierarchical relations between the poem and canon law digests, this study retrieves a "textual community" different from that reconstructed by those thinking through Brian Stock's influential concept of readership.[13] Whereas scholars such as Anne Middleton and Kathryn Kerby-Fulton have posited a community of socially and politically diverse readers drawn together by the material production and reception of *Piers Plowman*, I propose a community of concepts drawn together from among such diverse books as those owned by Walter de Brugge and John Wormyngton, and invoked by the flyleaves of MS 733B or even illustrated on a single leaf in MS Douce 104.[14] Reading *Piers Plowman* through the lens of such a conceptual community will uncover evidence for the co-production of canon law and literature – evidence for a history that lies hidden behind the recorded proximity of *Piers Plowman* to the *Decretum*, *Decretales*, and the *Oculus sacerdotis*.[15] This is a prehistory of the poetic means by which the versions of *Piers Plowman* are at once a product of the discourse of canon law and constitutive of it. The generative alliance between *Piers Plowman* and canonistic compilations, between literary and legal makings manifests itself best as we move across the B and C versions of *Piers Plowman* – to which we now turn.

During one wakeful moment in Sleuþe's confession in both B and C, this viciously and vividly protean character touches on his learning,

12 I adapt the concluding sentence of the romantic poet Percy Bysshe Shelly's *A Defense of Poetry* and echo John Alford's observation that *Piers Plowman* "was written at a time when knowledge of law seems to have been the common property of poets"; see Alford, *Piers Plowman: A Glossary of Legal Diction*, ix.

13 Stock uses the expression to designate "a group that arises somewhere in the interstices between the imposition of the written word and the articulation of a certain type of social organization"; see his *Listening for the Text*, 150.

14 For the textual community posited for *Piers Plowman*, see Kerby-Fulton and Despres, *Iconography and the Professional Reader*. See also Anne Middleton's distinction between the poem's "public" and "audience" in her "The Audience and Public of *Piers Plowman*."

15 I thank Jay Gundacker for suggesting to me "co-production" as a category through which to think about law and literature. For the concept of co-production, see Jasanoff's "The Idiom of Co-Production." She defines co-production as the "proposition that the ways in which we know and represent the world (both nature and society) are inseparable from the ways in which we choose to live in it. Knowledge and its material embodiments are at once products of social work and constitutive of forms of social life; society cannot function without knowledge anymore than knowledge can exist without appropriate social supports" (2–3).

or lack thereof. He confesses his inability to sing or read a saint's life despite having been "a preest and person passynge þritty wynter."[16] Only in B does Sleuþe disclose that he "kan noȝt rede a lyne" either in "Canoun" (canon law) or "in þe Decretals" (the *Decretales* or *Liber extra*).[17] In the corresponding passage in C, however, Sleuþe is less forthcoming. Not included in C are B's two pointed references to canon law, but present is a line indicating that Sleuþe "can nat construe Catoun ne clergialiche reden."[18]

Now flash forward to the memorable banquet hosted by Conscience in both B (passus 13) and C (passus 15) where yet another sinful cleric – a gluttonous friar – invokes academic lore.[19] In him, however, is not paucity but plenty of canon law. As guest of honour, the friar discourses learnedly about the doctrine of penance. He prescribes fasting while he himself feasts on costly fare. In both the B and C versions of the scene, the narrator exposes the gulf between the friar's deep learning and shallow living, between preaching penances and performing them. In C, however, the narrator spells out the friar's professional expertise in Gratian's *Decretum*. The narrator declares that the friar is "a decretistre of canoen" (a commentator on the *Decretum*) and "a mayster" although he "lyueth nat as a lereth."[20]

Such differences between the B and C versions can tell us as much about the uniqueness of either version's approach to the penitential institution as about a diversity of approaches to canon law in general. They can tell us about the relationship between the literary and the legal within B and C as well as in the late medieval world in which the poem's versions and canonistic treatises were composed and circulated. This study treats together two topics that typically have been explored separately: differences among the versions of *Piers Plowman* and the poem's engagement of the discourse of law. These topics drive two strands of current

16 Langland, *Piers Plowman: A Parallel-Text Edition of the A, B, C and Z Versions*. All quotations from the B and C versions of *Piers Plowman* are from this edition and are cited by version, passus, and line, as here, B 5.416; see also corresponding C 7.30. When quoting from a version of the poem, I first provide the reference to the quoted version and, wherever necessary, the reference to the corresponding words in the other version.

17 B 5.422.

18 C 7.34.

19 B 13.78–164; C 15.86–166.

20 C 15.86, C 15.91, and C 15.95.

scholarship on *Piers Plowman*. From individually authored monographs such as Sarah Wood's *Conscience and the Composition of Piers Plowman* and Lawrence Warner's *The Myth of Piers Plowman* to collaborative projects such as the ongoing multivolume *Penn Commentary on "Piers Plowman"* series, the interrelations between the poem's versions have been the site of fervent inquiry, but with only an occasional focus on law.[21] In such commentaries, law – more often the English common and civil legal traditions rather than their ecclesiastical counterpart – is treated as a context for explaining the differences between the poem's versions.[22] That is, legal discourse generally serves as an aid to study *Piers Plowman's* versional differences or even evolution rather than as an object of study within or across the poem's versions.[23]

Another strand of scholarship has centred on the interrelations between law and *Piers Plowman*. In the wake of Nicholas Gray's erudite "A Study of *Piers Plowman* in Relation to the Medieval Penitential Tradition," Richard Firth Green's monumental *A Crisis of Truth*, and Emily Steiner's influential *Documentary Culture and the Making of Medieval English Literature*, medievalists have done much to increase our knowledge of the poem's engagement of legal maxims and documents. Within the past decade, scholars such as Conrad van Dijk and Stephen Yeager have respectively deepened and broadened our understanding of *Piers Plowman's* conceptual and metrical debts to legal treatises.[24] But such interdisciplinary analysis has focused overwhelmingly on the poem as if it existed as one standard version (often B). Therefore, variations in the handling of ecclesiastical norms within and across the poem's versions have been understudied, and we have often looked past the history of canon law told by such versional variations.

---

21 See Sarah Wood, *Conscience and the Composition of Piers Plowman*; Warner, *The Myth of Piers Plowman*; and Galloway, *The Penn Commentary on "Piers Plowman."*

22 See, for instance, Andrew Galloway's stimulating reading of passus 4 in light of the common law courts of Common Pleas and King's Bench in his "*Piers Plowman* and the Subject of the Law."

23 I draw upon Eve Keller's distinction between the expressions "aids to study" and "objects of study in themselves" in her introduction to *Generating Bodies and Gendered Selves*, 6.

24 Conrad van Dijk briefly delves into the canonist thinking about equity in *Piers Plowman* in his "Giving Each His Due"; Stephen Yeager, in *From Lawmen to Plowmen*, sees in the alliterative style and metre of the *Piers Plowman* tradition evidence for the tradition's "participation in the post-Conquest continuation of Anglo-Saxon legal-homiletic discourse" (14); Archbishop Wulfstan's contributions to canon law are among the Anglo-Saxon legal and homiletic texts that Yeager explores.

By braiding together both of these strands of scholarship, I explore the ways in which two comparable versions of *Piers Plowman* – the B and C texts – court, extend, and even challenge the discourse of law invoked by the terms "Canoun," "Decretal," and "decretistre." The interrelations between B and C uncovered in this study bear witness to the poem's range of critical and creative approaches towards canon law, and not necessarily to any evolution of a single poet's thinking across the two versions.[25] Even as I distinguish the two versions, I neither endorse nor reject the consensus that B was revised by C – a consensus recently challenged by Lawrence Warner.[26] But I follow Warner to the extent that I treat "the A-B-C paradigm ... [as] a useful tool rather than a historically verifiable truth."[27] That is, I find the distinction between the versions useful as a basis for comparative analysis – i.e., for rendering visible the poem's versional reflections of and on canonist thought and practice. If we attend to how both B and C relate to canonistic writings we shall, above all, reveal the extent to which features of medieval literature that we understand as literary inform and transform our understanding of those we would distinguish as legal.[28] By "literary" I mean the formal properties of language that writers of fiction exploit to make meaning. Such properties include verse, voice, syntax, metaphor, mood, audience-orientation, and allegory. By "legal" I mean the norms or processes that canonists treat for the administration of ecclesiastical courts: conciliar rulings, papal rescripts, juridical or penitential procedures, and regulative maxims.

It is my contention that *Piers Plowman's* mobilization and modification of juridical properties not only engender a poetics informed by canonist thought but also express a vision of canon law alternative to and even critical of that offered by medieval jurists and recorded by modern medievalists. This is a vision of clerical reform formulated

---

25 I thank a reader for the University of Toronto Press for suggesting this point.

26 Warner, "The Ur-B *Piers Plowman*." For a review of the traditional dissension over the versions of *Piers Plowman*, see also Hanna, "On the Versions of *Piers Plowman*." See also Benson, "Another Fine Manuscript Mess."

27 Warner, "The Ur-B *Piers Plowman*," 27.

28 This claim is in part inspired by Helen Barr's chapter entitled "Legal Fictions" in her *Signes and Sothe*, 133–66; Barr notes that "*Piers* emerges as a text whose mode of thought and argument is substantially indebted to legal procedure and vocabulary," and that "*Piers* and its tradition are not unique in Middle English literature in using legal reference" (133).

through terms and concepts central to the academic discipline of law in the late Middle Ages. At the same time, it is a re-envisioning of such a linguistic and conceptual apparatus in a manner that, as this study argues, constitutes a poetic remaking of canon law – a reinvention that, I also argue, will add a chapter to the received history of canonist theory and practice and even revise some of that history.[29]

In the past few decades, interdisciplinary studies like this one have typically been associated with the so-called law and literature movement.[30] Despite its promising conjunction of law and literature, many of this movement's founders and followers tend to treat the literary and legal as though they were discrete or even antagonistic categories: the former proper to fictional compositions and the latter to prescriptive treatises. In this book, I call into question the method of dividing law and literature into "parallel forms of discourse, each with its own conventions and traditions" or into disciplines so separate as to have no more than a relationship based on properties of narrative or rhetoric.[31] To be sure, a summa on penance or a digest of decretals is not literature, if we restrict that term to cover only imaginative writings that deal in fictional characters. Equally assuredly, a dream-vision of the penitential forum or an allegorical representation of ecclesiastical rulings is not a work of legal discourse, if we understand that expression to denote only texts dealing with historically verifiable juridical matters like courts, litigants, and laws.

By challenging our discipline-specific categories of law and literature, however, I attempt to uncover intersections of, rather than just interrelations between, writings discursively labelled as legal and those equally discursively labelled as literary: intersections that will enable us to reconceptualize poetry as productive of, not just derivative from,

29 I thank Lenny Cassuto for this formulation.

30 For a current overview of the "law and literature" movement in premodern studies, see the introduction in Cormack, Nussbaum, and Strier, in *Shakespeare and the Law*, 1–18. As Bradin Cormack explains, the law and literature movement, "which was initially closely associated with the University of Chicago Law School, started in the early 1970s, when courses in law and literature began to be offered at a few U.S. law schools." See Cormack's introduction, in *Shakespeare and the Law*, 4.

31 For law and literature as "parallel forms of discourse," see Green, *A Crisis of Truth*, xvi. For law and literature as fundamentally separate disciplines, see Posner, *Law and Literature*. For a recent survey of both categories within law and literature studies, see Seaton, "Law and Literature." See also Green, "Medieval Law and Literature," 407, and Posner, *Law and Literature: A Misunderstood Relation*.

the discourse of canon law.[32] Such intersections include the practice of a shared hermeneutics and the pursuit of a common end. For instance, poet and canonist work alike when they interpret patristic and penitential sources not merely to record but also to reinvent normative authority – a point that we are more likely to concede to legislators of legal canons than to poets of our literary canons. No less than Gratian or the canonists that followed him, Langland mobilizes *sententiae* not just as statements of normative authority but also as sites within which to fashion approaches to problems or cases that could have been heard in the medieval church's penitential and judicial courts. Seen from this perspective, a canonist's *tractatus* on the penitential forum and the narrator's dream-vision of confession in *Piers Plowman* share moments when they emerge in concert or in conflict with each other, as if they were co-produced. By attending to such moments within the B and C versions of the poem, we will be able to see that canonist and poet employ common interpretative methods of engaging often identical textual sources in order to realize a common goal in their shared present. The method is dialectical interpretation, the goal justice, and the texts Latin *sententiae* drawn from sources ranging from the patristic to the papal.

All three shared properties – method, goal, and textual source – define the tradition of canon law towards which the poem explicitly gestures in its characterizations of Sleuþe and the portly friar. Starting from the mid-twelfth century and extending over the period of *Piers Plowman's* composition and circulation, canon law became more and more interpretatively ambitious and authoritative. With the second and vulgate "recensions" of Gratian's *Decretum* adopted as school texts, canon law emerged under its late medieval or "classical" aspect as an academic discipline and profession.[33] Best exemplified by the "second

32 I thank Carrie Hyde for this suggestion.

33 For the emergence of the "classical" character of canon law (from the mid-1100s to the mid-1300s), see the introduction in Helmholz, *The Spirit of Classical Canon Law*, 1–32. Given that the dating of the *Decretum* in its two recensions is still a matter of dissension, I suggest a broad range of forty years (1120–60) within which most scholars agree that the two recensions were composed. For a history of the first, second, and vulgate recensions of the *Decretum* and their significance for our understanding of the early teaching of canon law at medieval universities, see Winroth, *The Making of Gratian's Decretum*. For the latest survey of the scholarly dissension over the recensions of the *Decretum*, see Eichbauer, "Gratian's *Decretum*."

part" (pars secunda) of the *Decretum* was a dialectical method of making the law rather than merely handing it down as already and always made. In essence, such law-making consisted of the practice of reviewing disparate authorities and their opinions or their "canons" (canones) on a hypothetical "case" (causa) and then attempting to reconcile them.

Unlike its secular Roman counterpart, the classical canon law, as its great modern scholar Stephan Kuttner explains, "did not constitute a closed corpus" but "continued to grow" in order to create a "book of authority."[34] In the almost two centuries between Gratian's *Decretum* (which, although not originally officially authorized, inaugurated the academic study of canon law) and the *Constitutiones Clementinae* (the third and last authorized decretal collection to be added to the medieval academic curriculum), canon law burgeoned into a body of texts called the *Corpus iuris canonici*.[35] The openness of canon law lay not just in the absorption of prescriptive texts but also in the adoption of a methodological apparatus for reading them. More than "a collection of legislative enactments," canon law remained in Langland's day a dynamic method of constituting the norms themselves, with a view towards realizing justice on a case-by-case basis.[36]

As is evident in his treatment of the thirty-six "cases" (causae) that comprise the second part of his *Decretum*, Gratian typically opens with a hypothetical "case" (causa): a fictional narrative that illustrates a problem requiring adjudication in an ecclesiastical court.[37] He discusses it in

---

34 Although Kuttner cites Charles Homer Haskins's words, he elaborates upon the differences between Roman law as a closed system and canon law as an open one around the time of Gratian; see Kuttner, "The Revival of Jurisprudence," 306; see also Haskins, *The Renaissance of the Twelfth Century*, 215.

35 Brundage, "The Teaching and Study of Canon Law," 102. Although I reflect the general scholarly consensus that the authorized medieval *Corpus iuris canonici* closed with the *Consitutiones Clementinae*, the *Corpus* nevertheless continued to burgeon well into the the rest of the Middle Ages and into the early modern period.

36 I adapt Brundage's characterization of the classical canon law in his *Medieval Canon Law*, 47–8.

37 Unless otherwise stated, all quotations from the *Decretum, the Liber extra, the Liber Sextus*, the *Clementinae* as well as their surrounding apparatus are taken from the *Corpus juris canonici* [CJC], 3 vols (Rome, 1582) and, wherever relevant, I supply the corresponding volume number and column number(s) in Friedberg's edition of the *Corpus Iuris Canonici* [CIC], 2 vols (Leipzig, 1879–81; repr. Graz, 1959). Commissioned by the Council of Trent and brought out under the auspices of Pope Gregory XIII, the 1582 edition of *CJC* is now made digitally available by Professor Henry A. Kelly at the following UCLA Library website: http://digital.library.

light of "questions" (quaestiones) addressed and answered in different ways by various authorities who offer diverse reasons based on divergent "canons" (canones). To harmonize the discordant canons, Gratian offers his resolution in introductory, intermediate, and concluding "comments" (dicta), or lets the reader determine it. Take, for instance, the "third question" (quaestio 3) on penitential remission addressed in the discussion of penance introduced in the fictional "Causa 33" of a married man afflicted by magically induced impotence. Gratian introduces the question of remission briefly in his statement to the entire case and reformulates it more fully and differently at the outset of "Distinction 1" that discusses the third question.[38] As Atria Larson explains it, the "question" that Gratian raises in the two versions addresses the cause of remission, not "whether or not external confession is necessary."[39] Gratian responds with a "distinction" (distinctio) that broadly outlines and substantiates two authoritative positions – one defending the view that contrition and satisfaction alone without oral confession erase sin, and the other requiring oral confession as well for the remission of sin.[40] Gratian gathers various authorities and reasons to adduce support for each position but at the end of his exhaustive comparative analysis lets the reader settle which position to adopt:

---

ucla.edu/canonlaw/index.html. In my citations from Gratian's *Decretum*, I follow the practice exemplified by Brundage: "C" stands for "Causa" (i.e., case), "q" for "quaestio" (i.e., question,), "Dist" for "Distinctio" (distinction), and "c" for "canon/capitulum" (canon/chapter); the abbreviation "d.a.c" stands for "[Gratian's] dictum ante canonem/capitulum" whereas "d.p.c" stands for "[Gratian's] dictum post canonem/capitulum."

38 The case statement is at *Decretum*, II. C. 33 Dist. init.: "queritur ... tertio, si sola confessione cordis crimen possit deleri" (*CIC*, 1: 1148). That is, "It is asked in the third place if by confession of the heart alone sin can be erased." The reformulated question occurs at the beginning of "Distinction 1" at *Decretum*, II. C. 33 Dist.1 d.a.c. 1: "utrum sola cordis contritione et secreta satisfactione absque oris confessione quisque possit Deo satisfacere" (*CIC*, 1: 1159). That is, "[it is asked] whether by contrition of heart alone and secret satisfaction without oral confession anyone can make satisfaction to God." For a close reading of the two versions of the question and their delineation of "contritionist" and "confessionalist" positions, see John Wei, "The Two Questions" in his *Gratian the Theologian*, 103–12.

39 Larson, *Master of Penance*, 37; John Wei contests Larson's explanation, reading Gratian's "exposition of the contritionist position [as] set[ting] forth two separate and independently valid arguments for why confession is not necessary"; see John Wei's *Gratian the Theologian*, 108–10.

40 For a lucid summary of Gratian's exposition of the arguments for both positions in "distinction 1," see John Wei's *Gratian the Theologian*, 101–19.

> Quibus auctoritatibus, uel quibus rationum firmamentis utraque sententia satisfactionis & confessionis innitatur, in medium breuiter exposuimus. Cui autem harum potius adhaerendum sit, lectoris iudicio reseruatur. Vtraque enim fautores habet sapientes et religiosos viros. (Gratian, *Decretum*, II. C. 33, q. 3, *De penitentia*, Dist. 1, d.p.c. 89, cols 2253–4; *CIC*, 1: 1189)

> We have briefly explained to all what authorities or what supporting arguments both opinions about confession and satisfaction rely upon. To which of these one should preferably adhere, however, is reserved to the judgment of the reader. For both have wise and religious supporters.[41]

This open-ended invitation to reach a conclusion in view of opposed but learned perspectives on the same "case" illustrates canon law as a method of dialectical interpretation. In the preface to his *Summa decretorum* (a commentary on Gratian's *Decretum*), the canonist Huguccio describes the method thus: "Lest therefore from such a variety of canons either the diverse canons appear adverse or the various canons are believed to be contrary, master Gratian, looking to common utility, proposed to gather together into one [book] the dispersed canons and reconcile them, if contrariety appeared to be within them" (Ne igitur ex tanta uarietate canonum aut diuersa viderentur aduersa aut uaria crederentur contraria magister Gratianus communi consulens utilitati dispersos canones in unum colligere, et si que videbatur inesse contrarietas, proposuit soluere).[42] The scholastic maxim "differences are not contradictions" (diversa sunt, non adversa), as Kuttner explains, encapsulated "one of the most powerful elements" in the lawyer's process of dialectical argumentation, with the "solution of contraries" (solutio contrariorum) as the terminal product.[43]

The glosses on the *Decretum* – from Gratian's own pronouncements ("dicta Gratiani") to subsequently added or interpolated canons (the so-called paleae or straws) and exhaustive apparatus (like the *Glossa ordinaria* of Johannes Teutonicus and Bartholomew of Brescia) – furthered the dialectical methodology of canonical jurisprudence.[44]

---

41 The translation is taken from Larson's *Master of Penance*, 92.

42 Huguccio, *Summa decretorum*, 6.

43 Kuttner, "The Revival of Jurisprudence," 310–11.

44 For a succinct account of the *Glossa ordinaria* to Gratian's *Decretum*, see Weigand, "The Development of the *Glossa ordinaria* to Gratian's *Decretum*"; for a recent history of the "paleae," see Weigand, "Versuch einer neuen differenzierten Liste der Paleae und Dubletten im Dekret Gratians."

Subsequent collections of decretals in the thirteenth and fourteenth centuries substantiated this methodology. The *Liber extra* commissioned by Pope Gregory IX, the *Liber Sextus* by Pope Boniface VIII, Pope Clement V's *Constitutiones Clementinae* authorized by Pope John XXII, and the *Extravagantes Johannis XXII* compiled by the canonist Zenzelinus de Cassanis – and their accompanying standard glosses – no doubt contained positive rulings such as papal decretals on cases, but they also constituted a vast cross-referential hermeneutic apparatus by which to interpret and implement them.

To think of canon law less as a static compendium of norms than as a continuous process of interpreting them is to grasp more than its "[un]closed" textual character.[45] It is to perceive that canon law shares a common ground with fictional writings that also interpret norms and thereby shape them, even if only at the level of concepts. Such a perception will liberate us from seeing the law as an already reified institution constituted solely by professional jurists and only subsequently reproduced or reflected by others such as the socially and institutionally diverse fictional actors in *Piers Plowman*.[46] At the same time, it will enable us to witness the law as produced from within the poem – namely, as something malleable that, as the narrator in the Prologue to *Piers Plowman* B eloquently expresses, sundry agents, including the "Commune," shape ("shopen"): "The Kyng and þe Commune and Kynde Wit þe þridde / Shopen lawe and leaute – ech lif to knowe his owene."[47]

45 I am deliberately recalling Kuttner's citation of Haskins about canon law as not a "closed corpus" in the classical or formative period of its evolution; see Kuttner, "Revival of Jurisprudence," 306.

46 For a telling example of the reception and transformation of canon law by "diverse actors" for ends other than those for which it was originally envisioned by the lawgivers or enforcers, see Jay Gundacker's seminal article "Absolutions and Acts of Disobedience." For the role of professional jurists in the constitution of canon law, see Brundage, "The Rise of the Professional Jurist in the Thirteenth Century." The word "commune," as used in *Piers Plowman*, denotes a motley of referents drawn from diverse social orders. Most recently, Emily Steiner interprets it as referring to any or all of the following: "the parliamentary Commons, the community of the realm, and the third estate"; see her *Reading Piers Plowman*, 16.

47 Prologue B 121–2. Line 122 is not present in the C version of the Prologue but, as Galloway notes, "a parallel passage in C only, 3. 374–82, was perhaps inserted in tandem with C's omission of this one; there 'Lawe, loue, and leute' are what the 'commune' demand of the king (3. 379n)," in *The Penn Commentary*, 121. Other agents that shape the law include "loue": "Right so is loue a ledere and þe lawe shapeþ" (B 1.161); see also the corresponding line in C 1.156.

This book contends that literary compositions such as the B and C versions of *Piers Plowman* that "shopen" the "lawe" or "leaute" narrate a history of canon law that complements and complicates that told by legal scholars, whether they be medieval or modern.[48] In both B and C, "extraclergial" characters ranging from the vigilant Conscience to the dreaming narrator "constitute" the law in the manner of canonists.[49] In reflecting and reflecting on the practice and profession of canon law, they produce "legal fictions" that reveal how the normative apparatus of the church could be or could have been modified and mobilized.[50] Seen from the perspective of medieval rhetorical composition, the characters in the poem are "probable": they straddle the boundaries between the rhetorical categories "history" (historia) and "fiction" (fabula).[51] Despite being allegorical, such characters were composed "within history – if not within the sense of what did happen, at least

48 As Alford's entry on "leute" in *A Glossary* makes clear, the term has a "rich ambiguity" and encompasses meanings that range from "lawfulness" and "loyalty" to "justice" (83–4). For "leute" as a principle of justice, see Kean's "Love, Lawe and *Leute* in *Piers Plowman*." For a more recent understanding of "leute" as justice, see Conrad van Dijk's reading of the same passage in *John Gower and the Limits of the Law*, 120. See also Edwin D. Craun's discussion of the juridical associations of "leute" in "Ȝe, by Peter and by Poul!"

49 Although I borrow the term "extraclergial" from Fiona Somerset to indicate Langland's bestowal of clerical legitimacy upon his vernacular characters, I do not read them as necessarily opposed to the institutional clergy and "ally[ing] themselves with the laity." See Somerset's *Clerical Discourse*, 3–100. I draw upon Naomi Mezey's review of the constitutive theory of law: "[c]onstitutive theory is common law in its most literal sense: law crafted by ordinary people operating creatively under certain constraints. It is not unlike the formation of a coral reef: living, minutely made, symbiotic," in "Out of the Ordinary," 149.

50 Here, I echo the title of Mary Flowers Braswell's book on Chaucer's relations to law: *Chaucer's "Legal Fiction."*

51 In medieval rhetorical treatises such as *Rhetorica ad Herennium*, one of the sub-categories of narrative "that serves the exposition of affairs has three parts: fable, history, and argument. Fable is that which contains things neither true nor false such as those conveyed by tragedies. History refers to a deed done but remote from the memory of our age. Argument is a fictional thing, which could have happened – as, for example, the arguments of comedies" (Id, quod in negotiorum expositione positum est, tres habet partes, fabulam, historiam, argumentum. Fabula est, quae neque veras, neque verisimiles continet res, ut hae quae a tragoedis traditae sunt. Historia est res gesta, sed ab aetatis nostrae memoria remota. Argumentum est ficta res, quae tamen fieri potuit; velut argumenta comoediarum); while the translation is mine, see [Cicero] *Ad C. Herennium: De ratione dicendi* [*Rhetorica ad Herennium*] (I.8.13), trans. Harry Caplan, 22–4.

within the sense of what might have happened, of what could be imagined, of what commonly held interpretative structures permitted a late fourteenth-century audience to believe."[52] Just like the hypothetical characters in Gratian's probable cases that combine history and fiction, Langland's characters too construct law and justice (lawe and leaute), and, as we shall see, do so by means and for ends diverse from but not necessarily opposed to those pursued by the jurists schooled in the hermeneutics of the *Corpus iuris canonici*.

As the reader of any version of *Piers Plowman* can tell at a glance, the poem is replete with scenes of litigious debate over the interpretations of *sententiae* that frame cases at hand. Oftentimes, approaches to a case are buttressed by biblical or theological precepts and divergent readings of them. We need only think of the dissension between the priest and Piers over the Latin pardon-formula's meaning (interpreted by the former as no pardon and by the latter as an injunction to perform good deeds and avoid bad ones), the debate between Conscience and Mede on reading and reconciling biblical quotations on gifts (with the former stressing the perils to the gift-receiver and the latter the profits to the gift-giver), the confessors' conflicting interpretations of the same Latin dictum on penitential satisfaction for Wrong's punishment (with confessors in B construing the Latin words as favouring secular gain whereas those in C construe the same words as favouring spiritual gain), or even the playfully dissonant understanding of the English word "restitucion" offered by the penitent Covetise (who, unlike his confessor Repentaunce, reads it as a synonym for stealing from merchants "a-reste").[53] In such scenes, characters do more than merely invoke *sententiae* to point to a solution that has juridical force; they frequently adopt the same dialectical method of reading deployed by canonists to approach the same kinds of texts, although not always for the same ends.

At its broadest, this book explores the implications of overlapping interpretative practices for an understanding of motives and strategies common to both legal and literary discourses. In doing so, this study also complicates notions of "vernacular theology" and "vernacular legality" advanced by Nicholas Watson and Bruce Holsinger

52 I borrow Paul Strohm's words on the "historicity" of fictional writings; see "Introduction: False Fables and Historical Truth" in his *Hochon's Arrow*, 3.

53 B 5.230: "I roos whan þei were a-reste and riflede hire males!"; see the corresponding line in C 6.236: "Y roes and ryflede here males when they a-reste were!"

respectively, making the case for a multilingual poetics that serves as a fictional complement or, at moments, a supplement to the official Latinate legal culture in the time of *Piers Plowman's* composition.[54] Whereas Watson and Holsinger see in a medieval author's choice of writing in English a challenge to authoritative Latin discourses or even an appropriation of them, I find in Langland's choice of writing in English and Latin evidence for the participation of poet and canonist in a shared method of reflecting and reshaping legal thought. That is, this book substantiates the "less commonly acknowledged" point about *Piers Plowman*'s vernacularity – "which is that most of the texts that served as literary models for the poem *were not vernacular* [emphasis Kerby-Fulton's]."[55] Drawing at the same time on Fiona Somerset's argument about *Piers Plowman*'s creative usages of Latin, this book contends that the poem's incorporation of *sententiae* such as legal maxims in Latin makes for a "radical" rather than reactionary reading of the established church's discourse of law.

All this is to claim that the poem's relationship to its Latin canonistic sources is far from passive or deferential. At the outset of his recent book on conflicting models of sanctity in late medieval England, David Aers notes that "orthodoxy is always in the making," pointing to the process by which the medieval church constituted itself in continuous tension with heterodox modes of belief.[56] In an analogous fashion, I see canon law too as always in the making insofar as envisioning or expressing norms was not restricted to the activities of the canonists writing in Latin but was also available for equally dynamic bilateral multilingual treatment by poets such as Langland. In other words, poet and canonist – even if the latter did not know or care for the former – were engaged in a common approach to, and common pursuit of, writing, revising, and thereby co-producing the law. The story I tell about *Piers Plowman* B and C is, as it were, an *Ur*-story about such collective making or remaking of the law, and the implications of this poetic reinvention for revising our current understanding of legal and literary discourses in the Late Middle Ages.

My evidence for these claims about the intersection of poetic and canonistic makings most readily manifests itself in a comparative reading

54 Watson, "Censorship and Cultural Change in Late-Medieval England"; Holsinger, "Vernacular Legality."

55 Kerby-Fulton, "*Piers Plowman*" in *The Cambridge History of Medieval English Literature*, 526.

56 Aers, *Sanctifying Signs*, viii.

of the B and C versions of *Piers Plowman*. Because both versions are recursively invested in penitential administration, I read them alongside ecclesiastical norms that express a juridical or practical rather than merely a theological or theoretical approach to private sacramental penance. Throughout this reading, therefore, I attend to the poem's innovative engagement of the norms framing the stages of the penitential process: contrition, confession, restitution, and satisfaction. My focus on the canon law of penance has as much to do with *Piers Plowman*'s preoccupations with sin and redemption as with matters of internal evidence. In a poem as vast and various as *Piers Plowman* other areas of canon law, such as sex, marriage, ordination, and oaths, do receive poetic representation but because they are not as substantially and recurrently treated as penance is, they lie outside the scope of this study. But even in its focus on the penitential stages and procedures represented in B and C, this study does orient attention towards the extra-penitential implications of the reinvention of canon law by the poem's personified abstractions. Hence, I attend to socio-political questions of distributive justice and economic ethics that both allegorical poem and canonistic treatise alike approach in mutually illuminating ways.

My argument about the poem's construction of penance as juridical in character participates in a current conversation among historians on the reciprocal relationship between the legal and the penitential elements in Gratian and post-Gratian treatises on canon law. As recently as in 2014, Atria Larson's book-length study centres on the influence of Gratian's tract on penance (*De penitentia*) on canonists such as Huguccio, as well as on theologians such as Lombard, and argues against clear-cut boundaries in Gratian's day between canon law and theology or, more particularly, between legal procedure and pastoral care.[57] More recently, the historian John Burden has argued that German canon law collections that predate Gratian often integrate penitential material into the application of a singular episcopal justice, rather than using it to provide a separate manual for private confession.[58] Taking the methodological cue from Larson and Burden, my study makes a similar claim but for a later period and within a poem, reading the B and C versions of *Piers Plowman* in light of canonistic advice for administering private sacramental penance.

57 Larson, *Master of Penance*. See also Larson's "The Reception of Gratian's *Tractatus de Penitentia*."

58 I thank John Burden for discussing a section of his "Between Crime and Sin."

To study *Piers Plowman's* versions or the differences between them alongside canonistic treatises as well as handbooks for confessors is to discover the reinvention of canon law within and beyond the poem. By "reinvention," I mean two things: both finding ("inventio" in Classical Latin rhetoric) and founding ("invention" in contemporary English usage).[59] The reinvention of canon law occurs in the poem when a character mobilizes expressions drawn from the legally marked terminology found in prescriptive writings. When, in B, the narrator cites the biblical proscription of usury (central to canonistic discussions of the topic) to assail reckless gift-giving, or when, again in B, Repentaunce quotes a maxim on restitution (central to canonistic discussions of absolution from usurious sins) to exhort his penitent to restore misappropriated goods to their owners, both fictional characters find in the two authoritative pronouncements a basis for founding their reformed visions of gift-giving and restitutive justice. Reinvention also occurs when a character mobilizes modes of legal thought in novel ways or for novel ends. For instance, in C, Conscience forges his vision of legitimate gift-giving by reworking the canonistic concepts of earthly and spiritual usury without ever citing any legislative ruling. And, likewise in C, Patience deploys a common legal instrument (a "chartre") in order to court and challenge the sign-system peculiar to late medieval penitential discourse.[60] Attending to both kinds of reinvention within and across the B and C versions will ultimately enable us to witness the poem's intervention in the extra-textual world and, above all, to rethink the classical canon law from a poetic perspective.

The evidence I offer for the twofold sense of reinvention in either version leads to the book's subclaim that the C text, as presented in its modern editions, exhibits a sharper or more substantial engagement and enrichment of canon law than does B. More than in B, in C we see the penitential forum approached from the perspective of the clerics ordained to administer it. In comparison to B, C is more censorious of negligent clerics, offering a more technical approach to the procedures for instilling contrition, for inquiring into usury, for enforcing restitution, and for interpreting satisfaction. Even as both versions of the poem register and represent a rich diversity of approaches to canon

59 "Inventio" in classical rhetoric is typically associated not only with "invenire" or "reperire" but also with "excogitare" (to reflect). See Ullrich Langer's entry on "Invention."

60 The "chartre" occurs in C 16.22–41.

law, C expresses a poetically generative principle that is also legally generative and more explicitly so than B.[61]

The reinvention of canon law in the poem is made manifest at two levels: one at the level of concept and the other at that of letter. Conscience's treatment of usury in his denunciation of Mede in passus 3 exemplifies the former and Covetise's confession in passus 5 the latter. In Conscience's critique of Mede in C, we shall discover a far more unified understanding of illicit commercial exchanges than is found in B. In C, as explored in chapter 2, Conscience interprets the canonistic prohibition of usury to denounce not just interest on loans but also advance payments for services. Expanding the usury prohibition to cover inequitable exchanges of services as well, Conscience adapts the canonistic concept of earthly usury to critique the worker's demand for advance wages. In corollary fashion, he substantiates the canonistic concept of spiritual usury to envision an equitable relation between wage-giver and worker, between "maister" and "a leel laborer."[62] Although his words do not refer to the biblical prohibition of usury, they are nevertheless grounded in concepts through which canonists detected illicit profits hidden under potentially legitimate commercial exchanges and through which they proposed suitable remedies. In short, the reinvention of canon law inheres in the poem's creative mobilization and modification of the canonist thought on usury in the interests of reform at law.

But the poem's allegorical characters also reinvent canon law by radically transforming the structures of legal thought. In the C version of Covetise's confession, as discussed in chapter 3, the allegorical confessor Repentaunce creates a law out of a canonical maxim on a "rule of law" (regula iuris) on restitution. Although Repentaunce invokes the same maxim in both B and C, there are crucial differences in his treatment of it between the two versions. In B, he treats the maxim as a form of moral exhortation directed immediately at the penitent. In C, by contrast, he treats it under the aspect of a concrete law directed not just at the penitent but also at confessors ranging from the parish priest to the pope himself. In thus deriving a law from a rule, Repentaunce argues for the supremacy of the "rule of law" over and above the papal law-maker. Likewise, in the C version of Reason's trial of Wrong, which is the focus of chapter 4, we shall encounter a canonist's approach to a quotation on

61 I owe this formulation to Andy Galloway, who offered feedback on a version of this introduction.

62 C 3.347.

penitential satisfaction. In the passage in C, the addressed confessors are reported to have interpreted a quotation "kyndeliche" for the king's spiritual benefit whereas their counterparts in B read in the same quotation a justification of material gains made for the king but at the expense of his soul. Passages such as this in C are at once audience-centred and content-based. They invoke specific audiences – at one time royal and at another clerical – to enable them to comprehend and even creatively complicate the readings espoused by the narrator and Reason.

This study is contextual but without ignoring *Piers Plowman's* reworking of the canonical materials that both versions draw upon. Throughout the book I endeavour not only to uncover texts germane to the two versions' treatment of canon law but also to reread those texts that have already been identified as the poem's sources and analogues. Ever since Skeat's edition of *Piers Plowman*, there has been a considerable body of scholarship on the poem's relation to penitential literature in general and to confessors' manuals in particular. Scholars from John Alford to Nicholas Gray have painstakingly identified Langland's many "debts" to penitential treatises, including those composed by canonists.[63] Their contributions share the methodological conviction that a poetic passage can best be understood from the perspectives of the sources that it alludes to or explicitly draws upon.[64] Despite the light they have shed on the larger contexts of the poem, these source studies, premised as they are on a binary distinction between poetic text and normative treatise, overlook *Piers Plowman's* active participation in or co-production of the discourse of canon law. Hence, they tend to read the poem's relation to its putative sources as passive – as one of derivation or reflection, rather than of co-production or reinvention.

The following chapters challenge this mode of reading not by discounting the relevance of source studies, but by reassessing the relationship between *Piers Plowman* and its putative sources in ways that enable us to recognize a creative agency inherent to the poem itself.

---

63 Alford, "More Unidentified Quotations in *Piers Plowman*," and *Piers Plowman: A Guide to the Quotations*. See also Quick, "The Sources of the Quotations of *Piers Plowman*"; Braswell, *The Medieval Sinner*; Burrow, "The Action of Langland's Second Vision"; and Gray, "Langland's Quotations from the Penitential Tradition."

64 In the summary of his illuminating dissertation and in its first chapter, Nicholas Gray "argues the *prima facie* case for Langland's having known such texts [penitential manuals and *summae confessorum*], by examining a number of his Latin quotations and showing that they were probably drawn from technical penitential sources" ("Summary of Dissertation," in "A Study of *Piers Plowman*" unnumbered).

In this, I seek to complement the invaluable service that Nicholas Gray has rendered to any reader interested in "Langland's indebtedness to penitential texts."[65] To be clear, I do not dispute *Piers Plowman*'s debts to the body of theological and canonistic writings that scholars have painstakingly uncovered. After all, that is one sense in which I intend to use the word "reinvention." Rather, I argue that the places in *Piers Plowman* where we detect the poet's debts to his sources are, at the same time, *loci* of invention in the sense of the interpretation and transformation of those sources (the second sense in which I intend to use the word "reinvention"). This book tarries awhile at such places in the poem, especially with regard to the differences between the B and C versions, to observe how elements apparently borrowed from treatises – ranging from Gratian's *Decretum* to the anonymous *Memoriale Presbiterorum* – are transmuted by an interpretative logic internal to the poem. Even as it opens access to canonistic treatises germane to the poem's handling of law, this study explores how *Piers Plowman* also engenders an understanding of them different from that obtained from the medieval canonists themselves or, for that matter, from their medievalist commentators.

This book goes beyond arguing for the reinvention of canon law from within the poem: it also explores the extra-textual implications of the two versions' internal reworking of any source or surrounding materials. The different ways in which, and ends for which, the B and C versions mobilize canonistic words and concepts can help us rethink the official discourse of canon law and recover a history of it alternative to that told by medieval canonists and medievalist historians alike. Conscience's expansion of the canonistic prohibition of usury to cover advance payment for work, Repentaunce's making of a "law" from a "rule" on restitution, Reason's redefinition of satisfaction as at once manual and hermeneutic labour – all emerging into sharper relief in the C version – need not be viewed as solely internal to or sealed off within the poem. These actions of allegorical characters bear witness to a mobilization of canonistic categories to imagine and hence invent normatively intelligible ways of re-forming canonistic thought and practice in the historically real penitential forum of the poet's England.

---

65 Gray, "A Study of *Piers Plowman*," unnumbered page from "Summary of Dissertation." Gray argues "that Langland was indebted for a great deal of material to some text or texts of the many which make up the 'medieval penitential tradition,'" 25.

In envisioning legal reform by having characters narrate it as realizable, *Piers Plowman* embodies the kind of virtual history or "textual providentiality" recently ascribed by Matthew Fisher to medieval history writing from Bede's *Historia Ecclesiastica* to Geoffrey of Monmouth's *Historia Regum Britanniae*.[66] Although generated within the B and C versions of the poem, this providentiality is inter-textual and, just as important, outward-looking or action-seeking in the world inhabited by readers such as Walter de Brugge. At the end of an important survey of law and literature in medieval England, John Alford asserted: "[Langland] was not the first, of course, to look at law and theology simultaneously – their histories had long been intertwined – but he pushed the analogies between them further than anyone else dared."[67] Building on Alford's insights into the poem's recourse to legal maxims, this book turns his perceptive assertion into a polemical argument about an analogical poetics of legal thought engendered within *Piers Plowman* but also capable of impacting the legal fora outside the poem.

In advancing this argument, I make a case for the poem's continual engagement of, and even embeddedness in, the established church's institutions, and thereby call into question many of Aers's recent conclusions about the poem's disjunctive relationship to institutions in his most recent book on *Piers Plowman*.[68] For instance, Aers concludes that, by *Piers Plowman*'s ending, we can no longer imagine the poetic satire of the institutional abuses "in a familiar incitement to a traditional model of reformation ... [as] the [poetic] work's dialectic has shown, time and again, the resilience of such abuses and the ineffectuality of numerous attempts at reform."[69] Aers goes on to reason that the poem moves away from any reformist engagement with the late medieval church institutions and towards "present absences" that he identifies as "congregationalism."[70] Unlike Aers's argument about the poem's commitment to a vision of the pre-Constantine congregationalist church, mine claims quite the opposite: *Piers Plowman* continually thinks with or through post-Constantine or, more specifically, the late medieval

66 Fisher, *Scribal Authorship*, 79; Fisher defines "textual providentiality" as the "miraculous textualization of history" whereby "Bede's *Historia* creates its own *auctoritas*," 79.

67 Alford "Literature and Law," 947–8.

68 Aers, *Beyond Reformation*?

69 Aers, *Beyond Reformation*? 136.

70 Aers, *Beyond Refomation*? 160.

institution of canon law, even in places where the poem may exhibit a movement away from it. In a sense, this book offers a riposte to Aers's reading of the poem's adversarial or indifferent relationship to the late medieval church, uncovering ways in which the B and C versions court, complicate and co-produce the institutional discourse of penance.

Composed of five chapters and an epilogue, this study is structured thematically around the movements of the penitential process: contrition, confession, restitution (when necessary), and satisfaction. In chapter 1, I deal with the narrator's critique of fraternal confessors in terms of the poem's courting and critique of the canon law on contrition and confession. In chapters 2 and 3, I uncover the ways in which the poem draws upon but also supplements the received canonistic thinking around restitution; in chapter 4, I make the case for the poem's recuperation of superseded ideas of penance to reinvent a theory of penitential satisfaction; and in the last chapter, I argue that the poem courts and at the same time contests the received canonistic thought on the entire process of sacramental penance in Langland's day.

Chapter 1, "*Contritio cordis*: The Laughter of Mede and Tearlessness of Contricion" introduces the canon law pertaining to contrition as a set of procedures that confessors were required to follow to elicit and evaluate the penitent's remorse. Not unlike stage directions, such procedures, if properly followed, enabled the penitent to perform her/his penitence before the confessor, who judged the presence or absence of contrition in view of the penitent's gestures and postures. Signs of shamelessness, laughter, and tearlessness comprised hard evidence for the lack of contrition.

Attending to the signs of impenitence in Mede's and Contricion's confessions to fraternal confessors, the chapter makes the case for the extent to which performance and penance intersect, suggesting that the C version of Mede's confession is more procedurally canonistic in its focus on contrition than is B. The poetic reinvention of canon law at stake resides in the inversions of canonistic procedures relating to the signs of contrition. In reading the scenes of fraternal confession, I adopt what would in American legalese be called a "textualist" or "originalist" method of interpretation.[71] To establish the presence of canon law in the poem's confessional scenes, I first outline the procedures for eliciting

71 For a recent discussion of textualism and originalism in American jurisprudence, see Epstein, "Beyond Textualism."

and evaluating contrition in the penitent – procedures best elaborated by the canonist Raymond of Peñafort's *De Paenitentiis et Remissionibus*, a treatise that served as a model for confessors' manuals after Lateran IV. While scholars have argued that the C text is largely reformist in its concentration on restitution or on linking contrition with confession and satisfaction, I claim that a number of C passages are equally reformist in foregrounding criteria for contrition (to a greater degree than the corresponding passages in B). Reading Mede's and Contricion's confessions alongside Raymond of Peñafort's treatise will enable us to see that C's treatment of Mede's confession sharpens the focus on these criteria as a means of reforming friars. At the same time, however, the poem also reveals the abuses of such canonistic knowledge insofar as the friars and their penitents mobilize the procedures of canon law for their own material ends.

Whereas the previous chapter attends to the procedural letter of canon law, chapter 2, "Dreams of Avarice: The Absent Presence of the Usury Prohibition," explores the logic of canon law in the C passages that pertain to usury and its prohibition in Conscience's denunciation of Mede in passus 3. The reinvention in C, I argue, occurs within the canonistic framework of corporeal and spiritual usury. Reading the C version of passus 3 alongside canonistic treatises on usury by Hostiensis and John of Freiburg among others, I demonstrate that the usury prohibition, although terminologically absent from the passus, is nevertheless conceptually present as an underlying ground for a far more unified handling of Mede's varied acts of avarice than is to be found in the corresponding passages in the B version of the same passus (where the usury prohibition is spelled out). Furthermore, in comparing the B and C versions of the same passus, we shall see that C adapts the canonistic thought on usurious loans to construct a model of wage-labour to govern the relations between lords and tenants. Exemplifying the biblical ideal of spiritual usury, such a model offers a solution to a pressing socio-economic issue in the conceptual terminology of canon law. In proposing such a solution, *Piers Plowman* is no less legalistic than a canonistic treatise: although the latter is backed by an extra-textual institutional authority, the former is nevertheless performing novel work, even if the work is that of envisioning a reform of labour relations on the basis of concepts developed by canonists.

Juxtaposing the B and C versions of Covetise's confession to Repentaunce, chapter 3, "*Restitutio*: From Rule to Law to Justice in Covetise's Confession," argues that, in C, one encounters an invention of a "law" from a "rule" within the framework of canonistic thinking on rule-making and law-making. Specifically, this chapter compares Repentaunce's treatments of a Latin maxim or rule on restitution in B and C in light of commentaries on the same maxim in legal texts such as the *Liber Sextus*, its *Glossa ordinaria*, and Dynus Muxellanus's *Commentarius mirabilis super titulo de regulis juris*. What in the juristic commentaries is treated as no more than a "rule" on restitution for penitents, is, I argue, innovatively treated by Repentaunce, in C, as a strict "law" applying to confessors, including the papal penitentiary. I contextualize Repentaunce's poetically engendered law in terms of the widespread socio-legal *mentalité* of restorative justice best expressed in the penitential manual *Memoriale presbiterorum*. In reading the poem and penitential manual together, I argue for the shared conceptual means by which Repentaunce broadens the case for reparations to the human victims of sin (rather than to God himself). More specifically, the legal invention in question arises from Repentaunce's addition to, and, at the same time, replacement of, normative elements in the received canonist thought about restitution. The C version of Covetise's confession, I also argue, has wide-ranging implications for revising our understanding of the poem's preoccupation with papal indulgences and its participation in the late medieval conversation about the relations between the pope's adherence to canon law and his transcendence of it, between the "rules of law," on the one hand, and the supreme lawmaker's discretion to dispense with them, on the other.

In chapter 4, "*Satisfactio operis*: Maxim and Metaphor in Wrong's Trial," I explore the poem's resourceful combination of both contemporary and traditional notions of satisfaction found in the penitential tradition of Langland's day. Examining Reason's trial of Wrong in passus 4 of both the B and C versions, I establish the poetic site of innovation in Reason's interpretation of a Latin maxim ("Nullum malum inpunitum ... nullum bonum irremuneratum") that frames the discussion of satisfaction in penitential treatises across the Middle Ages. Whereas most scholars have read the quotation from the perspective of its usages within penitential sources, I take up Jill Mann's cue about addressing the same quotation in terms of its internal "dynamic" and hence examine it from the perspective of its usages by Reason from within the poem.[72]

72 See Jill Mann's comment on the scholarly neglect of the quotation's usage from within the "dynamic" of the poem; Mann, "Some Observations on 'Structural Annotation,'" 6.

Specifically, I focus on Reason's usage of the image of law as labourer within a metaphor to clarify how he wants the confessors to construe the Latin quotation. This metaphor, I argue, synthesizes disparate ideas of satisfaction found in two different phases of the medieval penitential tradition. Such a synthesis, expressive of a logic intrinsic to the passage, results in a redescribed idea of penitential satisfaction. To move from the B to C versions of the same passage, I further argue, is to move towards a canonist's perspective on the interpretation of satisfaction – a perspective present in both versions but sharpened in C in order to reform the confessors' widespread neglect of satisfaction in fourteenth-century England.

Unlike the previous chapters that explore canonical procedures pertaining to individual penitential stages, the final chapter, "*Contritio Cordis, Confessio Oris, et Satisfactio Operis*: From Symbol to Sign in Patience's Sermon," takes for its frame of reference the canon law governing all three stages (contrition, confession, and satisfaction) that comprise the typical penitential process. I address questions that emerge from the meeting of the penitential and the poetic. Which aspects of penance do B and C single out in order to clarify the poem's affiliation with Christ and the church? Conversely, what allegorical mode of clarification or representation do both versions deploy to highlight those aspects of penance? In approaching these questions, the chapter refines our knowledge of both the penitential tradition that certain understudied C passages foreground and the allegorical language used for this purpose. In particular, I compare a passage from Patience's sermon centring on a document described in B as Christ's covenantal "patente" against a comparable passage from C in which the analogous document is designated as a "chartre" authorized by the institutional church. The B and C versions of Patience's sermon offer two distinct approaches to canon law and its documentary representation: B describes the patent as a visual interpersonal symbol, whereas C defines the charter as an institutional sign. I argue that the C version of Patience's sermon both courts and even challenges the semiotics informing the documents of canon law.

Individually, then, each chapter offers an intersectional mode of reading *Piers Plowman* and canon law – one that highlights the mutual constitution of the literary and the legal within the poem's versions but with implications beyond them. Collectively, my readings describe a poetic-legal state of affairs that remains relevant up until "the closing of the Middle Ages."[73] In the epilogue that follows, I offer a retrospective glance at *Piers Plowman* and canon law from the perspective of Luther's incendiary reaction to the *Corpus Iuris Canonici* in the 1530s. I do so in order to suggest that the legal reinventions that I recognize in the poem belong to a historical moment that flickers and fades forever in the wake of the Reformation, when canon law ceased to hold the institutional power and imaginative potential that once allowed for its shaping by "the Kyng and þe Commune and Kynde Wit þe þridde."[74]

73 The expression is taken from the title of Richard Britnell's book *The Closing of the Middle Ages: 1471–1529*, and suggests that the end point of the Middle Ages is the 1520s around which time, as my epilogue notes, the tradition of the classical canon law underwent a radical change at the hands of Luther and his disciples.

74 Prologue B 121.

1 *Contritio Cordis*: The Laughter of Mede and Tearlessness of Contricion

Looking downcast, lying prostrate, sitting sideways, kneeling, weeping, and blushing are among the dramatic actions expected from the sinner confessing in the late medieval penitential forum. Confessional manuals present them as conduct conducive to as well as indicative of the penitent's heartfelt remorse for her/his sins. In his *Pars oculi* (the first part of the *Oculus sacerdotis* that deals with penitential procedures), the canonist William of Pagula advises that the confessor should teach the penitent, "however great a lord he might be" (quantumcumque fuerit magnus dominus), to sit "humbly at the feet of the confessor" (humiliter sedeat ad pedes sacerdotis) and, if the penitent is female, specifies that she position herself "sideways" (ex transuerso) so that the priest "not see her face" (nec faciem suam respiciat).[1] In the *Pupilla oculi,* a confessional manual that "digested complex and sometimes confusing legal texts"[2] and "summarized and systematized William's *Oculus sacerdotis*,"[3] the canonist John Burgh (1370–98) reinforces the linkage between posture and penitence. Under the section "on the mode of

1 William of Pagula, *Pars oculi*, 28–9: "Et debet sacerdos docere eum, quantumcumque fuerit magnus dominus, quod, quociens confitetur peccata sua humiliter sedeat ad pedes sacerdotis; et si femina sit, doceat eam ut sedeat ex transuerso nec faciam suam respiciat quia dicitur Habacuc, idest, Facies earum uentus urens." All quotations from *Pars oculi* are from *An Edition of the "Judica Me Deus" of Richard Rolle*, ed., J.P. Daly. Accompanying the edition of Rolle's *Judica Me Deus* is the corresponding text of *Pars Oculi*, which is based on the Ohio State University Latin MS. 1 [of the *Oculus sacerdotis*] collated with New College Oxford MS. 292; I have cross-checked the quotations with London, British Library Royal MS 8 C II.

2 Helmholz, "Notable Ecclesiastical Lawyers," 67–72.

3 Kelly, "Penitential Theology," 243.

hearing a confession and the mode of confessing," John enjoins the priest to receive "the penitent who is about to confess humbly and readily in such a way that with his [the confessor's] deportment and example, the penitent will be induced to make a humble confession" (*De modo audiendi confessiones et modo confitendi*. Suscipiat itaque sacerdos penitentem confessurum humiliter et mature vt suo gestu et exemplo ad confessionem humilem inducatur).[4] To help confessors commit to memory the signs of remorseful conduct, William, for instance, cites a mnemonic verse-composition that characterizes a "pure faithful confession" as psychosomatically performative: "willing, humble, shameful, secret, and tearful," to name its most dramatic features.[5]

Piers Plowman is no stranger to displays of remorseful as well as remorseless conduct in the penitential forum. The postures and gestures that Mede, Sleuþe, and Contricion exhibit before their confessors dramatize the view – one writ large in manuals for confessors – that conduct makes manifest contrition or the lack thereof. Not just what penitents say but also how they say it and act determines the depth or shallowness of their contrition. Enacting the advice to penitents found, for instance, in William's *Pars oculi*, Mede first "kneled"[6] before she confessed to the friar, but the narrator's remark about her "shamelees" deportment[7] and her "laghynge" (mentioned only in C)[8] manifest her lack of contrition. Levity rather than gravity marks her manner of confession: she offers no signs of shame that canonists deemed indubitable evidence of remorse. Another penitent, Sleuþe, approaches his confessor "al bislabered, wiþ two slymed eiȝen," but before he confesses he asks if he "moste sitte" lest he "nappe," as he "may noȝt stonde ne stoupe

4 John Burgh, *Pupilla oculi*: Capitulum vii; all quotations from *Pupilla oculi* are taken from the Paris 1527 edition, which is unpaginated. For a summary of its contents, see Kelly's "Penitential Theology."

5 In *Pars oculi*, William sums up the characteristics of an ideal confession thus: "Et qualiter debet esse confessio his versibus continentur: Sit simplex, humilis, confessio pura fidelis / Sit frequens, nuda, discreta, libens, uerecunda. / Integra, secreta, lacrimabilis, accelerata. / Fortiter accusans, et sic parere parata" (35). [And how confession ought to be is contained in these verses: A pure faithful confession should be simple, humble/ it should be frequent, bare, discreet, willing, shameful. / [It should be] complete, secret, tearful, quickly performed / Strongly accusing oneself and thus ready to obey.] John cites the same verse but with a slight variation: he adds "atque" before "frequens," and replaces the adverb "fortiter" with the adjective "fortis."

6 B 3.43; see corresponding C 3.45.

7 B 3.44; see corresponding C 3.46.

8 For Mede's laughter, see C 3.55.

ne wiþoute stool knele."[9] In wondering aloud about sitting, standing, and kneeling, Sleuþe treats contrition as a theatrical performance with sets like a "stool."[10] In this, Sleuþe dramatizes the stage-like directives on remorseful conduct outlined in handbooks on confessional procedures. For instance, the *Cum ad sacerdotem*, a thirteenth-century formulary for Dominican confessors, stipulates that the penitent should "stand inclined toward the ground" (stet inclinatus ad terram).[11] The handbook further instructs the confessor to see if "the penitent acts hesitantly or dubiously" (si uiderit penitentem cespitare et dubitare) and, if so, to comfort him with the following script: "Brother, you may securely say whatever you wish, as God is with you."[12] Sleuþe's deportment before his confessor as well as his comments on physical posture stage the penitent's mental impediments to expressing contrition.

No character in the poem stages penitence as theatrical performance more spectacularly than the allegorical figure that signifies it and bears the name of Contricion. At the end of the poem, Contricion invokes the signs of remorseful conduct detailed in confessors' handbooks precisely at moments when he inverts them and thereby enacts his own failure to play his allegorical role. Contricion steps out of character, as it were, when he "clene foryeten to crye and to wepe" or when "[f]or confort of his confessour, contricion he [Contricion] lafte."[13] To the narrator, Contricion's tearlessness and abandonment of "contricion" for his confessor's "confort" make manifest a failure in performance, exposing the distinction or even difference between external conduct and internal character, between playing a penitent and being a penitent. From a theatrical point of view, if only Contricion had not forgotten his part of crying and weeping, he would have remained true to the meaning of his name.

In the scenes that star Mede and Contricion in the penitential forum, the narrator sheds further light on the contrast between playing a penitent and being one, between the production of signs and the presence or absence of contrition. In both Mede's and Contricion's confessional

---

9 B 5.386–8; see corresponding C 7.1–3.

10 B 5.388.

11 *Summa "cum ad sacerdotem,"* 27.

12 I have paraphrased the following Latin sentences: "Sacerdos, si uiderit penitentem cespitare et dubitare et quasi palpando pertransire dicat ei, 'Frater, dicas secure quicquid uoluerit quia Deus uobiscum est,'" 27; all quotations from the *Cum ad sacerdotem* are taken from Goering and Payer's edition.

13 B 20.370–2; see corresponding C 22.370–2.

scenes, contrition is more dramatically than discursively treated.[14] Unlike the allegorical seven deadly sins whose public confessions to Repentaunce in the poem unfold as elaborate narratives of their sinful deeds, Mede and Contricion do talk but do not offer any account of their sins. The narrator hardly tells us that they confess, let alone what sins they recount. The absence of Mede's and Contricion's confessional narratives serves to throw into relief their non-verbal actions: actions that pertain to contrition. Above all, we see how Mede and Contricion as well as their confessors act: how they speak, how they look, who gives what to whom or, for that matter, who gropes whom. It is in the context of his commentary on their role-playing that the narrator presents the practice of canon law as a kind of performance: a play of signs enacted before the discerning narrator who, chorus-like, comments on the presence or absence of contrition in the penitent.

Not surprisingly, scholars of *Piers Plowman* have read Mede's confession as no more than a "vivid demonstration" or "stylish display" of the antifraternal parody or satire that John Yunck and Penn Szittya have long identified as integral to the poem's meaning.[15] This chapter, however, finds in the vividly demonstrative aspects of the poem's confessional scenes not so much parody as the performance of canon law.[16] Such scenes, I contend, dramatize the canonistic procedures for contrition – procedures for the signs that the confessor as "spiritual judge" (iudex spiritualis) should elicit to determine the remorse of his penitents.[17] Precisely at moments when penitents and even confessors act like players – especially bad ones – they stage the canon law pertaining to contrition. In other words, this chapter

14 Elsewhere in the poem contrition is, of course, discursively treated, as in the narrator's discussion of baptism and contrition where he cites the *sententia* "Sola contricio delet peccatum" (B 11.79–84).

15 Derek Pearsall reads the actions of Mede's confessor as comprising a "vivid demonstration of the friar-confessor in action." Pearsall, *A New Annotated Edition of the C Text*, 81. Galloway elaborates on Pearsall's point about the obviousness of the fraternal confessor's actions in the penitential forum: "[t]he friar's negotiations with Meed are a stylish display of bribery." Galloway, *The Penn Commentary*, 295. Yunck, John A. *The Lineage of Lady Meed*; Szittya, *The Antifraternal Tradition in Medieval Literature*.

16 This chapter revises my article "Canon Law and Fraternal Subversions."

17 In *Pars oculi*, William of Pagula considers the confessor a "spiritual judge that should not lack in the gift of expertise; it is necessary that he knows how to recognize whatever he needs in order to judge" (Iudex enim spiritualis non debet carere munere scientie; oportet ut sciat cognoscere quicquid debet iudicare) (37).

uncovers in the narrator's attention to signs of levity such as Mede's laughter and Contricion's tearlessness the contritionist framework that canonists outlined for the handling of sin and sorrow within the penitential forum. In doing so, I conclude that for *Piers Plowman*, as for the handbooks on confession, contrition is about the psychosomatic expression of remorse before a priest in the role of an ecclesiastical judge.

In moving beyond a surface level reading of the two confessional scenes, I deepen Nicholas Gray's reading that *Piers Plowman's* contritionism derives from "the pastoral penitential tradition" that "was already decidedly contritionist."[18] At the same time, I re-situate and enlarge Traugott Lawler's claim about the poem's preoccupation with contrition, which Lawler names the "silent middle term" underlying the poem's pardon formula ("do well and go to heaven, do evil and go to hell").[19] Whereas Lawler tracks numerous intimations of the "silent middle term" throughout the B and C versions, I scrutinize its vocalization or visualization in the narrator's comments on the conduct of penitents and confessors. In so doing, I discover a canonist's approach to contrition that is far more pervasive and pronounced in C than in B, and than previously thought by scholars. A.V.C. Schmidt and Derek Pearsall have argued that a number of C passages foreground a reformist conservatism by deemphasizing contrition and explicitly linking it to other parts of the orthodox penitential process.[20] I argue the opposite, contending that the stress on penitential orthodoxy is always and already present in both versions, if one reads the poem's first and last confessional scenes in light of confessors' manuals. Far from deemphasizing contrition, the narrator, I contend, addresses it but under the aspect of expressive conduct informed by the institutional procedures of private sacramental penance. In pointedly identifying Mede's or Contricion's failure to produce evidence of contrition, the narrator stages a performative but canonistically orthodox recuperation of contrition from those Wycliffite followers who rejected

18 Gray, "A Study of *Piers Plowman*," 83; see also section 2 of ch. 2 (66–86) for Gray's discussion of contrition in late medieval penitential manuals.

19 Traugott Lawler, "The Pardon Formula in *Piers Plowman*: Its Ubiquity, Its Binary Shape, Its Silent Middle Term."

20 Such passages include words that link contrition to satisfaction (C 3.396–400) and those that link contrition to confession (C 12.71), as well as those that link contrition to confession and satisfaction (C 16.25–32). See Schmidt, "Langland's Visions and Revisions," and Pearsall, "Langland and Lollardy."

oral confession or even the entire ecclesiastical institution of penance on the grounds that heartfelt remorse alone remits sin.[21]

This chapter first identifies and describes the contritionist procedures expounded by the canonist Raymond of Peñafort under the title *De paenitentiis et remissionibus* in his *Summa de paenitentia* and then reads both Mede's and Contricion's confessions in light of Raymond's title and William of Rennes's gloss to Raymond's treatise.[22] To strengthen my argument about the poem's engagement of canonistic advice pertaining to contrition, I also discuss other penitential works influential in England such as Thomas of Chobham's *Summa confessorum*.[23]

Composed initially between the years 1222 and 1225[24] but reworked "to reflect the Decretals of Pope Gregory IX, between the years c. 1235 and 1236," Raymond's *Summa de paenitentia* expounded a technical approach to penance that was to serve as a template for the prescriptive literature on penance ranging from treatises such as Hostiensis's *De poenitentiis et remissionibus* and John Burgh's *Pupilla oculi* to confessional manuals.[25] As early as in the "Prooemium" to the *Summa*, Raymond outlines the juridical tenor of his treatise to his audience of fraternal

---

21 See, in particular, the Wycliffite tract "Of Confession," in *The English Works of Wyclif Hitherto Unprinted*, 325–45. For the centrality of contrition to Lollardy, see Barr, "Wycliffite Representations of the Third Estate"; and Hudson, *The Premature Reformation*.

22 All references to Raymond of Peñafort's *De paenitentiis et remissionibus* are from Book 3, Title 34 of *Summa de paenitentia*, vol. 1, pt. B, 793–884, hereafter cited in the text by section and column number. All references to William of Rennes's gloss apparatus to Raymond's *Summa* are from Book 3 of *Summa sancti Raymundi de Peniafort … de poenitentia, et matrimonio cum glossis Ioannis de Friburgo* [i.e., William of Rennes, as the gloss is wrongly attributed by the editor to John of Freiburg] and are indicated by section and page number.

23 Thomas of Chobham's *Summa confessorum* circulated widely in England and on the continent. See *Thomae de Chobham Summa confessorum*, lxxiv–lxxv. All quotations from Thomas's *Summa* are from Broomfield's edition, and are cited by reference to the article number, the distinction (where applicable), the question, and the page number.

24 Kelly, "Penitential Theology," 240.

25 Newhauser, "The Parson's Tale," 1: 531. For Hostiensis's treatment of penance, see *Summa aurea, 5, De poenitentiis et remissionibus*, cols 1549–1666; all quotations from Hostiensis's *Summa* pertain to this edition, and are cited by reference to the book, the book number, the title, the section (where applicable), and the column number respectively. For confessional manuals, see Michaud-Quantin, *Sommes de casuistique et manuels de confession*; Muzzarelli, *Penitenze nel Medioevo*; and Goering, "The Internal Forum."

confessors.[26] But, as Henry A. Kelly has observed, despite being a "very sophisticated" work, Raymond "deals directly with penitence, confession, and absolution only in the final title."[27] In book 3, title 34 of the *Summa*, Raymond treats the administration of the penitential sacrament in a manner not different from how a discerning judge would look for outward signs of guilt and remorse in, say, the external forum of justice. Called *De paenitentiis et remissionibus*, the title comprises an independent "treatise on confession, contrition, absolution, and satisfaction"[28] and one that despite sometimes being deemed "obsolete" in Langland's day continues to be consulted, cited, and even circulated in part, as, for example, in translation in Chaucer's "The Parson's Tale."[29] In *De paenitentiis et remissionibus*, Raymond portrays the confessor as a spiritual judge – entrusted with the task of adjudicating the souls of his penitents. Under this title, Raymond addresses what he in the *Summa*'s "Prooemium" terms the "many problems" or "difficult and perplexing" cases that the fraternal confessor might confront in the "judgment of souls in the penitential forum."[30] In so doing, he lays out the procedures that the confessor should follow: the interrogation of the penitent about her/his sins and their circumstances; the inducement of the penitent to remorse for the sins confessed; the discernment of the penitent's contrition via the signs s/he produces; and the imposition of works of satisfaction to be carried out outside the penitential forum.

As a confessional treatise, *De paenitentiis et remissionibus* offers above all a pragmatic methodology for eliciting and evaluating signs of contrition within the penitential forum. Opening with invocations of Ambrose's

26 Raymond, *Summa de paenitentia*, 277.

27 Kelly, "Penitential Theology," 242.

28 Boyle, "The Summa for Confessors as a Genre," 106. See also Blanco, "Prassi sacramentale della riconciliazione."

29 Kelly, "Penitential Theology," 244; Kelly notes that L.E. Boyle considers it obsolete by 1300; see Boyle, "Summa confessorum," 268. As numerous scholars have noted, a section of Chaucer's "The Parson's Tale" is indirectly dependent upon Raymond's title.

30 Raymond, *Summa de paenitentia*, 277: "… summulam ex diversis auctoritatibus et maiorum meorum dictis diligenti studio compilavi, ut si quando fratres Ordinis nostri vel alii circa iudicium animarum in foro paenitentiali forsitan dubitaverint, per ipsius exercitium, tam in consiliis quam in iudiciis, quaestiones multas et casus varios ac difficiles et perplexos valeant enodare" (… with diligent study, I composed a little work out of diverse authorities and the words of my betters so that if friars of our [Dominican] order or others should have doubts concerning the judgment of souls in the penitential forum, through its exercise with regard to both advice and judgments, they would be able to untangle many problems and various cases both difficult and perplexing).

and Augustine's definitions of "penitence" (paenitentia), Raymond foregrounds the centrality of contrition to private sacramental penance.[31] He presents contrition as bidirectional in its action. On the one hand, contrition refers to the remorse for past sins; on the other, it pertains to the avoidance of future deeds that would have to be rued again.[32] Further on, in another section, Raymond defines "contrition to be that which is universal and continuous, with the intention of confessing and making satisfaction" (contritio, scilicet, quod sit universalis et continua, habens propositum confitendi et satisfaciendi).[33] Although Raymond acknowledges "diverse opinions" (variae sunt opiniones) on "whether, namely, contrition alone without confession removes sins or contrition with confession" (utrum scilicet sola contritio sine confessione tollat peccata, an contritio cum confessione), he leans towards what he calls "the more celebrated view" (opinio est celebrior), namely that "for any adult contrition of heart alone remits sin, if s/he is truly crushed and proposes to abstain from other sins and to confess that sin and make satisfaction for it according to the judgment of the church."[34] For Raymond, contrition is not just about feeling remorse inwardly: it is also about exteriorizing it according to the norms governing the penitential forum. "Confession," as Raymond puts it succinctly and semiotically, "is the sign only, namely, of contrition" (Confessio est signum tantum, scilicet, contritionis).[35] Thus, the penitent should not only experience remorse for her/his sins but also relate them according to the canon law governing the penitential forum, for "confession is a lawful declaration of sins before the priest" (confessio est legitima coram sacerdote peccatorum declaratio).[36] William of Rennes, glossing the words "before the priest" (coram sacerdote) underscores the judicial role of the priest: [he should be the one] "having the use of the keys with regard to him who confesses to him" (habente usum clavium quoad illum, qui ei confitetur).[37]

31 Raymond 1.796; the word "paenitentia" can be translated either as "penitence" or "penance," and, in my book, I have let the context of its usage determine the English translation.

32 Raymond 1.796.

33 Raymond 10.807.

34 Ibid., 12.809: "Tertii vero dicunt sola cordis contritione dimitti peccatum cuilibet adulto, si vere conteritur et proponit ab aliis abstinere et illud confiteri et de eo satisfacere secundum iudicium Ecclesiae. Haec ultima opinio est celebrior."

35 Ibid., 13.811.

36 Ibid., 14.811.

37 William of Rennes, Gloss ad v. *Coram sacerdote*, 13.447.

In the late Middle Ages, as the historian Maria Giuseppina Muzzarelli observes, the penitent's expression of contrition, not the performance of restitution, was the "central moment of remission from sin" (il momento centrale della remissione).[38] Raymond assigns to contrition pride of place by identifying it as the first "rule" (diaeta) of penance, with confession and satisfaction regarded as the second and third rules, respectively.[39] He goes on to consider contrition the logical motivation behind confession and satisfaction, and reiterates the primacy of contrition by defining it as the "intention" (propositum) of confessing and making satisfaction.[40] Raymond recommends that the confessor guide the penitent through three steps in order to ensure that the "penitence" ("paenitentia") be "true" (vera) and "complete" (perfecta).[41] The steps are "contrition of heart" (cordis contritio), "confession of mouth" (oris confessio) and "satisfaction of work" (operis satisfactio).[42] True and complete penitence originates from contrition initially expressed in an oral confession of sins, and subsequently expressed in acts of satisfaction that exteriorize the penitent's remorse for the confessed sins. That is, just as the confessor should elicit verbal and nonverbal signs of contrition during the penitent's confession, so he must ensure that the penitent continues to express signs of contrition outside the forum of penance. To this end, Raymond recommends that the confessor calculate appropriate penances according to the penitential canons. Such penances, which include giving alms and lacerating the flesh, are called "exterior penance" (paenitentia exterior): prayer, fasting, and alms-giving that the penitent undertakes

---

38 Muzzarelli, *Penitenze nel Medioevo*, 82.

39 Raymond 8.803: "Prima diaeta est contritio … Contritio est dolor pro peccatis assumptus cum proposito confitendi et satisfaciendi" (The first rule is contrition … Contrition is the sorrow taken up on account of the sins and with the intention of confessing and making satisfaction).

40 Ibid., 10.807: "Sequitur qualis debeat esse contritio, scilicet, quod sit universalis et continua, habens propositum confitendi et satisfaciendi" (It follows of what kind contrition should be, namely that it should be universal and continuous, with the intention of confessing and making satisfaction).

41 Ibid., 7.802.

42 Ibid., 7.802: "Sequitur videre quae sint necessaria in paenitentia vera et perfecta. Et quidem tria, videlicet: cordis contritio, oris confessio, operis satisfactio. Ioannes, Os aureum [John Chrysostom]: 'Perfecta paenitentia cogit peccatorem omnia libenter sufferre; in corde enim contritio, in ore confessio, in opere tota humilitas, haec est fructifera paenitentia.'"

to oppose the threefold wickedness of the Devil, i.e., pride, lust, and avarice.[43]

In *De paenitentiis et remissionibus*, Raymond also offers a semiotic theory of contrition that underlies the poem's depictions of Mede's and Contricion's confessions. For Raymond, contrition is at once a sign and a thing:

> Sunt enim ibi tria notanda, scilicet, confessio, contritio et mundatio. Confessio est signum tantum, scilicet, contritionis. Contritio est res et signum: res signi confessionis, signum mundationis. Mundatio est res signi tantum, scilicet, contritionis. (Raymond 13.811)

> There are three matters to be noted here, namely, confession, contrition, and purgation. Confession is a sign only, namely, of contrition. Contrition is thing and sign: the thing of the sign of confession, and the sign of purgation. Purgation is the thing of the sign only, namely, of contrition.

The glossator William of Rennes substantiates the verbal expressiveness of confession. His gloss to *Confessio est signum* explains the signifying aspect of confession: [confession is a sign] "on account of the grief and great lamentation that appear in the words of the one confessing and accusing himself" (propter dolorem & planctum enormem, que apparent in verbis confitentis, & se accusantis).[44] Seen in light of Raymond's exposition of penance as a semiotic system, Mede's and Contricion's conduct in the penitential forum and the narrator's commentary on it render vivid the procedures for the performance of contrition: procedures that receive more dramatic foregrounding in C than in B at moments when penitent and confessor generate signs that invert those that canonists such as Raymond and his commentator William deem evidence of heartfelt remorse.

---

43 Ibid., 36.835: "Restat ut de satisfactione, quae paenitentia exterior dicitur, aliqua supponamus. Videamus ergo in quibus consistat satisfactio; deinde visuri qualiter sacerdos debeat procedere circa ipsius impositionem. Consistit satisfactio in tribus, scilicet, oratione, ieiunio et eleemosyna, ut iste ternarius contra illum nefarium diaboli ternarium opponatur: oratio contra superbiam, ieiunium contra carnis concupiscentiam, eleemosyna contra avaritiam. Aliter etiam potest dici, videlicet, quod satisfactio consistit in duobus, scilicet, in largitione eleemosynae et carnis maceratione."

44 William of Rennes, Gloss ad v. *Confessio est signum*, 12.447.

Mede's Confession

We begin with Mede in passus 3 in both B and C. Mede first appears in a secular court and then in the penitential forum. At the opening of the passus, Mede stands "bifore þe Kynge," who summons a "clerk" to "maken hire at ese."[45] Although by no means a spiritual judge, the king uses expressions denoting justice and forgiveness that are subsequently ascribed to Mede's confessor. The king asserts that he "shal assayen hire [himself]" and that, if "she werche bi [his] wit and [his] wil folwe, [he] wol forgyuen hire þis[e] giltes."[46] The "clerk" then "curteisly ... took Mede ... into chambre" where "the iustices somme" "confort[ed] en hire kyndely by Clergies leue" and Mede "mildely" or "myldeliche" (in C) "merciede hem alle."[47] Differing little in both B and C, courtly clerics continue to "conforte" Mede by bidding her to "be blythe" and she, in turn, "hendeliche behyhte hem þe same."[48] The language of comfort and consolation that the narrator has used thus far to describe Mede's encounter with secular justices recurs in his description of her encounter with the confessor that shows up "coped as a frere"[49] but is otherwise left unannounced and unintroduced.

As soon as the fraternal confessor encounters Mede, he speaks to her just like the courtly clerics who have comforted her:

> To Mede þe mayde myldeliche he sayde:
> "Thow lewed men and lered men haued layn by the bothe,
> And Falshede yfonde the al this fourty wyntur
> Y shal assoyle the mysulue for a seem whete
> And ȝut be thy bedman, and brynge adoun Consience." (C 3.39–43)

Gray sees in the confessor's humility and obedience before Mede a thorough inversion of the proper conditions of humility, obedience, and shame that the penitent should show: "for far from accepting her penance meekly, Mede clearly regards it as a matter of pride and an opportunity to vaunt herself, while it is her confessor who bows

45 B 3.2–4; see also corresponding C 3.2–4.
46 B 3.5–8; see also corresponding C 3.5–8.
47 B 3.9–20; see also corresponding C 3.9–21.
48 C 3.27–30; see also corresponding B 3.26–9.
49 B 3.35; see also corresponding C 3.38.

humbly, promises obedience, and speaks 'softly, in shrift as it were,' to her, the penitent, thus thoroughly inverting the proper conditions."[50]

The "inversion of proper conditions" can, however, at the same time be read from the fraternal confessor's perspective. Doing so will enable us to witness the extent to which the confessor – despite his humble deportment – is already complicit with the proud penitent in their complementary efforts to adapt the canonistic advice on contrition to make mutual material profit. To be sure, the friar's speaking "myldeliche" or "softely" enacts Raymond's advice that confessors adopt "a pius, sweet, and pleasant speech to induce him [the penitent] to remorse and confession" (pio, dulci ac suavi alloquio inducere ipsum ad compunctionem et confessionem) in the penitent for her/his sins.[51] Presenting the confessor as a diligent inquirer, Raymond advises the confessor to "be benevolent" (adsit benevolus) and "ready to raise and bear the burden with the penitent" (paratus erigere, et secum onus portare); the confessor must be "sweet in disposition" (habeat dulcedinem in affectione), "always softening or placating the penitent" (semper eum iuvet leniendo), by "consoling" (consolando), "by offering hope" (spem promittendo), and "when necessary, by rebuking [and] [b]y speaking he may express grief, [and] by toiling he may instruct" (et cum opus fuerit etiam increpando. Doleat loquendo, instruat operando).[52] In his gloss to *Doleat*, William of Rennes portrays the confessor's sorrowful deportment as expressive of empathy for the penitent: "that is, he [the confessor] shows himself to sorrow for his [the penitent's] sin" (id est, se dolere pro peccato eius ostendat).[53] Filtering Raymond's penitential treatise via John of Freiburg's *Summa confessorum*, William of Pagula, likewise, recommends that the confessor "initially use sweet and persuasive talk" (primo quod dulci ac suavi colloquio) when addressing the penitent not, of course, to encourage mirth in the penitent but "to move him to contrition and confession of his sins" (moueat eum ad compunccionem et ad confitendum peccata sua).[54] The friar's mild

50 Gray, "A Study of *Piers Plowman*," 103.

51 The narrator uses the expression "ful softely" in B 3.37 and "myldeliche" in the corresponding line in C 3.39. Gray, "A Study of *Piers Plowman*," 103. See Raymond 32.831 for the advice on how the confessor should speak to the penitent.

52 Raymond 30.827–8.

53 William of Rennes, Gloss ad v. *Doleat*, 28.463.

54 *Pars oculi*, 31. In his "Penitential Theology," Henry A. Kelly sees William of Pagula as one of the "unacknowledgers" that drew on John of Freiburg's immensely popular *Summa confessorum*, which, in turn, drew on and updated Raymond's penitential work, 242–3.

disposition towards Mede at once exemplifies and inverts Raymond's, William of Rennes's, and William of Pagula's advice on the the confessor's deportment. Whereas Raymond, William of Rennes, and William of Pagula recommend mildness of speech to elicit signs of contrition from the penitent, the friar adopts such a mode of address to elicit "a horse-load of wheat" (a seem whete) and a monetary fee for Mede's absolution.[55]

In his discussion of Mede's "bad confession," Gray has eruditely commented on the poet's skilful use of prosody to parody the penitential process in general.[56] Here, I shall draw upon Gray's commentary in order to uncover more evidence for Mede's dramatic inversion of the norms governing contrition expounded in *De paenitentiis et remissionibus* or, for that matter, in any other post Lateran IV handbook on penitential procedure. These contrition-specific violations are demonstrated by the steps that the friar and Mede together follow in the scene, and the words they exchange as well as by the narrator's remarks on their actions.

The friar's gentle offer to grant Mede absolution in return for wheat no doubt amounts to simony. Underlying the friar's simoniacal offer is the less evident violation of a sequence of procedures whereby the confessor knowingly poses questions to obtain evidence of the penitent's remorse. In *De paenitentiis et remissionibus*, the confessor is portrayed in the character of a "spiritual judge" (spiritualis iudex) who should beware of committing the "crime of negligence/wickedness" (crimen nequitiae) and "therefore should not lack in the gift of knowledge" (ita non careat munere scientiae).[57] For "judicial power" (iudiciaria enim potestas) requires that the confessor "discern" (discernat) what he should "judge" (iudicare).[58] Put in another way, "it is necessary for him to know to recognize whatever he has to judge" (oportet ut sciat cognoscere quidquid debet iudicare).[59] Furthermore, the confessor should be "a diligent inquisitor, a subtle investigator, who questions the sinner wisely and, as it were, astutely even about that [sin] that the sinner might perhaps

55 C 3.42; see corresponding B 3.40.

56 Gray, "A Study of *Piers Plowman*," 103–8. Gray contrasts Mede's confession with that of the penitents in the B version of passus 5.

57 Raymond 30.827: "Caveat spiritualis iudex, sicut non commisit crimen nequitiae, ita non careat munere scientiae."

58 Ibid.: "Iudicaria enim potestas hoc expostulat, ut quod debet iudicare, discernat."

59 Ibid.

not be aware of, or wish to conceal because of shame" (Diligens igitur inquisitor, subtilis investigator sapienter et quasi astute interroget a peccatore quod forsitan ignoret, vel verecundia velit occultare).[60] Mede's fraternal confessor commits not only simony but also fails to exemplify Raymond's ideal of the confessor as diligent and subtle inquisitor. Rather than inducing Mede to a canonistically valid expression of contrition and confession, the friar underscores the ubiquity of sin, and negotiates absolution for a monetary fee. In so behaving, the friar excuses Mede from the necessity of expressing any verbal and visual signs of remorse.

Just as the confessor ignores procedures for seeking out evidence for contrition, so Mede displays her lack of remorse in the manner in which she confesses and thereby subverts the "form" (forma) that Raymond recommends for expressing contrition.[61] The narrator invokes such a form in remarking on Mede's "shamelees" mode of confessing: "[Mede] ... shrof hire of hire sherewednesse – shamelees, I trowe, / Tolde hym a tale and took hym a noble."[62] The word "tale" used to characterize Mede's confession may, of course, mean no more than an oral form of narration – the general sense of the word in Middle English, as, say, in Chaucer's work.[63] But the narrator may also intend "tale" in the sense of "an oral account or falsehood" – a meaning active in the poem, as, for instance, in the name of the character "Tomme Trewe-tonge-tel-me-no-tales."[64] That Mede's "tale" is an act of false tale-telling is indicated not just by her "shamelees" manner of confessing but also by the verbs "told" and "took" that alliteratively connect in a single line her verbal confession and her physical conveyance of the coin. As Gray has argued, the line's terse brevity encapsulates the speed or shortness of Mede's "tale," and calls attention to its "levity" and thereby the paucity of contrition.[65] In Raymond's

60 Ibid.

61 Ibid., 28.825: "Confiteatur ergo paenitens integre iuxta formam praedictam explicans omnia." The "formam praedictam" refers to the manner of confession discussed by Raymond in the preceding sections.

62 B 3.44–5; see corresponding C 3.46–7.

63 Strohm, "Some Generic Distinctions in the *Canterbury Tales*," 322; see also Strohm's "*Storie, Spelle, Geste, Romaunce, Tragedie*."

64 B 4.18.

65 In "A Study of *Piers Plowman*," Gray notes that "Mede's confession begins and ends within the space of one of Langland's tersest and most summarily dismissive half-lines – she 'told hym a tale' [and that] [b]oth by prosody and by diction (the use of the word 'tale'), and with the greatest economy, Langland condemns Mede's confession out of hand for its levity and cursory manner, without even troubling to repeat a word of it," 107.

treatise, "contritio" derives from the deliberate and slow form of confessional speech – one that should be "detailed" (discreta); that is, the penitent "should confess clearly and individually each of the sins, [and] not all together" (ut distincte ac separatim confiteatur singula peccata, non confuse).[66] Raymond emphasizes that "contrition and shame" are all the greater when the sins are narrated with "slowness and deliberation":

> Item, morosa, ut non dicantur peccata in transcursu, sicut campsores computant nummos, sed cum mora et deliberatione, ut ex hoc accendatur devotio, et maior habeatur contritio et verecundia. (Raymond 27.825)

> Also, [the confession should be] deliberate, so that the sins should not be told in haste, as money-changers count coins, but with slowness and deliberation so that from this devotion may be kindled, and more contrition and shame may be obtained.

Mede's stenographically brief "tale" invokes Raymond's conditions for remorseful speech by failing to fulfil them. Likewise, the swift exchange of a coin ("noble") between Mede and the confessor recalls Raymond's numismatic analogy between unrepentant penitents and money-changers ("campsores") and thereby makes manifest her lack of contrition.

The narrator's choice of the expression "shamelees" to characterize Mede's swift confession also invokes the sign of "shame" (verecundia) that Raymond sees as the form and function of a deliberate and detailed confession:[67]

> Sequitur quae sint necessaria ad veram confessionem. Ad hoc dicas quod quattuor, videlicet, quod sit amara, festina, integra et frequens. De primo, scilicet de amaritudine ... Signa huius amaritudinis sunt quinque: Verecundia, humilitas, lacrimae, fortitudo vincens pudorem, et pronitas oboedientiae. De primo signo, scilicet verecundia, Augustinus: "Laborat mens patiendo erubescentiam, et quoniam verecundia est magna poena, qui erubescit pro Christo, fit dignus misericordia." (Raymond 23.817–18)

---

66 Raymond 27.824.

67 In the *Templum dei*, a source for the late fourteenth-century English penitential work "The Clensyng of Mannes Soule," Robert Grosseteste enjoins the confessor to look for signs including shame in the penitent's mode of confession: "vere, scilicet, integer, plane, nude, amare, verecunde" (250).

> Next: what things are necessary for a true confession. Answer that there are four: that confession be sorrowful, speedy, whole, and frequent. Concerning the first, namely, about sorrow ... the signs of sorrow are five: shame ("verecundia"), humility, tears, fortitude overcoming reticence, and readiness for obedience. Concerning the first sign, namely, shame, Augustine says: "The mind labors by suffering shyness; and, because shame is a great penalty, one who blushes before Christ is rendered worthy of mercy."

Raymond's sense of "verecundia" may not exactly match the "shame" meant by the narrator in his comment on Mede's "shamelees" behaviour but both the narrator and the canonist identify shame as a first sign expressive of "a true confession" (ad veram confessionem).

Late medieval penitential manuals elevated the penitent's expression of shame to the status of punishment. Discussing the shift in emphasis from the early medieval penitentials to the later ones, Haren notes that shame or "the embarrassment involved in confession was also regarded as a penance in itself ... It was this 'erubescentia' that made a virtue of confession to the laity in the absence of a priest and that prompted some theologians to assert that in such a case, confession to a layman was essential for forgiveness."[68] In a scene that follows Mede's confession, the penitent Envy uses the word "shame" in the sense of "shrifte," underscoring the interchangeability of the two penitential stages: "'Ne neiþer shrifte ne shame, but whoso shrape my mawe?'"[69] Linking the "sh" words, the alliteration and syntax collocate "shrift" and "shame" in one semantic continuum. Earlier in the same penitential forum, Envy underscores the interchangeabilty of "shame" and "shrift": "'I wolde ben yshryue,'" quod þis sherewe, "'and I for shame dorste.'"[70] In admitting to his confessor that he would like to be shriven but dare not do so on account of "shame," Envy foregrounds the centrality of shame to the entire penitential process.

In the C version of Mede's confession, the narrator goes on to include a slight but significant emphasis on her failure to manifest shame. In a line not present in the corresponding section in B, the narrator notes

---

68 Haren, "A Study of the *Memoriale presbiterorum*," 1: 37. See also Quera, "De contritionismo et attritionismo."

69 B 5.123; see corresponding C 6.90. The majority of instances of "shame" or its cognates in the poem occurs in the context of penance; see *Piers Plowman: Concordance*, 585.

70 B 5.90; there is no corresponding line on "shame" in C.

Mede's laughter in her mode of acceding to the confessor's request for material support for decorating the church: "Loueliche þat lady laghynge sayde."[71] The present participle "laghynge" casts Mede as the antithesis of the contrite penitent, since her mirth stands out as egregious in light of Thomas of Chobham's discussion of "signs and proofs" (signa et indicia) of contrition in a "questio" in his *Summa confessorum*.[72] Contrasting signs such as tears and blushes with those expressive of denial of or indifference to sin, Thomas names laughter as a sign that an impenitent sinner might express and that a confessor must look for and correct with the imposition of penance:

> Primo ergo debet inquirere si vere peniteat, sicut ait Augustinus: *qui penitet omnino peniteat*. Et sicut medicus corporalis multa signa et indicia inquirit de morbo patientis utrum possit curari vel non, ita medicus spiritualis per multa signa debet considerare circa penitentem si vere peniteat vel non, veluti si gemat, si ploret, si erubescat, et cetera talia faciat. Vel si rideat vel se peccasse neget vel peccata sua defendat et similia.
>
> Si autem sacerdos per confessionem penitentis vel per alia certa indicia perpendat ipsum non vere penitere, nullam potest vel debet ei iniungere penitentiam.[73]
>
> Therefore, he [the priest) must first of all inquire whether s/he [the penitent] truly repents, as Augustine says: *who repents should do so completely*. Just as the physical doctor investigates many signs and marks concerning the sickness of the patient whether he can be cured or not, so the spiritual doctor must determine through many signs whether or not the penitent truly repents, such as if he sorrows, cries, blushes, and makes other such signs. Or if he laughs or denies to have sinned or defends his sins and suchlike.
>
> But if the priest determines by means of the penitent's confession or by other definite signs that the penitent does not truly repent, he cannot or should not impose penance upon the penitent.

So egregious are signs of mirth in the penitential forum that the Dominican manual *Cum ad sacerdotem* warns that the priest "should beware

71 C 3.55. For a learned treatment of laughter in *Piers Plowman*, see Goldstein's "Ve Vobis qui ridetis (Lk. 6.25)."

72 Thomas of Chobham, *Summa confessorum*, art. 6, dist. 1, q. ia, *Si peniteat*, 240.

73 Thomas of Chobham, *Summa confessorum*, art. 6, dist.1, q. ia, *Si peniteat*, 240–1.

of boisterous guffawing and laughter and beware of the desire to spit when he confesses, lest perchance he should cough" (Caueat autem a cachinno et risu et ne spuere uelit cum audierit peccata, nisi forte tusseat).[74] Mede's fraternal confessor, of course, could not care less: he lets her speak on in her merry tone.

The laughter of Mede is all the more indicative of the inversion of the sign of contrition on account of her gender. The contemporary penitential manual, the *Memoriale presbiterorum*, singles out female penitents as most lachrymose in their expression of contrition, and contrasts them with those penitents who are unable to shed any tears and have stony hearts:

> Ecce enim quod plerique in confessionibus suis ubertim / effundunt lacrimas et potissime mulieres que pro quolibet vento flent et promittunt quod a peccatis prius commissis iterato non committendis firmiter se et perpetuo abstinebunt. Alii vero non possunt flere dum confitenter, corda habentes lapidea; bene tamen promittunt quod de cetero non committent peccata prius commissa et sic tamquam vere penitentes et contriti absolvuntur per confessores suos. Tamen postea ad ipsa peccata redeunt. Tales igitur "irrisores" vocantur in iure, quia non dicuntur vere contriti set ficte. (in the section "b. lxxiii. De contricione peccatoris," 276)[75]

> Now, then, many in their confessions copiously shed tears and, specially, women who cry at whatever occasion [literally, whatever gust] and promise that they will not commit the sins again that they had committed and will firmly and perpetually abstain from doing so. Others, however, are not able to cry while they confess, having stony hearts; they, however, promise well that they will not commit the sins that they had earlier committed and thus, as if they were true and contrite penitents, they are absolved by their confessors. However, later they return to the self-same sins. Such [penitents] therefore in the law are called "mockers," described as not truly but falsely contrite.

Seen in light of this passage on false penitents, Mede's "laghynge" renders audible – albeit in a psychosomatic vein – the "mockers" (irrisores)

74 Summa *"cum ad sacerdotem,"* 26.

75 Unless otherwise stated, all quotations from the *Memoriale presbiterorum* are from Michael Haren's unpublished edition of the text in volume 2 of his D Phil dissertation, "A Study of the *Memoriale Presbiterorum.*"

denounced in the *Memoriale*: the poem's English word translates the root verb form of the Latin "ridere" (to laugh) underlying the nominal "irrisor." In passing uncorrected from shamelessness to laughter, Mede performs her lack of contrition and thereby renders audible and risible the canonistic advice concerning the signs of contrition.

Furthermore, the friar allows Mede to invert the pedagogical hierarchy that Raymond establishes between confessor and penitent, between instructor and the pupil: the confessor is to teach the penitent about the heinousness of sin and the necessity of remorse. During Mede's confession, the friar makes no effort to educate his penitent but requests her to finance the decoration of his church, a request that emboldens Mede to usurp the pedagogical role of the confessor.[76] In the *Memoriale*'s rubric "On the mutual contract by law between confessor and the confessing penitent" (De obligacione mutua contracta de iure inter confessorem et sibi confitentem), the author bases upon the "authority of law" (Iuris auctoritate) the pedagogical terms by which the confessor and penitent are bound.[77] Noting that the people of God should not argue with those from whom they desire to be instructed, blessed, and saved, the *Memoriale* author states: "For the people should be taught, by the same people and chastised, but not the other way around because the disciple is not above the master nor ought to be by law" (Populus enim docendus est ab eisdem et corripiendus, set non e converso, eo quod discipulus non est supra magistrum nec de iure esse debet).[78] It is this law that Mede's confessor subverts by letting the penitent play the teacher to him for material gain. Indeed, the poem's invocation of this law is all the more specific to friars when we bear in mind that the *Memoriale's* author goes on to exhort confessors "especially from the

76 C 3.50–4: "And he assoilede here sone and sethen a sayde, / 'We han a wyndowe a worchynge, wol stande vs ful heye; / Wolde ȝe glase þat gable and graue ther ȝoure name, / In masse and in mataynes for Mede we shal singe / Solempneliche and softlyche as for a suster of oure ordre.'"

77 Here is the full sentence with which the section on mutual obligation between confessor and penitent opens in the *Memoriale presbiterorum*: "Iuris auctoritate inducitur quoddam obligacionis vinculum quo ex effectu sacramenti penitencialis confessor et sibi confitens invicem astringuntur et si alter uter offenderit vel non observaverit ea ad que astringitur in hoc graviter delinquere comprobatur" (By the authority of law a certain bond of obligation is introduced by which from the performance of the penitential sacrament the confessor and the one confessing in turn to him are bound, and if either one or the other should offend or not observe the [terms] to which each is bound, he is shown to fail in this gravely), 2: 279.

78 *Memoriale presbiterorum*, 2: 279.

mendicant orders, who acquire many illicit goods from such gain by imposing light penances for cases in which a certain penance is established by the canon and mostly in cases in which by law they are not permitted to absolve or bind" (maxime illi de ordinibus mendicancium qui ex tali questu bona plurima illicita sibi adquirunt, penitencias leves iniungendo in casibus in quibus certa penitencia a canone est statuta, et maxime in casibus in quibus de iure sibi non permittitur absolvere vel ligare).[79] The *Memoriale* author's specification of the contract between confessor and penitent as legal ("de iure") casts Mede and the mendicant friar's reversal of roles as a legal infraction and not just as a pastoral oversight.

Intent on obtaining an easy absolution for her sinning protégées, Mede now offers to be the confessor's "frende" and promises never to "fayle" him so long as "ȝe [the friar] louyen this lordes that lecherye haunteth, / and lacketh nat this ladyes þat louyeth þe same."[80] Mede's offer to be the fraternal confessor's "frere" punningly reinforces her appropriation of fraternal authority, and thereby reinforces the inversion of the hierarchical relationship between penitent and confessor mandated by Raymond for the exteriorization of remorse. Offering to decorate the confessor's friary, Mede now teaches the friar a lesson about lechery:

> "'Hit is but frelete of fleysche, ȝe fyndeth wel in bokes,
> And a cours of kynde, wherof we comen alle.
> Ho may askape þe sclaundre, þe skathe myhte sone be mended;
> Hit is synne as of seuene noon sonner relesed.
> Haueth mercy,' quod Mede, 'on men þat hit haunteth.'" (C 3.59–63)[81]

Mede deploys terms such as "sclaundre," "mercy," and "amende" that penitential writers commonly use to speak of contrition, but she wrenches them out of their normative context. Arguing for the irrelevance of Repentaunce, Mede instructs the friar that the sinner who commits lechery may evade the shame inherent in ill fame ("sclaundre"), and that the damage ("skathe") caused by lechery is soon amended ("þe skathe myhte sone be mended").

79 *Memoriale presbiterorum*, 2: 279–80.
80 C 3.56–8; see corresponding B 3.52–4.
81 See corresponding B 3.55–9.

Mede's characterization of "sclaundre" as something that may be avoided once again invokes and inverts the normative requirement of "shame" (verecundia) that, as we have discussed above, Raymond singles out as a first sign of contrition.[82] Raymond makes clear that the penitent must experience and express the shame ("verecundia") that accompanies her/his sins in order to be repentant. Mede, by contrast, argues for the dissociation of shame ("sclaundre") from the sin of lechery by underlining that a sinner "may askape þe sclaundre." In Middle English usage, the word "sclaundre" includes "an action or a situation bringing disgrace or shame," and "shameful distress."[83] The context of lechery and the confessional setting within which Mede deploys the term "sclaundre" hold in tension two opposed senses of the same word: "sclaundre" as a sin kindred to lechery and "sclaundre" as a penitential sign expressive of contrition, as in Raymond's "verecundia." The Middle English poem *Ipotis* defines the word "sclaundre" as "shame" within a penitential context, although it does not endow it with the redemptive sense of Raymond's "verecundia": "Sclaundre is a noþer shame, / To brynge a man in yuell fame, / But giff he hym make þer off clere / His soule goþ to heell fire; / Þan is pryde also anoþer, / Lecherie is the thirde broþer."[84] To escape "þe sclaundre" in the latter penitential sense of the word is to avoid the disgrace or shame that, according to Raymond's citation of Augustine, comprises "a great punishment" (magna poena).[85]

Mede invokes another penitential term – "mercy" – but invests it with a meaning that mocks (and hence manifests) the contrition-laden valence conferred upon it by Raymond. Raymond cites Augustine to argue that mercy ("misericordia") is the result of the "great punishment" (magna poena) that the contrite penitent endures and that the penitent's contrition justifies the mercy that Christ grants the penitent.[86] Mede, by contrast, argues for "mercy" not because the penitent endures

82 Raymond 23.818.

83 *Middle English Dictionary*, s.v. "sclaundre."

84 *Ipotis*, lines 366–71, in Sutton, "Hitherto Unprinted Manuscripts of the Middle English *Ipotis*," 126.

85 Raymond 23.818.

86 Ibid., 23.818: Concerning the first sign, namely, shame, Augustine says: "The mind labours by suffering embarrassment, and because shame is a large penance, the one who becomes embarrassed in front of Christ is worthy of mercy."

the punishment for sin, but because of the sin's triviality. Because Mede holds the sin of lechery so frivolous that a penitent guilty of it is "as of seuene noon sonner relesed," she recommends that the friar grant "mercy" to such a penitent.

Mede's simultaneous invocation and subversion of contrition-centred procedures find sharper expression in certain words found in C but not present in B:

> And Y shal cuuere ȝoure kyrke and ȝoure cloustre make,
> Bothe wyndowes and wowes Y wol amende and glase,
> And do peynten and purtrayen ho payede for þe makyng,
> That euery seg shal se Y am a sustre of ȝoure ordre. (C 3.64–7)[87]

Both the B and C versions of this passage are alike in their mention of Mede's offer to refurbish the friar's church. The versions differ, however, with regard to two words – "amende" and "ordre" – that are unique to the C passage (as cited above). Seen in light of the corresponding passage in B, both words confer on the C passage a more technical cast: C's inclusion of "ordre" rather than "house" does not change the meaning in B but sharpens the focus on the friar's technical or institutional status, and C's use of "amende," likewise, is discursively marked. In vernacular confessional manuals, the term "amende" and its cognates designate the third and last penitential stage: satisfaction. For instance, the fourteenth-century *Ayenbite of Inwyt* defines amendment specifically as the "þridde" penitential step: "hit behoueþ þet he habbe þri þing þet byeþ ine zoþe penonce. Þe uerste þing is: uorþenchinge of herte. Þe oþer: ssrifte of mouþe. Þe þridde: is ynoȝ amendement be dede. Of þise þri þinges is y-hol: þe hauberk of penonce."[88] Under the section "Of Ynoȝbote," the author goes on to clarify that this "ynoȝ amendement" finds expression in terms of spiritual action ("dede") that follows "ssrifte" (absolution) and includes "uestinges," "elmesse," and "benes."[89] Likewise, *The Book of Vices and Virtues*, a fourteenth-century translation of the French Dominican penitential work *Somme des vices et*

87 See corresponding B 3.60–3: "And I shal couere youre kirk, youre cloistre do maken,/ Wowes do whiten and wyndowes glaȝen, / Do peynten and portraye and paie for þe makynge, / That euery segge shal see I am suster of youre house."

88 *Dan Michel's Ayenbite of Inwyt*, 170–1.

89 Ibid., 180.

des vertus, relates "amendes" to the labour of satisfaction ("sufficiaunt amendes in dede doynge") undertaken for the profit of the soul ("þe profiȝt of here soules").[90] Identifying amendment with the third stage of the penitential process, Raymond defines it as a series of spiritual actions performed to further exteriorize contrition:

> Restat ut de satisfactione, quae paenitentia exterior dicitur, aliqua supponamus ... Consistit satisfactio in tribus, scilicet, oratione, ieiunio et eleemosyna ... Eleemosyna autem est triplex. Prima consistit in cordis contritione, quando aliquis seipsum offert Deo, iuxta illud: "Miserere animae tuae placens Deo" ... Est autem oratio pius affectus mentis in Deum tendens ... item non debent peti in oratione temporalia, saltem principaliter, sed spiritualia, aeterna, et ad salutem pertinentia ... Item exiguntur in oratione ista decem et tria scilicet: quod sit fidelis, secura, humilis, discreta, devota, verecunda, secreta, pura, lacrimosa, attenta, fervida, operosa, et assidua. (Raymond 36, 37.835–7)

> It remains to add something about satisfaction, which is called exterior penance ... [it] consists in three things: prayer, fasting and alms ... [A]lms are threefold. The first kind consists in contrition of the heart when someone offers himself to God, according to the words: "Pleasing God, have mercy on your soul" ... For prayer is a pious feeling of the mind inclining towards God ... Again, temporal things ought not to be requested in prayer, at least, principally, but things that are spiritual, eternal and pertinent to salvation ... These thirteen things are required in prayer, namely that prayer be faithful, untroubled, humble, discreet, devout, abashed, secret, pure, tearful, attentive, fervid, energetic, and assiduous.

Although Mede follows an appropriate procedural step by turning to amendment after her absolution, she alters the meaning of that step substantially when she removes "amende" out of the contritionist context in which Raymond and the vernacular penitential writers who follow him locate it. For Mede, to "amende" is not to undertake, as Raymond recommends, contrite, pious, humble, and discreet acts of satisfaction directed towards spiritual matters ("spiritualia, aeterna, et ad salutem pertinentia"). Rather, as Mede makes clear, making amends is performing acts for temporal gain, acts that make manifest pride and impunity

90 *The Book of Vices and Virtues*, 171, 183–4.

(the "temporalia" that, as Raymond advises, the penitent should not pray for). She will "cuuere" the "kyrke," "glase" the "wyndowes and wowes," and "do peynten and purtrayen."[91] Mede's shameless audacity invokes and inverts the figure of Mary Magdalene as characterized in the canonist Hostiensis's treatment of the signs of an exemplary confession. Identifying fortitude as the fourth sign of confession, Hostiensis in the section "Qualis debet esse confessio" (Of what kind a confession should be) characterizes it in the personality of Magdelene:

> Quartum signum est fortitudo, sicut patet in Magdalena, que adeo fortis fuit in confitendo, quod nullo pudore obstante, publice confessa fuit turpitudinem peccatorum, neque timuit. (*Summa aurea*, 5, *De poenitentiis et remissionibus*, 4, col. 1564)

> The fourth sign is fortitude, as it appears in Mary Magdalene, who was so courageous in confessing that, notwithstanding any shame, publicly confessed the filthiness of sins, and was fearless.

Needless to say, Mede's fortitude, shamelessness, and forthright advocacy of lechers serve as a stark counterpoint to or inverted illustration of the canonistically valid signs of contrition.

The violations of contrition-centred procedures in Mede's confession in passus 3 are intensified by none other than the allegorical figure of Contricion in his confession to Frere Flatrere in passus 22. Seen from the perspective of Mede's confession in C, both the B and C versions of Contricion's confession offer all the more explicit evidence of the "silent middle term" that is affirmed or enacted in its very subversion.

Contricion's Confession

Unlike Mede's confession that takes place near the outset of the narrator's wanderings, Contricion's confession occurs at their end and is almost identical in both B and C.[92] The narrator arrives at the recently instituted ecclesiastical setting (Vnitee) for Contricion's confession by himself wandering through "Contricion and Confession."[93]

91 C 3.64–6; see corresponding B 3.60–2.

92 Hence, in the block quotations that follow, I cite only from C.

93 B 20.212–13: "And þere by conseil of Kynde I comsed to rome / Thoruȝ Contricion and Confession til I cam to Vnitee."

The "Vnitee" is Piers's "newly constructed Church, the Barn of Unity"[94] but, not unlike the corrupt church of the poem's Prologue that it replaces, "Vnitee" is already susceptible to widespread clerical and fraternal neglect of the *cura animarum*. Parish priests and friars alike turn out to be ineffectual confessors. Indicting the parish clergy ("inparfit prestes and prelates of Holy Churche")[95] for their inability to administer penance properly, Conscience calls out for able confessors. Friars hear the call and arrive in droves. Conscience, however, "forsoek hem," as he considers them no more competent ("Ac for they couthe nat wel here crafte") than the "inparfit" parish confessors.[96] As Nede's advice makes clear, Conscience accuses the friars of incompetence not because they lack skill ("crafte") in hearing confessions, but because they profit illegally from their craft, and because they lack "patrymonye."[97] Nede informs Conscience that the friars come "for couetyse to haue cure of soules: / And for thei aren pore, parauntur, for patrimonye hem faileth."[98] Understandably, Nede enjoins Conscience to "charge hem [the friars] with no cure."[99]

In his account of the curatorial crisis expressed by Conscience and Nede, however, the narrator shifts the focus from profit to penitence. Distinguishing between parish and fraternal confessors, he denounces both within the framework of contrition:

And euele is this yholde in parsches of Yngelond;
For persones and parsche prestes, þat sholde þe peple shryue,
They ben curatours cald, to knowe and to hele,
Alle þat ben here parschienes penaunses enioynen
And be aschamed in here shryft; ac shame maketh hem wende
And fle to þe freres – as fals folk to Westmynstre,
That borweth, and bereth hit theddere, and thenne biddeth frendes
Ȝerne of forȝeuenesse or lengore ȝeres leue. (C 22.280–7)

"Shame" is the reason why "þe peple" flee from their proper "persones and parsche prestes" to "þe freres." In order to distinguish parish

94 Simpson, "Religious Forms and Institutions in *Piers Plowman*," 109.
95 C 22.229. See corresponding B 20.229.
96 C 22.231. See corresponding B 20.231.
97 B 20.231 and 234; see corresponding C 22.231 and 234.
98 C 22.233–4.
99 C 22.237.

confessors from fraternal confessors, the narrator, as Gray notes, invokes two opposed or paradoxical kinds of shame theorized by canonists.[100] Raymond designates the shame proper to (and productive of) oral confession as "verecundia," which, as we have already seen, is deemed the foremost sign of contrition in the penitential forum.[101] This is the laudable shame that penitents experience and express when they are "aschamed in here shrift" – the contrition that the "parsche prestes" as "curatours" "enioynen" upon them.[102] At the same time, there is the shame that hinders one from going to confession and expressing contrition. Raymond designates the shame that impedes oral confession and contrition as "pudor," which he singles out as one of the four impediments to the penitential process:

> Sunt autem quattuor praecipua impedimenta, scilicet: pudor, timor, spes et desperatio ... Pudor scilicet confitendi. Hic quidem pudor retrahit multos a paenitentia. (Raymond 69.877)

> There are, however, above all four impediments, namely, shame, fear, hope, and desperation ... shame, namely, of confessing. This shame, indeed, holds many back from penance.

As the foremost impediment, "pudor" is the kind of shame that the narrator evokes in his complaint about the "shame" that "maketh hem [the parishioners] wende / And fle to þe freres."[103] The narrator focuses

---

100 Gray briefly discusses the paradoxical nature of shame expressed in this passage, calling attention to Langland's reference to shame as both proper to and an impediment to confession; see Gray, "Study of *Piers Plowman*," 100.

101 See Raymond 23.817–18, 27.824–5. Raymond does not restrict the term "verecundia" to mean solely the laudable penitential shame, for he uses the verbal form of "verecundia" to mean "pudor," as, for instance, in the use of "verecundetur" in the following line of advice to the confessor: "Item, suadeat ei quod non verecundetur confiteri, quia non homini confitetur sed Deo" (Also, [the confessor] should persuade him not to be ashamed to confess because he confesses not to man but to God) (Raymond 32.831).

102 C 22.281–3. See corresponding B 20.281–3.

103 C 22.284–5. See corresponding B 20.284–5. It is worth noting that the word "pudor" itself elsewhere in the penitential tradition takes on a positive role and is used alongside "verecundia" and, hence, only context indicates the valence of the word; see, for instance, Hostiensis's collocation of "pudor" and "verecundia" when citing John Chrysostum in order to elaborate on tears as a sign of contrition: "Lachrimae lavant delictum, quod pudor est confiteri, id est, cum pudore et verecundia confitendum" (*Summa aurea*, 5, *De poenitentiis et remissionibus*, 4, col. 1564.

on contrition and its avoidance, leaving aside the contention over confessional rights that Conscience has been explaining as dividing friars and parish priests. He does so by stylistically foregrounding in one line the laudable ("verecundia") and the reprehensible ("pudor") kinds of shame distinguished by Raymond: "And be aschamed in here shryft; ac shame maketh hem wende."[104] In the first hemistich, the word "aschamed" refers to Raymond's "verecundia" as it is the sign of contrition that the penitent is expected to show "in here shryft." In the second hemistich, the word "shame" refers to Raymond's "pudor" as it causes the penitents not to confess to their proper priests/curators (that "[are able] to hele and know") but to flee to the friars. In his long gloss to *Proprio sacerdoti* in Raymond's text, William of Rennes notes that "rational cause" (rationabilis causa) may excuse a parishioner from confessing to his proper priest but, significantly, concludes that "he does not believe that shame is a sufficient cause for which a penitent should be absolved unless he confess to his proper priest" (nec credo quod erubescentia sit causa sufficiens, quare paenitens absolui debeat, ne confiteatur proprio sacerdoti).[105] In another gloss pertaining to the same feeling of "shame" (erubescentia), William contemplates the situation in which the penitent happens to be the priest's own concubine to underscore Raymond's view that shame is itself the greatest part of contrition:

> Quid de sacerdote habente socariam parochianam suam, numquid debet eam admittere ad confessionem, de illo peccato maxime? Respondeo: credo quod non, quia aufertur ei erubescentia, quae est maxima pars paenitentiae; quia non erubesceret ita coram eo, sicut coram alio: debet ergo eam mittere ad alium sacerdotem, sicut notavit H. circa presbyterum & vxorem propriam. (William of Rennes, Gloss ad v. *Laborat*, 21.455)

> What about the case of a priest with his concubine, shouldn't he allow her to confess to him especially concerning that sin? I answer: I do not believe so, because the shame is removed from her, which is the greatest part of penitence; because she would not be ashamed before him [her own priest] as before another [priest]; therefore, he [her own priest] should send her to another priest, as noted by H concerning the case of a priest and his own wife.

104 C 22.284. See corresponding B 20.284.

105 William of Rennes, Gloss ad v. *Proprio sacerdoti*, 14.449.

Read in light of both Raymond's and William's emphasis on the centrality of shame to contrition, the fleeing penitents in the poem are evidently not required by their fraternal confessors – who are not their proper priests – to show shame ("verecundia" or "erubescentia"). Such penitents are thus like the "fals folk" who seek sanctuary in Westminster in order to avoid the requirements of settling their debts to their own creditors.[106]

The canon law pertaining to contrition is also invoked in Conscience's initial selection of a parish priest for parishioners and in Conscience's consequent invitation of Frere Flatrere. In an attempt to provide spiritual care to the exodus of parishioners to Westminster, Conscience "calde a leche, þat couthe wel shryue."[107] In doing so, Conscience recalls canon 21 of Lateran IV: "the priest must, however, be discreet and cautious so that by that custom of a skilled physician he may ... understand prudently what counsel he must offer to him and what remedy to apply, using diverse experiments to heal the sick person."[108] Conscience's "leche" is such a "skilled physician," for he knows how "to salue tho þat syke were and thorw synne ywounded. / Shrift schop scharp salue, and made men do penaunse / For here mysdedes that thei wrouht hadde."[109] To formulate a "scharp salue" is to induce the penitent to undergo contrition about her/his past sins. The "leche" chosen by Conscience, however, finds little favour among the penitents: "Somme liked nat this leche, and letteres they sente, / Yf eny surgien were in þe sege that softur couthe plastre."[110] What the dissatisfied penitents want is a confessor who will not follow the procedures that require the penitent to experience contrition. They want "eny surgien"

106 Barney explains that the simile "compares making ineffectual confession to friars, and hence avoiding the onerous repayment of the debt of sin with taking sanctuary in the precincts of Westminster Abbey in order to escape financial debt" (*The Penn Commentary*, 237).

107 C 22.305. See corresponding B 20.305.

108 *Decrees of the Ecumenical Councils*, 245. Making annual confession to one's proper priest obligatory, canon 21 of Lateran IV, as Winfried Trusen notes, accelerated and accentuated the legalization of the sacrament of penance: "Der Einbruch der Jurisprudenz in die Praxis des *forum internum*, den wir zunächst an wenigen Stellen beobachten können, wird nun durch ein Ereignis beschleunigt und intensiviert. Im Jahre 1215 erlässt das 4. Laterankonzil die berühmte Konstitution 21 *Omnis utriusque sexus.*" See Trusen, "*Forum internum*," 90.

109 C 22.306–8. See corresponding B 20.306–8.

110 C 22.310–11. See corresponding B 20.310–11.

who "softur couthe plaster," that is, who would save them from the sorrow or sharpness of contrition.

The "surgien" who can answer their wish is none other than Frere Flatrere, the friar whom the penitent Contricion recommends and introduces as "fiscicien and surgien."[111] Whereas, as I have just argued, Conscience's "leche" fulfils canon 21's ideal of the confessor-physician, the fraternal "surgien" that the penitents desire exemplifies the kind of cleric or priest denounced in canon 18 of Lateran IV: "And no cleric should be put in command of either mercenaries or crossbowmen or this kind of men of blood. Nor should the sub-deacon, deacon, or priest practise that art of surgery which leads to searing or incision."[112] In light of the sharp canonistic distinction drawn between physic and surgery, Frere Flatrere's personification of both professions already raises questions about the legitimacy of the actions he will perform as a confessor to Contricion: will Frere Flatrere behave as the physician-confessor praised by canon 21 or as the surgeon of canon 18?

The narrator's antifraternal critique answers this question by centring on the manner in which Frere Flatrere fails to behave as the skilled physician in treating Contricion. The narrator gradually shifts the attention from the issue of Frere Flatrere's legal right to hear confessions to that of his spectacular abuse of that right. The narrator first clarifies that the friar has recourse to canon law to obtain a "lettre, leue to haue to curen / As a curatour a were, and kam with his lettre / Baldly to þe bishope, and his breef hadde."[113] Frere Flatrere's procurement of such a "breef" – a legal term that Alford glosses as "letter of authority" – is in keeping with papal bulls such as Boniface VIII's *Super cathedram*.[114]

---

111 C 22.316. See corresponding B 20.316.

112 "Nullus quoque clericus rottariis aut balistariis aut huiusmodi viris sanguinum praeponatur, nec illam chirurgiae artem subdiaconus, diaconus vel sacerdos exerceant quae ad ustionem vel incisionem inducit." See *Decrees of the Ecumenical Councils*, 244. Citing from other sources such as the *Memoriale* (for example, Liber III, cap. xxvi), Gray notes that "regulars and priests were specifically prohibited by canon law from practising or studying 'physica' and especially 'chyrurgia'" (263).

113 C 22.326–8. See corresponding B 20.326–8.

114 Alford, *A Glossary*, 19; for the text of *Super cathedram*, see *Corpus iuris canonici, constitutiones Clementis papae V*, 3.7.2 (*CIC*, 2: 1161–4). See also Barney's note that "Pope Boniface VIII issued a bull [*Super cathedram*] that required friars to receive a bishop's formal licence in order to hear confessions." *The Penn Commentary*, xxx. For a detailed survey of the contemporary papal history of such licences to friars, see Haren, "Friars as Confessors." For a pastoral background to the same, see also Haren's "Social Ideas."

Already in Raymond, we read that confessors are required to obtain legal permission from the bishop of the diocese or the apostolic see before they engage in any curatorial activity with parishioners who do not belong to them.[115] With the acquisition of the letter, Frere Flatrere enjoys the legal status of a limitour-friar: by canon law, he now has the right to hear confessions within the jurisdiction of the bishop who gave him permission ("breef").

Although Frere Flatrere follows the established canonistic procedure of obtaining episcopal permission to hear the confessions of lay parishioners, he violates the canonistic procedures that require him first to elicit contrition from them and then to determine whether or not to grant absolution. Even before he has gathered evidence of the penitent's remorse, Frere Flatrere hastens to the final stage of the penitential process:

> And [the friar] goeth, gropeth Contricion, and gaf hym a plastre
> Of "A pryué payement, and Y shal preye for ȝow,
> And for [alle] hem þat ȝe aren holde to, al my lyf tyme." (C 22.364–6)

Whereas Raymond's exemplary confessor poses verbal questions to elicit signs of contrition, Frere Flatrere investigates in a dramatically physical manner: he ("gropeth") to procure "a pryué payement." Evoking the idea of secrecy, the adjective "pryué" recalls the fraternal subversion of the canon law mandating that the confessional narration, not the penitent's payment to the confessor, be kept secret.[116]

Evidence of contrition in Contricion's confession is conspicuous by its absence:

> Thus he goeth and gedereth, and gloseth þer he shryueth –
> Til Contricioun hadde clene forȝete to crye and to wepe,
> And wake for his wikkede werkes as he was woned bifore.

---

115 For the canon law on the confessor's power of binding and loosing souls, and the episcopal and papal jurisdiction governing it, see Raymond 15.812: "Licet enim omnes sacerdotes recipiant hanc potestatem, ligata est tamen, ita quod non possunt eam exsequi nisi data sibi auctoritate et potestate ab episcopo dioecesano vel ab Apostolica Sede" (For although all priests receive this power, it is so bound that they cannot exercise it except by the authority and power granted to them by the diocesan bishop or the Apostolic See).

116 For the canon law requiring that confessions be kept secret, see Raymond 61.866.

For confort of his confessour, contricioun he lefte,
That is the souereyne salue for alle kyne synnes. (C 22.369–73)

The alliteration of the words "gooth," "gedereth," and "gloseth" as well as the anaphoric "and" underscores the speed with which Frere Flatrere administers the sacrament. There is no mention at all here of Contricion's confessional account, much less one marked by the slowness and deliberation that Raymond considers the hallmarks of a true and perfect confession, that is to say, a confession emanating from contrition.[117] The verb "gloseth" used to characterize the confessor's handling of the penitent also carries a sense of mockery of the law, for, as Alford, explains, the term specifically means "to adapt a standard form (e.g., a writ or charter) to individual circumstances."[118] Consequently, Frere Flatrere's ministrations result in the penitent's forgetting to cry and weep: "Til Contricioun hadde clene forȝete to crye and to wepe."[119] The narrator notes further that Frere Flatrere forgets to "wake for his wikkede werkes as he was woned bifore," for the friar administers the sacrament in such a way as to turn Contricion away from his habitual modes of expressing contrition – the tears that penitents had to show in the penitential forum and the vigils that, as Raymond explains in his discussion of satisfaction, they had to keep to further exteriorize their contrition.[120]

The narrator holds Frere Flatrere's "confort" culpable for Contricion's abandonment of contrition: "For confort of his confessour, Contricion he lefte." As we have already discussed, Raymond and William (of Pagula) instruct the confessor to comfort his penitent to induce him/her to express remorse, and not the other way around. Likewise, instead of "the souereyne salue for alle kyne synnes," Frere Flatrere gives the penitent a different kind of salve – "a fisyk" that "this folk hath enchaunted."[121] Frere Flatrere's "fisyk" has an effect directly contrary to what a confessor's physic, according to Raymond, should have. Far from pricking the penitent into a bitter and vigilant remembrance of

117 Raymond 27.824–5.
118 Alford, *A Glossary*, 65.
119 C 22.370. See corresponding B 20.370.
120 C 22.371; see corresponding B 20.371. For vigils as another canonistic expression of contrition, see Raymond 38.837.
121 C 22.379. See corresponding B 20.379.

past sins, Frere Flatrere's "fisyk" enchants Contricion among his other penitents: "And doth men drynke dwale, þat men drat no synne."[122] The "men" ministered to by Frere Flatrere drink a sleeping potion ("dwale") and cease to show that they rue sin. In short, the narrator exposes to ridicule the consequences of the fraternal administration of confession by invoking and inverting the signs of contrition that canonists required confessors to elicit.

Given the poem's ending with Contricion's inability to show contrition, and given the consequent collapse of the "hous Vnitee," what is one to make of the poem's attention to the inversion (and hence invocation) of the signs of contrition? What are we to make of the gulf that the poem exposes between the procedural theory of contrition expounded, say, by Raymond and the practice of it, as in the performances of Mede and Contricion? And, more broadly, what kind of reinvention of canon law does the poem's handling of contrition offer?

One answer to such questions is that the poem finds fault not with the procedures of canon law but with those entrusted with their implementation. The friars that hear Mede and Contricion are no doubt schooled in the canonical procedures governing sacramental confession, but, as we have seen, choose not to act appropriately on their procedural knowledge. Rather they take advantage of their schooling and the secrecy afforded by the forum of penance to elicit material profits at the expense of their penitents' spiritual welfare. The narrator in *Piers Plowman*, in turn, takes advantage of his knowledge of canon law and his privileged role as an observer of the proceedings or performances in the penitential forum to forge, as it were, an internal critique of the fraternal abuses in the academic language the friars were trained in and would therefore understand.

In a number of other instances of antifraternalism to be discussed in the chapters that follow, the poem exposes to critique the contrast between canonistic theory and practice, with C going farther than B in laying bare the chasm between the depth of the friars' canonistic learning and the shallowness of their implementation of it. Although in both B and C the friars appear as academically learned, C offers a more specific sense of their scholarly credentials than does B, and, hence, a sharper contrast between their training and penitential practice. For instance, in passus 10 words found in C but not present in B show a

---

122 C 22.380. See corresponding B 20.380.

friar correctly expounding the doctrine of three penitential stages to a non-comprehending narrator.[123] Likewise, in passus 15, another set of words found only in C portrays a preaching friar as a decretist ("decretistre of canoen").[124] In both these passus, the friar does not practise what he learnedly preaches. We shall return to the chasm between fraternal learning in canon law and fraternal practice in chapter 4 that focuses on penitential satisfaction (and the fraternal neglect of it).

How, then, do the B and C versions of the fraternal confessions reinvent canon law? Surely, not by promulgating norms to govern the penitential forum! Nor, for that matter, by contributing to the doctrine of contrition that confessional manuals translated into procedural steps for the confessor to follow. Rather, B and C reinvent by means of a poetic mimesis: by having fraternal confessor and penitent act in ways that recall and reinforce the evolving canon law on confession. Dallas G. Denery II observes that late medieval confessional treatises "reveal an overwhelming and systematically conceived interest in appearances ... not only does the confessor see the penitent, the penitent is taught to see himself through the confessor's gaze."[125] The fraternal confessions discussed above render vivid the procedures for regulating such appearances in the penitential forum.

If this chapter has been successful in uncovering norms that inform the poem's handling of contrition, then it has, at the very least, demonstrated the reinvention of canon law in the derivative sense of finding procedures that have already been formulated within the normative discourse on contrition. In the poetic passages we have examined the reinvention of canon law in the extended sense of founding something new pertains not to the canonical procedures themselves but to their rhetorical forms or dramatic adaptations. In the next chapter (as well as in the rest of the book), we shall explore the poem's reinvention at the level of substance as well: both as finding and founding within the terms of the official discourse of canon law.

---

123 C 10.52–3: "To repenten and to arise and rowe out of synne / To contricion, to confessioun, til he come til his ende."

124 In C 15.86, the friar is described as a "doctour and dyvynour" and a "decretistre of canoen."

125 Denery II, *Seeing and Being Seen*, 7.

2 Dreams of Avarice: The Absent Presence of the Usury Prohibition

Gifts, goods, payments, and profits: wherever they appear in the poem, Mede is either ahead of or behind them. Whether personifying or promoting them, Mede matters. She motivates friars to take it easy on their lecherous but lordly penitents. She moves Conscience to take a hard line on rampant royal giving. To regraters, she is a boon; to their customers, a bane. She is both giver and given.[1] At one point, she appears literally as a penitent granting her confessor a coin; at another, she stands metaphorically for the privy payment for which the confessor gropes his penitent. At yet another point, she is a bride ceremoniously handed over to False "moore for hire goodes."[2] A figure of infinite variety, she vacillates between sign and referent, abstract quality and concrete matter, between subject and object positions. Distinguished from Mercede or the just wage openly given for the labour already done, Mede also embodies and expresses the gift surreptitiously advanced for work yet to be undertaken. Mede has the elusiveness, indeterminacy, and illegality that epitomize the covert gift which theologians denounced eloquently, which canonists theorized elaborately, and which the B version of passus 3 engages explicitly and the corresponding C subtly but more substantially: namely, usury.

In this chapter, we return to Mede to focus on the protean usurious gift she concretizes and circulates – a gift overtly present in the B version of passus 3 but hidden in plain sight in the C version of the same passus. In the debate between Mede and Conscience over gift-giving

1 For a survey of Mede's passive and active roles, see Helen Barr, "Major Episodes and Moments in Piers Plowman B," 15–18.

2 B 2.76; the corresponding line in C 2.80 has "more for here richesse."

and gift-receiving, the prohibition of usury is explicitly quoted in B but conspicuously absent from C. With characteristic aplomb, Mede shows little awareness of the biblical proscription of loans granted for interest-bearing offerings. Asserting that gifts of any kind are indispensable for secular or sacred offices, she argues that they are morally value-neutral. While eliciting the king's support for her argument, she provokes Conscience to launch into a lengthy debate with her on the moral valence of gifts.

In both B and C, Conscience refutes Mede's apology for gifts by means of a value-based distinction between two kinds of gifts – one laudable and the other reprehensible.[3] In the B version of the refutation, Conscience applauds the "firste mede" by opposing it to usury:

> "That oon God of his grace graunteþ in his blisse
> To þo þat wel werchen while þei ben here ...
> ....
> And han ywroȝt werkes wiþ right and wiþ reson,
> And he þat ne vseþ noȝt þe lyf of vsurie
> And enformeþ pouere men and pursueþ truþe:
> *Qui pecuniam suam non dedit ad vsuram, et munera super innocentem ...*
> And alle þat helpen þe innocent and holden with þe riȝtfulle,
> Wiþouten mede doþ hem good and þe truþe helpeþ –
> Swiche manere men, my lord, shul haue þis firste mede
> Of God at a gret nede, whan þei gon hennes." (B 3.232–45)

Conscience presents "þis firste mede" as God's posthumous gift of "his grace" offered to those who have lived "riȝtfulle" and are "at a gret need." The prospective recipients of such divine grace would "helpen" the "innocent" and "doþ hem good" "wiþouten mede," and hence their "werkes" would be performed with "right" and "reson." While Conscience does not gloss the nouns "right" and "reson," he does specify what "werkes" would disqualify one from meriting such divine "mede." He explains in English and Latin that anyone who "vseth" "þe lyf of vsurie," gives money ("pecuniam") towards usury ("ad vsuram"), and grants gifts ("munera") at the expense of the innocent

3 B 3.231–54; C 3.285–311.

("super innocentem") will not be eligible for God's "mede." In light of this specification, "werkes" done with "right" and "reson" are necessarily free from usury, whether given as money ("pecuniam") or as gifts ("munera").

In the corresponding C version of his refutation of Mede, Conscience differentiates between two kinds of mede ("mede" and "mercede") but, curiously enough, without ever mentioning usury by name:

> "Ac there is 'mede' and 'mercede' – and bothe men demen
> A desert for som doynge, derne oþer elles.
> Mede many tymes men ȝeueth bifore þe doynge,
> And þat is nother resoun ne ryhte ne in rewme lawe
> That eny man mede toke but he hit myhte deserue,
> And for to vndertake to trauaile for another
> And wot neuere witterly where he lyue so longe
> Ne haue hap to his hele mede to deserue.
> Y halde hym ouer-hardy or elles nat trewe
> That *pre manibus* is paied or his pay asketh.
> Harlotes and hoores and also fals leches –
> They asken here huyre ar thei hit haue deserued,
> And gylours gyuen byfore and goode men at þe ende.
> When þe dede is ydo and þe day endit;
> And þat is no mede but a mercede, a manere dewe dette,
> And but hit prestly be ypayed, þe payere is to blame." (C 3.290–305)

In contrast to the comparable passage in B, the C passage expresses a more sustained treatment of "mede." Stating that both "mede" and "mercede" represent reward "for som doynge, derne oþer elles," Conscience dwells on the former ("mede") at greater length than on the latter ("mercede"), which he regards as a kind of debt owed ("dewe dette"). In the same passage, Conscience also narrows the focus on the reprehensible "mede," which he describes as a "pre manibus" (advance) payment. But, strikingly enough, Conscience does not make any mention, much less offer a treatment, of the laudable or the "firste mede" that dominates the corresponding passage in B. Words denoting usury or its prohibition such as the English word "vsurie" and the Latin words "vsuram" and "munera" do not occur in the passage in C and, indeed, are not present elsewhere in the C version of the passus.

Let me open with two questions stimulated by a juxtaposition of the B and C passages quoted above: first, what role do the Latin and English words about the prohibition of usury play in the B version of passus 3? And, second, to what extent and to what ends does the C version of the same passus engage usury despite not using the words denoting it and its prohibition? Apart from J.A.W. Bennett and Andrew Galloway, few have approached the first question, much less accounted for the second. Bennett reads the Latin words about usury in B as referring to the biblical proscription found in Luke 6:35: "Do good, and lend to one another, expecting nothing in return."[4] Disagreeing with Bennett's reading, Galloway finds "no reason to take the English lines in B as a reference to Luke 6:35," because "Conscience's point is quite different from the Lucan passage."[5] Galloway argues instead that the B passage's Latin words about the prohibition of usury and "[m]any of the English lines appearing next to the Latin can be matched to lines in Psalm 14 or seen as summarizing its point."[6] He goes on to claim that the English lines before the Latin words construe "the Vulgate *munera super innocentem non accepit* as 'He [who] does not take money from the innocent' rather than (its literally correct meaning, which the poet likely knew), 'He [who] does not take bribes against the innocent.'"[7] His concluding comment is "[t]hat C drops all these passages does not necessarily show a full rejection of this construal, as [passus] 2.38 shows, but it may show a retreat from emphasizing that eccentric interpretation of the psalm's monetary ethics."[8]

In situating the B passage alongside biblical sources on the usury prohibition, both Bennett and Galloway overlook other equally germane canonistic sources alongside which the same passage can be just as, if not more, fruitfully read. In this, to be sure, they follow a well-established tradition of interpreting the poem's scriptural invocations in light of their material rather than formal sources. Historians of canon law distinguish between the two kinds of sources in terms of composition and circulation. The "material sources" of law are its "original sources" such as "the Biblical passages, papal decrees, conciliar canons and patristic writings"; the law's "formal sources," by

4 Bennett, *Piers Plowman*.
5 Galloway, *The Penn Commentary*, 329.
6 Ibid.
7 Ibid.
8 Ibid.

contrast, are the "vehicles through which the law is transmitted, that is, the [contemporary] books and collections where someone can find it."[9] Medieval "canonists generally used formal sources rather than returning to material sources, even when they were available and could have been used."[10]

Given the poem's invocations of Gratian's *Decretum* and Gregory IX's *Liber extra*,[11] and Nicholas Gray's documentation of the poem's references to late medieval penitential texts, Langland too may have encountered the psalmic prohibition of usury and, more significantly, its interpretations not just within its material sources but also in other equally pertinent formal sources that conceptualize it variously.[12] In the time of the poem's composition, the most influential among such sources included Gratian's *Decretum*, Johannes Teutonicus and Bartholomew of Brescia's *Glossa ordinaria* to it, Raymond of Peñafort's *Summa de paenitentia*, William of Rennes's *Glossa* to Raymond's *Summa*, Hostiensis's *Summa aurea*, and John of Freiburg's *Summa confessorum*. Unlike any of the material sources of the usury prohibition, these formal sources, as T.P. McLaughlin has comprehensively shown, embody the evolving teaching of usury across the later Middle Ages.[13] Rather than the Bible's authors themselves, as John Baldwin has argued, "it was chiefly the canonists who formulated the major principles of usury in the late twelfth and early thirteenth centuries."[14] The canonists do more than cite the biblical prohibition of usury as uniformly self-evident. They

9 Somerville and Brasington, *Prefaces to the Books of Canon Law*, 3. As Greta Austin puts it, "canon law collections, penitentials, and excerpts of theological writings, [and] the books from which a compiler took his canons were called his 'formal sources'" (*Shaping Church Law*, 11); see also Austin's paragraph on the difference between material and formal sources in the context of medieval canon law in *Shaping Church Law*, 34.

10 Somerville and Brasington, *Prefaces to the Books of Canon Law*, 4.

11 As touched on in the preceding chapter, references to the *Decretum* and the *Decretals* are found in both B and C texts: see C 15.86 and B 5.422.

12 In his "Study of *Piers Plowman*," Gray observes that "Langland's treatment of usury likewise echoes that of the penitential manuals," but he notes that "in effect neither offers more than a partial or summary treatment of the far more detailed and extensive discussion conducted elsewhere by both theologians and canonists," (325).

13 McLaughlin, "The Teaching of the Canonists on Usury."

14 Baldwin, *Masters, Princes, and Merchants*, 270; I have rearranged the clause without changing Baldwin's words; the exact words are: "In the late twelfth and early thirteenth centuries it was chiefly the canonists who formulated the major principles of usury."

interpret it variously. To move chronologically and cross-referentially across the *Decretum*, the *Liber extra*, their *Ordinary Glosses*, as well as the titles on usury by Hostiensis and John of Freiburg is to witness enlargements as well as specifications of the usury-prohibition. In the hands of the canonists, usury's referential range extends from manifestly interest-bearing loans to sales covertly driven by avarice, and, consequently, the usury prohibition varies in meaning according to the nature of and motivations behind such transactions. Our poet or, properly speaking, Conscience and the narrator too contribute to this changing discourse on usury in their conceptualization and critique of the varied species of profiteering advocated by or associated with Mede.

To read the usury prohibition in the B and C versions alongside its formal rather than material sources is to read it laterally, with an attention to verbal and conceptual intersections of literary and legal understandings of usury. This mode of reading will reveal that the C version of passus 3 exists not in a relation of nominal reference or, if you will, deference to a temporally distant "original" source but in a relation of conceptual participation within a vibrantly dynamic contemporary discourse about avaricious profiteering.[15] What interests me, then, is not so much how precisely the narrator's wording of the usury prohibition in B matches that found in any of his sources as how the narrator and Conscience in the C version of the corresponding passus co-produce canonistic concepts of usury without ever naming it or its prohibition. In their critiques of Mede, both fictional characters think and speak like the canonists but in ways that shape the canonist thought on usury for novel ends unique to the poem. As we shall first see, the narrator in the C version mobilizes the canonist thought on usurious retail trade to shape his denunciation of secular regraters that profit from the poor. As we shall subsequently see, Conscience goes on to modify the canonist thought around usurious time-sales regarding merchandise to critique advance payments regarding labour yet to be undertaken. Together both critiques of the varied forms of corporeal usury personified by Mede prepare the grounds for Conscience's invention of a corrective model of spiritual usury. Unlike the canonists, who hold up spiritual

15 My methodological move is both inspired by and expressed in terms of Paul Strohm's reading of the debate between Roger Chartier and Robert Darnton: "The cat massacre and the Revolution may, that is, exist not in a relation of reference but a relation of participation within a larger system of events and signs" ("Lad with Revel to Newgate" in *Theory and the Premodern Text*, 57).

usury as an ideal for the relationship between the divine Lord and the faithful Christian, Conscience goes on to translate this ideal into interpersonal terms that, for him, could or should govern the relationship between the human lord and his faithful vassals.

This chapter is divided into three parts. Part I sheds light on the "formal sources" that discuss the psalmic prohibition of usury invoked in the B passage of passus 3. Part II attends to the narrator's and Conscience's critiques of Mede in C, paying close attention to a C passage that does not contain the wording of the usury prohibition found in the corresponding passage in B. Part III focuses on passages of Conscience's speech found only in C (and not in B) and that succeed the same C passage that does not have the wording of the usury prohibition.

Part I

The Psalmic Usury Prohibition in "Formal Sources" from Gratian's *Decretum* to Hostiensis's *Summa aurea*

Gratian offers the standard canonistic exposition of the biblical proscription of usury. As John T. Noonan has observed, Psalm 14:5 – the Latin verse on usury cited in the B version of passus 3 – comprised the "only biblical reference" for the prohibition of usury in the section devoted to the same subject in the *Decretum*.[16] With venal clerics in mind, Gratian includes a ruling from the Council of Nicea (AD 325) that cites the psalmic prohibition of usury but extends its semantic scope to condemn commercial activities in addition to "interest-dependent loans" (usuras):

> [Item, Ex Nicaeno Concilio (c. 17)]: Qvoniam multi clerici, auaritiae causa turpia lucra sectantes, obliti sunt diuini praecepti, quo dictum est: *Qui pecuniam suam non dedit ad vsuram*, foenerantes, centesimas exigunt; statuit hoc sanctum concilium, ut, si quis inuentus fuerit post hanc definitionem usuras accipere, uel ex quolibet tali negotio turpia lucra sectari, uel etiam species frumentorum ad sescuplum dare; omnis, qui tale aliquid conatus fuerit ad quaestum, deijciatur a clero, & alienus ab ecclesiastico habeatur gradu. (Gratian, *Decretum*, II. C. 14, q. 4, c. 8, cols 1401–2; see also Gratian (ed. Friedberg), *CIC*, 1: 737)

16 Noonan, *The Scholastic Analysis of Usury*, 19.

Also, from the Nicene Council [c. 17]: Seeing that many clerics who seek after filthy profits out of avarice have forgotten the divine precept – which says: *who has not given his money to usury* [Psalm 14:5] – they, lending on interest, demand a hundredfold interest; this sacred council has mandated that, if anyone subsequent to this decree is found to take usury, or to seek after filthy profits by a similar tactic, or even to give any kind of grain at fifty percent interest – anybody who has tried any such thing in order to make a profit is to be removed from the clergy, and regarded as estranged from the ecclesiastical rank.]

In the passage above, usury ranges beyond the interest expected or exacted on a loan: it extends to any activity inspired by "turpe lucrum" (filthy profit). The coordinating conjunction "uel" (or) broadens the semantic reach of the psalmic prohibition to cover "loans on interest" (usuras) "or" (uel) the pursuit of "wicked gains" (turpia lucra) in a similar kind of activity "or" (uel) even "anything similar" (tale aliquid) sought after "for profit" (ad questum). Gratian's explication of "turpe lucrum" and Johannes Teutonicus's subsequent gloss to *Quaestum* understand usury as including trades (not just loans on interest) motivated by the profit-motive for its own sake.[17] In the gloss, Johannes explains that taking usury is prohibited "on account of desire for gain" (causa lucri captandi) but, significantly, adds that the same is permitted "for the sake of avoiding a loss" ([causa] uitandi damni).[18] In the subsequent "chapter" or "canon" (capitulum / canon), Gratian sheds further light on such "wicked profit" (turpe lucrum) in the activity of buying an item cheap in order to sell it dear:

[Gratian] *Turpe lucrum sequitur, qui minus emit, vt plus vendat.* Item Iulius Papa. Qvicumque tempore messis vel vindemiae non necessitate, sed propter cupiditatem comparat annonam vel vinum, verbi gratia de duobus denarijs comparat modium vnum, & seruat, vsque dum vendatur denarijs quattuor, aut sex, aut amplius, hoc turpe lucrum dicimus. (Gratian, *Decretum*, II. C. 14, q. 4, c. 9, *Quicumque*, cols 1403–4; see also Friedberg ed., *CIC*, 1: 737)

---

17 *Glossa ordinaria* ad v. *Quaestum* col. 1402: "videtur hic quod prohibeamur sumere usuram causa lucri captandi, non autem uitandi damni." For convenience's sake, I assume that the *Glossa ordinaria* is as Johannes Teutonicus left it but, as we know, Bartholomew of Brescia modified a good deal of it.

18 *Glossa ordinaria* ad v. *Quaestum* col. 1402.

> *He seeks after filthy profit who buys cheaper so that he may sell dearer*. [Gratian's rubric for the canon that he and Ivo of Chartres attribute to Pope Julius I] Likewise, Pope Julius: Whoever in the time of harvest or of vintage, not by necessity but out of greed, buys produce or wine, for example, a measure of grain for 2 *denarii*, and keeps it until he can sell it for 4, or 6, or more, this we call filthy profit.

Pope Julius's definition of "turpe lucrum," which Gratian incorporates and hence endorses, notes that the "profit" (lucrum) is "turpe" not on account of the actions of buying cheap at one time and selling dear at a later time but "on account of cupidity" (propter cupiditatem). But, as Gratian also implies, to engage in the same mercantile activity on account of "need" (necessitate) would not render the profit "filthy" (turpe).[19] In his gloss to *Modium* ("measure"), Johannes Teutonicus identifies "doubt" (dubium) concerning the future market value as another criterion to determine whether or not the profit is usurious:

> ***Glossa ordinaria* ad v. *Modium*:**
> si aliquis vendat merces quae modo valent quattuor, & facit pactum, vt ei dentur quinque ad terminum praefixum: illud non est vsura, si dubium est quantum possunt valere merces illae ad terminum praefixum, ut extra de vsura *in ciuitate*, licet si venderet longe cariori foro, quam modo valeant tunc esset vsura vt extra eo. tit. *consuluit*. Io." (Gratian, *Decretum*, II. C. 14, q. 4, c. 9; *Glossa ordinaria* ad v. *Modium* cols 1403–4)
>
> If someone should sell merchandise which is now valued at four and makes a deal so that five be given to him at a prefixed time: that is not

19 In his *Summa de paenitentia* 2.7, *De usuris et pignoribus*, 9, col. 547, Raymond of Peñafort considers a similar context in which the "lucrum" made from buying cheap and selling dear is "turpe" unless the buyer acted from necessity: "De quibusdam autem qui tempore messis vel vindemiae emunt annonam vel vinum vilius ut postea vendant carius, dico quod peccant et turpe lucrum est. Secus si aliquis propter necessitatem emat, et postea non indiget sicut credebat; hic potest licite vendere prout venditur communiter in foro, licet carius quam emerit" (Concerning those, however, who in the time of harvest or grape-gathering buy the year's produce or wine cheaper so that they may afterwards sell dearer, I say that they sin and the profit is filthy; it is otherwise if someone sells on account of necessity, and afterwards does not want, as he was supposing; in this case, he can licitly sell it at the going price in the marketplace although he sells dearer than he bought). In this chapter, all quotations from Raymond's *Summa de paenitentia* are cited by reference to the book, the title, the section, and the column.

> usury, if there is doubt about how much the merchandise be worth at the prefixed time, as in X 5.19.6 *In ciuitate*; however, if one were to sell the merchandise far dearer in the marketplace than the value they have then, it would be usury, as in X 5.19.10 *Consuluit*.[20]

Referring to the decretal *In ciuitate* first issued by Pope Alexander III (1159–89), and later included in the *Liber extra*, Johannes Teutonicus invokes the criterion of doubt as an exception to the usury prohibition: selling on credit at a price higher than the item's value in the present would not be usurious, if the seller had genuine "doubt" (dubium) about the future value of the item offered for sale.[21] Referring to another decretal, *Consuluit*, issued by Pope Urban (1185–7) and also later included in the *Liber extra*, Johannes suggests that certainty about the future value of the merchandise would make the transaction usurious – i.e, the gain made by selling in the present would be far more than the gain the seller knows he would certainly obtain at a specific time in the future.

When we bear in mind that Johannes Teutonicus's glossarial comments on the *Decretum* were written sometime after 1214 (i.e., nearly seventy-five years after the first recension of Gratian's *Decretum*) and already cites two decretals issued after the publication of the *Decretum*, we can see that the canonist thinking about usury has already expanded to include "doubt" (dubium) as a criterion for the determination of the usuriousness of buying cheap and selling dear.

Likewise, elaborating on the concept of "doubt" (dubium) about the future value of commodities sold on credit, canonists such as Raymond and Hostiensis go on to deem a credit-sale exempt from the charge of usury in case the seller is not genuinely certain about the value of the object at the (future) time when the buyer will pay for it. Take, for instance, Raymond's inclusion, in the *Liber extra*, of Pope Alexander III's decretal *In ciuitate* that deems credit-based sales sinful in cases where buyers buy on credit items like pepper or cinnamon which, say, do not have a value above 5 librae but promise to settle their debt at a fixed

20 The "X" in translation above and elsewhere in my book refers to the *Decretales Gregorii IX* (= *Liber extra* = X). It is worth noting that Johannes Teutonicus interpreted Gratian in light of later decretals.

21 For a lucid account of the context in which Alexander III's decretal was issued, see Kaye, *History of Balance*, 35.

time in the future by paying the creditors 6 librae.[22] "Although such a contract," Alexander argues, "may not be reckoned usurious in name, the sellers commit sin unless there be doubt about the value of the merchandise at the time of the settlement of the debt" (Licet autem contractus huiusmodi ex tali forma non possit censeri nomine vsurarum, nihilominus tamen venditores peccatum incurrunt, nisi dubium sit, merces illas plus minusve solutionis tempore valituras).[23] Raymond, however, invokes the psalmic prohibition of usury to deem a credit-sale usurious, if the seller knows with certainty the future value of the object in question. Having treated such exceptions to usury in his *Summa de paenitentia*, Raymond cites the line on usury in Psalm 14:5 as the sole biblical source for his opposition to any laws that permit usury in its narrow sense of loans on interest:

> Quid de legibus quae permittunt usuras exigi, numquid tenent? Dico breviter quod non: immo sunt omnes abrogatae. Quod probo auctoritate, ratione, et civili iure. Auctoritate Psalmi: "Qui pecuniam suam non dedit ad usuram," etc. (Raymond, *Summa de paenitentia* 2. 7. col. 547)

> What about laws that permit usury to be exacted – do they not hold? Briefly, I say no: indeed, they are all abrogated. Which I prove by authority, by reason, and by civil law. By authority of the psalm [Psalm 14:5]: "Who has not given his money to usury," etc.

In his slightly controversial treatment of usury, Hostiensis makes allowances for seeking or receiving more than is lent because of "interesse" or "interest" in the technical sense of loss/damage. Hence, in discussing cases of loans where one can legitimately charge "interesse," Hostiensis distinguishes it from usury and justifies it on the grounds of recovering a loss.[24] At the same time, however, he, like Raymond, enlists Psalm 14's

---

22 X 5.19.6, col. 1736; see also Friedberg, *CIC*, 2: 813: "In ciuitate tua dicis saepe contingere, quod quidam piper, seu cinamomum, seu alias merces comparant, quae tunc vltra quinque libras non valent, & promittunt se illis, a quibus illas merces accipiunt, sex libras statuto termino soluturos."

23 X 5.19.6, cols 1736–7; see also Friedberg, *CIC*, 2: 813. See also the decretal *Nauiganti* in X 5.19.19, cols 1744–45; see also Friedberg, *CIC*, 2: 816.

24 For such cases of legitimate "interesse," see Hostiensis, *Summa aurea*, 5, *De vsuris*, 8, col. 1439–42. I am also indebted to Joel Kaye's discussion of Hostiensis's treatment of interest as an external title rather than as a justification of usury; see *A History of Balance*, 31–3.

usury prohibition as among other biblical mandates to condemn not just the manifestly usurious loan but also "usurious fraud" (in fraudem usurarum):

> Illud in mutuo, & quod dicitur, quicquid sorti accedit, usura est, illud est verum, quando ex pacto datur, vel aliquid excogitatur in fraudem usurarum, divina etiam pagina in mutuo tantum usuram prohibere videtur, unde in Evangelio, Mutuum dantes, nihil inde sperantes. Psal. Qui pecuniam suam non dedit, id est, mutuo ad usuram tradidit. (*Summa aurea*, 5, *De vsuris*, 8, col. 1441)

> In a loan, as has been said, anything that exceeds the principal is usury, and that is true when anything is explicitly given or excogitated [manipulated] by a usurious fraud [literally, "into a fraud of usuries"] – also divine scripture appears to prohibit usury in a loan only, whence in the Gospel, "those lending and hoping for nothing from it," Luke 6:35; Psalm 14:5: "who has not given his money," that is, who, in a loan, has not given "to usury."

By introducing the concept of the "usurious fraud" (in fraudem usurarum), Hostiensis extends the referential range of the usury prohibition to cover actions that conceal usurious loans under the aspect of sales-transactions.[25]

As we move from Gratian to Raymond and Hostiensis, we see the psalmic prohibition of usury interpreted more and more diversely to govern a variety of profit-driven transactions from overt loans given on interest to sales disguising interest-bearing loans. The usury-prohibition invoked in the B version of passus 3 occurs within a similarly expansive denunciation of all kinds of illicit profit that canonists would understand as, at the very least, concealing usury. Read in the context of canonistic discussions of usury, the C version of passus 3 too – despite not quoting the usury-prohibition – will emerge as thematically and structurally more

25 A little later in the same title on usury and in the same section distinguishing legitimate interest from illicit usury, Hostiensis offers an example of a sales transaction undertaken for a loan to justify it only when it accords with the "just price" criterion and has nothing of "usurious fraud": "Si vendo tibi rem meam tali pacto, quod si solvo tibi usque ad duos annos res revertatur ad me, hoc enim facis fructus tuos, *ut C. de pac. inter emptorem & venditorem. l. commissoriae* quod intelligas, quando pretium justum est, & nihil sit in fraudem usurarum, alias contra, *sup. de contrahenda emp. ad nostram*, ad hoc C. *de pac. inter emptorem si fundum*" (*Summa aurea*, 5, *De vsuris*, 8, col. 1441).

cohesive and co-productive of the canonist thought on usury than does the B version. The C version draws upon the canonistic logic of usury to knit together the narrator's and Conscience's critiques of Mede in passages on topics as thematically diverse as simony and regrating – passages that occur structurally well before the usury prohibition is invoked in the B version, and will be read as anticipating it, not overtly by the literal name of usury, but covertly by its conceptual logic. And in so doing, C sets the foundation for offering – in passages not present in B – a vision of realizing the ideal of spiritual usury mentioned by the canonists.

Part II

Initial Intimations of Usurious Commercial Behaviour

In both B and C, passus 3 opens in a legal space, whose jurisdiction, as we have seen in the previous chapter, shifts from the secular to the ecclesiastical.[26] Arraigned in the court of Westminster,[27] Mede is "wiþ bedeles and baillies brouȝt bifore þe Kynge"[28] who orders "a clerk" to put her "at ese"[29] before her confrontation with the fraternal confessor and Conscience. While under the king's care in a "chambre"[30] or "boure,"[31] Mede "of hire grete goodnesse" gives the "iustices" visiting her "coupes of clene gold and coppes of siluer, / Rynges wiþ rubies and richesses manye ... [and] a moton of golde."[32] Meanwhile, "clerkes," coming "to conforten hire,"[33] claim that they belong to her to work her will ("For we beþ þyne owene / For to werche þi wille þe while þow myȝt laste").[34] In response to the clerics' offer to work her "wille," Mede promises the same ("behiȝte hem þe same"), specifying to "louen [them] lelly and lordes to make."[35] She then promises to have the names

26 Given that B and C differ little in their characterization of Mede in the early part of passus 3, I cite mainly from B but refer to C wherever necessary.

27 Helen Barr specifies the setting of the opening of passus 3 as "the court of Westminster." See Barr's "Major episodes," 16.

28 B 3.2.

29 B 3.3–4.

30 B 3.10.

31 C 3.11.

32 B 3.21–4.

33 B 3.26.

34 B 3.27–8.

35 B 3. 29–30.

of lords called in the consistory courts and to ensure that ignorance on their part would not hinder them from advancement.

But for two lines in C, both versions of the passus are almost identical in their representation of the deals suggested or struck between Mede and her visitors. In the two lines unique to C, Mede expresses her intent to commit simony, an offence prosecutable by canon law. We would be well served to examine these lines as their conceptualization of simony is strikingly similar to that of the canonists in one crucial respect. Both the poet and the canonists articulate their critique of simony on the same logic of illicit intention underlying their shared denunciation of usurious forms of exchange associated with Mede. Here are the lines in C:

> And purchace ȝow prouendres while ȝoure panes lasteth
> And bygge ȝow benefices, pluralite to haue, (C 3.32–3)

The "prouendres" that Mede promises, as Galloway explains, "are stipends from membership in cathedral or collegiate churches, whose purchase was commonly complained of as simony," and the "purchase of benefices – from the twelfth century on the generic term for any ecclesiastical office or living to which was attached an endowment – was a basic definition of simony."[36] Marking a sudden break in the narrator's denunciatory report of Mede's activities, these words do more than represent Mede's simoniacal intention: they enact it in the manner of a speech act. Helen Barr has observed that, unlike in the previous passus where Mede

36 Galloway, *The Penn Commentary*, 293. Such a view is expressed in the 1287 Statutes of Exeter II, "Summula of Bishop Peter," where simony is defined as a purchase or giving or selling of a spirituality or anything pertaining to it for oneself or for another: "Item, symoniacus, scilicet qui emit vel dat aliquid ut habeat aliquod spirituale, vel qui vendit spirituale vel etiam spirituali annexum, vel etiam qui procurat aliquid dari ut ipse vel alius habeat aliquod spirituale sicut beneficium ecclesiasticum vel etiam ordines" (ed. Powicke and Cheney, 2: 1073). Although the received learned view on simony was that it was the zealous will or desire to buy or sell spiritualities or things pertaining to them ("studiosa voluntas, sive cupiditas emendi vel vendendi spiritualia, vel spiritualibus annexa"), Hostiensis dissents from it, asserting that he does not find this view good: because the definition treats simony as committed on the basis of intention alone, it is false with regard to the church but may be true with regard to God: "sed haec descriptio non videtur bona: quia innuit quod sola intentione simonia committatur, hoc tamen falsum est, quo ad ecclesiam, licet quo ad Deum verum sit …"; see Hostiensis, *Summa aurea*, 5, *De simonia*, 1, cols 1320–1.

is a passive object in the arrangements made for her marriage, here in the court of Westminster Mede acquires agency in that "she is not only what is given but also a giver herself."[37] From the perspective of canon law, Mede's offers to give gifts alone express culpable illocutionary agency: she commits simony by verbalizing her intention to do so, and hence attracts the suspicion of usury. In his early fourteenth-century commentary on Peter Lombard's *Sentences*, the Dominican theologian Durandus de Saint-Pourçain distinguishes between simony based on intention and that based on action.[38] Durandus specifies that the latter is subject to the penalty of law and that one of the three ways of committing it is by a speech act such as "a verbal offer" (munus a lingua).[39]

What relates simony to usury is the same intention (voluntas) to profit materially from gifts that ought to be given or received gratuitously. Mede, of course, does not stop at committing simony with regard to "wille" or "voluntas." A few lines later, she commits simony in deed as well: she offers her fraternal confessor a coin ("a noble") in return for absolution. Here again, the giving of the coin is not per se simoniacal but her giving it before the end of the confession suggests that she intends to purchase the sacramental gift of absolution that by canon law ought to be freely given. Hostiensis reviews several learned views on the priest's taking of anything material or monetary from the confessing penitent, reporting among other things that he could do so for good reason: if the priest is a pauper, the penitent is specifically bound to give something ("Quod si sacerdos, cui quis confitetur, pauper sit, tunc dixit Joannes de Deo, quod confitens, & poenitens tenetur praecise aliquid dare").[40] Hostiensis also considers a case pertaining to a fraternal confessor who,

---

37 Barr, "Major Episodes," 16.

38 Durandus, Liber 4, Dist 25, Quaestio 5, col. 821: "cum omne peccatum essentialiter consistat in actu voluntatis, sed talis simonia non inducit penam iuris sed sola poenitentia purgatur, sicut habetur extra de simonia circa finem" (since every sin essentially consists in an act of will, but such simony does not lead to the penalty of law but is purged by penance alone, as is dealt with at the end of the title on simony in the *Liber extra*).

39 Durandus, Liber 4, Dist 25, Quaestio 5, col. 821: "Simonia autem quae inducit poenam iuris committitur tripliciter, scilicet per munus a lingua, & per munus a manu, & per munus obsequio" (But simony which incurs the penalty of law is committed in three ways, namely by a verbal offer, by a gift, and by service); see *D.N Durandi A sancto porciano in sententias theologicas Petri Lombardi commentariorum.*

40 "Hostiensis," *Summa aurea*, 5, *De poenitentiis et remissionibus*, 54, col. 1620.

as in the case of Mede's unnamed mendicant confessor, is offered money by the penitent. Asking what a Franciscan confessor, who should neither touch the money nor refuse what is offered, should do, Hostiensis answers that "he can refuse" not because of pride but because his order does not tolerate it, advising, however, that "he should not refuse the offer; but he should not receive it in his own hands but he should say 'I am not able to take it but you should hand it over to the provisor or the procurator of our order'").[41] Mede's confessor not only accepts the monetary gift but goes on to induce her to give to his fraternal order for refurbishing the window and the gable of his friary.[42] At any rate, Mede's simony – with regard to either intention or action – is in one sense conceptually indistinguishable from usury as understood in canon law, for common to both simony and usury is the intent to make an unjust profit.

C's lines on simony do more than interpolate a canonistic afterthought on Mede's illicit conversion of spiritual gifts into objects of commerce: they restructure the critique of Mede in B by articulating it in terms of the canonist thought on usury. That is, C recasts B's treatment of Mede's illicit deeds in a way that parallels that of similar crimes in the *Decretum* and canonistic digests. As James Brundage has observed, the increase of concern "over the inadequacy of the procedural system [of canon law] to cope with essentially private matters such as sexual behavior and simony" that led Gratian to "move directly from his treatment of simony to deal with criminal procedure may reflect the connection that he saw between these two topics."[43] The lines in C too express a causal movement from simony to Mede's other acts of avarice such as usury and regrating.[44] In short, underlying the C lines is a cohesive

41 Here are the relevant lines paraphrased above: "Sed quid faciet frater minor, qui non debet tangere denarium, nec debet refutare, quod sibi offertur. Respondeo: refutare potest, quia hoc non facit ex superbia: sed quia ordo suus hoc non patitur, consulo tamen sibi, quod non refutet, nec in propria manu recipiat: sed dicat. Ego non possum recipere, sed tradas hoc provisori, sive procuratori ordinis nostri"), *Summa aurea*, 5, *De poenitentiis et remissionibus*, 54, col. 1621.

42 B 3.48–9; see also the corresponding C 3.51–2.

43 Brundage, *Medieval Canon Law*, 93–4; as he notes, "[i]n Part II of the *Decretum*, C. 1 is devoted primarily to the crime of simony, while C. 2 deals with the problem of proof in a criminal process," 94, n. 45.

44 It is pertinent to note the association of simony with canon law elsewhere in the C text, as in C 2.243–4 where "Symonye" appears as a personified abstraction knowledgeable of the canonical process of appealing to the pope: together with "Syuile," "Symonye" sends "Lyare" to Rome and "putte hem thorw appeles in þe Popes grace" (C 2.243–4).

or continuous structure undergirded by the canonist thought on illicit profits.

Nowhere is the conceptual continuity between simony and usury clearer than in their common end, which canonists identify as "turpe lucrum" (filthy lucre). In offering to buy "prouendres" and "benefices," Mede seeks to profit illicitly from the church. Despite their spiritual significance, the clerical stipends she offers are economic assets vulnerable to the same charge of "turpe lucrum" to which any other secular trade is susceptible. Not surprisingly, theologians and canonists proscribe simony by the same criterion of "turpe lucrum" that they use to proscribe usury among other crimes of misappropriation. For instance, Thomas Aquinas collocates "plunder, usury, and simony" (rapina, usura, et simonia) as criminal activities similar to each other with regard to "filthy lucre" (turpe lucrum) or "iniquitous profit" (iniquum lucrum).[45] And, in the "question" devoted to usury in the *Summa confessorum*, Thomas of Chobham introduces the topic of usury by relating it to simony and naming both as "the two detestable kinds of avarice that are punished in the judicial forum through ecclesiastical sentence" (duo detestabilia genera avaritie que puniuntur in iudicio per sententiam, scilicet usura et simonia).[46]

"Regratorie" and Usury: Contextual Evidence for Their Kinship

The narrator denounces the activities denoted by "regratorie" just as the canonists denounced them under the increasingly capacious rubric of usury. As Mike Jones has recently argued, "the group of commercial ploys with which Langland surrounds the term 'regratorie' are more numerous than the dictionary definition of 'forestalling'" or, for that matter, any general meaning of retail trade.[47] Typically linked to the offices of civic government after the 1380s, "regratorie," Jones points out, signified a cluster of fraudulent practices: "issues of over-pricing,

45 Here is the full sentence: "ad tertiam quaestionem dicendum quod quando lucrum ipsum est lege prohibitum, ut rapina, usura, et simonia, non solum dicitur turpe lucrum sed iniquum" (to the third question it must be said that when the profit itself is prohibited by law, as in pillage, usury, and simony, the profit is said to be not only filthy but iniquitous) (*Scriptum super sententiis magistri Petri Lombardi*, ed. M.F. Moos, Parisiis, 1947, tom.4, lib. 4, dist. 15, quaest. 2, art. 4).

46 Thomas of Chobham, art. 7, dist. 6, q. xia, *De usura*, 504.

47 Jones, *Radical Pastoral*, 28.

manipulating weights, and measures, and of setting substandard produce all reappear in civic legislation in the fourteenth and fifteenth centuries."[48] These are also the activities that fall under ecclesiastical jurisdiction and within the purview of the usury prohibition. "Canon law," as Brundage observes, "punished regraters, who bought commodities in bulk at the market town and then resold them in the countryside at many times the purchase price."[49] But, as Joel Kaye has eloquently argued, given that the canonistic understanding of economic balance changed from being "arithmetic" to "geometric" in the period between the 1280s and the 1360s, canonists examined forms of retail trade on a case-by-case basis to determine whether or not they were usurious and in what circumstances they might even be licit.[50] In the title on usury in his *Summa confessorum*, John of Freiburg considers a number of such forms by summarizing and synthesizing the positions on them by canonists such as Raymond, his glossator William of Rennes, and Hostiensis. To read the narrator's treatment of "regratorie" in light of John's discussion of retail trade is to uncover the poem's cooption of and contribution to the evolving canonist thought on the usury prohibition.

Take, for instance, one of the many questions that John raises about retail trade. Asking "in what cases usury is permitted" (in quibus casibus usura sit permissa), John, following Raymond, identifies a number of criteria (including interest and doubt) that canonists such as Hostiensis and Innocent IV consider in order to determine whether or not receiving more in value than what was lent or paid for is usurious.[51] John goes on to take up the question of regraters that the narrator in *Piers Plowman* addresses and that we touched on above: "concerning those, who in the time of grain-harvest or grape-harvest buy a year's produce or wine cheaper so that they may later sell them dearer" (Quid de quibusdam qui tempore messis vel vindemie emunt annonam vel vinum vilius ut postea vendant carius?).[52] John initially answers by

48 Jones, *Radical Pastoral*, 28.

49 Brundage, *Medieval Canon Law*, 76.

50 Kaye, *A History of Balance*, 1–19.

51 All quotations from John of Freiburg's *Summa confessorum* are from John A. Lorenc's edition of the title *De usuris* in his "John of Freiburg and the Usury Prohibition in the Late Middle Ages," and refer to book number, title number, title, question, and page number, as in Freiburg, 2.7 *De usuris*, q. 16, 282–3 at which "interest" or indemnity for damage is addressed; for "doubt" as a justification for buying cheap and selling dear, see Freiburg, 2.7 *De usuris*, q. 16, 284.

52 Freiburg, 2.7 *De usuris*, q. 40, 300.

citing Raymond, who says that "they [such traders] sin and it is filthy profit" (dicit quod peccant et turpe lucrum est).[53] At the same time, John notes that William of Rennes's gloss (to Raymond's *Summa*) "says that it is extremely difficult, if it [Raymond's opinion] should be understood without any distinction" (Glossa dicit hic quod hoc nimis durum est si sine distinctione intelligatur).[54] "Whence," John cites "canon XIIII, q. III," reproducing in full Gratian's citation of Pope Julius's canon *Quicumque*, which, as we have already discussed, only deems "wicked profit" (turpe lucrum) the gain made by trading for the sake of "cupidity" (cupiditatem) and not on account of "necessity" (necessitate).[55] However, unlike Gratian or even Johannes Teutonicus, whose gloss to this canon focuses only on the word "modium," John of Freiburg dwells at length on the motivations underlying acts of regrating. He justifies regrating if it is undertaken for a just cause – say, if one does so for the common good or for the private good but on account of prudent necessity. He cites Ulrich of Strasbourg's *Summa de summo bono* to offer an example of licit regrating for the common good: "or [when] such a purchase is done for the sake of the common good, just as Joseph bought grain in order that he could keep it and hence provide for the people in time of famine, and this is meritorious."[56] Likewise, John cites Ulrich again to offer a parallel example of licit regrating for a private good: "or it is done on account of private good, [for example], out of foresight, as, for example, if someone buys in this manner from fear that, if he were in

53 Ibid., 300–1.

54 Ibid., 301.

55 Freiburg, 2.7 *De usuris*, q. 40, 301: [John cites from the *Decretum*] "Quicunque temporis messis vel vindemie non necessitate, sed propter cupiditatem, comparat annonam vel vinum, verbi gratia, de duobus denariis comparat modium vini, et servat usque dum vendatur denariis IIII aut VII aut amplius, hoc turpe lucrum dicimus." John uses the conjunction "unde" (whence) to transition to his citation of Gratian's invocation of the canon *Quicumque*; see Gratian, *Decretum*, II. C. 14, q. 4, c. 9, *Quicumque*, cols 1403–4; *CIC*, 1: 737.

56 Freiburg, 2.7 *De usuris*, q. 40, 301: "Sed Ulricus plenius et planius, §. Est etiam turpe, distinguit dicens, 'Quia vel talis emptio fit propter commune bonum, sicut Joseph emit frumenta ut haberet unde provideret populis tempore famis, et hoc meritorium est'" (Ulrich of Strasbourg, *Summa de summo bono*, 6.3.4, *De llliberalitate*, Quartus modus est, fol. 105v); All references to Ulrich's *Summa* follow Lorenc, who cites Ulrich according to the incipit of each of the sections of manuscript he consulted (Erlangen, Universitätsbibliothek MS 530, II) and the folio number.

need of it afterwards, he would have to pay a dearer rate, and, nevertheless, he sells it afterwards at the dearer price at which it is sold in the marketplace, because he does not need it as he thought he would, this also is licit" (sicut si aliquis emat huiusmodi timens quod postea oporteat eum carius emere si indiguerit, et nihilominus tamen postmodum carius vendit sicut in foro venditur, quia non indiget sicut credebat, et hoc etiam licitum est).[57] John buttresses Ulrich's position by referring to Raymond's *Summa de poenitentia et matrimonio*, William of Rennes's *Glossa ad Summam Raymundi*, as well as Innocent IV's *Apparatus Super quinque libros decretalium*.[58] Reinforcing the licitness of regrating on grounds of private necessity or public charity, he once again cites Ulrich. For Ulrich and, hence, for John, regrating "is much more assuredly licit if he [the regrater] does not buy more than he needs or [if he] buys out of pity so that he may provide for the poor with the profit of the sale, on the condition that he does this moderately so that the community be not hurt by the increase in price" (multo fortius licitum est hoc si non emit ultra suam necessitatem vel emit ex pietate ut ex lucro venditionis habeat unde provideat pauperibus, dummodo ita moderate hoc faciat quod per caristiam communitas non ledatur.)[59] Regrating done from avarice and to the detriment of the community, however, as John's citation from Ulrich again reveals, is sinful:

> Vel fit ex avaricia, ita quod unus tantum de huiusmodi congregat quod compelluntur homines ab ipso emere ad libitum suum, et ideo vendit adeo care sicut vult. Et patet quod isti enormiter peccant, non solum contra proximum, sed etiam contra communitatem proximorum.[60]
>
> Or it is done from avarice, so that one only hoards [items] together in such a manner that people are compelled to buy at his pleasure, and so he sells as dearly as he wishes. And it is clear that they [such regraters] sin enormously not only against the neighbour but also against the community of neighbours.

---

57 Freiburg, 2.7 *De usuris*, q. 40, 301; see also Ulrich, *Summa de summo bono*, 6.3.4 *de illiberalitate*, Quartus modus est, fol. 105v.

58 Ibid., "Idem Raymundus et glossa hic. Idem etiam Innocentius dicit, Extra. ne clerici vel monachi, in glossa super c.I."

59 Ibid.

60 Ibid., 302; as the editor notes, John cites from Ulrich of Strasbourg, *Summa de summo bono*, 6.3.4 *De illiberalitate*, Quartus modus est, fol. 106r.

In the hands of John, the usury-prohibition is no longer interpreted as a unilateral condemnation of all acts of regrating. Rather personal motivations of the regrater as well as public consequences of his actions on the larger community of neighbours are to be considered to determine if regrating is usurious or permitted. It is in light of such circumstance-related determinations of usury in retail trade that Langland's narrator presents and judges regraters and usurers.

In both versions of passus 3, the narrator does not mention usury by name at the outset of his denunciation of regrating but he does go on to name a characteristic that John of Freiburg identifies as distinctive usury: the unjust price charged from avarice. Identified as "brewesters and baksters, bochiers and cokes,"[61] regraters, the narrator complains, enrich themselves at the expense of the poor: "þat moost harm wercheþ / To þe pouere peple þat parcelmele buggen ... richen þoruȝ regratrie."[62] The narrator calls notice to the unjustness of the profit made by the regraters by hypothesizing that they would not build such lofty edifices if they "toke" [profits] "trewely" ("For toke þei on trewely, þei tymbred nouȝt so heiȝe").[63] Clearly, the regraters undertake their trade not out of necessity for survival but out of cupidity. Both the profits from not taking "trewely" and the resultant pains or "moost harm" to "þe pouere peple" exemplify the "turpe lucrum" that John of Freiburg among other canonists deem usurious.

In his pioneering work on late medieval commerce in England, R.H. Britnell calls attention to proclamations that condemn various kinds of retail trade on the analogy with usury. Among the documents that Britnell examines is a certain "Composicio ad puneniendum infringentes assisam panis et cervisie, forestallarios" that likens forestallers (a certain kind of regrater, who intercepts goods on the way to market before reselling them) to usurers insofar as both seek after unjust profits at the expense of the poor:

> Moreover, several quirks of the drafting suggest that he [the author of the "Composicio"] knew the fundamental texts relating to usury and had them in mind while formulating his ideas on forestalling. *Lucrum viciosum* recalls the phrase *turpe lucrum* from the principal text relating to unjust trade in canon law. And the initial requirement that "No forestaller should

---

61 B 3.79; see corresponding C 3.80.

62 B 3.80–3; see corresponding C 3.81–2.

63 B 3.85; see corresponding C 3.84.

be allowed to remain (*commorari*) in town, being manifestly (*manifeste*) an oppressor of the poor" takes its emphasis from the Lyons Council of 1274, which had decreed that no one was to allow usurers from other parts to settle in his lands. Manifest usurers of this sort (*huiusmodi usurarii manifesti*) should be expelled within three months; lands in which usurers were allowed to settle should be subjected to ecclesiastical interdict so long as the usurers stayed there (*quamdiu in eis iidem usurarii commorantur*). Echoes of this ecclesiastical thinking give the "Composicio" its powerful appeal, even though its practical content owes nothing to canon law.[64]

Like the "brewesters and baksters, bochiers and cokes" in both B and C,[65] the forestallers condemned in the "Composicio" oppress the poor by seeking after "lucrum vitiosum" – an expression also cited by John of Freiburg to signify the usurious "turpe lucrum" in his discussion of the canonist Gottofredo da Trani's view on the justness or unjustness of receiving more than the principal lent in a loan.[66] The "Composicio"'s denunciation of forestallers rests on the same "ecclesiastical thinking" as the narrator's denunciation of the regraters that do "most harm þe mene peple."[67] In both cases, unjust profit is conceived of as injustice to the poor. While Hostiensis reserves sharper criticism for usurers of clerical status rather than of lay status, the narrator shifts the focus from the status of the regraters to the effects of their regrating and thereby articulates a more socially attentive critique than the canonist.[68]

---

64 Britnell, "Forstall, Forestalling and the Statute of Forestallers," 94–5.

65 B 3.79; see corresponding C 3.80.

66 While discussing just and unjust gifts offered by a debtor to a creditor, John of Freiburg summarizes Gottofredo da Trani's view and uses the expression "vitiosum" to signify "turpe lucrum": "Goffredus tamen dicit quod non est hoc vitiosum" (However, Gottofredo says that this is not vicious); see Freiburg, 2.7 *De usuris*, q. 8, 278; see also Gottofredo, *Summa super titulis decretalium*, X 5.19 *De usuris*, n. 1. In citing Gottofredo da Trani, I follow Lorenc, who cites from the *Summa super titulis decretalium*, X 5.19 *de usuris*, n. 1 (Lyons, 1519; reprint Darmstadt, 1968).

67 C 3.81.

68 Hostiensis attends to the status of usurers in a number of places in his title of usury. Noting that although the Nicene Council's prohibition of usury speaks only of clerics and therefore it seems that it permitted lay people to practise usury ("illud tantum de clericis, & non de laicis loquitur, & ideo videtur laicis concessum"), he argues that the prohibition applies to both laiety and the clergy, given that the sacred authority of the Council is common to all ("sed certe quamvis illud concilium de clericis tantum loquatur, authoritas tamen sacra, quae in eo inducitur, generalis est, & tam in clericis, quam in laicis locum habet"; see *Summa aurea*, 5,

Regrating and Usury: Evidence for Their Kinship within the C Version

I have thus far discussed the relationship between usury and regrating in canonist thought to establish an external ecclesiastical context for the B and C versions' critiques of Mede. In what follows, I argue that C goes further than B by adapting such canonist thought for secular ends – an adaptation that comprises a reinvention of the canon law governing usury. At first sight, of course, the narrator in C does not appear to invoke any canon at all when he turns from the condemnation of Mede's support of simony to that of her advocacy of regrating. To be sure, in the narrator's initial approach to regrating in either version of the passus there is nothing explicit that expresses the link theorized by canonists between usury in its formal sense of a loan on interest and, as discussed above, any sales-transaction inspired by "turpe lucrum." Thus, the narrator at first invokes secular rather than ecclesiastical jurisdiction to assail regrating: corrupt mayors, not ecclesiastical administrators, are held responsible for usurious regrating. Excoriating the practice of "regratrie" and "rentes"[69] that takes advantage of the "pouere peple,"[70] the narrator accuses Mede of asking the secular "mair," in B, to maintain regraters ("þe regratiers to mayntene")[71] and, the same "mayre," in C, to take pity on them ("haue reuthe on this regraters þat han riche hands").[72]

Much like the poem's narrator, historians such as Anthony Musson and Britnell have seen regrating and other allied forms of retail trade throughout late medieval England as a matter regulated largely by secular laws (whether by the assize or by royal statute). Drawing on

---

De vsuris, 8, col. 1438. However, in a subsequent section on another species of usury, Hostiensis clarifies that although usury is execrable with regard to the laiety, it is more execrable with regard to the clergy on the grounds that an illicit thing ought to be much less allowed to the clergy than to the laiety ("Si illicitum, multo minus debet concedi clerico, quam laico: licet usura respectu laicorum sit execranda: respectu clericorum est execrabilior"); see *Summa aurea*, 5, *De vsuris*, 8, col. 1439. Likewise, distinguishing between penalties for clerical and lay usurers, he notes that the former is "suspended from office and benefice" (usurarius clericus ab officio, beneficioque, suspenditur) and the latter is "excommunicated" (excommunicatur); see *Summa aurea*, 5, *De vsuris*, 10, col. 1447.

69 B 3.83; see corresponding C 3.82.

70 B 3.84, see corresponding C 3.83.

71 B 3.90.

72 C 3.118.

Judicium pillorie (c. 1266), Musson observes that "consensual forestalling and regrating were penalized by statute from at least the reign of Henry III ... [and both] were regularly to be found in the commissions of the Justices of the Peace from 1364 onwards."[73] Literary scholars such as Galloway, Pearsall, and Vance Smith have, likewise, also pointed to the abundant records of secular legislation – both local and royal – such as the statutes of Edward III as bound up with the poet's treatment of regrating.[74] Although "the microscopic practices of 'regraterye' were not criminalized in city and guild ordinances," it was, as Pearsall and Vance Smith argue, regulated by the royal initiative, for "the economic imaginary of *Piers Plowman* is inseparable from the deep interest that Edward took in managing the political economy of England."[75]

To approach the narrator's critique of regrating in both versions of the passus solely from the perspective of secular legislation, however, is to overlook the ways in which C goes on to shape the critique on conceptual grounds on which the canonists thought about usury. In a set of lines found in C (but not in B) on the mayoral regulation of mercantile franchise, the narrator returns to the subject of regrating but now links it with usury in a manner that recalls the canonists' view of regrating as a form of usury. In the C lines, the narrator exhorts mayors to verify the nature of trade engaged by prospective "fremen":

Forthy mayres þat maketh fremen, me thynketh þat ȝe ouhten
For to spyre and to aspye, for eny speche of suluer,
What maner muster oþer marchandise he vsed
Ar he were vnderfonge fre and felawe in ȝoure rolles.
Hit is nat seemely, for sothe, in citee or in borw-toun,
That vsurers oþer regraters, for enys-kynes ȝeftes,
Be yfranchised for a freman and haue a fals name. (C 3.108–14)

With these words, which have no parallel in the corresponding section in B, the narrator identifies the prospective citizens ("fremen") as

73 Musson, *Expectations of the Law*, 120–1.

74 In his gloss to the lines on regrating, Galloway observes that although "regrating" or "profitable retailing by victuallers" was "repeatedly subject to civic regulation in the fourteenth and fifteenth centuries," it was "perfectly legal" (*The Penn Commentary*, 300).

75 Smith, "*Piers Plowman* and the National Noetic of Edward III," 246.

standing for "vsurers oþer regraters." The narrator's use of the coordinating conjunction "oþer" to link usurers and regraters can be read as establishing equivalence in two senses. In one sense, "oþer" can mean "that is to say," signifying that a usurer is another word for a regrater: they are interchangeable persons. In another sense, "oþer" can mean that, for the narrator, both usurers and regraters practise trades that are identical in concealing fraud. Either reading of the coordinating conjunction contains evidence for the narrator's adaptation of the canonist thought on usury to confer on secular "mayres" (not on ecclesiastical judges) the charge to scrutinize ("to spyre and to aspye") the manner of trade ("eny speche of suluer / What maner muster oþer marchandise he vsed") of a candidate for the position of "fremen." The ruling from the Nicene Council, collated by Gratian and cited above, also uses the Latin conjunction "uel" that corresponds to the English "oþer" in order to broaden usury's meaning to include all forms of trade that result in "turpe lucrum."[76] The ruling condemns "usuras" in their denotative sense of loans given on interest but does not stop at that. Using the coordinating conjunction "uel" (or), it also condemns any business similar to usury ("tali negotio") with regard to the pursuit of "filthy profits" (turpia lucra): "usuras accipere, uel ex quolibet tali negotio turpia lucra sectari, uel etiam species frumentorum ad sescuplum dare."[77] In citing from the Nicene Council to frame his discussion of usurious transactions, Gratian expands the category of usury to include any "affair" (negotium) motivated by illicit profits. My point is not so much about lexical equivalence: that the poem's "oþer" is a translation of the "uel." Rather, my point is about the conceptual equivalence that Gratian and Langland establish between diverse forms of exchange with regard to usury: that, in the C lines discussed above, the narrator conceives of regrating as an extension or even exemplification of usury in the sense that both activities share the same logic of an avaricious profit-motive underlying the evolving canonistic understanding of usury.

But where there is a samesness of logic, there is also a difference of audience. The narrator in C does not address ecclesiastical judges or, for that matter, any ecclesiastical context for the prosecution of usury. Rather,

76 Gratian, *Decretum*, II. C. 14, q. 4, c. 8, cols 1401–2; see also Emil Friedberg, ed., *CIC*, 1: 737.

77 Gratian, *Decretum*, II. C. 14, q. 4, c. 8, cols 1401–2; see also Friedberg, *CIC*, 1: 737.

he addresses secular mayors.[78] Unlike the canonists who tended to judge usurious clerics more culpable than their lay counterparts, the narrator judges the laity – specifically, lay officials but, as I shall argue, from the perspective of canonist thought. The narrator expresses the suspicion that traders seeking citizenship might be engaging in usury. While he appeals to the secular jurisdiction, he does so in the language of canonists. Specifically, he asks the mayors to examine prospective citizens ("fremen") for speche of suluer ("any persuasive language of money")[79] and for any illicit "vse" of "merchandise." The narrator deploys a cluster of expressions that resonate with those used in canonistic explanations of usury: "ȝeftes," "eny speche of suluer," "vse," and "vsurers." Discussing the gifts tainted by usury, Hostiensis and John of Freiburg distinguish one kind that bears a striking similarity to "eny speche of suluer." John makes clear that any "verbal offer" (munus a lingua) exacted or even implicitly expected for a loan is just as illicit as a material gift taken from hand ("munus a manu"). Citing Thomas Aquinas, he explains that if the "munus a lingua" "can be valued in terms of money" (pecunia estimari potest), then it is not licit to expect or exact such a gift:

> Quid si pro pecunia mutuata exigatur munus a lingua vel ab obsequio? Respondeo secundum Thomam, ibidem, art. II, arg. III dicendum quod sicut munus a manu non licet expectari vel exigi pacto tacito vel expresso pro mutuata pecunia, ita nec munus a lingua vel ab obsequio, "quia utrumque pecunia estimari potest, ut patet in his qui locant operas suas quas manu vel lingua exercent." (John of Freiburg, 2.7 *De usuris*, q. 5, 276–7)

> What if for a monetary loan, a verbal offer or service could be exacted? I respond according to Thomas Aquinas in the same place art.ii, arg.iii, that it should be said that just as it is not licit that a material gift be expected or exacted by a tacit or expressed agreement for a monetary loan, so also with a verbal offer or service, "because either [the verbal offer or service] can be estimated in terms of money, as it appears with those who hire out the work they do by hand or speech."

78 Noting that "the poem's voice of public chastisement of usurers comes very close to the 1384 anti-usury London programme," Galloway has argued that the narrator's appeal to the mayors is "predicated on financial transparency and legal equality, a new and more precise and ethical mercantile accounting directly based on the documentary technologies that allowed the very practices such efforts for transparency assailed"; see Galloway, "Non-literary Commentary," 19.

79 Galloway, *The Penn Commentary*, 303.

Placed within the narrator's denunciation of those usurers or regraters who offer "enys-kynes ȝeftes," the expression "eny speche of suluer" reads as a compressed translation of "munus a lingua," and the "suluer" the "pecunia" for the monetary estimation of such a gift. Just as Mede had previously committed simony by promising to buy clerics benefices, so here, the prospective "fremen," the narrator fears, may have committed usury in their verbal offers of something of monetary value to the mayors.

The conceptual equivalence between literary and legal approaches to usury is reinforced in the narrator's play on the word usury. In speaking of the "maner" and the "marchandise he vsed," the narrator echoes the canonists' play on the etymology of "usura." Both the narrator and the canonists pun on the word "use" (usus) or its cognates to illustrate that usury inheres in the manner in which an object is "vsed" in exchange. Among the senses of "usurie" recorded in the *Piers Plowman Concordance*, two pertain to the punning relationship between the verbal "use" and the nominal "usury."[80] In the lines on the prohibition of usury in the B passage in passus 3, we may recall, Conscience relates the verb "vseþ" to the noun "vsurie" when claiming that one is eligible for God's mede, if one "vseþ noȝt þe lyf of vsurie."[81] Likewise, in a later passus in Covetise's confession, Repentaunce recalls and reinforces the link between the verbal "Vsedestow" and the nominal "vsurie" when he asks Covetise: "Vsedestow euere vsurye in al thy lyf tyme?"[82] The syntactical link between "use" (vseþ) and "usury" (vsurie) in the alliterative formulation "vseþ ... vsurie" creates a kind of self-interested *mis-en-abime* that reflects, and reflects on, a similar link canonists draw between "usus" and "the use of goods" (usus rei) or "use of money" (usus aeris).[83] For instance, Hostiensis singles out "usus" (use) when he parses "usura" into "usus" (use) and "rei" (of goods), deriving the meaning of usury from the manner of the use of goods. He reinforces his focus on "usus" when he subsequently distinguishes in the term "usura" between "usus" (use) and "aeris" (bronze / money):

> Et unde dicatur. Et quidem dicitur "usura," ab "usu rei," quia datur ob usum rei, id est, pecuniae; vel dicitur "usura," quasi "usurea," sive "usueta," id est, "usus aeris," hoc est pecuniae, quod ad idem recidit. (*Summa aurea*, 5, *De vsuris*, 2, cols 1433–4)

80 *Piers Plowman: Concordance*, 711.

81 B 3.240.

82 C 6.239; see also corresponding B 5.236.

83 I thank an anonymous reader for this formulation.

> And, whence its name: it is called "usura" from "usu rei," [from the use of goods], because something is given for using goods, that is, money. Or, it is called "usura" for "usurea" connected with "usueta" [accustomed], meaning a combination of "usus" [use] and "aes" [copper], that is "use of money," which is the same idea.

Teasing out the extended senses of the name "usura," Ranulph Higden, a fourteenth-century English Benedictine commentator on canon law and *pastoralia*, also understands usury's location primarily in the "use of goods" (usu rei) or "any unjust usurpation of another's goods" (omnis iniusta usurpatio rei aliene).[84]

While John of Freiburg, Hostiensis, and Ranulph Higden's etymological explications of the word "usura" help uncover the usurious connotations of the narrator's diction in C, English attitudes towards foreign merchants may also shed light on the larger mercantile context in which usury was understood in Langland's day and in which Conscience's concern about the prospective "fremen" is articulated. In her examination of the usury prohibition in late medieval England, Gwen Seabourne notes that "[u]sury was particularly associated with unpopular foreigners and Jews in a way in which the other offences to be considered were not," even as "there was an element of differentiation between 'insiders' and 'outsiders' in many urban rules concerning pricing."[85] Just as, in the later scene of Covetise's confession, Repentaunce identifies usurers explicitly as non-English residents such as Jews and Lombards ("Y lernede among Lumbardus a lessoun [about usury], and of Iewes"),[86] so here, in passus 3 too, the narrator forges a kinship between usurers and "outsider" merchants, whose acquisition of citizenship and the concomitant trading "franchise" would cause the English merchants to face stiff competition.[87]

---

84 Higden, *Speculum Curatorum*, 280. Higden defines "theft" (furtum) as committed not only in the thing itself but also in the "use" of the thing: "Ipsam rem vel usum vel possessionem ponitur quia furtum non solum committitur in ipsa re, set eciam in usu rei, quamuis sit cum animo restituendi."

85 Seabourne, *Royal Regulation of Loans and Sales*, 69.

86 C 6.241; see also corresponding B 5.238.

87 In a footnote on page 69, Seabourne observes that "[u]sury might be used as a xenophobic insult" and points to Mandeville's *Travels* and *Piers Plowman* as two fourteenth-century texts that depict usurers as foreigners; see the description of Constantinople and the Greek faith in Mandeville's *Travels* (9–13), and see Covetise's confession in passus 6.

Establishing the poem's participation in "new literacies"[88] of mercantile accounting in Ricardian London, Galloway sees in the narrator's address to the mayors a telling example of "the prospect of transparent discourse, direct speech to the powerful, as well as financial exchanges."[89] Seen from a canonist perspective, what is transparent or evident is the narrator's targeting of non-transparent or covert usury – i.e., the narrator seeks to expose those non-English merchants whose transnational "manners" of mercantile "use" disguise usury.

C's linkage of usurers and regraters in the context of local franchise cannot be dismissed as an isolated instance of a broader sense of usury found among later medieval canonists such as Hostiensis than, say, in Gratian's *Decretum*. In further C lines about the buying and selling advocated by Mede, the narrator returns to and reinforces the framework of local legislation from which to denounce regraters. In the B and C passages following his appeal to mayors, the narrator condemns Mede's maintenance of "regratiers"[90] by means of "presentȝ wiþouten pens – as pieces of siluer."[91] In B, the narrator deplores regrating as a violation of "reson" given that Mede urges mayors to allow regraters to "selle somdel ayeins reson"[92] and the narrator mentions the law only in the context of Solomon's sermon admonishing mayors and law-keepers to reform themselves ("amenden maieres and men þat kepen lawes").[93] The corresponding passage in C, however, includes two lines (not present in B) in which the narrator shifts the focus from "reson" to "lawe" and assails Mede's request to the mayor to "soffre hem [regraters] som tyme to selle aȝeyne þe lawe."[94] In these lines, Mede pleads for leniency towards regraters that violate the "lawe" rather than, as in B, "reson." For regraters to "selle aȝeyne þe lawe" is to violate the just price: a standard not just promulgated by local legislation but also integral to the theological and canonistic determination of usury in

88 Galloway, "The Account Book," 69.

89 Ibid., 88. Galloway has argued that the "C-text indeed shows even more direct address to the London world than the other versions" (82).

90 B 3.90.

91 B 3.89; see corresponding C 3.116–17.

92 B 3.92.

93 B 3.94.

94 C 3.120.

retail trade.[95] To be sure, Mede does not identify the "lawe" that the regraters break as either secular or canon law, for it could have been both or either. Indeed, my point here is that contemporary retail activity and the just price are framed in the poem not just by secular statutes but also, as I have been arguing, by concepts drawn from canonistic and theological thought.[96]

Back to C: Omitting Usury by Name

Just as the narrator denounces Mede as a violator of the law concerning retail trade, so Conscience continues his critique of Mede in the same legal vein when he mentions the usury prohibition in the passage (in B 3.231–54 as well as in C 3.285–311) that was addressed at the outset of Part I of this chapter. The intimations of canon law in C discussed so far

---

95 Citing Thomas Aquinas, John of Freiburg reads or reinforces Raymond's definition of usury as covering any trade that violates the just price: "Dicit Thomas, in *Summa* art. II, arg. VII, quod 'si aliquis carius velit vendere res suas quam sit iustum precium ut de pecunia solvenda emptorem expectet manifeste usura committitur, quia huiusmodi expectatio precii solvendi habet rationem mutui. Unde quicquid ultra iustum precium pro huiusmodi expectatione exigitur est quasi precium mutui, quod pertinet ad rationem usure. Similiter etiam si quis emptor velit rem emere vilius quam sit iustum precium, eo quod pecuniam ante solvit quam possit ei res tradi, est peccatum usure, quia etiam ista anticipatio solutionis pecunie habet rationem mutui, cuius quoddam precium est quod minuitur de iusto precio rei empte.' (Freiburg, 2.7 *De usuris*, q. 16, 285; for the citation from Aquinas, see also *ST* IIa-IIae q. 78 a. 2, ad 7)" [Thomas says in *Summa* article II, argument VII, that if someone wishes to sell his things at a price higher than the just price, and so waits for the buyer to pay the money, usury is manifestly committed, because such waiting for the price to be paid has the character of a loan. Whence whatever is demanded beyond the just price on account of this kind of waiting is akin to the price of a loan, which pertains to the character of usury. Similarly also, if a buyer should wish to buy a thing cheaper than the just price by paying the money before the goods can be handed over to him, it is the sin of usury because again this delay of the payment of the money has the character of a loan, whose price is made less than the just price of the item bought]. According to Werner Goetz, "the medieval academics gathered the concept of the just price from the new Latin translations of Aristotle's writings. The major scholastics were also the influential theoreticians of the 'just price'" (Den neuen Übersetzungen seiner Schriften ins Lateinische entnahmen die mittelalterlichen Gelehrten den Begriff des gerechten Preises. Die grossen Scholastiker waren auch die einflussreichen Theoretiker des "pretium iustum"); see Goetz, "Das Ringen um den gerechten Preis," 21–32.

96 See Richard Britnell's essay on canon law and borough price-fixing, "Price-Setting in English Borough Markets, 1349–1500."

are intensified in further C lines in which Conscience elaborates on the reprehensible "mede." These lines in C, as we shall see, adapt concepts of credit, time, risk, and doubt used by canonists to theorize usury lurking behind credit sales such as advance ("pre manibus") payments.

To begin with, the C lines about "mede" have no parallel in the corresponding passage in B.[97] They shift the focus of attention from the laudable mede to the reprehensible mede. Whereas, in B, Conscience explains the nature of the "werkes" that will merit the good God-given mede, Conscience, in the corresponding passage in C, laments the "many tymes" when "mede" is asked or given temporally before "som doyng" is actually accomplished. Judging "mede" given for "som doyng" from the perspective of time, Conscience applauds "goode men" who give mede temporally after an action has been completed ("þe ende").

In the passage in C, then, Conscience assails "mede" in relation to time rather than to work: at the centre of his critique is when one receives mede rather than what exactly it is given for. In the passage in B, by contrast, what work one does – whether it be just or unjust – determines whether or not one is eligible for the divine "mede." Absent from the C passage, thus, is any reference to what purposes or at whose expense such "mede" is given (i.e., whether, as in the corresponding place in B, something is given "ad usuram" or against an innocent borrower "super innocentem"). Thus, even when he speaks of "mede" passing the hands of "harlots and hoores and also fals leches" and "gylours," Conscience assails neither the morality of their "werkes" nor the acts themselves of receiving and giving "mede" or even their impact on the innocent – all of these are the criteria for the reception of the divine mede in the corresponding passage in B. Rather, he deplores the practice of asking and receiving "mede" or "huyre" temporally before one has merited or worked for it: "That *pre manibus* is paied or his pay asketh." Harlots and false doctors "asken" for their "huyre" before ("ar") they have "deserved" it; likewise, "gylours" are critiqued because they gyuen" before ("byfore"). By contrast, those who give temporally after the deed is done are good: "goode men at þe ende. / When þe dede is ydo." In sum, for Conscience, the time of giving or receiving "mede" – whether "byfore" or "at ende" of "som doying" – determines whether or not the "mede" given is good or bad.

97 For the passage in B, see B 3.231–54.

Conscience's critique of "mede" in the C passage complements that expressed in the corresponding B passage in the same way in which covert usury complements overt usury. Whereas in the B passage Conscience assails the usurious loan overtly by its denotative name, in the C passage, Conscience assails usury covertly in the connotative sense that it carried for canonists who regarded a "pre manibus" transaction usurious if "mede" rather than need was the underlying motivation. Identifying the Latin expression "pre manibus" as "a legal formula," Alford traces it to a number of sources including the *Liber extra* where it is associated with "the form of usury known as 'time-selling.'"[98] In his more recent discussion of "Meed mesureless," Galloway argues that "pre manibus" payments amount to "a form of venture" that "unlike the other forms of venturing that Langland's poem pervasively praises ... relies on a more or less deliberate obscuring of the full terms and consequences of the transaction, a conscious acquiescence in deception that allows Conscience to claim that such transactions are intrinsically tied to further ethical and social deceptions."[99] Seen against the corresponding passage in B, the C passage's "pre manibus" exchanges that Galloway identifies as "deceptions" exemplify a form of disguised usury or "in fraud of usuries" (in fraudem usurarum) singled out for censure by canonists such as Hostiensis. To move from B to C is to move from a denunciation of manifestly named usury ("usura aperta" or "usura manifesta") to that of disguised usury – a usurious venturing that, to adapt Galloway's words, is not equitable or mutually transparent, for neither party has "as much information as possible about the values in the transaction before its completion."[100]

Canonists came up with the idea of disguised usury in order to combat mercantile exchanges that sought to circumvent the usury prohibition by charging interest covertly – often in the guise of a legitimate sale or "pre manibus" payment. In the thirteenth and fourteenth centuries, as Joel Kaye has recently argued, "merchants continued to invent new contractual forms of credit, in part because the dynamic of commercial expansion called them into being, and in part, to disguise interest-bearing loans (*in fraudem usurarum*)."[101] Usury disguised "in

98 Alford, *A Glossary*, 120; see also his *Piers Plowman: A Guide to the Quotations*, 38; and Alford, "More Unidentified Quotations in *Piers Plowman*," 284.

99 Galloway, "The Account Book," 84.

100 Ibid.

101 Kaye, *A History of Balance*, 19.

fraudem usurarum" took the form of contracts. As Kaye observes, one of "two of the most complex and problematic of contracts" that "came under the watchful eye of the canonists over the course of the thirteenth century" was "time sales (*venditio ad tempus*), connected primarily to commercial goods."[102]

A common variant of the time sale is the "pre manibus" payment at the centre of Conscience's critique of the reprehensible "mede." In medieval England, "pre manibus" payments were judged as usurious if there was a difference between the amount the buyer paid in advance for merchandise (to be delivered in the future) and the market price of the same merchandise at the time of its delivery. Here is a report of disguised usury in the guise of a "pre manibus" sale from the Eyre of Westmorland in 1292:

> Villa de Appleby. De usurar[ariis] etc. dicunt Johannes de Goldington emit premanibus de Thom[a] fil[io] Mag[istri] Will[elmi] de Goldinton tres saccos lane pro decem mar[cis] et dim[idio] quos ad certum terminum videlicet ad pent[ecostem] debuit recepisse; quo termino adveniente idem Thom[as] soluit ei unum saccum de precio novem mar[carum] et pro residuis duobus saccis soluit sibi xvii mar[cas] etc.[103]

> The Town of Appleby. Concerning usurers etc. They say that John Goldington bought "premanibus" from Thomas, son of Master William Goldington by making [an advance] payment of 10.5 marks for 3 sacks of wool which he was to receive at a certain point, that is, at Pentecost when Thomas gave him 1 sack of wool valued at the price of 9 marks, and, for the remaining 2 sacks, he gave 17 marks.

This "pre manibus" payment on the buyer John's part disguises a loan of 10.5 marks to Thomas, for which John as buyer gets back the value of 26 marks [one sack of wool valued at 9 + 17 marks cash for the other two sacks]. In sum, John gets back an excess in the value of 15.5 marks.

Conscience forges his critique of "pre manibus" payments for services by adapting the canonistic critique of "pre manibus" payments for goods. That is, whereas the canonists denounce the usurious greed or gain hidden under the payments that buyers advance to sellers for

102 Ibid., 69. The other contract is annuities, which are connected primarily with real property.

103 See Appendix 1 in Seabourne, *Royal Regulation of Loans*, 176.

goods not yet procured or produced, Conscience denounces as usurious the advance payments for labour not yet performed and that could bring unearned profit to the already paid-for workers at the expense of their masters. In other words, Conscience's critique does more than reflect the canonistic notion of disguised usury that underlies the credit that buyers give to sellers for fungible items: it refashions that notion to theorize usurious intent hidden within the context of services yet to be undertaken for wages already advanced.

Usury in the C version: Doubt and Risk

More specifically, to view Conscience's critique of Mede from the perspective of canonist thought on disguised usury is to uncover a poetic adaptation of concepts of risk and doubt found in canonistic condemnations of hidden usury in trade. Considering the complex attempts by merchants to conceal usury in credit sales, the pope and canonist Gregory IX issued a decretal that approached such transactions through two other related concepts: "risk" (periculum) and "doubt" (dubium). Published in 1234 in the *Liber extra*, the decretal *Naviganti* specifically answers a query about the legitimacy of obtaining interest on a loan advanced to a merchant setting sail or travelling to a market:[104]

> Gregorius IX. Fratri R. Nauiganti, vel eunti ad nundinas, certam mutuans pecuniae quantitatem, pro eo, quod suscipit in se periculum, recepturus aliquid vltra sortem, vsurarius est censendus. Ille quoque, qui dat decem solidos, vt alio tempore totidem sibi grani, vini vel olei mensurae reddantur, quae licet tunc plus valeant, vtrum plus vel minus solutionis tempore fuerint valiturae, verisimiliter dubitatur: non debet ex hoc vsurarius reputari. Ratione huius dubii etiam excusatur, qui pannos, granum, vinum, oleum, vel alias merces vendit, vt amplius, quam tunc valeant,

104 The larger mercantile context of this decretal is a certain kind of "pre manibus" payment called the "sea loan" (foenus nauticum), which Kaye describes as "a very common contract of the time … in which a sedentary party acting as a creditor lends a sum of money to a travelling merchant to trade with, while retaining all the risk involved in the future transaction. If, for instance, the ship were to sink or the merchandise were to be ruined, the sedentary merchant would absorb the loss of the entire sum he had invested. In return for assuming all the risk of the venture ("periculum sortis"), the sedentary merchant contracts to receive a certain portion of the profit made from the trade, in addition to the original sum he lent" (Kaye, *History of Balance*, 35–6).

> in certo termino recipiat pro eisdem; si tamen ea tempore contractus non fuerat venditurus. (*Liber extra* 5.19.19, cols 1744–5; see also Friedberg, ed., *CIC*, 2: 816)

> Gregory IX to Brother R: If a person lends money to another who is setting sail or going to market, and the lender is to receive in return something beyond the principal because he has assumed the risk, he should be judged a usurer. But he who gives 10 shillings in order that at some future time just as many measures of grain, wine, oil should be returned to him, even though at a higher value at that future time, should not be considered a usurer if it is truly doubted whether they will be worth more or less [than the sum lent] at the expiration of the time fixed. By reason of this doubt, one is also excused, who sells cloths, grain, wine, oil, or other merchandise so that he may receive more for them at some certain time in the future than they are now worth, if in the time of the contract, he had not been about to sell them.[105]

Clearly, for the canonist, doubt about the future value of the goods rather than any risk attendant on lending excuses the merchant-lender from receiving more than the principal from the borrower. "Risk" (periculum), as the *Glossa ordinaria* on the word makes clear, "should pertain not to the lender but to the borrower, but nevertheless it is usurious to receive more than the principal."[106]

At first sight, the diction of Gregory IX's decretal about sea loans has little in common with that of Conscience's critique of "pre manibus" payments. The commonalities between the two are circumstantial and

105 The translation has been adapted in light of that found in Chandler's article "Recent French Works on Insurance," 58–9.

106 Gloss ad v. *Periculum*, *Liber extra* 5.19.19, col. 1745: "quia iste recipiebat in se periculum, videbatur quod quasi quadam compensatione licite aliquid vltra sortem recipere posset: quia periculum pecuniae mutuatae pertinebat ad debitorem, cum sua facta fuisset: sed nihilominus est vsurarius, cum excedat naturam mutui: vt dictum est supra, eodem [titulo], cap. *Conquestus* [X.5.19.8]. quia si nullum periculum sequutum fuit, & aliquid vltra sortem recepit, illud fuit vsura" [because that person was undertaking the risk onto himself, it seemed that he could receive something beyond the loan, as some compensation: because the risk regarding the money lent pertained to the borrower, since the money was made his [the borrower's]: but nevertheless it is usurious when it goes beyond the nature of a loan, as it is mentioned above in the same [title], chapter *Conquestus* [X.5.19.8]. Because if no risk followed and he received something beyond the loan, that was usury.]

conceptual rather than lexical. Although Conscience does not identify the "pre manibus" payment anywhere with a sea loan, the temporal circumstances of the sea loan parallel those of the "pre manibus" payment. Just as the creditor in Gregory's narrative lends money to the "one setting sail" (naviganti) or to the "one travelling (eunti) to the market" to invest it and make profit for both in the future, so Conscience's creditor makes (or is requested to make) an advance payment to someone who will "vndertake to trauaile" in the future for his creditor (the one who pays him in advance).[107] In both poetic and canonistic examples, credit is offered for the work to be undertaken in the future. Likewise, in both examples, such work is indicated by words similar in meaning: Conscience's "trauaile" and Gregory's "naviganti vel eunti," although linguistically different, have at least one semantical and, by extension, structural similarity. In Middle English, the verb "trauaile" means both "to work" and "to travel" just as the Latin "naviganti vel eunti" refers to the one "travelling (by sea)" or "setting out." That is, the travelling merchant-borrower of Gregory's decretal is structurally in the same position as the travelling or travailing-worker of Langland's poem.

Conceptually as well, there are parallels between Gregory's decretal and Conscience's denunciation. Conscience critiques the "pre manibus" payment through the concepts of doubt and risk that underpin Gregory's pronouncement on the sea loan. The merchant-borrower and the paid-for worker are presented as facing one thing in common: risk to their lives and loan. The risk (or what Gregory calls "periculum") to the travelling merchant pertains to the entire enterprise for which the loan has been sought or offered. A recent study of documents of late medieval sea loans concludes that the risk involved the sea voyage itself and piracy, and "for extremely dangerous voyages, the borrower paid high interest rates, sometimes up to fifty percent."[108] Conscience too characterizes the paid-for worker as confronted by doubt and risk: the pre-paid worker does not know for certain ("wot neuere witterly")[109] whether he will live long enough ("where he lyue so longe")[110] nor

107 C 3.295.

108 See Hazard and Zacour, *The Impact of the Crusades*, 403. The loans and the risks involved are discussed in Raimondo Morozzo della Rocca and Attilio Lombardio, *Documenti del commercio veneziano nei secoli XI-XIII* (Rome: Istituto italiano per il Medio Evo, 1940), I, nos. 183, 223, 228.

109 C 3.296.

110 C 3.296.

may he have the chance or fortune ("hap") to merit ("to deserue") the already paid-for "mede."[111]

Seen together, Conscience's critique and Gregory's decretal participate in a shared language of usury. Despite the similarties between the two, there are also crucial differences that reveal a poetic adaptation of the canonist thought on usury. When juxtaposed alongside Gregory's decretal, Conscience's ruling comprises an invention – one that is expressed in the familiar canonist terms of doubt and risk to propose a novel solution to the problem of advance wages for labourers. Whereas Gregory deems obtaining any excess for such a loan usurious (except in case of doubt about the merchandise's future value), Conscience rules the credit or a request for it unreasonable or illicit ("nother resoun ne ryhte ne in no rewme lawe")[112] as "he [the borrower] myhte [not] deserue" it.[113] Whereas Gregory invokes doubt to exculpate the creditor's acceptance of an excess value beyond the principal, Conscience combines doubt and risk to question the probability of the outcome of the paid-for work to be undertaken, and, more important, to make no allowances for the legitimacy of "pre manibus" payments or requests for them. In deeming the worker who seeks such a payment "ouer-hardy or elles nat trewe,"[114] Conscience reworks Gregory's decretal about the mercantile sea loan that, as we may recall, allows the creditor to expect beyond the principal from the travelling merchant, not because of the "risk" (periculum) involved in the latter's acquiring the merchandise, but because of the "doubt" (dubium) about its price at the time of selling it.

My argument is not so much that Conscience's critique of a "pre manibus" payment derives from a source like a historically documented sea loan as that Conscience thinks through a commonly available conceptual language of loans for ends different from those that canonists like Gregory IX had in mind. Conscience's critique of labour-centred advanced-wage payments repurposes concepts through which canonists discerned and denounced usury concealed in merchandise-centred

111 In his *Commentary* on lines 296–7, Schmidt, correcting Pearsall's misreading of the referent "he," reads that "the referent of *he* 296 is the *he* of 294" ("Langland's Visions," 504).

112 C 3.293.

113 C 3.294.

114 C 3.298.

time-sales. The reinvention of canon law that I attribute to Conscience occurs in the double sense of extraction and production. Conscience draws upon the same concepts of doubt and risk found in canonist thought about usurious exchanges of goods but goes on to shape a novel condemnation of a profit-oriented basis of labour-relations. This twofold sense of reinvention finds elaborate expression in the C version of Conscience's exposition of the laudable mede, to which we now turn in Part III of the chapter.

Part III

Repurposing the Canonist Logic of the Usury Prohibition

Having denounced gifts associated with Mede, Conscience introduces those that he deems laudable. In lines that are found in C but not in B, Conscience identifies such gifts, their givers, and the basis of their giving:

> And thow the kyng of his cortesye, cayser or pope,
> ȝeue lond or lordschipe or oþer large ȝeftes
> To here lele and to lege, loue ys the cause;
> And yf the lele and lege be luyther men aftur,
> Bothe kyng and cayser and þe crouned pope
> May desauowe that thei dede and dowe þerwith another,
> And bynyme hit hem anone, and neueremore aftur
> Noyther [hy] ne eny of here ayres hardy to claymen
> That kyng oþer kayser hem gaf, catel oþer rente.
> ....
> So God gyueth nothyng þat *si* ne is the glose,
> And ryhte so, sothly, may [cesar] and pope
> Bothe gyue and graunte there his grace lyketh
> And efte haue hit aȝeyne of hem þat don ylle. (C 3.314–31)

Although these lines do not have any parallel in the corresponding place in B, Conscience's characterization of laudable gifts recalls and substantiates the "firste mede" briefly described in an earlier passage in B but not present in the corresponding passage in C. As in that B passage, so here: Conscience differentiates the good mede from the reprehensible one personified by Mede but, as Galloway affirms, "Conscience's effort to define good gifts is not so much an answer to Meed as an answer to his own B text condemnation of all gifts, by which he typically means payments for maintenance and bribes."[115]

Building on Galloway's claim, I argue that "Conscience's effort to define good gifts" is indeed "an answer to his own B text condemnation of all gifts," but by the same logic by which he and the narrator have already condemned Mede so far in the passus. That is, the canonist logic of usury that I have been arguing underlies Conscience's logic and the narrator's earlier critique of Mede's illicit gifts can be discovered here too in Conscience's substantial introduction to, and celebration of, good gifts: the two contrastive categories of gifts are mirror images anchored in the same canonist thought.

Conscience's good gifts differ from Mede's bad gifts on the same grounds on which canonists distinguish between a fungible item given in a "loan" (mutuum) and a non-fungible item given as a "lease" (locatum). In their discussions of usury, canonists understand fungible items as "those that exist in terms of number, weight, or measure" (que consistunt in numero, pondere, vel mensura).[116] With regard to the loan of a fungible item, no distinction can be drawn between the "ownership" (dominium) of the item and its "use" (usus). This is because using a fungible item results in its consumption. Therefore, when a creditor lends a fungible item s/he grants the borrower complete ownership of the item and can only expect an item of equivalent value. In his treatise on usury, *De usura*, Robert Courçon, an English papal legate trained in canon law, points out that the etymology of the Latin word "mutuum" encodes the concept of transference of ownership from creditor to debtor: in a fungible "loan" (mutuum), what is "mine" (meum), in being lent to you, becomes "yours" (tuum).[117] John of Freiburg quotes Thomas Aquinas, who draws upon the same concept of fungibility and its concomitant notion of ownership to deem any interest charged on a fungible loan unjust:

> [John's citation of Aquinas] Dicendum quod accipere usuram pro pecunia mutuata est secundum se iniustum, quia vendit id quod non est ... sciendum est quod quedam res sunt quarum usus est ipsarum rerum

115 Galloway, *The Penn Commentary*, 337.

116 Raymond, *Summa de poenitentia, et matrimonio*, 2.7, *De usuris*, n. 1 (as quoted in John of Freiburg, 2.7, *De usuris*, 280).

117 "Dicitur enim mutuum quia de meo fit tuum vel e converso." Robert Courçon, *De usura*, 15.

> consumptio, ut vinum, et panis, et huiusmodi. In talibus non debet seorsum computari usus rei a re ipsa, sed cuicumque conceditur usus rei ex hoc ipso conceditur ei res. (John of Freiburg, 2.7 *De usuris*, q. 3, 275)
>
> It must be said that to receive usury for the sake of a monetary loan is in itself unjust because one sells what does not exist [what one does not have – as a loan results in the transference of the thing from creditor to borrower] ... it must be known that there are certain things whose use results in their consumption, such as wine, bread, and things of this kind. In such cases, the use of the thing ought not to be computed separately from the thing itself but whoever is granted the use of the thing is thereby granted the thing.

Returning to the passus in light of the canonist understanding of fungible loans, we can see at least three levels at which Mede's gifts differ from Conscience's. First, Mede's "coupes of clene gold, coppes of syluer / Rynges with rubees and othere riche ȝeftes"[118] and the "noble" (that she gives her fraternal confessor) are fungibles as they are all expressible in terms of number, or weight, or measure. Second, because they are fungibles, the lender of Mede's gifts cedes ownership of them to his recipient(s) and cannot reclaim them in the same form nor charge for their use. Third, as fungibles, Mede's gifts are inherently unproductive: they cannot yield fruit.

In sharp contrast to Mede's fungible gifts, those given by Conscience's triadic gift-givers ("kyng and cayser and þe crouned pope") are non-fungibles: "lond or lordschipe," "catel" (chattels), "rente" (property-yielding revenues) and "oþer large ȝeftes."[119] All such gifts are not completely used up when used by those to whom they are lent. In affirming that they can be reclaimed at any point, Conscience underscores their non-fungibile status. Unlike a loaned fungible item ("mutuum"), a loaned non-fungible item ("locatum") does not result in

---

118 C 3.23–4; see corresponding B 3 22–3.

119 The word "rente" in the late fourteenth century carries the sense of "property yielding revenue." The *Middle English Dictionary* offers examples of rent as property thus: "b) ?a1160 *Peterb.Chron.*(Ld Misc 636) an.1137: Martin abbot … wrohte on þe circe & sette þar to landes & rentes, & goded it suythe. c. 1230(?a1200) *Ancr.*(Corp-C 402) 87/24: Trussen & purses, baggen & packes beoð ... alle eorðliche weolen & worltliche rentes [Nero: renten]."

its complete consumption when used but only in its deterioration. Consequently, the loan or, properly speaking, lease of a non-fungible item does not necessarily result in the transference of ownership of the item from creditor to borrower. John of Freiburg cites Aquinas to explain these two salient features of a non-fungible item as follows:

> Quedam vero res sunt quarum usus non est ipsa rei consumptio, sicut usus domus est inhabitatio, non autem dissipatio. Et ideo in talibus seorsum potest utrumque concedi: puta, cum aliquis tradit alteri dominium domus, retento sibi usu, ad aliquod tempus, vel econverso cum quis concedit alicui usum domus, retento sibi eius dominio. Et propter hoc licite potest homo accipere precium pro usu domus. (John of Freiburg, 2.7 *De usuris*, q. 3, 275)

> There are, however, certain things the use of which does not result in their consumption, as living in a house is using the house but not using it up. And, therefore, in such cases alone either [handing over ownership and retaining use or handing over use and retaining ownership] can be conceded separately: say, when anyone hands over the ownership of a house to another for a certain period, but retains the use of it; or, by contrast, when one concedes to another the use of a house, but retains the ownership. And, on account of this, one can licitly accept a price for the use of a house.

John of Freiburg's exposition of the loan of a non-fungible item under the aspects of use and ownership informs Conscience's vision of licit gifts. As with John's non-fungible item, so with Conscience's "lond or lordschipe or oþer large ȝeftes." Conscience's gift-givers separate the ownership of their gifts from their use: as leases, the gifts are granted for use only, as long as the recipients are loyal. Even in the case of the gift of "lordship," which could be read as equivalent to ownership, Conscience deems the giving conditional and hence revocable. Conscience spells out the contingent terms of such gift-giving: "si" (if) the recipients become "luther" (disloyal), the gift-givers "may desauowe" (disawow) or "bynyme of them" (deprive them of the gifts) and "dowe þerwith another" (deal with them differently or hand them over to another). Conscience's mention of the legal terms "desauowe" and "bynyme" evokes notions of escheatment or attainder that pertain to fiefs whereby the lord can reclaim land held of him by his tenant should he (the tenant) cease to serve him faithfully. Conscience also clarifies that gifts once received are not heritable, if they are revoked because of disloyalty, and consequently the "ayres" of the initial recipients cannot lay claims to them.[120]

Analogous to fiefs, Conscience's good gifts are given on the condition of loyalty or non-"luther" behaviour towards their gift-givers. Indeed, Conscience's characterization of conditional gifts granted out of courtesy or love has much in common with the understanding of the "feudum" (fief) as offered by Hostiensis in a title devoted to the subject:

> [Rubric] "Quid sit feudum." Est itaque feudum beneficium, id est, benevola actio, tribuens gaudium capienti, capiensque tribuendo in id quod facit prona & sua sponte parata. Vel est feudum illud beneficium, quod ex benevolentia alicujus ita traditur alicui & proprietate ejus rei, quae in feudum datur penes dantem remanente, id est, domino. (Hostiensis, *Summa aurea*, 3, *De feudis*, 1, col. 854)

> [Rubric] "What a fief might be." A fief is thus a benefit, that is, a benevolent action, bestowing joy to the one receiving, and receiving joy from bestowing it, which he does readily and willingly. Or a fief is that benefit which, out of the benevolence of one, is handed over to another, in such a way that its ownership remains in the power of the one granting it as a fief, that is, to the lord.

Distinguishing various kinds of fiefs, Hostiensis addresses at one point the conditional fief, whose terms are almost identical to those on which Conscience's gift-givers grant gifts:

> [Rubric] "Qualiter feudum distinguatur." Quod quidem ita potest distingui: feudorum aliud dicitur paternum, aliud novum: aliud etiam dicitur maternum seu foemineum. Item feudorum aliud est cum fidelitate, aliud sine fidelitate. Item feudorum aliud est conditionale, aliud non. Item feudorum aliud perpetuum, aliud non ... Cum fidelitate dicitur illud, de quo fidelitas juratur, vel jurari debet: & intelligas, quod de omni feudo debet fieri fidelitas, nisi per pactum remittatur ... Feudum conditionale est illud, quod datur ad certum servitium, ut, vel ad conditionem certam

---

120 For this clarification, I thank Stephen A. Barney, who suggested that the emphasis on the word *si* may "recall specifically the idea in biblical scholarship of God's conditional granting (to Noah, Abr., etc.) of land and progeny" (email correspondence, 21 August 2017).

faciendam, quod fieri potest ... inde est quod alias dicitur, quod si vasallus negaverit conditionale feudum quod ipsum amittere debet ... Non conditionale feudum dicitur illud, quod sine aliqua conditione datur, ut ex praemissis patet ... Non perpetuum vero feudum dicitur illud, quod non transit ad heredes. Sunt enim quaedam feuda quae ad heredes non transeunt. (Hostiensis, *Summa aurea*, 3, *De feudis*, 6, col. 857)

[Rubric] "In what ways a fief may be distinguished." It can be defined thus: one kind of fief is called paternal, another new, and another is called maternal or feminine. Also, one kind of fief entails fealty, another does not. Also, one kind of fief is conditional, another not. Also, one kind of fief is perpetual, another not ... A fief over which fealty is sworn, or ought to be sworn, is called "cum fidelitate" and you should understand that fealty should be established for every fief unless it is remitted by agreement ... A conditional fief is that which is given for a certain service: as, for a certain condition to be fulfilled ... whence it is otherwise said that if the vassal should deny the conditional fief, he should lose it ... A non-conditional fief is that which is given without any condition, as is evident from what has been said above ... But a non-perpetual fief is one that does not transfer to heirs. For there are fiefs that do not transfer to heirs.

In the passages above, Hostiensis treats the conditional fief as given on the basis of the fief-recipient's service towards the fief-grantor. Like Conscience, Hostiensis too thinks of such a gift in terms of a distinction between use and ownership – a distinction made clearer in their discussions of the conditional gift. Although Conscience and Hostiensis do not here deploy the terms "usus" and "dominium" to designate the characteristics of the gifts they discuss, they nevertheless describe the conditional gift as non-heritable and revocable should the gift-recipient be, as in the poem, "luther" or, as in Hostiensis, violate the terms of the relationship to his fief-giver. Unlike fee simples, which in Langland's day could be inherited or even alienated to other tenants in accordance with the 1290 *Quia emptores* statute, Conscience's gifts are akin to fee tails: temporary and conditional leases of land or cattle, which can neither be inherited nor alienated without the principal lord's permission, as the rights of ownership of property remained solely with the original lordly gift-giver.

As fee tail leases, Conscience's gifts counter Mede's gifts on another conceptual ground on which canonists distinguish between a fungible loan ("mutuum") and a non-fungible lease ("locatum"): fruitfulness. Quoting

Raymond's threefold distinction between a "mutuum" and a "locatum," John of Freiburg affirms that "fructus" and "utilitas" are the distinguishing marks of the latter: "because the use of money produces no fruit or utility to the user, it is otherwise for the use of land, or of a house, or of a horse, or of any other leased item" (quia usus pecunie nullum fructum vel utilitatem parit utenti, secus in usu agri, vel domus, vel equi, vel alterius rei locate).[121] Whereas Mede's gifts can neither deteriorate with use nor produce any fruit ("fructus") on their own, the gifts granted by the "kyng and cayser and þe crouned pope" are among those that canonists place under the category of fertile or inherently productive objects with use-value: "land," "lordship," "catel," and "rente" yield "fructus" with their "usus." In sum, Mede's sterile gifts are associated with money or its exchange-value, Conscience's with land or cattle and their use-value.

If I have been successful in demonstrating that Conscience's and Mede's gifts are sharply differentiated along canonistic lines separating fungible and non-fungible objects, then how differentiated are Mede and Conscience's gift-givers along the same lines? To what extent does the C version of the passus continue to adapt canonistic ideas of gift-giving in distinguishing between Mede and Conscience's gift-givers?

Within passus 3, Conscience's triadic gift-givers mirror Mede with regard to the cause of their gift-giving. Both Mede and Conscience spell out a common motive for giving: "grete goodnesse"[122] is the cause of

---

121 Here is the full excerpt that John cites from Raymond on the distinction between a loan and a lease: "Ponit etiam hic Raymundus tres differentias inter mutuum et locatum: 'Prima, quia in mutuo transfertur periculum in accipientem, secus in locato. Secunda, quia pecunia non deterioratur per usum, secus in domo, vel equo, vel alia re locata. Tertia, quia usus pecunie nullum fructum vel utilitatem parit utenti, secus in usu agri, vel domus, vel equi, vel alterius rei locate.'" ("Raymond also puts forward three differences between a loan and a lease: 'First, because in a loan risk is transferred to the borrower, it is otherwise for a lease. Second, because money does not deteriorate with use, it is otherwise for a house, or for a horse, or for any other leased item. Third, because the use of money produces no fruit or utility to the user, it is otherwise for the use of land, or of a house, or of a horse, or of any other leased item.'"), John of Freiburg, 2.7 *De usuris*, q. 28, 291; in footnote 124 on page 291, Lorenc provides the following reference to Raymond's text: *Summa de poenitentia et matrimonio*, 2.7 *De usuris*, n. 7 (All of Lorenc's citations from Raymond's *Summa* reproduced in my book refer to *Summa sancti Raymundi de Peniafort Barcinonensis, ordinis praedicatorum, de poenitentia, et matrimonio cum glossis Ioannis de Friburgo*).

122 B 3.20–2: "Mildly Mede þanne merciede hem alle / Of hire grete goodnesse, and gaf hem echone / Coupes of clene gold and coppes of siluer"; see also the corresponding C 3.21–3.

Mede's giving, and, likewise, "cortesye" or "loue," "ys the cause" why the king, caesar, and pope give generous gifts.[123] Whereas the prospective recipients of Mede's gifts promise to follow her "wille" (with her also reciprocating by promising to do the same),[124] those receiving the gifts granted by the triadic gift-givers too have to obey the "wille"[125] of their gift-givers to retain them. Just as, in Conscience's analogy, God deprived Solomon of the gifts given him when he "seyh a sewed nat his wille," so the triadic gift-givers would deprive their recipients of the gifts they have given them if they (the recipients) do not follow their (the gift-givers') will.[126]

The two kinds of gift-givers are, however, different in one crucial respect that Conscience elaborates: intention. Whereas the gift-givers personified by Mede give in order to make the kinds of illicit profits that canonists associate with the usurious "turpe lucrum," Conscience's triadic gift-givers have no intention or hope to obtain any profit at all. The triadic gift-givers give in a context outside of any profit-motive: their very lack of intention to make any profit – whether licit or illicit – marks their giving as radically apart from Mede's but exemplary of the non-usurious gift-giving theorized by the canonists.

In the same treatises of usury that I have been citing from to contextualize the critique of Mede's gifts, one finds provisions for the non-usurious giving or receiving of gifts. For instance, John of Freiburg, citing Raymond, Ulrich and Gottofredo, embeds his definition of non-usurious gifts within a discussion of usurious gifts:

> "Non enim puto usuram committi si gratis oblatum gratis accipitur, arg. XIIII, q. III, *Usura*; dist. XVIII, *De eulogiis*. 'Nulla enim oblatio suscipienti culpe maculam ingerit que non ex ambigentis petitione processit,' I, q. II, *Sicut* [Gratian, *Decretum*, II. C. 1, q. 2, c. 4, *Sicut episcopum*]."[127] Concordat Ulricus, lib. VI, tract. III, c. IIII. Et addit quod hec liberalis donatio est "cum non datur a debitore nec recipitur a creditore intuitu mutui, et ex neutra parte est corrupta intentio. Et hoc precipue constat quando, soluto mutuo,

123 C 3.314–16.

124 B 3.28–9; see corresponding C 3.29–30.

125 C 3.325.

126 C 3.323–31.

127 John of Freiburg is here citing Raymond's words in *Summa de poenitentia et matrimonio*, 2.7 *De usuris*, n. 1; see footnote 1 on page 273 in Lorenc's edition of John of Freiburg's text.

aliquid datur."[128] Unde et Gottfredus, lib V, tit. XIX, *De usuris*, sic dicit, "Usura est quicquid sorti accedit intentione precedente vel pacto. Sola enim spe vel expectatione vitium contrahitur usurarum, ut *Extra*. eodem tit., c. I et c. *Consuluit*; XIIII, q. III, *Si feneraveris*. Quod intelligo verum esse cum causa mutuandi principaliter ponitur in spe vel in expectatione lucri vel emolumenti. Alias, si non principaliter super hoc moveatur mutuator ad mutuandum, sed ob charitatem et dilectionem, secundario autem sperat de aliqua retributione, non puto hoc vitiosum, arg. ad hoc LXXVII dist., *In singulis*; LIX dist., *Si officia secularia*; LXI dist., *Quid proderit*."[129] (John of Freiburg, 2.7 *De usuris*, q. 1, 273)

"For I think usury is not committed, if something freely offered is received freely, as is argued in the canon *Usura* in arg. *XIIII*, q. III [Gratian, *Decretum*, II. C. 14, q. 3, c. 4, *Usura est*], and in the canon *De Eulogiis* in dist. XVIII [Gratian, *Decretum*, I. D. 18, c. 8]: 'For no gift that does not proceed from the request of a petitioner brings a stain of guilt on the recipient,'I, q.II [*Decretum*, II. C. 1, q. 2, c. 4, *Sicut episcopum*]"; as Ulricus agrees in lib. VI, tract. III, c. IIII. He adds that a free gift is that "which is neither given by the debtor nor received by the creditor with the loan in mind, and there is no corrupt intention on either side. And this obtains particularly when something is given after the loan is paid off." Whence Gottfredus too in the title *De usuris*, X, lib. V, says thus: "usury is whatever exceeds the principal with a prior intention or pact because in hope alone or expectation the vice of usury is contracted, as in the *Liber extra*, under the same title, c.i and the canon *Consuluit* [X 5.19.1 & c. 10]; XIIII, q.III, *Si feneraveris* [Gratian, *Decretum*, II. C. 14, q. 3, c. 1]. Which I understand to be true when the cause of lending lies principally in the hope or in the expectation of profit or emolument. It is otherwise, if the lender does not act principally for this reason but rather on account of charity and love and only secondarily expects some compensation. I do not consider this to be vicious, as is established in Gratian, Distinction LXXVII *In singulis* [Gratian, *Decretum*, I. D.77, c. 2], Distinction LIX *Si officia secularia* [Gratian, *Decretum*, I. D. 59, c. 2], Distinction LXI *Quid proderit* [Gratian, *Decretum*, I. D. 61, c. 7.]"

---

128 John of Freiburg is here citing Ulrich of Strasbourg, *Summa de summo bono*, 6.3.4 *De illiberalitate*, Quartus modus, fol. 105v; see footnote 2 on page 273 in Lorenc's edition of John of Freiburg's text.

129 John of Freiburg is here citing Gottofredo da Trani, *Summa super titulis decretalium*, X 5.19 *De usuris*, n. 1; see footnote 3 on page 273 in Lorenc's edition of John of Freiburg's title on usury.

For John of Freiburg, a gift is non-usurious if "something offered freely is received freely" (gratis oblatum, gratis accipitur). A "gift is free" (liberalis donatio) if it is offered with "no corrupt intention" (corrupta intentio) to gain more than the loaned principal. John of Freiburg explicitly names "charity and love" (charitatem et dilectionem) the motivation to lend freely with no expectation of any interest. Conscience is likewise explicit about why his triadic gift-givers give, or properly speaking, lease their large gifts. In the first three lines in which he introduces the gift-givers, he foregrounds their motivation: "cortesye" and "loue."[130] Both these terms parallel the terms "charitatem et dilectionem" that John identifies as the motivation behind non-usurious giving.[131] Furthermore, Conscience's use of the word "cause" to clarify the causal role played by "loue" mirrors John of Freiburg's use of the term "ob" to underscore the same causal role played by "charitatem et dilectionem."

In a later passage on lending even spiritually designated lands such as prebends (i.e., what the "pope" – one of Conscience's three gift-givers – might grant to his loyal clerics), John of Freiburg invokes canonists such as Raymond and Tancred to elaborate on the defining characteristics of the usurious gift: hope or intention:

> "Ad hoc dico, salvo meliori iudicio, cum Alano et Tancredo quod creditor nullo modo debet pactum apponere nec principaliter spem vel intentionem in tali retributione habere, sed propter Deum et ex charitate principaliter debet mutuare proximo indigenti. Et tunc si forte secundario speret quod ille debitor sibi remutuet vel aliquid simile rependat si opus fuerit, forte non est reprobandum, arg. Dist. LXI, *Quid proderit*, cum suis concordantiis."[132] (John of Freiburg, 2.7 *De usuris*, q. 6, 277)

> "To this I say, with all due respect to better judgment, with Alan [Alanus Anglicus] and Tancred that the creditor in no way should create a pact nor principally have hope or intention in such a reward but ought to lend to his needy neighbour on account of God and principally out of charity. And then if, secondarily, he should hope that the debtor would repay him or

130 C 3.314–16.

131 In the fourteenth century, the word "courtesye" when used in the context of gift-giving carried the sense of a charitable offering.

132 As noted in footnote 22 on page 277 of Lorenc's edition, John of Freiburg is quoting Raymond, *Summa de poenitentia et matrimonio*, 2.7 *De usuris*, n. 4.

> compensate him with something similar, if necessary, perhaps that should not be reproved, as in the canon *Quid proderit* [Gratian, *Decretum*, I. D. 61, c. 7.] and concording canons."

Although John does concede that the creditor's necessity exempts him from reproof for hope of compensation from the borrower, he is clear that the creditor's motivation to offer the loan should not be principally hope or intention to have any reward but charity on account of God. As we have already discussed, canonists understand usury as inhering in hope and/or intention: "only hope or intention makes the man [creditor] a usurer" (sola spes vel intentio facit hominem usurarium).[133] From the vantage point of canon law, usurious gift-giving involves lending on account of the "hope" (spe) or "expectation" (expectatione) of "gain" (lucri vel emolumenti). By the same logic, non-usurious gift-giving would be devoid of any such usurious hope or intention. It is this corollary that Conscience, in C, substantiates.

In the C passage discussed above what governs licit gift-giving can best be expressed in terms of a "relacioun rect" – an expression that Conscience coins in a preceding passage in the same passus and defines as "a record of treuthe"[134] and subsequently as "a ryhtful custume, / As a kyng to clayme the comune at his wille / To folowe hym and to fynde hym and fecche at hem his consayl / That here loue to his lawe thorw al þe lond acorde."[135] It is this "relacioun rect" that Conscience exemplifies by drawing on the usury-centred concepts of hope and intention but associating them not with the lenders but with the borrowers and hence purging them of their illicitness. He likens the "relacioun rect" between gift-giver and gift-recipient to that between "maister" and "a leel laborer" where the latter "parforme[s]" his work and the former pays him only afterwards.[136] Although Conscience appears to be merely presenting the opposite of Mede's model of illicit "pre manibus" payment, he takes care to explain that the "rect" nature of the "relacioun" binding master and labourer, as Robert Adams has argued, is not the actual payment itself (or the promptness with which he pays – a salient feature of licit wage-payment that Conscience had earlier raised in

133 Here John is citing Raymond; see John of Freiburg, 2.7 *De usuris*, q. 1, 274.

134 C 3.343.

135 C 3.373–6.

136 C 3.347–9.

response to Mede's "premanibus" transactions) but, as Galloway puts it, "a theory of contract."[137]

What makes for "relacioun rect" is the belief or trust in payment: "as a leel laborer, byleueth with his maister / In his pay and in his pite ... / So of hol herte cometh hope ... "[138] Far from suggesting what or how much such "paye" should be, Conscience makes clear that the loyal labourer's trust in being paid by his master (even if the labourer has not done satisfactory work) is the enabling condition for the "hope" or expectation that comprises the basis of the analogous relationship between the believing man and God.[139] Deploying the causal conjunction "so," Conscience, in the subsequent exposition of the relationship between gift-giver and gift-receiver, relates "hope" to the expectation of "sustantif sauacioun"[140] The analogy between merciful master and loyal labourer thus gives way to one between God and man as Conscience merges the concepts of "hope" with that of "belief" – "*credere in ecclesia*, in Holy Kyrke to bileue."[141]

Obvious in Conscience's exposition of the "relacioun rect" between gift-giver and recipient is the general vocabulary of economic exchanges: the labourer's trust in earthly "paye" from his master, on the one hand, and man's trust in some kind of spiritual debt-relief and salvation ("sauacioun") on the other. The Latin infinitive verb "credere," with its mercantile connotations of trust reposed in credit sales, invests the English equivalent "to bileue" with the sense of an economic trust even as such trust is reposed in spiritual referents such as posthumous redemption. Less obvious in Conscience's economic lexicon, however, are the usurious connotations of the pair of terms ("hope," "credere"/ "to bileue,") – terms that are central to the determination of usury in canonist thought but now resourcefully repurposed to invent a non-usurious model of gift-based relations between lord and labourer, on the one hand, and those between God and man, on the other.

Conscience's model of non-usurious giving invites comparison with the biblical model of spiritual usury ("usura spiritualis"). Explicitly invoked in Latin in the B version of passus 7 (but, notably, absent from the corresponding place in the C version), spiritual usury is a

137 Galloway, "The Account Book," 85.
138 C 3.347–51.
139 C 3.351.
140 C 3.352.
141 C 3.356.

biblical ideal that canonists prescribed as an antidote to corporeal usury ("usura corporalis" – i.e., the earthly usury proscribed by canon law).[142] In all the tracts on usury that have been discussed so far, the distinction between spiritual and corporeal usury occurs at the very outset. As may be inferred from my quotations, the treatises dwell at length on the latter but devote little attention to the former, often offering no more than a few words such as follows:

> Sunt autem duae species principales usurae: una est bona et est in praecepto, altera in prohibitione. Prima scilicet spiritualis est in multiplicatione talenti tibi traditi. De qua dominus in Evangelio: "Oportebat te pecuniam meam dare nummulariis et ego veniens exegissem eam cum usuris." (Robert Courçon, *De usura*, 7)

> There are two principal kinds of usury: one is good and a matter of precept; the other is prohibited. The first, namely, is spiritual in the multiplication of the talents given unto you. Concerning which, the Lord says in the Gospel: "You should have given my money to the money-changers so that at my coming I would have got it back with usury (interest)."

Here Robert Courçon deems spiritual usury "good" (bona) as it is authored and prescribed by Christ.[143] Like Robert, John of Freiburg cites Raymond to contrast "equitable" (equa) spiritual usury with "inequitable" (iniqua) corporeal usury, and praises the former.[144] Drawing on the canonist terminology used to distinguish the two kinds of usury above, we may recast our claim about the C version of passus 3 thus: Conscience constructs his model of spiritual usury by repurposing the canonist logic

---

142 B 7.82–3: "Quare non dedisti pecuniam meam ad mensam, vt / ego veniens cum vsuris exigissem vtique illam?"

143 As noted above, this view of spiritual usury is echoed at B 7.82–3.

144 John of Freiburg, 2.7 *De usuris*, q. 14, 280: "due sunt species, quia alia spiritualis et equa, de qua in evangelio Mat. XXV, 'Nonne oportebat te pecuniam dare nummulariis, et ego veniens cum usuris exegissem eam,' alia vero corporalis et iniqua de qua hic agitur." [There are two kinds of usury: one spiritual and just, concerning which is found in the Gospel Matthew 25: "Wasn't it necessary for you to give money to the money-changers so that at my coming I would have claimed it with usury (interest)," but the other kind of usury is fleshly and unjust, concerning which it is treated as follows]; as noted in footnote 42 of page 280 of Lorenc's edition, John of Freiburg is quoting from Raymond's *Summa de poenitentia et matrimonio*, 2.7 *De usuris*, n. 2.

of corporeal usury. If this claim is tenable, then the poem reinvents canon law by way of substantiating "spiritual usury" (usura spiritualis) – a form of usury that the canonists applaud but rarely elaborate. For all its ingeniousness, the poem's reinvention nevertheless takes place in the same conceptual field shared by the canonists writing on usury.

The B and C versions of passus 3 represent different ways of engaging the canonist thought on usury. By viewing both versions side by side, my aim has been to suggest a dialectical interrelation – one that results in throwing into relief C's otherwise not immediately visible contribution to the canonist thought on usury and its handling. Although C lacks the words that in B name corporeal usury, the concept of usury serves as the unnamed ground for C's innovative vision of spiritual usury in passus 3. For, in C, the omission of the "name" of corporeal usury does not eradicate its conceptual logic, which informs the critique of Mede's model of usurious gift-giving as well as the construction of Conscience's model of non-usurious gift-giving. At the same time, within the unfolding of passus 3 in C too, there is a process of erasure and preservation, or perhaps even production. Mede's corporeal usury is gradually erased or used up to engender Conscience's spiritual usury, thereby enacting, to borrow a felicitous expression from a contemporary theorist, usury's "double bearing" of exhaustion and surplus.[145]

Conclusion

In the C version of passus 3, the poetic reinvention of canon law occurs in the double-sense of the word: *finding* within canon law the means of *founding* something new. Conscience finds in the categories through which canonists thought about usury a method of generating a model of spiritual usury designed to ensure a "relacioun rect" between lenders and borrowers. But, in what sense does Conscience's model contribute to the history of canon law, given that we have not yet found

145 In his essay in "White Mythology: Metaphor in the Text of Philosophy," Jacques Derrida comments on "the double bearing of the French word *usure*" to argue that it has two senses: "first, 'wear' [that is] erasure by rubbing, or exhaustion, or crumbling; but secondly, it has also the sense of 'usury' – the additional product of a certain capital, which, far from losing the stake, would make that original wealth bear fruit, would increase the return from it in the form of income, of higher interest." Derrida and Moore, "White Mythology," 7.

(and may indeed never find) any acknowledgment of such a poetic reinvention in any legal records?

One answer would be that Conscience contributes to the history of probable causes: options that might have been realizable within the institutional system of canon law but, for reasons of historical contingency, never came to be actualized but still remained part of the poem's present meaning. That is, although Conscience's model of spiritual usury was not ratified or incorporated into the official records of canon law, it belongs to the history of "what might have been" in the sense that *Piers Plowman's* contemporary readers would have seen it as intelligible and probable – just as probable as other canonically analogous models of commercial exchange that were approved and acknowledged.[146]

For instance, in the year 1404, the lawyer Lorenzo d'Antonio Ridolfi too came up with a model of a non-usurious relation between creditor and debtor under the guise of the insurance-contract ("contractus assecurationis") to respond to the problem of risk in any enterprise.[147] Just as Conscience characterizes good gift-givers as leasers of non-fungible items to their tenants, so Ridolfi presents the insurer as a giver not of a fungible loan but of a non-fungible lease ("locatum") to the travelling merchant, and so makes him (the lender) automatically responsible for any risk involved in the enterprise. Put in another way, Ridolfi's insurer is foreshadowed in Conscience's gift-giver, who too is presented as automatically responsible for paying the labourer even if he does not perform the assigned work satisfactorily. Conscience's defence of non-fungible leases as an answer to Mede's fungible gifts can thus be seen as having near contemporary implications for devising non-usurious insurance for risk (which otherwise cannot be licitly charged on any fungible loan). That is, only when the insurer leases a non-fungible item rather than loans a fungible item to the merchant can s/he separately charge for the risk of the enterprise (the "periculi susceptio") as such risk could be canonically justified as a charge for the "use" of the item. In other words, Ridolfi's model of insurance is already nascent in Conscience's conceptually similar treatment of good-gifts as lease contracts rather than as loans. Even though Conscience's model of "relacioun rect" was at the time of its inception yet to be realized in another's

146 I borrow the expression from the title of a recent collection of essays on counterfactual history; see Cowley, *What If*.

147 For my comments on Lorenzo d'Antonio Ridolfi's concept of insurance, I draw on Ceccarelli's essay "Risky Business."

hands, it was nevertheless available for readers to think through the canon law governing restitutive justice and, thereby, to envision change for the future.

The great historian of canon law F.W. Maitland is famously said to have remarked "it is very difficult to remember that events now in the past were once far in the future."[148] Seen through the lens of *Piers Plowman* and its politically engaged readers, one such "event" was indeed Conscience's vision of the "relacioun rect" that spiritual usury embodies: the temporally closed historical past in which I have read the poem was still for them an open future, and the vision was one of many alternatives awaiting realization "far in the[ir] future."

---

148 I have not been able to find the original source of Frederick Maitland's words; although they have been frequently quoted, they have never been cited: see Schlesinger, *Cycles of American History*, 216, and Nielson, *Paths Not Taken*, 53.

3 *Restitutio*: From Rule to Law to Justice in Covetise's Confession[1]

Corporeal usury takes on many forms in *Piers Plowman*. It proceeds not from the abject Nede but from the protean Mede.[2] Its antithesis and antidote is spiritual usury, which is all about establishing or restoring a "relacioun rect," which, as Conscience explains is "a record of treuthe."[3] But this "relacioun rect" extends elsewhere in the poem as much to fungible things as to their fallible handlers. To relate rightly is no doubt to trade licitly in the right merchandise and at the right price established by "[m]aires and maceres, þat menes ben bitwene/ The kyng and þe comune to kepe þe lawes."[4] At the same time, it is to deal justly with the "comune" in all its complex senses, or with "þe pouere peple."[5] It is not to defraud one's fellow Christian creditor or debtor or, in the still familiar expression, to beggar one's own neighbour.

But what if one does covet, claim, and even retain what belongs rightfully to one's neighbour(s), as the poem's personified sins confess to have done? How do the less fallible instructors in the poem seek to correct those who, like Covetise, follow Mede and "richen þoruȝ regratrie

1 While the passages from *Piers Plowman* examined in this chapter include those found in my essay "The Subject of Canon Law," this chapter challenges the claim made in that essay about Langland's reflection of the canon law in the *Memoriale*, and offers a fundamentally new argument about the poet's invention of a law from a rule.

2 For the relationship between the allegorical figure of "Nede" and the legal principle of necessity in *Piers Plowman*, see Hewett-Smith's article "'Nede ne hath no lawe'"; her article also surveys the wide scholarship on "Nede." For a more recent examination of "nede" in the poem, see Dijk's "'Nede hath no law.'"

3 C 3.343.

4 B 3.76–7; see corresponding C 3.77–8.

5 B 3.81; see corresponding C 3.83.

and rentes hem[selves] biggen"?[6] What, then, are the implications of Conscience's critique of usurious "regratrie" for the poem's broader preoccupation with the restoration of "relacioun rect" between sinner and victim? Or, to pose a question of method, if Conscience's vision of "relacioun rect" in C adapts the canonist thought on corporeal usury as futuristically as I have argued, then, to what extent does the adaptation have a "projective horizontality" of meaning beyond passus 3 in *Piers Plowman* B and C, as well as in the extra-textual world in which both versions were composed and circulated?[7]

Questions such as these have a familiar ring to the reader of *Piers Plowman* today. They speak to the poem's preoccupation with equitable interpersonal relations and echo a long-standing scholarly interest in the subject of commutative justice. After all, "relacioun rect" or its violation by usury recurs as a resonant theme in later passūs, and, as the reader may know all too well, under the Latin motif "redde quod debes" (render what you owe). Equally familiar to the same reader would likely be the context of spiritual economics within which scholars have approached the motif. As Roger A. Ladd observes, Conscience uses this oft-repeated Latin phrase to balance "material and spiritual economies."[8] Illustrating "the blurring of the recording of debts repaid between the earthly and heavenly spheres" in Covetise's confession, James Simpson argued that Langland conceives of the relations between man and God "in fundamentally economic terms."[9] Langland's vocabulary of spiritual economics, as Simpson went on to demonstrate, has much in common with that used by theologians ranging from the Franciscan Thomas of Celano to Durandus of St Pourçain.[10] More recently, Traugott Lawler has uncovered the interpersonal and material basis of the injunction "redde quod debes" in both B and C, arguing that the motif is "present not only at the end" but runs throughout the passus, and is more pronounced in C.[11] "*Reddite Cesari*," quotes Holy Churche

6 B 3.83; see corresponding C 3.82.

7 I borrow Ralph Hanna's concept of "projective horizontality" to specify the impact of canonistic adaptations across a single version of the poem. See Hanna, "The Versions and Revisions of *Piers Plowman*," 49.

8 Roger A. Ladd, *Antimercantilism in Late Medieval Literature* (NY: Palgrave Macmillan, 2010), 43–4.

9 Simpson, "Spirituality and Economics," 88–9.

10 Simpson, "Spirituality and Economics," 91–5. See also his *Piers Plowman: An Introduction to the B-text*, 70–1, 229; see also 161–5.

11 Lawler, "Harlots' Holiness," 142.

magisterially to the narrator in the opening passus, "þat Cesar byfalleth, / *Et que sunt Dei Deo*, or ellys ȝe don ylle."[12] "Horizontal fraternalism," to borrow David Aers's felicitous phrase for the directionality of Holy Churche's injunction or, for that matter, of the poem's preoccupation with restitution, epitomizes the core principle of "relacioun rect" between man and God.[13]

Glossed over in such extensive and erudite scholarship on the "redde quod debes" principle, however, are canonistic grounds upon which the poem founds its socially attentive or horizontal vision of restorative justice.[14] They may be less visible to the reader today but, as I shall argue, they are just as fundamental to the poem as the theological and economic ones illuminated by Ladd, Simpson, Lawler, and Aers. Attending to such grounds in the B and C versions will uncover the latter's innovative treatment of a "rule" (regula) or maxim on restitution as well as an equally innovative recasting of the received canonistic distinction between "rules" (regulae) and "laws" (iura) in general. Such a poetic invention in turn, I argue, "supplements" the canonist thinking on restorative justice within the *cura animarum* by placing or recognizing limits upon the pope's plenary power to dispense with the canonistic rule on restitution.[15]

As early as in Covetise's confession in passus 6, the allegorical confessor Repentaunce offers a realization of Conscience's vision of "relacioun rect" that was explored in the previous chapter. In his rambling account of mercantile sins in both B and C, Covetise confesses the sin of usury. Repentaunce's initial response to Covetise varies across both the versions not so much in its content as in its mode of orientation. In B, as we shall explore in detail, Repentaunce focuses on the contrition that Covetise needs to feel for the victims of usury, and only then exhorts him to make restitution. He asks if Covetise has "pite on pouere men þat [borwe mote nedes]."[16] With sneering contempt, Covetise replies

12 C 1.48–9; see corresponding B 1.52–3.

13 Aers, *Faith, Ethics and Church*, 74; see also his more recent *Sanctifying Signs*, 50.

14 For late medieval "horizontal" and "vertical" models of justice, see Biller, "Confession in the Middle Ages: Introduction," and Bossy, "The Social History of Confession."

15 I invoke Jacques Derrida's sense of the "supplement" as that which "adds only to replace" or one that "intervenes or insinuates itself *in-the-place-of* [and] whether it adds or substitutes itself, the supplement is *exterior*, outside of the positivity to which it is super-added, alien to that which, in order to be replaced by it, it must be other than it" in *Of Grammatology*, 145.

16 B 5.253.

that he has "as muche pite of poure men as pedlere haþ of cattes, /That wolde kille hem, if he cacche hem myȝte, for coueitise of hir skynnes!"[17] Assiduous in his pastoral office, Repentaunce inquires if he is "manlich among þi neȝebores of þi mete and drynke," to which the unrepentant Covetise retorts that the "neȝebores" regard him "as hende as hound is in kichene."[18] In inquiring whether Covetise has "pite"[19] or is "manlich," Repentaunce seeks to determine the presence and nature of Covetise's concern for those whom he has defrauded. On failing to detect any signs of remorse, Repentaunce urges Covetise to "repente," admonishing him about God's abandonment of him: "Now [but þow repente þe raþer," quod Repentaunce, "God lene þee neuere]."[20] Only after he has failed to induce contrition in Covetise does Repentaunce cite a Latin quotation (italicized below) that John Alford has identified as a "maxim of canon law, derived from Augustine":[21]

"Thow art an vnkynde creature – I kan þee noȝt assoille
Til þow make restitucion" quod Repentaunce, "and rekene wiþ hem alle,
And siþen þat Reson rolle it in þe Registre of heuene
That þow hast maad ech man good, I may þee noȝt assoille:
Non dimittitur peccatum donec restituatur ablatum." (B 5.269–72)

In the corresponding section in C, Repentaunce neither inquires into Covetise's "pite" for his victims nor invokes "þe Registre of heuene" to exhort him to repent. Rather Repentaunce cuts to the chase, as it were, by zeroing in on restitution rather than on contrition as soon as Covetise admits to having lent on interest. Hoping that neither the executor will settle Covetise's "syluer" nor his [Covetise's] "heyres" will profit from the usurious winnings, Repentaunce focuses not only on the penitent's obligation to make restitution but also on the confessor's duty to impose it on usurious penitents.[22] Citing a version of the same Latin maxim much earlier in C than in the corresponding

17 B 5.254–5.
18 B 5.256–7.
19 B 5.254.
20 B 5.259.
21 Alford, *Piers Plowman: A Guide to the Quotations*, 46.
22 C 6.254–5.

passage in B, Repentaunce reads into its words the pope's and the papal penitentiary's lack of power to absolve a usurious penitent that has not made restitution:

> "Now redily," quod Repentaunce, "and by þe Rode, Y leue,
> Shal neuere seketoure wel bysette the syluer þat thow hem leuest,
> Ne thyn heyres, as Y hope, haue ioye of þat thow wonne;
> For þe Pope with alle his pentauncers, power hem fayleth
> To assoyle the of this synne *sine restitucione*:
> *Numquam dimittitur peccatum, nisi restituatur ablatum.*" (C 6.253–7)

The two excerpts quoted above appear alike in their shared commitment to restitutive justice: the usurer Covetise must needs make restitution to his victims in order to obtain absolution in the penitential forum. Seen, however, within their internal contexts respectively, the excerpts differ from each other in emphasis and perspective. To move from the B to the C versions of Covetise's confession is to encounter a shift in emphasis from contrition to restitution, and at the same time, a shift in perspective – from the perspective of the penitent obligated to make restitution (in B) to that of the confessor required to impose it upon the usurious penitent (in C). By attending to this twofold shift in emphasis and perspective across B and C, we shall orient our attention to a substantial instance of reinvention within the framework of the maxim – C's reinvention of a law from a rule in order to regulate the "relacioun rect" between priest and penitent.

Precisely because Repentaunce in C affirms that the pope and his penitentiary are subject to the Latin maxim, his affirmation invites investigation alongside canonistic commentaries on versions of the same maxim already incorporated by two popes: Pope Gregory IX in his *Liber extra* and Pope Boniface VIII in his compilation of eighty-eight regulative maxims or "rules of law" (regulae iuris), which are appended to the *Liber Sextus*. Situating Repentaunce's handling of the maxim alongside its papally authorized usages will reveal the process by which an allegorical confessor both draws on and departs from the canonists in order to invent a "law" (ius) on restitutive justice from a "rule" (regula) on it. Repentaunce's invention reconceptualizes the canonistic distinction between "rule" and "law" in order to prioritize the literal power of the law over and above "the men of lawe" including even the supreme ecclesiastical lawmaker:

the pope himself.[23] More generally, as I shall argue, the C version of Covetise's confession, unlike the B version of the same confession, courts, complicates, and thereby contributes to the canonist thinking about the "rules of law" (regulae iuris), and about the power or powerlessness of the papal lawmaker to dispense from them.

Let me clarify the two terms "rule" and "law" as distinguished by canonists in their treatment of regulative maxims. The Roman jurist Julius Paulus provided the frame of reference for the canonistic distinction between both terms in the "law" (lex),[24] *Regula est*: "the law should not be taken from the rule but the rule should be made from the existing law" (non ex regula ius sumatur, sed ex iure quod est, regula fiat).[25] Canonists beginning with Bernard of Pavia followed the legists (authorities of the civil law based on the *Corpus iuris civilis*) in their characterization of rules. As Peter Landau notes, Bernard was aware of introducing something new into canon law when he treated regulative maxims not as independent laws or concrete statutes but as rhetorical commonplaces or aphorisms.[26] Addressing the title *De regulis iuris* in his *Summa decretalium*, Bernard "gave the first canonist discussion of *regulae*."[27] Bernard analogizes the "rules of law" (regulae iuris)

23 The expression "the men of lawe" is found at B 4.152/C 4.148 and B 7.39/C 9.44.

24 Here the word "lex" refers to the actual legislation or law mentioned in the *Digest* (of the *Corpus iuris civilis*).

25 All quotations from civil law (*Corpus iuris civilis*) are cited by reference to its part, book number, title number, and then the individual law as well as its incipit, as here, *Corpus iuris civilis*, Dig. 50.17.1, *Regula est*. In citing the *Corpus iuris civilis*, I use the following abbreviations: Cod., Dig., Nov. = Codex, Digest, Novels of Justinian. Here is the complete definition of a rule offered by Paulus: "*Paulus libro sexto decimo ad Plautium*. Regula est, quae rem breviter enarrat: non ex regula ius sumatur, sed ex iure quod est regula fiat" (In the sixteenth book, Paulus to Plautius: a rule is that which relates a matter briefly: a law should not be derived from a rule but a rule should be formulated from a law already in place). (*Corpus iuris civilis*, Dig. 50.17.1, *Regula est*).

26 Peter Landau observes that "Bernard is aware that he is introducing something new into the existing canon law and designates, in his textbook, *Regulae iuris* as aphorisms, that is, as propositions that ought to be there in jurisprudence just as they must be in physics" (Bernhard ist sich bewußt, daß er im kanonischen Recht etwas Neues einbringt und bezeichnet in einem von ihm verfaßten Lehrbuch die Regulae iuris als *Aphorismi*, also als Lehrsätze der Rechtswissenschaft, die es in der Rechtswissenschaft ebenso wie in der Physik geben müsse); see "Die Bedeutung des kanonischen Rechts," 34.

27 Stein, *Regulae iuris, From Juristic Rules to Legal Maxims*, 144.

with those specific to grammar and dialectic, as well as to aphorisms in physics. "But just as," he clarifies, "in other arts there are certain specific rules such as the ones governing gender and case in grammar, and commonplaces and syllogisms in dialectic, and like aphorisms in physics, thus also in this [legal] science, there are rules of law, as it were, aphorisms of laws or of canons" (Sicut autem in aliis artibus sunt quaedam regulae speciales, ut in grammatica de genere et casu, in dialectica de locis et syllogismis, in physica aphorismi, sic et in hac scientia regulae iuris quasi legum vel canonum aphorismi).[28] Bernard goes on to elaborate four different senses of "regula," identifying it with a "rod" (virga), a "canonical constitution" (constitutio canonica), a "code of conduct" (norma), and finally, a "pithy definition" (diffinitio compendiosa) that is "universal in scope" (complectens universitatem).[29]

Commenting on the title *De regulis iuris* in his *Glossa ordinaria* to the *Liber Sextus*, Johannes Andreae first offers the grammarians' succinct definition of the rule and then cites the equally succinct legal definition of the rule offered in the *Digest*:

> Regula secundum Grammaticos est multorum similium collectio. Lex autem describit regulam eam esse, quae rem quae est, breuiter enarrat, ff. *eod.l.1*. Dicitur autem regula, quia regit vel normam recte viuendi praebet. (Johannes Andreae, *Glossa ordinaria in Librum Sextum*, col. 776)[30]
>
> According to the grammarians, a rule is a gathering of many similar things. A civil law, however, defines a rule to be that which briefly states what a thing is; as is established in the [Justinian] *Digest* in the same title

---

28 All quotations from Bernard of Pavia's *Summa decretalium* are from the edition by Ernst Adolph Theodor Laspeyres (Regensburg: Josef Manz, 1860; reprint Graz: Akademische Druck-u. Verlagsanstalt, 1956), and are cited by reference to the book number, the title number and name, and (where appropriate), the paragraph, and the page number, as here, 5.37, *De regulis iuris*, 282.

29 Bernard of Pavia, *Summa decretalium* 5.37, *De regulis iuris*, ¶1, 282–3: "Regula pluribus dicitur modis. Dicitur enim regula virga, unde Achor furatus est regulam auream i.e. virgam; dicitur etiam regula consititutio canonica, ut Di. XI *Hoc vestrae* (c. 10); item dicitur specialis norma vivendi, ut regula monachorum vel canonicorum; quarto modo dicitur regula diffinitio compendiosa rerum complectens universitatem, ut C. VI. qu. 1 *Quaero* (c. 21) et Dig. eod. l. 1 [Digest 50.17.1, *Regula est*]; accipitur autem in hoc loco in hac quarta significatione."

30 Johannes Andreae, *Apparatus in Librum Sextum* (c. 1304) = *Glossa ordinaria in Librum Sextum, Corpus juris canonici (CJC)*.

> [*De diversis regulis iuris antiqui*] in the first law. Now, it is called a rule because it rules, that is, it offers a norm of right living.

Johannes Andreae goes on to distinguish "law" (ius) from "rule" (regula) on the grounds of prior causal authority: the former precedes and produces the latter. He ponders the question of the rule's nature ("Quae sit potestas regulae"), doubting "whether it makes a new law or repeats a law" (an scilicet constituat ius de nouo, an antiquum recitet dubitatur).[31] And, although he does eventually concede the argument to the contrary (i.e., a rule makes a law) he affirms that the rule "never establishes a new law, which is proved by law and by the fact itself" (ius de nouo nunquam constituat: quod iure & ipso facto probatur).[32] For the proof "by law," Johannes refers to the first law [i.e., *Regula est*] of the same title in the *Digest*.[33] For the proof "by fact," Johannes reasons that "because in the eighty-eight rules put forward here below, not even one can be found which establishes a law *de novo*, as will be evident in what follows" (quia in octoginta octo regulis infra positis non est vnam etiam solam inuenire, quae ius nouo constituat, vt in prosecutione patebit).[34] In true dialectical fashion, however, Johannes does admit one exception: a certain "rule of Cato" (regula Catonia) that "established a new law" (de nouo statuit), and he concedes that "this rule itself established a new law" (ipsa regula constituit ius de nouo). To support this conclusion, he refers to "infinite laws that the pope judges on the basis of rules" (Ad haec faciunt infinita iura, in quibus Papa iudicat ex regulis).[35] We shall return to this concession at the end of the chapter but, as Giulio Silano, in what is perhaps the most substantial and stimulating article in English on the title *De regulis iuris* in the *Liber Sextus*, notes, "[d]espite what seems like his own overwhelming evidence for the view that rules make law, Johannes remains reluctant to admit it."[36] For, as Johannes affirms:

> ego tamen non recedo a verbis legis & dico quod per regulam non statuitur ius, sed ex iure sumitur regula, alias non video quomodo posset dici regula iuris.[37]

---

31 Johannes Andreae, *Glossa ordinaria* in *Librum Sextum*, col. 777.
32 Ibid.
33 Ibid.: "Iure: ff. *eodem.l.1*" [Digest 50.17.1, *Regula est*].
34 Ibid.
35 Ibid.
36 Silano, "The *Regulae Iuris* and the Jurists,"184.
37 Johannes Andreae, *Glossa ordinaria* in *Librum Sextum*, col. 777.

> I nevertheless do not depart from the words of the law and I say that a law is not established by a rule but a rule from a law; otherwise I do not see how it can be called a rule of law.

In the passage above, Johannes uncovers a grammatical understanding of the phrase "regula iuris." The genitive case in the expression enables two readings of the relationship between "rule" (regula) and "of law" (iuris). As a subjective or possessive genitive, the "regula" (in regula iuris) is generated by the "ius" (i.e., rule from the law); as an objective genitive, the "regula" in the same expression also regulates the "ius" (i.e, rule for the law). Either reading grammatically expresses the almost unanimous canonistic position that the rule derives from or serves the law.

The B and C versions of Covetise's confession invoke the maxim designated as the fourth rule in Pope Boniface VIII's *Liber Sextus* ("Peccatum non dimittitur, nisi restituatur ablatum").[38] In both B and C, Repentaunce follows Boniface VIII and the other canonists insofar as he quotes versions of the same maxim to clarify restitution as a condition for absolution from the usurious sins personified by Covetise. But to whom, where, and how exactly Repentaunce words and interprets the maxim differ significantly across B and C, and it is by attending to such differences that we can discern the poem's invention of a law out of a rule. Briefly, in B, Repentaunce takes a pastoral approach to the maxim: he mobilizes it to elicit from Covetise enough remorse to induce him to make restitution of his own accord. In C, however, Repentaunce takes a more juridical approach to the maxim. He mobilizes it not as a "rule of law" (regula iuris) but as a "law" (ius) that is binding on not just the penitent but also on the most powerful confessor and lawmaker: the pope himself. In enunciating the maxim as a sentence to punishment rather than as a means of persuasion, Repentaunce challenges the received canonistic distinction between regulative maxims and laws, and thereby promulgates a law on restitution. That is, Repentaunce, in C, confers on the maxim a stipulative and even punitive force that it does not have in B or in its treatment by the canonists.

Such law-making from a rule is poetically generated in at least three ways in the C version of Covetise's confession: 1) in Repentaunce's orientation of the maxim on restitution to the pope and his penitentiary;

38 *Liber Sextus* 5.13.4, cols 786–7; see also Friedberg, *CIC*, 2: 1122.

2) in Repentaunce's wording of the maxim that makes no allowances for mitigating exceptions to the requirement of restitution; 3) in Repentaunce's prescription of penalties to clerics that fail to enforce the letter of the maxim. In these three ways, Repentaunce in C shapes a vision of restitutive justice in which even the supreme ecclesiastical rulemaker – the pope himself – is, as it were, denied the power to dispense with a strict reading of the maxim.

Covetise's Confession: From the "Rule" in B to the "Law" in C

To make visible the poetic making of a law from a rule, we need to step back to compare the internal contexts in both B and C in which the maxim occurs. In B, Repentaunce invokes the maxim only after he has followed the procedures of eliciting contrition elucidated by canonists such as Raymond of Peñafort, William of Pagula, and John Burgh. In B, as we have already seen, Repentaunce seeks to know whom Covetise has defrauded and whether or not he feels "pite" for his victims, who borrow on account of necessity or "nede."[39] On failing to detect any signs of contrition, Repentaunce urges Covetise to "repente," admonishing him about God's abandonment of him: "Now [but þow repente þe raþer," quod Repentaunce, "God lene þee neuere]."[40] Carrying a note of exasperation, Repentaunce's "Now" exhorts Covetise to repent lest he lose God's help, and only at this point does the confessor quote the maxim but still in the same pastoral vein. Even after quoting it, Repentaunce continues to focus on repentence rather than restitution. For, when Covetise subsequently fears damnation and expresses a suicidal impulse, Repentaunce hastens to "reconfort" him in order to prevent him from falling into "wanhope."[41] As Covetise teeters perilously on the verge of despair, Repentaunce exhorts him to think of "mercy"

39 B 5.253: Hastow pite on pouere men þat [borwe mote nedes]?

40 B 5.259.

41 B 5.279–81: "Thanne weex þe sherewe in wanhope and wolde han hanged hymselue / Ne hadde Repentaunce þe raþer reconforted hym in þis manere / 'Haue mercy in þi mynde, and wiþ þi mouþ biseche it.'" Repentaunce's attempt to prevent Covetise from falling into despair, as Gray notes has a parallel in penitential manuals such as the *Memoriale presbiterorum*, which "insist that the confessor must keep the penitent from falling into despair, by assigning him no more penance than was tolerable, requiring only such restitution as was practicable, and comforting the penitent with gentle and encouraging words and assurance of God's mercy" ("A Study of *Piers Plowman*," 129–30).

and to ask for it "wiþ þi mouþ." In all his efforts to steer Covetise away from damnation towards salvation, Repentaunce is more preoccupied with the remorse that Covetise needs to express for his victims than the restitution that the penitent needs to make to them.

In the corresponding lines in C, Repentaunce, likewise, does initially inquire into Covetise's lending to lords ("Lenedestow euere eny lord for loue of his mayntenaunce?") and Covetise does answer in the affirmative in like fashion ("Y haue lent lordes and ladyes þat louede me neuere aftur, / And haue ymad many a knyht bothe mercer and draper, / Payed neuere for his prentished nat a payre gloues! /That chaffared with my cheuesaunces cheued selde aftur").[42] Thus far, both Repentaunce and Covetise behave in C just as they do in B. But in the lines that follow – in which Repentaunce responds to Covetise's abovementioned admission of usury – the C passage differs significantly from the corresponding one in B. Not present in C is Repentaunce's exhaustive inquiry into Covetise's contrition discussed above but present are words with which Repentaunce emphasizes the confessor's (not the penitent's) obligation to heed the maxim on restitution:

> "Now redily," quod Repentaunce, "and by þe Rode, Y leue,
> Shal neuere seketoure wel bysette the syluer þat thow hem leuest,
> Ne thyn heyres, as Y hope, haue ioye of þat thow wonne;
> For þe Pope with alle his pentauncers, power hem fayleth
> To assoyle the of this synne *sine restitucione*:
> *Numquam dimittitur peccatum, nisi restituatur ablatum.*" (C 6.253–7)

Unlike their corresponding lines in B, these lines focus on restitution rather than on contrition, and turn to the confessor's rather than just the penitent's obligations to repair the "relacioun rect" broken by sinners like Covetise. By shifting the emphasis from concern with Covetise's "pite" (in B)[43] to the amends to be made for the penitent's victims (in C), Repentaunce mobilizes (in C) the Latin maxim in order to affirm that even the "Pope with alle his pentauncers, power hem fayleth" to absolve a usurious sinner who does not make appropriate restitution.[44]

42 C 6.248–52.
43 B 5.253–4.
44 C 6.256.

The legislative innovation of Repentaunce's mobilization and, as we shall see, even modification of the maxim would be lost on us, if we read the maxim solely alongside Augustine's Epistle 153 – the material source to which the Latin quotation has been traced.[45] Reading Repentaunce's version of the maxim not within its temporally distant material source but within more contemporary formal sources (such as the *Decretum* and the papally promulgated *Liber extra* and *Liber Sextus*) would render vivid not only Repentaunce's conversion of a rule into a law but also the poem's larger contribution to the discourse of what we would today call "the rule of law."

The Formal Sources of the Canonical Rule on Restitution

I begin with Gratian's *Decretum* (1120–60). The context for Gratian's use of the maxim is the genuineness of penitence felt by a sinner guilty of theft. Questio 6 in Causa 14 opens with Gratian's linking of restitution to penitence in his citation of the canon *Si res aliena* (by Augustine in his Epistle 153): "when the item of another that is the basis of the sin can be restituted and is not, penitence is not done but pretended" (Si res aliena, propter quam peccatum est, cum reddi potest, non redditur; non agitur paenitentia, sed fingitur).[46] Gratian proceeds to cite the maxim drawn from Augustine as well as rest of Augustine's words that significantly restrict its scope with a "but" (sed) clause on the penitent's ability to do so:

> Si autem veraciter agitur; non remittitur peccatum nisi restituatur ablatum: sed, ut dixi, cum restitui potest. Plerumque enim qui aufert, amittit, siue alios patiendo malos, siue ipse male viuendo: nec aliud habet, unde restituat. Huic certe non possumus dicere, redde quod abstulisti; nisi cum habere credimus, & negare. (*Decretum* II, C. 14. q. 6. c. 1, cols 1411–14; see also Friedberg, *CIC*, 1: 742)

45 Augustine, Epistola 153.6.20 in *Patrologia Latina*, vol. 33, col. 0662. Most recently, Anna Baldwin refers to Augustine's Epistle 153 as a possible source; see her *A Guidebook to Piers Plowman*, 84.

46 For the exact passage that Gratian quotes from Augustine, see Augustine's Epistle 153.6.20 in *Patrologia Latina*, vol. 33, col. 0662; Gratian follows Augustine's wording of the maxim in all respects except with regard to one word: whereas Augustine has "remittetur" (in "non remittetur peccatum"), Gratian has "remittitur" (in "non remittitur peccatum").

> If, however, it [penance] is truly done, sin is not remitted unless restitution of the stolen item is made: but, as I said, when it can be restituted. For the most part, he who steals loses it, whether by permitting other sinners [to take it] or by his own bad living, and he does not have anything with which he can make restitution. To him, certainly, we cannot say: "restore what you took," unless we believe him to have it and deny it.

The gloss to *Redde* in the *Glossa ordinaria* (1214–17; and 1234–41)[47] to the *Decretum* clarifies that Gratian's injunction must be understood in terms of the penitent's solvency: "understand this when a thief or plunderer is insolvent; but if he should be solvent, even though the item he stole perished without his fault, he is however held to make restitution of like value" (hoc intellige quando fur vel raptor non est soluendo sed si esset soluendo, licet res quam abstulerit, sine culpa sua periisset, tamen tenetur reddere aestimationem ipsius).[48] To vary the memorable analogue in *Piers Plowman*, the penitent must "reddere quod debet" but, in the *Decretum* and its *Glossa ordinaria* among other contemporary prescriptive texts only when s/he possesses the material means to do so.[49] Likewise, the gloss to *Peccati* goes on to note that such a penitent "is not freed from the debt but only from the penalty" (non est liberatus a debito, sed tantum a poena).[50]

---

47 According to Rudolf Weigang, Johannes Teutonicus's initial contribution to the *Glossa ordinaria* belongs to the period between 1214 and 1217 whereas Bartholomew of Brescia's revision and completion of it to the period between 1234 and 1241; see Weigang's "The Development of the *Glossa ordinaria* to Gratian's *Decretum*," 84–91.

48 *Glossa ordinaria in Decretum*, II. C. 14, q. 6, c. 1 *Res aliena*, ad v. *Redde*, col. 1413.

49 One such prescriptive text is Alain de Lille's *Liber poenitentialis*: in a chapter concerning the appropriate penance for usury that the priest should impose, Alain cites a version of Augustine's maxim on restitution but goes on to make restitution contingent upon the truly confessed usurious penitent's means to make restitution, and, failing that, his/her willingness to do so as well as doing so to his/her victim or kin or the poor, when s/he has the means: "Si vero confessus fuerit peccatum usurae consulat ei sacerdos, ut ea quae per usuram rapuit restituat, si restituendi facultatem habeat. Aliter enim ei non est salus, quia ut ait Augustinus 'Non datur venia, nisi restituantur ablata.' Si vero facultatem reddendi non habeat, voluntatem offerat, quia sufficit affectus, ubi deest effectus, his autem spiritualiter reddat quibus rapuit; si desunt, eorum proximis, si nec proximi inveniuntur, pauperibus eroget." See *Liber poenitentialis* 2: 10, 52; all references to Alain de Lille's penitential manual in this book are cited by book, chapter, and page number respectively.

50 *Glossa ordinaria in Decretum*, II. C. 14, q. 6, c. 1 *Res aliena*, ad v. *Peccati*, col. 1413.

Following the *Decretum*, the *Liber extra* (1234) includes a decretal that cites the maxim with a subtle variation on Gratian's wording of it but, likewise, underscores the conditionality of the maxim. Included in the title on usury, the decretal *Cum tu* deploys the maxim to enjoin usurers to make restitution of usuries "provided they have the means, whence they [usuries] can be restituted to them: since according to the word of the St. Augustine, 'sin should not be remitted, unless what is taken is restored'" (dummodo in facultatibus habeant, vnde ipsis possint eas restituere: cum iuxta verbum beati Augustini: Non remittatur peccatum, nisi restituatur ablatum).[51] The subsequent lines of the same decretal clarify that "those who do not have the means to be able to make restitution of usuries should not be punished with any penalty, since the state of poverty clearly excuses them" (Illi autem, qui non habent in facultatibus, vnde vsuras valeant restituere, non debent vlla poena mulctari: cum eos nota paupertatis euidenter excuset).[52] In the *Glossa ordinaria* (1234–66)[53] to the *Liber extra*, Bernard of Parma's gloss to *In facultatibus* affirms this exception to the rule of restitution by noting that the usurers "are entirely freed from the obligation to make restitution, if they have nothing" (sed si nihil habent, liberantur ex toto).[54]

In the papally promulgated *Liber Sextus* (1298) that followed the *Liber extra*, the maxim acquires the status of a rule.[55] The fourth "rule" (regula) that Pope Boniface includes among the eighty-eight rules (under the title *De regulis iuris*) is none other than the Latin maxim cited by Repentaunce and, as already mentioned, found originally in Augustine's Epistle 153. Pope Boniface's inclusion of the Augustinian maxim among his rules of law updates or even upgrades it; what functioned in a fifth-century epistle as a moral exhortation to penitents acquired

---

51 *Liber extra*, 5.19.5, *Cum tu*, col. 1735–6.

52 Ibid., col. 1736.

53 In "The 'Glossa ordinaria' to the Gregorian Decretals," Kuttner and Smalley argue that Bernard of Parma's glossatorial work on the *Liber extra* can be mapped out in four redactions: "first redaction 1234–c. 1241; second 1243–5; third 1245–c. 1253; final 1263–6," 101.

54 *Glossa ordinaria in Librum extra* 5.19.5, *Cum tu*, ad v. *In facultatibus*, col. 1736; but the glossator goes on to note that, as he has already mentioned earlier, the usurers would nevertheless be bound to make restitution should they arrive at a richer fortune: "Si tamen ad pinguiorem fortunam peruenerint, tenentur vt prius."

55 Thematically structured like the previous collection the *Liber extra*, the *Liber Sextus* was not really a sixth book, but rather added five more books to the already existing five books of the *Liber extra*.

the status of a canonical norm from 1298 (the year of the *Liber Sextus*'s promulgation) onwards. This status was not just confirmed by the pope but also reaffirmed by the earliest authoritative commentators on the papal rules of law: the secular jurist Dynus Muxellanus (1254–1303) and canonist Johannes Andreae (1270–1348).

Dynus Muxellanus's treatise on Boniface's title *De regulis iuris* served as a basis for subsequent thinking about regulative maxims not just by canonists but, as we shall see, possibly by Langland himself.[56] Given that Johannes Andreae and other canonists absorb and expand Dynus's concept of the rule as having regulative rather than legislative status, their glosses can serve as a foil to foreground the novelty of Repentaunce's contrarian reading of the same rule – a reading that casts the "rule" in the role of a "law" rather than as a derivation from it. To foreground the legislative (rather than merely regulative) nature of Repentaunce's dictum out of the regulative maxim on restitution, I shall now establish in greater detail the extent to which the canonists treat the same maxim as a contingent rule rather than as a binding law.

Let me begin with Dynus Muxellanus's comments on the rule on restitution in his *Commentarius mirabilis super titulo de regulis iuris*, since they may have influenced Johannes Andreae's discussion of the maxim. Dynus's opening reading of the maxim is almost identical with that of Repentaunce. Elaborating the sin of aggravated robbery or extortion by "usurious wickedness" (usurariam pravitatem) and affirming that such a sin is not remitted, Dynus adds that it follows that neither is the "penalty of sin" (pena peccati) remitted unless restitution of the stolen item is made.[57]

56 Dynus Muxellanus, *Commentarius mirabilis super titulo de regulis iuris* (Lyons, 1540). All quotations from this commentary are taken from this edition. Peter Landau considers Savigny's claim that the Bolognese professor Dynus Muxellanus's commentary on the title *De regulis iuris* is the first and goes so far as to hold it possible that he too might have also been the actual redactor of the title but adds that the authorship of it is a much debated matter ("Man kann daher immer noch die besonders von Savigny vertretene Vermutung wahrscheinlich halten, dass dieser legistische Professor [Dynus] der eigentliche Redaktor der 'Regulae iuris' war; diese Frage ist in der rechtshistorischen Literatur häufig diskutiert aber bisher nicht geklärt worden"); see Landau's *Die Bedeutung des kanonischen Rechts*, 37–8.

57 Here is the full sentence of Dynus's text: "Si rem meam surripuisti vel violenter abstulisti vel aliud a me extorsisti per usurariam pravitatem, non remittitur peccatum, et consequenter nec pena peccati, nisi restituas rem ablatam" (If you stole my item or took it away by force or extorted something from me by means of depraved usury, the sin is not remitted; consequently, nor is the penalty for it, unless you should return the stolen item) *Commentarius*, s.v. *Peccatum non remittitur*, fol. 29v.

When Dynus goes on to consider possible exceptions to the rule, he, like Gratian, Gregory IX, and Raymond, parts ways with Repentaunce in the C version of the poem. Offering a far less literal or absolutist reading of the maxim than does Repentaunce, Dynus treats the maxim less as a law to be enforced unconditionally than as a general principle to be interpreted in light of the sinner's material circumstances or the victim's forgiveness. For instance, Dynus considers the situation where the sinner ("a thief or plunderer, or usurer") has the means to make restitution to his victim but is released from the debt by him/her.[58] Dynus offers two diametrically opposed readings of the maxim. "Some," he reports, "say that the sinner is absolved, because to pay a debt and have it forgiven are the same thing" (quidam dicunt quod sit absolutus: quia solvere et consequi remissionem eius quod erat solvendum paria sunt).[59] "Others," he adds, "say that the person is not freed because the words of the rule have to be adhered to in a doubtful case when sin is at issue" (Alii dicunt quod non liberatur quis quia verbis regule inherendum est in dubio cum de peccato agatur).[60] Considering, however, the scenario in which the sinner "does not have the ability to make restitution of the item," Dynus argues that "then, restitution would be impossible for him, and, then too, he should be absolved without restitution because no one can be obliged to do an impossible thing" (Sed si non habeat facultatem rei restituende: tunc esset sibi impossibilis restitutio. Et tunc sine restitutione absolvetur quia nemo potest ad impossibile obligari).[61] Dynus argues that the rigour of the civil law would probably not release such a sinner on account of personal hardship rather than on account of natural impossibility, adding,

58 Dynus Muxellanus, *Commentarius*, s.v. *Peccatum non remittitur*, fol. 29r: "Queri autem solet si fur vel raptor vel usurarius habet facultatem rei restituende etiam si fiat eius remissio absque eo quod restituat rem an intelligat a peccato absolutus."

59 Dynus Muxellanus, *Commentarius*, s.v. *Peccatum non remittitur*, fol. 29r.

60 Here is the full passage: "Queri autem solet si fur vel raptor vel usurarius habet facultatem rei restituende: etiam si fiat eius remissio absque eo quod restituat rem an intelligatur a peccato absolutus: et quidam dicunt quod sit absolutus: quia solvere et consequi remissionem eius: quod erat solvendum paria sunt. *ff.de re iud.l. iiii soluisse, et.l.intra dies*, et quia satisfactum accipimus per eum modum quem creditor acceptaverit. *ff. de actio.l. si rem;* satisfactum autem, *tit. ex quibus modis pignus vel hypo. solui.l.item liberatur*, in principio. Alii dicunt quod non liberatur quis, quia verbis regule inherendum est in dubio cum de peccato agatur" (*Commentarius*, s.v. *Peccatum non remittitur*, fol. 29r).

61 Dynus Muxellanus, *Commentarius*, s.v. *Peccatum non remittitur*, fols 30v–30r.

however, that "the sinner could be excused without the rigour of the civil law – it matters greatly if the giving or the deed was made under an obligation – for, if the giving was made under an obligation, then even personal hardship does not release the one in debt."[62] Dynus's consideration of such circumstances reveals the centrality of discretion (say, that of a priest or a pope) in the interpretation and implementation of the maxim.

In the *Glossa ordinaria* (completed in 1304) to the *Liber Sextus*, Johannes Andreae, likewise, reinforces Dynus's circumstantial approach to the rule.[63] To be sure, glossators including the fictional Repentaunce, initially read the regulative maxim as an unambiguous and non-negotiable demand for restitution but then, like Dynus, they consider several scenarios where the rule can or should be read more moderately or even dispensed with. For instance, the initial glosses to *Peccatum non dimittitur* locate the expression within a dual frame of reference "concerning the remission of sin with regard to God" (de remissione peccati quo ad Deum) and then "with regard to the church or the priest's granting of absolution" ([de remissione peccati] quo ad ipsam Ecclesiam, id est, de absolutione facienda sacerdoti).[64] Johannes Andreae presents a hypothetical case involving a certain Titius, who, like Covetise, knowingly deprives people of what belongs to them and thus profits at their expense. Like Covetise, Titius too feels contrite enough about his sin to confess to a priest but not to make either satisfaction or restitution.[65] Johannes then interprets the maxim's opening words as requiring the

62 "Licet forte secundum rigorem iuris civilis non esset excusatus: quia naturalis impossibilitas non persone difficultas debitorem excusat. vt *ff. De verborum obligatione l.continuus actus.*§. *illud*. Sed mihi videtur quod etiam sine rigore iuris civilis potest excusari: multum enim refert utrum sit in obligatione datio vel factum. Nam si est in obligatione datio, et difficultas persone non excusat debitorem" (Dynus Muxellanus, *Commentarius*, fol. 30r).

63 In this section, it has been almost impossible to neatly distinguish Johannes Andreae's comments from those of later canonists as the 1582 *Apparatus* does not always distinguish them.

64 Johannes Andreae, *Glossa ordinaria in Librum Sextum* 5.13.4, *Peccatum*, ad v. *Peccatum non dimittitur*, col. 785.

65 *Glossa ordinaria in Librum Sextum* 5.13.4, *Peccatum*, ad v. *Peccatum non dimittitur*, col. 785: "Aliquis Titius subtraxit rem alienam scienter: facta subtractione, ipse forte ad cor rediens habuit displicentiam de huiusmodo peccato, & de illo fecit confessionem suo sacerdoti: tamen vult remanere in simplicibus, contritione & confessione absque satisfactione & restitutione rei: licet habeat facultatem, & possit rem ipsam

penitent to make restitution to be eligible for remission from God and absolution from the priest. "Or the question can also be understood to be asking whether the sin is remitted before God on account of contrition alone" (Vel etiam potest intelligi vtrum sit dimissum peccatum quo ad Deum per solam displicentiam?); the answer is "no, because sin is not remitted unless restitution is made" (Respondetur quod non: quia non dimittitur peccatum nisi restituatur ablatum).[66]

In subsequent comments on the regulative maxim, Johannes shifts the emphasis from a literal to a discretionary reading of its words. Rather than insisting on the letter of the rule, he calls attention to its spirit: he addresses various circumstances in which the maxim can and should be set aside and, hence, treated as a general principle for thinking through restitution rather than as a specific law in the sense of an enforceable statute. When he goes on to treat exceptions to the rule, we begin to see the rule's peculiarly contingent nature, and will be able to detect the novelty in Repentaunce's handling of the same rule as a non-contingent and, hence, non-negotiable obligation – that is, as if it were a law. One such exception concerns the sinner's inability but intent to make restitution: "whether it is without question true that sin is not remitted unless restitution is made" (Vtrum sit verum indistincte quod non dimittitur peccatum, nisi restituatur ablatum?) and the answer is "no" (Respondetur quod non).[67] But, this answer "is understood" (sed intelligitur) insofar as "the misappropriator should have the ability to make restitution" (si subtractor habeat facultatem restituendi.)[68] He then spells out the conditions for an exception to the rule: "but if the misappropriator should not have the ability to make restitution because he is poor [and] if he should have the intent to do so when he arrives at

---

restituere: & petit impendi sibi beneficium absolutionis: vtrum suus sacerdos licite possit eum absoluere?" [A certain Titius knowingly took away another's item: with the item having been taken away, he himself perhaps returning to his heart had remorse concerning the sin of this kind, and confessed it to his priest: however, he wishes to remain just in contrition and confession, without satisfaction and restitution of the item, although he has the ability and can return the item itself, and he seeks the benefit of absolution: can his priest licitly absolve him?]. Although some of the glosses to the *Liber Sextus* are not by Johannes Andreae's hand and probably postdate him, they nevertheless expand the exceptions already present in Dynus Muxellanus's gloss, and, hence can be brought to bear upon the poem.

66 *Glossa ordinaria in Librum Sextum* 5.13.4, *Peccatum*, ad v. *Peccatum non dimittitur*, col. 785.

67 Ibid., col. 786.

68 Ibid.

a richer fortune, the sin is remitted from him" (sed si non habeat facultatem restituendi quia est inops: si habeat propositum restituendi dum peruenerit ad pinguiorem fortunam, peccatum ei remittitur).[69]

Johannes Andreae or a later commentator sheds light on yet another exception to the rule, describing a scenario in which the sinner has misappropriated goods that were themselves illicitly obtained. He introduces the exception with a query about whether or not to follow the strict letter of the regulative maxim:

> Vtrum sit verum indistincte quod indebite subtractum debet restitui illi, cui est subtractum, si sit praesens, vel eius haeredibus ... Respondet glossa quod quando in subtractione sit turpitudo ex parte subtrahentis tantum: tunc est facienda restitutio illi cui res subtracta, vel eius haeredibus ... sed si sit turpitudo ex parte vtriusque, vt in eo quod est lucratus in ludo prohibito: quia ludens non potest licite retinere nec restituere illi a quo lucratus est: tunc debet illud erogare pauperibus. 14.q.5. *non sane*. vel Ecclesiae, si illi facta est iniuria. supra X, *de simo*, cap. *de hoc* in *antiq*. (*Glossa ordinaria in Librum Sextum* 5.13.4, *Peccatum* ad v. *Peccatum non dimittitur*, col. 786)

> Is it without question true that the wrongfully appropriated item ought to be returned to him from whom it was taken away, if he is alive, or to his heirs... The gloss answers that when there is turpitude in the act of misappropriation only on the part of the one misappropriating [the item], then restitution should be made to him from whom the thing was removed or to his heirs ... but if there should be turpitude on the part of both [the sinner and his victim], as with the winnings in a prohibited game since the player cannot rightly keep what he has won or return it to the one he won it from, then he should give it to the poor, as established in causa 14, quaestio 5, chapter *Non sane*, or to the Church, if it has been injured. See above in the title, *De simonia*, chapter *De hoc* in *Quinque compilationes antiquae decretalium extravagantium*.

In the explication above, the glossators understand the rule not as a self-evident law requiring restitution to be made to the victim at any cost but as a frame of reference within which to think about the legitimacy of the obligation to make restitution. In circumstances where the strict application of the canonical rule might, in effect, promote illicitness, the

69 Ibid.

rule should be interpreted less literally and in ways that do not violate prior laws such as the one proscribing gains through an illicit game.

For the canonists, then, the rule derives from and must serve already existing laws, and not the other way around. In his *In titulum de regulis iuris commentarii* (or *Novella commentaria*) Johannes Andreae clarifies the derivation of the rule from its subservience to the law. Invoking the canonist Johannes Monachus, Johannes Andreae defines the rule of law (regula iuris) as a rule *for* law ("regula iuri") in the way the "cap of Socrates" (cappa Socratis) is "a Socratic cap" (socratica cappa).[70] He adds that "in the definition of the rule of law, the law and the rule ought to be conjoined" (dicit autem, quod in diffinitione regulae iuris sunt coniungenda ius & regula).[71] By this contrast, the rule, as Johannes Andreae makes repeatedly clear in his treatment of every exception discussed above, is equated with something dependent upon and serving the law's power.

Dynus Muxellanus's commentary on the rules of law and the glosses by Johannes Andreae as well as later canonists to the same title in the *Liber Sextus* constitute the standard canonist distinction between the category of rules and that of laws, between regulative maxims and legislative norms that they are derived from or dependent on. More pertinent to *Piers Plowman*, the glosses comprise the canonist thought on rules that Repentaunce in C at once courts and complicates in his transformation of the regulative maxim into a law, and in his "curtailment" of the power of the papal penitentiary. Juxtaposing the B and C passages that quote the maxim in light of the varied canonistic glosses on it will reveal that, in C, Repentaunce invests it with a quality of indispensability or authoritative rigour characteristic of laws rather than of rules.

C's Wording of the Regulative Maxim

Granted, there are slight variations of the wording of the maxim across the manuscripts of *Piers Plowman*. But the poem's modern editions such as Schmidt's allow for conclusions to be drawn – not so much about any absolute differences between the B and C versions of the poem as about

70 That is, Johannes Andreae treats the "regula iuris" as an objective genitive; Johannes Andreae, *In titulum de regulis iuris novella commentaria, vulgo mercuriales*. Facsimile edition, 1581 (Turin: Bottega d'Erasmo, 1966), A2. All quotations from the *Novella commentaria* are from this edition.

71 Johannes Andreae, *In titulum de regulis iuris*, A2.

different approaches to the maxim across the poem's versions, manuscript or editorial. To compare, then, the wordings of the maxim in the B and C versions of the poem as presented in Schmidt's edition: in B, the maxim reads as: "*Non dimittitur peccatum donec restituatur ablatum*" (B 5.272) whereas in C the maxim reads as: "*sine restitucione: Numquam dimittitur peccatum, nisi restituatur ablatum*" (C 6.257).[72] As Nicholas Gray has observed, in the grammatical location where B has "*donec*," C has "*nisi*," and thereby C's formulation of the maxim is lexically closer to that found in legal discourse, as "[n]o parallel from earlier or contemporary texts has yet been reported for Langland's reading of '*donec*.'"[73] C's use of "nisi" rather than "donec" also renders the maxim almost into a leonine hexameter – a form often used by canonists for expressing "brocardica" (pairs of diametrically opposed arguments), and other *sententiae* that students of canon law could easily commit to memory.[74] In and of themselves, such lexical and metrical differences between the B and C versions of the maxim may do no more than align C with the canonistic passages that contain the maxim cast in a similar form.

But the expression "sine restitucione" in C (and not present in B) that Repentaunce prefixes to the Latin maxim emphasizes a reading of the maxim that makes no allowances for absolution without restitution. Not only the Latin prefix but also the maxim's wording in C casts the rule as possessing the rigour of positive law that it does not carry in B or in the canonistic glosses on it. Rather than opening with the adverb "non" (as in B's version "non dimittitur" or in Augustine's "non remittetur" in Epistle 153), the maxim in the version that Repentaunce deploys in C opens with the adverb "numquam" (never) and therefore is divested

72 For the canonistic sources of such changes, see Gray, "Langland's Quotations from the Penitential Tradition."

73 Ibid., 54. In his dissertation, Nicholas Gray offers a more detailed sense of the manuscripts that have "nisi" or "donec": "B V 273a (as quoted, except that MSS R and F, together with Crowley's printed editions, read 'nisi' for 'donec'); C VI 257a ('Numquam dimittitur peccatum nisi restituatur ablatum', abbreviated in most MSS); B XVII 310a (abbreviated to 'Numquam dimittitur peccatum & c.' in all MSS except Y and Cot, which add 'donec', and MS F, which reads 'Numquam dimittitur peccatum nisi restituatur ablatum'); and C XIX 285a ('Nunquam dimittitur peccatum')" (27 footnote 3).

74 The parenthetical definition of "brocardica" or brocards offered above is my translation of Peter Weimar's observation that medieval jurists treated them as "argumenta" in the sense of evidence in classical and medieval rhetoric: "Sie waren Paare von entgegengesetzten Argumenten." Weimar distinguishes three types of brocardica: "loci generales," "generalia," and "solutiones" (91). See "Argumenta Brocardica."

of the potential for moderation present in its formal sources.[75] We may recall that the *Decretum*, the *Liber extra*, the *Liber Sextus* and the *Ordinary Glosses* to them use "non" rather than "numquam" to modify the verbal force of the maxim. More absolutist than "non," the adverb "numquam" leaves no latitude for the numerous exceptions to the rule that the canonists painstakingly detail. Together, these three differences between B and C present two distinct poetic usages of the maxim. Whereas B handles the maxim as a provisional rule (in the same way in which the canonists that I have quoted treat the maxim), C casts the maxim less in the nature of a provisional rule ("regula iuris") or a moral exhortation than in that of a strict law ("ius") that, as Repentaunce goes on to claim, binds even the pope and his penitentiary (pentauncers).[76] To be clear, my point is that, in C, Repentaunce deploys the maxim to hold primarily confessors – from the papal to the parochial – to a strict reading of the maxim, for he does suggest that he may absolve Covetise so long as "by thy [the penitent's] myhte," Covetise makes restitution to all men – a view that Gray notes is echoed in the medieval penitential tradition.[77]

75 In his Epistle 153, Augustine's wording of the maxim has "non" rather than "numquam": "non remittetur peccatum, nisi restituatur ablatum"; see *Epistola* 153.6.20 in *Patrologia Latina*, vol. 33, col. 0662. In footnote 3 in his "A Study of *Piers Plowman*," Nicholas Gray observes that, elsewhere in B, the maxim has "Numquam" rather than "non": "B XVII 310a (abbreviated to 'Numquam dimittitur peccatum & c.' in all MSS except Y and Cot, which add 'donec', and MS F, which reads 'Numquam dimittitur peccatum nisi restituatur ablatum'); and C XIX 285a ('Nunquam dimittitur peccatum')" (27).

76 John Alford explains that a "pentauncer" "is a priest appointed by a pope or bishop to administer the sacrament of penance, esp. in cases reserved to the bishop or pope"; see his *A Glossary*, 113. The "pentauncers" refer to the *paenitentiarii* who, as W.P. Müller explains, "were the principal representatives of the Apostolic Court (Curia) ... papal confessors [who] counted it among their main duties to hear confessions of contrite pilgrims who had come to Rome (or the pope) to ease their troubled consciences," and "[u]pon having consented to acts of penance, the repentant individuals would receive priestly absolution, which was believed to free them from spiritual guilt" ("The Price of Papal Pardon," 459). For a comprehensive study of the papal penitentiary, see Emil Göller, *Die päpstliche Pönitentiarie von ihrem Ursprung bis zu ihrer Umgestaltung unter Pius V*, 4 vols (Rome, 1907–11); see also Salonen and Schmugge, *A Sip from the "Well of Grace."*

77 C 6.295; see also Gray, "A Study of *Piers Plowman*," 239–41. Noting that Langland's inclusion of "by thy myhte" "recalls how the penitential tradition requires a sinner to make restitution 'iuxta posse suum' or 'pro posse suo,'" Gray cites evidence from a range of manuals including the *Memoriale Presbiterorum* and *Pupilla Oculi*; see his exhaustive footnote 75 on page 241.

As with the maxim's lexical and metrical forms, so with its location and the concomitant imagery. Comparing the internal context of the maxim in B with that of the maxim in C will provide additional evidence, in C, of the process of law-making from a rule. In B, we may recall, Repentaunce invokes the regulative maxim precisely at the point where he assails Covetise for his fraudulent activities:

"Thow art an vnkynde creature – I kan þee noȝt assoille
Til þow make restitucion" quod Repentaunce, "and rekene wiþ hem alle,
And siþen þat Reson rolle it in þe Registre of heuene
That þow hast maad ech man good, I may þee noȝt assoille:
Non dimittitur peccatum donec restituatur ablatum." (B 5.269–72)

Here, Repentaunce's admonitory words to Covetise are located towards the end of the confessional process (and not much earlier on, as in the corresponding passage in C). This is the place where the parish confessor would typically decide whether or not to grant absolution to his penitent: if the sinner confessed to one of the reserved sins such as usury, the confessor would withhold absolution and send the penitent to the bishop or to superior confessors.[78]

What occasions Repentaunce to resort to the regulative maxim in B is to spell out to Covetise the condition for absolution: the confessor cannot ("kan þee noȝt") and may not ("may þee noȝt") grant him absolution without the penitent's having made restitution. Addressed solely to Covetise, Repentaunce's words do not emphasize the confessor's obligation to follow the maxim. Rather, they focus on the penitent's obligation to abide by it for his own spiritual and social good. More particularly, they exemplify a pastoral rhetoric suited to persuade penitents to repent and to make restitution rather than to admonish confessors about fulfilling their office with diligence. Such a penitent-oriented approach explains why Repentaunce substantiates the rule on

78 For instance, Richard Rolle, in his confessional manual, advises the parish priest to send the sinner who commits grave sins such as usury to the bishop or his penitentiary, observing that he cannot absolve such a penitent unless he is in danger of death: "In istis uero casibus non potest sacerdos parochialis absoluere nisi in periculo mortis, sed debet mittere peccatorem ad episcopum seu eius penitenciarium, uidelicet, blasfematores, clandestine matrimonium contrahentes … usurarius … Hii et huiusmodi ad superiores debent mitti"; see *Judica Me Deus*, 66.

restitution by invoking allegorical figures like "Reson" and the "Registre of heuene" rather than, as in the corresponding C passage, to the referential ones of institutional authority such as the pope and his papal confessors. The former have a vividly dramatic or even demotic appeal whereas the latter would appear bureaucratic – perhaps even a trifle bland – to the vivacious audience that Covetise typifies. All these examples of Repentaunce's concentration upon, and care for, Covetise's soul underscore, in B, the penitent's need to repent and make restitution to his victims rather than the confessor's conditional power to grant or withhold absolution.

The lexical differences between the B and C versions of the Latin maxim point to Repentaunce's inventive treatment of the sources of the quotation in C. Commenting on the use of Latin in *Piers Plowman*, Fiona Somerset notes that the "variations between Langland's putative 'sources' and the Latin text within his poem are not errors in quotation or copying but deliberate changes designed to fit the 'quotation' to its surroundings."[79] In B, the canonistically less formal or rhetorically less emphatic version of the maxim "fits" (or is made to fit) the curatorial context of exhorting the penitent Covetise to first express contrition and then make restitution: the maxim works more like a moral exhortation than like a legal enforcement. In C, the "deliberate changes" made to the maxim's Latin wording in its putative canonistic sources "fit" the context of turning the rule into a law and explaining its indispensability not just to the penitent but also to papal confessors: the maxim works more like a statutory law than like a moral principle. In C, thus, Repentaunce invents in the sense of "finding" a common rule and formulating it as a law to a clerical audience – perhaps one even aware of the canonistic distinction between rules and laws in light of Pope Boniface VIII's title on the eighty-eight rules of law. Repentaunce also invents in the sense of "founding" something radical from a normatively common maxim: he invests it with a legislative authority to curb the papal privilege that the narrator, as early as in the Prologue of both B and C, perceives as deriving from the "þe power that Peter hadde to kepe – / to bynde and to vnbynde, as þe Boke telleth."[80] Towards the end of the chapter, we shall return to the implications of Repentaunce's invention in its

79 Somerset, "'Al þe comonys with o voys atonys,'" 108–9.
80 *Piers Plowman* Prologue C 128–9.

twofold sense for the papal power of binding and loosing under the aspect of "ordo" (the confessor's power to grant absolution from the "culpa" of sin) and "jurisdictio" (the power in the external forum to grant indulgences from the "pena" of sin).[81] For now, however, let us consider a set of lines in the C version of Covetise's confession that critique or curb the power of priestly ministry (i.e., the key of "ordo").

C's Investment of the Rule with the Punitive Power of Law

Having cast the regulative maxim as a law, Repentaunce goes on to expound and extend its punitive force to the unnamed and absent parish priest in lines in C that do not have any parallel in B:

> "ȝe, þe prest þat thy tythe toek, trowe Y non other,
> Shal parte with the in purgatorye and helpe paye thy dette,
> Yf he wiste thow were such, when he resseyued thyn offrynge.
> And what lede leueth þat Y lye, look in þe Sauter glosed,
> On *Ecce enim veritatem dilexisti,*
> And there shal he wite witterly what vsure is to mene,
> And what penaunce the prest shal haue þat proud is of his tithes.
> For an hore of here ers-wynnynge may hardiloker tythe
> Then an errant vsurer, haue God my treuthe,
> And arste shal come to heuene, by [Hym] that me made." (C 6.298–307)

Reinforcing the shift in focus from the penitent to the pope and his penitentiary, these lines present Repentaunce here as digressing from hearing Covetise's confession to apostrophizing Covetise's own parish priest about any potential abuses of the *cura animarum*. With the exclamation "ȝe," Repentaunce interrupts the dialogue between penitent and confessor (which in B version proceeds with no such interruption): he introduces a new addressee that, though visibly absent from the immediate setting of the penitential forum, is nevertheless "hailed"

81 "jurisdictio" also pertains to the penitential forum insofar as the confessor should have the legal right to hear confessions: the parish priest possesses the right to hear confessions of his own parishioners whereas regulars like friars must seek and obtain such permission from the bishop of the diocese where they wish to serve as confessors. Likewise, within the penitential forum, the penances that the priest imposes can also go toward satisfying the "pena" of sin.

from within it.[82] At this juncture, Repentaunce shifts the focus from the parishioner Covetise to his parish priest, from the forum of penance to the parish in which the latter would have external as well as internal jurisdiction over the former. Just as Repentaunce had earlier on (in the C passage discussed above) asserted the papal penitentiary's lack of "power" to grant absolution without restitution in an effort to persuade Covetise to make restitution, so he now invokes the parish confessor to admonish him about his [the priest's] subjection to the rule on restitution: both the parish confessor and the parishioner will together have to share and expiate the debt of usury in purgatory.

Repentaunce's promulgation of the law in the form of penalties binding on the priest that profits from penitents' ill-gotten gains invites comparison with, and, I argue, supplements a received ecclesiastical view on the parish priest's intermediary role in dispensing restitutive justice. For instance, in the third question of the twenty-first disputation (drawn from his compilation *Quaestiones disputatae*), Simon of Tournai (c. 1130–1201/1216), "who in his youth had attended the classes (and disputations) of the lawyers in Bologna," underscores the responsibility for restitution to be shared not only by the penitent but also by his own [the penitent's] confessor.[83] In a scenario analogous to the one dramatized by Repentaunce in his critique of Covetise' parish priest, Simon introduces the obligation that a thief like Covetise owes to his victim, and frames it within the same maxim on restitution (italicized below) that we have been discussing so far:

> Quod autem tertio queritur, an fur teneatur ei cui damnum dedit, sacerdote retinente furtum sibi commissum, probari videtur. Ait enim auctoritas: *Non remittitur peccatum, nisi restituatur ablatum.* Sed non est ei restitutum cui ablatum. Non est ergo dimissum peccatum. E contra docetur. Sufficienter confessus est, et in quantum in se est restituit, quando ut restitueret sacerdoti commisit. Ergo peccatum remissum est; non ergo tenetur ei cui damnum dedit.[84]
>
> A third question is: it remains to be proved whether a thief should be held [to make restitution] to him from whom he stole, if the priest retains the

82 Here, I am indebted to Jocelyn Wogan-Browne's treatment of Althusser's concept of hailing or "interpellation" in the context of medieval literature; see Wogan-Browne, Watson, Taylor, and Evans, *Idea of the Vernacular*, 111.

83 Novikoff, *The Medieval Culture of Disputation*, 136.

84 Simon of Tournai, "Disputatio xxi," 71–2.

> stolen item entrusted to him. Authority has it that "sin is not remitted unless restitution is made." But the stolen item was not returned to him from whom it was taken away. Therefore, the sin is not remitted. On the contrary it is taught that he confessed sufficiently and, insofar as he was able, he made restitution, when he committed it to the priest to make the restitution. Therefore, the sin is remitted; he therefore has no obligation to him to whom he caused damage.

In the presentation of the "question," Simon, like Repentaunce, distinguishes the spiritual remission of sin in the penitential forum (i.e., the absolution from the "culpa" of sin) from the material remission of the debt owed by the penitent to the defrauded person. More strikingly, both Simon and Repentaunce imagine a situation in which the confessor acts as an intermediary between penitent and victim, and both underscore the penitent's obligation to make restitution to the defrauded victim.

In Simon's answer to the question, however, we can see that he and Repentaunce differ in their treatment of the intermediary figure of the priest. Attending to their differences will reveal the extent to which Repentaunce goes beyond Simon's thinking to produce a poetic invention of legal import. Answering the "third question" cited above on the obligations of the penitent, Simon proposes the following solution:

> Redditur. Obligatio duplex est: peccati et debiti. Obligatione peccati tenebatur apud Deum, sed illa soluta est per confessionem. Obligatione debiti tenebatur et tenetur apud proximum; illa enim soluta non est, quando furtum sacerdoti est commissum. Distinguitur enim, utrum rem tuam tibi mittam per meum vel tuum nuntium. Si enim per meum, et meus nuntius tibi non reddat, non liberor; sed si per tuum, sive tuus nuntius tibi reddat sive non, absolvor. Sacerdos autem cui furtum commissum est, nuntius fuit furis, non eius cui res subrepta est. Si ergo sacerdos rem retinet, fur non liberatur ab obligatione debiti, sed ab obligatione peccati; si tamen adhuc habet animum restituendi si possit.[85]

> Here is the response: the obligation is two-fold: of sin and the debt. By sin, he was obliged to God. But that was remitted through confession. For the obligation of debt, he was obliged and is obliged to the neighbour.

85 Simon of Tournai, "Disputatio xxi," 71–2.

> The obligation was not settled when he committed the stolen item to the priest. For a distinction is made: between sending your thing to you through my messenger or sending it through your messenger. If [the item to be restored is sent] through my messenger, and my messenger does not return it to you, then I am not freed [from the obligation to make restitution]. But if it is sent through your messenger, whether or not he returns it to you, I am absolved [from the obligation of the debt]. Now, the priest to whom the stolen item was committed was the messenger of the thief, and not the messenger of the one from whom it was stolen. Therefore, if the priest retains it, the thief is not released from the obligation of debt but from the obligation of sin, provided that he still has the intention of making restitution, if he can.

In this answer to his "questio," Simon regards the penitent's own priest as a personal "messenger" who represents the penitent, not the victim's interests (unless, of course, restitution is made to the victim's priest). But, unlike Repentaunce, Simon makes no mention of the priest's obligation to return the item [to the rightful owner] entrusted with him [the priest] by his own parishioner. Nor does Simon touch on the priest's culpability in case he benefits from the stolen item given to him [the priest] by the penitent. Although both Repentaunce and Simon regard the relationship between penitent and his own confessor as one of complicity, as between a person and his own messenger, Repentaunce differs from Simon in making the priest [Covetise's own priest] answerable for such complicity as well, and it is this difference that reveals the poem's addition to the received canon law that is otherwise silent about the culpability of confessors on the matter of restitution.

Repentaunce reinforces his point about clerical answerability towards the end of Covetise's confession in both B and C. Repentaunce asserts that even the bishop to whom is entrusted the penitent's unrestituted gains "shal onswerie" for the penitent at divine judgment:

> And ȝif thow wyte neuere to whom ne where to restitute,
> Bere hit to the Bischop, and bide hym of his grace
> To bysetten hit hymsulue as beste be for thy soule;
> For he shal onswerie for the at the hey dome,
> For the and for many mo þat man shal ȝeue a rykenynge. (C 6.343–7)[86]

86 The corresponding lines in B are almost identical: see B 5.290–4.

While advising Covetise to make restitution to the bishop in case he does not know to whom or where to restitute, Repentaunce treats the bishop as playing an intermediary role structurally analogous to that played by Simon's messenger-priest who properly handles or disposes of the stolen item placed in his charge by his penitent. But unlike Simon, Repentaunce holds the clerics entrusted with such unrestituted gains answerable in the afterlife: the confessor is subject to penalties in purgatory should he profit from them, and the bishop, likewise, is subject to "divine judgment" (the hey dome). Repentaunce's reinvention of canon law thus takes the form of finding in an academic question such as Simon's a means of fashioning posthumous penalties for the parish priest and also potentially for the bishop should either cleric disregard the rule on restitution.

Repentaunce's innovative critique of the parish priest in lines present in C (but absent from B) also broadens the regulatory scope of canon 21 of Lateran IV that was introduced in chapter 1 to point to the canon's explicit emphasis on the confessor's need for the physician-like skills of discernment. Here, we return to canon 21 to call attention to implications of that emphasis. The canon mandated that "every faithful member of either sex after having reached the age of discretion, should faithfully confess at least once a year to his own priest and with all his might set about performing the penance enjoined on him."[87] The canon's mandate that "at

---

87 For canon 21, see *Liber extra* 5.38.12 (*CIC*, 2: 887): "Omnis utriusque sexus fidelis, postquam ad annos discretionis pervenerit, omnia sua solus peccata saltem semel in anno fideliter confiteatur proprio sacerdoti, et iniunctam sibi poenitentiam propriis viribus studeat adimplere, suscipiens reverenter ad minus in Pascha eucharistiae sacramentum, nisi forte de proprii sacerdotis consilio ob aliquam rationabilem causam ad tempus ab huiusmodi perceptione duxerit abstinendum, alioquin et vivens ab ingressu ecclesiae arceatur, et moriens Christiana careat sepultura. Unde hoc salutare statutum frequenter in ecclesiis publicetur, ne quisquam ignorantiae caecitate velamen excusationis assumat. Si quis autem alieno sacerdoti voluerit iusta de causa sua confiteri peccata, licentiam prius postulet et obtineat a proprio sacerdote, quum aliter ipse illum non possit absolvere vel ligare" (Every faithful member of either sex, after having reached the age of discretion, should alone faithfully confess at least once a year to his own priest and should try to fulfil the imposed penance according to his ability, receiving reverently at least during Easter the sacrament of the Eucharist, unless perhaps, by the advice of his own priest on account of some reasonable cause, he should abstain from receiving the sacrament for a time; if he fails to obey this mandate, let him be kept from entering the church during his lifetime and let him be denied a Christian burial on his death. Whence, this salutary statute should be published frequently in the churches lest anyone with the blindness of ignorance should assume the veil of excuse. However, if anyone, with just cause, should wish to confess his sins to a priest other than his own, he should first request and obtain a licence from his own priest, since otherwise the other priest would not be able to absolve or bind him).

least once a year one should faithfully confess to one's own parish priest" (saltem semel in anno fideliter confiteatur proprio sacerdoti) implied that only the parish priest knew the parishioners under his charge best and that an intimate knowledge of their daily activities (and not just the sins they confessed) was integral to hearing their confessions. In requiring the priest to know his parishioners' activities from both their confessions and the sources of their tithes, Repentaunce's words, in C, "supplement" a canonical constitution that is already full but they also replace what is deficient in it.[88] Furthermore, Repentaunce's admonition to the parish priest within the penitential forum can be seen as tactically adapting a sacramentally sealed space to educate not just the penitent within the text, as do penitential manuals, but also the confessor himself or the secular clergy outside it. Repentaunce's choice of the penitential forum for such pedagogic work and not any other institutional setting (like the sermon by Reason or the trial of Mede that preceded the confessional scene) might have been dictated by the confidentiality that canon law granted to whatever is sincerely said within confession.[89]

Slight as the differences between the B and C versions of Covetise's confession may appear, they bear witness to C's more pronounced courting and co-producing of the canonist thought on restitution than B. When considered independently, the features peculiar to C (or absent from B) discussed so far may offer little evidence of legal innovation, much less of intervention in canon law. Taken together, however, the features express a vision of restitutive justice different from that extrapolated from the decretal collections and their glosses on regulative maxims. Oriented to an audience of papal "pentauncers" and the parish priests entrusted with the *cura animarum*, this is a vision of the rigour of the rule on restitution that cannot be mitigated, much less dispensed with. The papal penitentiary that Repentaunce invokes or the parish priest that he apostrophizes enables the very discourse about

---

88 I draw on Helen Barr's interpretation of Derrida's "supplement" in her reading of the "*Piers Plowman* Tradition." She explains that such "poems can be seen to supplement institutionalized discourse in the Derridean sense of 'supplement': that which is simultaneously both an enrichment of something already full and a replacement of something which is deficient" ("*Piers Plowman* and Poetic Tradition," 47).

89 Henry A. Kelly summarizes the range of canonist thought on circumstances where the seal of confession did not cover confessed sins: such circumstances include sins insincerely confessed; see his "Penitential Theology," 313–14; see also Lyndwood's *Provinciale*, 5.6.8, *Prohibemus*, 334, and discussed by Kelly in the same essay "Penitential Theology," 256–67.

restitution that gives it jurisdictional specificity, and, as I shall further argue, presents the poem as participating in the canonistic thinking about restorative justice and, more broadly, about the pope's power to dispense from divine or natural law.

From Law to Justice: Restorative Justice in *Piers Plowman* and the *Memoriale presbiterorum*

Recent scholarship has highlighted fourteenth-century anticlerical polemics as a context for understanding the poem's treatment of restitution. Wendy Scase and Michael Haren among others have understood Repentaunce's preoccupation with restitution in terms of the polemical strife between the mendicants and the seculars.[90] Scase argues that C extends the anticlerical scope of B by including parish priests as objects of censure for their neglect of canon law.[91] She sees in Repentaunce's attack on Covetise's parish priest evidence of a "new anticlericalism" that transforms the antifraternal polemics spearheaded in Archbishop of Armagh Richard FitzRalph's *Unusquisque, De pauperie salvatoris* and *Defensio curatorum*.[92] Michael Haren provides the larger

90 Scase, *"Piers Plowman" and the New Anticlericalism*; see also Lawler, "Harlots' Holiness," 141–89; Lawler points out that the subject of miswinnings – whereby absolution is granted for a donation – "grew in importance in Langland's mind as he wrote the B version, to the point that he made it the subject of the final scene … and in the C version expanded it still further" (142–3).

91 For the additions on restitution in the C text, see 6.298–307; commenting on the additions, Scase writes that "[i]n *Piers Plowman* an anticlerical development of this antifraternalism is apparent: antifraternal still, but with implications for other priests brought out too … especially (typically) in the C text revision where Repentaunce warns that any priest who knowingly accepts tithes from ill-gotten gains can discover from the gloss of Ps. 51: 8 'witterly what vsure is to mene' (C 6.304)." See *"Piers Plowman" and the New Anticlericalism*, 29.

92 The expression "new anticlericalism" is taken from the title of Scase's book on *Piers Plowman*; Scase notes that "[t]his [Repentaunce's attack on Covetise's parish priest] example is typical of how in *Piers Plowman* the reference of the polemical language is often wider, and with its implications more developed, than in FitzRalph's writings. What in FitzRalph's polemics was a language for addressing the limited problem of the friars' dominion became a language in which the dominion of all clerics might be discussed, when later political developments made this the more pressing question." See *"Piers Plowman" and the New Anticlericalism*, 29; see also pages 25–8 of Scase's book for a reading of Repentaunce's admonition to Covetise's parish priest concerning the canon on restitution.

historical background to the poem's preoccupation with restitution.[93] Haren explores the moral and satirical affinities between the *Memoriale* and *Piers Plowman*, and discusses in detail the former's recurrent concern with the canon law of restitution.[94]

Without quite acknowledging it, scholars such as Haren tend to treat the relationship between *Piers Plowman* and the *Memoriale* along lines of the influence model: the poem and penitential manual relate to each other unidirectionally and hierarchically. That is, *Piers Plowman* draws on or reflects concerns already articulated in historical sources such as the *Memoriale*. Given the obvious differences of language, genre, and form between *Piers Plowman* and the *Memoriale*, I propose that we treat the relationship between the two as lateral rather than vertical – i.e., in the same way as I treated the relationship between the poem and its formal sources on usury in the previous chapter. Thus, I start with the self-evident observation that both the *Memoriale* and the C version of passus 3 share a commitment to restitutive justice but then go on to explore the different forms in which that commitment is expressed. Doing so will help us see, as we did in the previous chapter's exploration of the poem's treatment of usury, that the C version is also productive of, rather than only derivative from, the received thinking about restitutive justice.

Written in England, the *Memoriale* is "a manual for confessors" and "a thoughtful application of the continental tradition to the mid-fourteenth-century English scene by a puritanical though sensitive observer."[95] The *Memoriale* expresses what Haren terms "a strong legalism in its approach to confessional technique ... by a punctilious, remorseless concern for abstract justice, as is particularly evident in its burning preoccupation with restitution."[96] Describing its approach to

93 In his *Sin and Society in Fourteenth-Century England*, Haren follows William A. Pantin, who long ago identified the *Memoriale presbiterorum* as one of a cluster of penitential works underlying *Piers Plowman's* vision of reform. For an overview of such works contemporary with *Piers Plowman*, see part three of Pantin's *The English Church in the Fourteenth Century*.

94 In his *Sin and Society in Fourteenth-Century England*, Haren notes that "the [*Memoriale*'s] author's contribution [to the subject of restitution] is considerable and he reveals a marked zeal for his subject. It is a trait which is shared by other moralists of the middle and later part of the century, notably Richard FitzRalph, Thomas Brinton, and William Langland" (75).

95 Haren, "Confession, Social Ethics and Social Discipline," in *Handling Sin*, 111.

96 Haren, *Sin and Society*, 4–5.

restitution, Haren writes that the "two outstanding characteristics of the *Memoriale* are its puritanical and legalistic approach to penance – as evidenced principally by the anonymous author's emphasis on the canonical penances and on the overriding necessity of restitution as a prerequisite of absolution in cases where the obligation has arisen."[97] Nowhere is the spirit of restorative justice more apparent than in the *Memoriale*'s section on usury ("De usurariis"). Denouncing the "modern confessors" as "blind or leaders of the blind," the author, like Repentaunce, asserts that they do not have the "power at all of absolving such a sinner [as one who caused his victims to suffer material loss] in this case; but gifted with some part of the booty or some other thing, they cling to the booty, and absolve the robber from the deed, caring not at all that the law demands that restitution be made."[98] Indeed, at one point the *Memoriale* author, like Repentaunce, singles out usury to admonish the reader and uses the second person form to directly address the confessor about the requirement of restitution:

> [Rubric] *De usurariis*[99]
>
> Hic scire debes quod usura singulis diebus, aliquando occulte, aliquando manifeste, exercetur a plerisque, tam clericis quam laicis, qui, recipiendo aliquid ultra sortem, in hoc non credunt se peccare, nec in foro

---

97 Ibid., 77.

98 Here are the relevant sentences from the section "De usurariis" in the *Memoriale*, vol. 2, 219–20: "Tenentur eciam ad restitucionem faciendam dampnum passis, in quantum dampnum dederunt per se vel familiam suam directe vel occasionaliter. Set quicquid hic vel alibi scribatur de materia ista, vix / reperitur aliquis qui de hoc peccato confiteatur, et si aliquociens forsan hoc contingat, plerique tunc confessores moderni et maxime de ordinibus mendicancium ceci et duces cecorum, nullam penitus talem peccatorem in hoc casu absolvendi potestatem habentes, data sibi aliqua parte huiusmodi prede, vel re alia, predonem et alios sibi adherentes absolvunt de facto, de restitucione prout ius exigit facienda / penitus non curantes." [They should also be held to the making of restitution to those having suffered loss insofar as they caused the loss themselves or through their people (servants/ extended family) directly or occasionally. But (despite) whatever is written here or elsewhere concerning this matter, hardly is anyone found who would confess concerning this sin, and if perhaps at times the confession should touch upon it, then the majority of modern confessors and, especially, those belonging to the mendicant orders, blind and leaders of the blind, having no power at all of absolving such a sinner in this case; but gifted with some part of the booty or some other thing, they cling to the booty, and absolve the robber from the deed, caring not at all about making restitution as the law demands.

99 The section is "b.lxii" in Haren's edition, 247.

penitenciali de hoc peccato confitentur, nec confessores moderni aliquid inquirunt de hoc peccato. In foro vero iudiciali, iusticia contra usurarios non redditur, eo quod omnes iudices moderni in exequenda iusticia circa hoc peccatum tepidi sunt et remissi, nec aliqualiter volunt punire hoc peccatum. Caveas igitur tibi, o confessor, ut consideres condiciones cuiuslibet persone tibi quoad hoc confitentis, videlicet, utrum fuerit mercator, sive fuerit clericus sive laicus, et utrum consuevit mutuare peccunias suas vel blada seu alia bona sua aliquibus gravatis, nichil penitus recipiendo a suis debitoribus ultra sortem, et si sic, tunc mutuans non est in culpa. Quod si taliter mutuans aliquid ex convencione receperit vel spem habuerit recipiendi ultra sortem, et postea quicquid ultra recepit, usurarius est censendus ... Multe sunt et alie species usure, quas hic omitto scribere causa brevitatis. Tenebis igitur pro summa quod omnes et singuli usurarii tenentur ad restitucionem usurarum, hoc est enim omnium bonorum illorum que pacto vel alio modo illicito receperunt ultra sortem, faciendam illis vel eorum heredibus a quibus huiusmodi bona sic illicite receperunt, quia usurarii raptores dicuntur, et secundum quod raptor tenetur ad restitucionem, sic et usurarius, qui secundum canones exercendo usuras infamia notantur, et gravi pena a iure statuta puniuntur, prout superius est scriptum suo loco.[100]

[Rubric:] "Concerning usuries." You should know that each day usury is perpetrated by many, sometimes secretly, and sometimes openly, both by clerics and by lay folk who do not believe themselves to sin when they receive more than the principal; neither do penitents confess this sin in the penitential forum nor do modern confessors inquire into this sin. In the judicial forum [i.e., the external forum], justice against the usurers is not rendered because all modern judges are tepid and remiss concerning the justice to be done concerning this sin, and they do not wish in any way to punish this sin. Take care, then, O confessor, that you [in the penitential forum] consider the circumstances of the person confessing to you, namely whether he is a merchant, or cleric or a lay person, and whether he is accustomed to lend his money or his grains or other goods to those in need of them, by receiving nothing beyond the principal from his debtors; and if this is so, then the one lending is not to blame. But if the one lending in such a manner should by agreement receive or have hope of receiving something beyond the principal, and afterwards receives something

100 *Memoriale presbiterorum*, 2: 247–9.

> beyond the principal, he must be regarded as a usurer ... Many are the other species of usury that I omit to mention on account of brevity. In short, you will require therefore that all and each of the usurers be bound to the restitution of the gains of usury – that is, all those goods which by pact or any other illicit mode they received beyond their proper share. It is to be made to them or their heirs from whom they illicitly received goods of this kind, because usurers are called plunderers, and just as a plunderer is held to make restitution, so are the usurers, who, according to the canons, are rendered infamous for practicing usury and are punished by a grave penalty by established law, as mentioned above.

At at least four levels, this passage from the *Memoriale* can uncover a common conceptual apparatus of restorative justice underlying Repentaunce's admonitions to the confessor about the proper handling of usury.[101] First, the *Memoriale* passage deplores the modern confessors' indifference to the sin of usury; second, it enjoins confessors to inquire into the circumstances of the penitent and sins confessed in order to determine whether or not usury is committed; third, it treats the sin of usury as requiring correction in accordance with the rigour of the established justice; fourth, it regards restitution as the appropriate response to usury not merely because it might help the penitent gain salvation but because it serves the social claims of restorative justice.

In passages such as the one quoted above, the *Memoriale* has much in common with the C version's handling of usury, Covetise, and his parish confessor. Like Repentaunce, the *Memoriale* writer addresses the confessor directly in the second-person about the "form you [the confessor] ought to observe and hold, when it pertains to you to impose in a case authorized by law restitution or satisfaction to be done," advising that "first you [the confessor] must always enjoin that the penitent make satisfaction concerning goods acquired wrongly or concerning damages done through him to those persons despoiled or those who have suffered damage or to their heirs or executors, if they can be found"].[102]

---

101 For other similar passages on usury/restitution from the *Memoriale*, see Haren's "The Interrogatories for Officials, Lawyers and Secular Estates of the *Memoriale presbiterorum*," in *Handling Sin*, 123–63.

102 Here is the full passage numbered "b.lxxii" and entitled "De forma restitucionis faciende penitenti iniungenda": "Ex quo supra vidisti de quibusdam personis que ad restitucionem male adquisitorum et satisfaccionem dampnorum datorum de iure obligantur, pro eo quod sic inique agendo mortaliter peccaverunt, quia

Not just the pedagogic form and force of the exhortation in the second-person singular to the confessor relate poem and penitential manual but also the invocation of the maxim of restitution attributed to Augustine. In another substantial passage on restitution, the *Memoriale* author employs both dialogue and the dicta of the maxim in ways that show him and Langland thinking together about restitutive justice but from different perspectives: the former more from that of the penitent and the latter more from that of the confessor.

> [Rubric] "De restitucione male adquisitorum, et dampnorum datorum iniuste."
>
> Circam istam materiam a diversis doctoribus tractatur varie et diffuse, et pauci sunt confessores qui considerando advertunt quid vel qualiter consulte agere debeant in hoc casu, cum quia pro maiori parte confessores moderni sunt iuris ignari, tum quia experti in iure, scripta / doctorum circa materiam huiusmodi in diversis voluminibus sparsa non habent, nec unquam respexerunt, et sic obumbrata acie sue mentis de facili errant in dando consilium salubre taliter delinquentibus, et letalia eorum vulnera / nonnunquam relinquunt / penitus incurata.
>
> Et licet soli episcopi et eorum penitenciarii de peccatis huiusmodi se debent intromittere de iure et nullus alius nisi auctoritate apostolica sibi fuerit specialiter hoc commissum, in casu tamen necessitatis tu presbiter parochialis poteris confessionem taliter delinquencium audire, et vel

---

peccatum proprie est voluntas consequendi vel retinendi quod iusticia vetat, et peccatum dicitur breviter, mali perpetracio, consequenter restat videre quam formam debes observare et tenere, quando iniungere te contingit in casu tibi a iure permisso, restitucionem seu satisfaccionem fore faciendam. Et / primo debes semper iniungere quod penitens satisfaciat de bonis male adquisitis vel de dampnis per ipsum datis, personis spoliatis vel dampnum passis aut eorum heredibus aut executoribus si poterunt inveniri" (Concerning the form of restitution to be imposed on the penitent: From what you have seen above concerning the persons who are obliged by law to make restitution of things acquired wrongly and to make satisfaction of damages given, because they have acted so wickedly that they have sinned mortally, since, properly speaking, sin is the desire of attaining and retaining what justice proscribes, and sin is defined briefly as the perpetration of evil; consequently, it remains to see what form you ought to observe and hold, when it pertains to you to require restitution or satisfaction to be done in a case authorized by law. And, first you must always enjoin that the penitent make satisfaction concerning goods acquired wrongly or damages done by him to those who have been despoiled or have suffered damage, or to their heirs or executors, if they can be found). See *Memoriale presbiterorum*, 2: 269.

consilium dare de modo restitucionis seu satisfaccionis faciende, vel restitucionem seu satisfaccionem confitentibus fore faciendam iniungere, considerata condicione cuiuslibet persone tibi confitentis, et criminis commissi qualitate.

Ut igitur tu confessor circa materiam huiusmodi restitucionis et satisfaccionis faciende lucidius instruaris, scire debes quod quilibet qui iniuste aliena invadit, occupat, consumit, alienat, seu alias de eisdem disponit illicite preter domini voluntatem seu cuiquam iniuriose dampnum dedit tenetur ea restituere seu de eisdem satisfacere illis a quibus illa bona extorsit vel alias qualitercumque maliciose ledit seu dampnum dedit, si vixerint et sciatur quales fuerint et ubi moram traxerint ... Ille tamen qui dampnum dedit, tenetur ad restitucionem in solidum faciendam si tantum habuerit in bonis unde de his competenter / satisfacere poterit. Alioquin frustroria erit sua penitencia quia sibi non dimittetur peccatum, nisi restituerit integre sic ablatum, secundum Augustinum.[103]

[Rubric]: "Concerning the restitution of items acquired wickedly and damages done unjustly." About the matter of restitution, different doctors have treated it in varied and scattered ways and few are the confessors who in considering take notice of what or how they should prudently act in this case, partly because, for the most part, modern confessors are ignorant of the law – and partly because experts in law [i.e., specialized canonists and commentators] do not have the writings of doctors on this matter, dispersed as they are in various books, and have never taken notice of them. And, thus with their mental acuity blunted, they readily err in giving salutary advice to those who sin in such matters, and they frequently leave their deeds and words completely uncured.

Furthermore, even though only bishops and their penitencers ["penitenciarii"] are legally allowed to deal with sins of this kind, and no one else without a commission by apostolic [papal] authority, nevertheless, in cases of necessity, you the parish priest can hear the confession of such sinners and either give them advice concerning the mode of restitution or of satisfaction to be made, or instruct them in confession that restitution or satisfaction must be made, with due consideration for the confessant and the quality of the crime committed.

Therefore, in order that you the confessor be more clearly instructed about such matters of making restitution and satisfaction, you should

103 The section is numbered "b.xxviii"in the *Memoriale presbiterorum*, 2: 195–7.

know that whoever unjustly takes possession of another's possessions, or occupies, consumes, or alienates it, or otherwise disposes of it illicitly against the will of its owner, or wrongfully causes harm to anyone, is held to restitute it or make satisfaction for it to those from whom he extorted those goods or otherwise hurt them maliciously in whatever way or inflicted injury, if they are alive and it can be known who they are and where they live ... One who has caused such harm, however, is held to making restitution for the whole only if he has the wherewithal to make proper satisfaction. Otherwise, his penitence will be in vain because the sin will not be forgiven unless he restitutes wholly what was taken away, according to Augustine.

In the passage above, the *Memoriale* author, like Repentaunce, invokes the "penitenciarii" as well as bishops but, unlike Repentaunce, only to deem bishops alone (apart from clerics permitted by papal authority) authorized to interpose themselves in cases requiring restitution. Likewise, the *Memoriale* author, like Repentaunce, addresses the parish confessor directly in the intimate second person form ("tu presbiter parochialis") but, unlike the allegorical character, only to allow him to give counsel to penitents about restitution in cases of necessity, and impose it (along with satisfaction). Likewise, the *Memoriale* author quotes a version of the same maxim on restitution invoked by Repentaunce in the poem but reads the requirement of restitution as conditional upon the penitent's means of doing so. Read alongside such passages from the *Memoriale*, Repentaunce's injunctions about restitution appear to express a common endeavour to educate the confessor who is wilfully negligent or woefully ignorant of the doctrine of restitutive justice. However, there are crucial differences between the poem and penitential manual – differences that reveal a poetic intervention in the received thinking about restitutive justice. Specifically, in the C passages on Covetise's confession discussed so far, Repentaunce does more than merely exemplify the doctrine on restitution that the *Memoriale* author deems necessary for the *cura animarum* of usurious penitents. Whereas the *Memoriale* author stops short at admonishing confessors about insisting on restitution, Repentaunce, in C, goes farther to spell out and, in effect, promulgate penalties for confessors that neglect the canon. (And, in both B and C, Repentaunce, unlike the *Memoriale* author, holds even bishops answerable in the after-life for those penitents that entrust them with their unrestituted gains). But, then, to what extent, if any, do Repentaunce's words about restitution or punishment for its neglect comprise a reinvention of canon law? Specifically, how does his interpretation of a canonistic rule contribute to or detract from the ideal of restorative justice to which the canonists in their rule-making aspired? And, on the basis of our answers to both questions, what kind of innovation do we see as we move from the B to the C versions of Covetise's confession?

One way to approach such questions is to pose them, as Bradin Cormack does, within the framework not of any concrete law or literary text but of jurisdiction – a principle which both legal and literary texts instantiate when they seek to clarify any matter of regulation. In his recent study of early modern common law and literature, Cormack explores "the intersection of the English legal and literary imaginations from Skelton to Webster" in terms of a premodern definition of jurisdiction as "a power to do justice."[104] To have jurisdiction is to have "*a* power, because it is, conventionally, a power among others, and because, as such, it entails the fundamental juridical dynamic by which the distribution of a given authority both stabilizes and makes contestable an authority's norms."[105]

By viewing jurisdiction as an *ur*-principle of power that legal and literary texts alike draw upon to regulate the world, Cormack provides us with a lens for discovering in other premodern literary texts possibilities of legal innovation. Seen through Cormack's lens, Repentaunce's reading into the maxim punitive consequences for negligent confessors comprises "a force for law."[106] But can Repentaunce's words about and to papal and parochial confessors be understood to have jurisdictional import in the sense of the canons promulgated by the popes themselves?

Pietro Costa and Paolo Grossi, as Cormack has recently argued in his book, offer answers that shed light on the intersection of language and jurisdiction at the very foundation of late medieval law.[107] Drawing on both Costa and Grossi, Cormack finds "in the twelfth-century writings of the earliest scholars (glossators) of the recently discovered Roman law" a means of legal production based on an already existing order.[108] Central to Cormack's reading (of Costa and Grossi) is the inventive role of the medieval glossators' verbal or vocal synthesis and exegesis:

104 Cormack, *A Power to Do Justice*, 1–6.
105 Ibid., 5.
106 Ibid., 1–6.
107 Ibid., 8.
108 Ibid.

"jurisdiction was a speaking of the law (*iuris dictio*)."[109] As Grossi puts it, "*speaking* the law means presupposing it as already created and formed, means rendering it explicit, making it manifest, applying it, not creating it."[110] In light of such a concept of jurisdiction and, adapting Grossi's words on medieval jurists, we may say that canonists spoke the law in order to at once find and found it. Like the maxim on restitution, many of the norms to which the canonistic glossators lent validity had long been in existence from the time of the Church Fathers. And by recording patristic as well as papal and episcopal rulings, the canonists saw their task as finding and harmonizing discordant ones already in existence and expounding their meanings to administrators of the church's courts. In thus verbalizing the norms old and new, of course, canonists demonstrated above all how the norms ought to work, who should implement them and on whom: they produced the law as a coherent jurisdictional system in the sheer process of inventing – in the dual sense of finding and formulating and hence founding – diverse canons.

In C, Repentaunce participates in such an enunciatory and inventive mode of law-making. He does so by challenging and reconceptualizing the hierarchical relationship not so much between members of the clergy as between the canon law thus verbally produced and its enunciating producers such as the popes themselves. That is, Repentaunce speaks the letter of the rule to the papal lawmaker that has the power to mitigate or dispense with the rigour of the rule on restitution. Such a prioritization of the letter of the rule over the dispensatory power of the ecclesiastical lawmaker may not be surprising, given that *Piers Plowman* was produced in a period when popes were the preeminent lawmakers (and rulemakers) and at the same time granters of exemptions from canons.[111]

The papal penitentiary that Repentaunce addresses was the highest authority to which were directed reserved cases that could not

---

109 Ibid.

110 Ibid.; see also Grossi, 131: "Orbene se v'è un concetto logicamente estraneo all'iurisdictio è la creazione del diritto: 'dire' il diritto significa presupporlo gia creato e formato, significa esplicitarlo, renderlo manifesto, applicarlo, non crearlo." I use Bradin Cormack's translation and discussion of Costa's and Grossi's explication of the canonist understanding of jurisdiction.

111 Kirsi Salonen observes, "from the time of Pope Innocent III (1198–1216), the office around the *penitentiarius* [the papal penitentiary] grew rather quickly due to the increasing number of cases submitted from all over the Christian West to the Apostolic See and delegated to the Penitentiary." See Salonen and Schmugge, *A Sip from the "Well of Grace,"* 14.

be resolved by the parish priest or bishop. As Kirsi Salonen explains, "[l]egally speaking, the popes had delegated to the penitentiary the powers to grant four kinds of grace" – two of which Repentaunce appears to allude to in his invocation of the papal penitentiary.[112] The first kind of grace was the power "to grant special absolutions to Christians who had violated the rules of canon law in a specially severe way" such as in "matters of papal reservation"; and "[s]econdly it could grant dispensations to those Christians who needed for some reason to act against the norms of the church and where the church could grant them the possibility to do so."[113] As for the other two papally granted types of grace – "licences and indulgences" – while they do not receive any mention in Covetise's confession, they, as we shall see, are taken up elsewhere in the poem in the narrator's discussion of fraternal licences and papal pardons.

Although we do not have access to the papal penitentiary's registers (especially under the title *De confessionalibus* that would have dealt with cases of restitution related to Covetise's sins) for around the time of the writing of C, historians have been able to reconstruct from contextual sources the nature of the penitentiary's powers to grant absolution. As Salonen and Schmugge point out, "the Penitentiary could grant confessors special licences [such as the *sententia generalis*] to absolve their parishioners from more severe violations ... for example, an ordinary priest could release his parishioners from a special excommunication, normally reserved to the papal authority."[114] All this is to say that by Langland's day canon law became increasingly the expression of papal power and thus dependent on the discretion of popes. Hence, for Repentaunce to speak of the pope or the papal penitentiary's lack of "power" to absolve penitents like Covetise is to verbalize an intervention in legal thought: the idea that a papal rule – indeed Pope Boniface VIII's own fourth rule – once promulgated is independent of its legislator, even as it was authorized by the pope himself. Put in another way, C's law-making from a rule can be seen as an articulate reaction to or even curtailment of the plenary power of the pope to grant absolutions in reserved cases or, for that matter, to take advantage of the many exceptions already built into canon law.

112 For the papal "letters of pardon" in the four canonical formats, see also pages 171–3 of Müller, "Pardons for Sexual Misconduct."

113 Salonen and Schmugge, *A Sip from the "Well of Grace,"* 17.

114 Ibid., 66.

My conclusion about Repentaunce's intervention in the extra-poetic discourse around the papal power of granting absolution (and indulgences) may at first sight seem brash, if not downright baseless. To be precise, even C's mention of the papal penitentiary's powerlessness to dispense with the rule on restitution extends barely over two lines and does not receive any further attention from Repentaunce in the rest of the passus. But, if we look beyond Covetise's confession to other parts of the poem (in both B and C) that address the papal power of binding and loosing souls, we shall see that Repentaunce's brief assertion does have a "projective horizontality" (to borrow Ralph Hanna's characterization of the "movement toward an end" of any of the three versions of the poem).[115] That is, Repentaunce's words foreshadow the preoccupation with the distinction or even disjunction between doing good deeds (whether by restitution or by satisfaction) and obtaining papal exemptions from them, between the demands of the law and the equally legal discretionary powers of the pope to mitigate its rigour by any of the four graces: absolution, dispensation, indulgence, and licence.

As early as at the close of the confessions of the seven deadly sins in B, for instance, Piers takes up the question of papal power to exemplify the penitent's obligation to feel contrition and perform the penances imposed by the confessor. When Reason's congregation of pilgrims are lost in their search of Truth, Piers offers them a succinct verbal "token" to be spoken to a "man" called "Amende-yow"; the token runs as follows: "I parfourned þe penaunce þe preest me enioyned / And am ful sory of my synnes and so I shal euere / Whan I þynke þeron, þeiȝ I were a pope."[116] Even if he "were a pope," Piers (or the penitent that speaks the "token") implies that he did not take advantage of any papal power to grant himself any pardons or exemptions from the penances required to be performed for his sins. Rather, as he affirms, Piers followed the letter of the law requiring "ful" contrition and the performance of penances "enioyned" by the priest. In speaking thus in the first person, Piers confesses like an exemplary penitent who follows the standard advice on contrition, confession, and satisfaction. And, in verbalizing his submission to the penitential process "þeiȝ [he] were a pope," he articulates a subjunctively safe critique of the papacy's power to grant exemptions.

115 Hanna, "The Versions and Revisions of *Piers Plowman*," 49.

116 B 5.598–600; see the corresponding lines in C 7.245–6: "Y am sory of my synnes and so Y shal euere, / And parformed þe penaunce þat þe prest me hihte."

In subsequent scenes in *Piers Plowman*, Repentaunce's pronouncement about the power or powerlessness of the pope is recalled and reinforced through two concepts formulated by canonists such as Hostiensis and elaborated by theologians such as Giles of Rome.[117] One is the concept of "absolute power" (potestas absoluta): the pope's exercise of his "full power" (plenitudo potestatis) to disregard, with cause, existing canonical norms and, hence, transcend the laws of the church. The other is the concept of "ordinary power" (potestas ordinata): the pope's exercise of his power in accordance with existing canonical norms and, hence, his adherence to the laws of the church. Together both concepts helped canonists and theologians speculate about the circumstances in which the pope could act like a secular prince by being freed from existing laws ("legibus solutus").[118] More pertinent to our reading of Covetise's confession is Pope Boniface VIII's pronouncement on the reach of papal power in his famous bull *Unam sanctam*, which is later gathered in the *Extravagantes communes* in the *Corpus iuris canonici*: favouring papal absolutism, the decretal concludes with the proclamation that "it is necessary for salvation that every person be subject to the Roman Pontiff."[119]

Read in light of such contemporary canonist thinking on papal power, passages in *Piers Plowman* such as the memorable pardon-tearing scene have retrospective significance for the coherence of the poem's vision of canon law: they hark back to Repentaunce's specific enunciatory act of law-making and tease out its implications for thinking about the subjection of powerful "men of law" to the law itself.

---

117 For Hostiensis's concept of "potestas absoluta," see Kenneth Pennington's discussion of the third book of the first and second recensions of Hostiensis's *Lectura* on the *Liber extra* in *The Prince and the Law*, esp. 48–58, as well as 65–73. For Hostiensis's "most detailed and coherent analysis of papal power," Pennington suggests also Hostiensis's comments on Alexander III's decretal *Ex publico* (X 3.32.7), and on three decretals of Innocent III, *Proposuit* (X 3.8.4), *Magnae devotionis* (X. 3.34.7), and *Cum ad monasterium* (X 3.35.6), 56. For a foundational theological contribution to the subject of papal power, see Giles of Rome (Aegidius Romanus), *De ecclesiastica potestate*.

118 For a recent discussion of the limits of papal power in Langland's day, see Canning, *Ideas of Power*, 11–59, and 143.

119 The papal bull is included in the *Extravagantes communes*, 1.8.1 (*CIC*, 2: 1245–6); the concluding sentence of the decretal is as follows: "Porro subesse Romano Pontifici omni humanae creaturae declaramus dicimus, definimus et pronunciamus omnino esse de necessitate salutis."

In his sustained meditation on pardons and penances (in B7/C9) that follows Covetise's confession and the disputation on pardons, the narrator takes up the question of the pope's absolute power when he distinguishes between the demands of the law and the power of the papal lawmaker to mitigate them. In the C version of the scene, the narrator speculates, albeit more dialectically than does Repentaunce, about the efficacy and, arguably, even the legitimacy of the pope's plenary or discretionary powers:

> ȝet hath þe Pope power pardoun to graunte
> To peple, withouten penaunce to passe into ioye,
> As lettrede men vs lereth and lawe of Holi Churche:
> *Quodcumque ligaueris super terram erit ligatum et in celis ...*
> And so Y leue lely (Lord forbede elles!)
> That pardoun and penaunce and preyeres don saue
> Soules þat haue syneged seuene sythes dedly.
> Ac to truste vp this trionales – treuly, me thynketh,
> Hit is nat so syker for þe soule, certes, as ys Dowel.
> Forthy Y rede ȝow renkes þat riche ben on this erthe:
> Vp truste of ȝoure tresor trionales to haue,
> Be ȝe neuere þe baldere to breke þe ten hestes;
> And nameliche ȝe maistres, mayres and iuges,
> That haen the welthe of this world and wise men ben holde,
> To purchace ȝow pardoun and the Popes bulles.
> At þe dredful dome when dede shullen ryse
> And comen alle bifore Crist acountes to ȝelde –
> How we ladde oure lyf here and his lawes kepte,
> And how we dede day be day the doem wol reherce.
> A pouheful of pardon there, ne prouinciales lettres,
> Thow we be founden in the fraternite of alle fyue ordres
> And haue indulgences doublefold – but Dowel vs helpe,
> Y sette by pardon nat a pese nat a pye hele! (C 9.324–45)[120]

Invoking the "power" of "the Pope," the narrator initially affirms the "Pope['s] power pardoun to graunte" on the grounds of canon law ("the lawe of Holi Churche"). (It is worth remarking that the corresponding line in B makes no reference at all to any canonistic basis of papal power,

120 The corresponding lines in B are 7.174–95.

as it does not include the line referring to canon law.) Much like Boniface VIII's papal bull proclaiming that each human's salvation depends upon obedience to the pope, the narrator affirms the salvific force of papal pardons and of "preyeres." Indeed, he substantiates his affirmation by invoking Christ's bestowal upon Peter the authority to spiritually bind and loose people on earth, quoting the Latin "*Quodcumque ligaueris super terram erit ligatum et in celis*" (whatsoever you shall bind on earth will also be bound in heaven). Commenting on this passage from *Piers Plowman*, Alastair Minnis helpfully points out that "a standard late medieval exegesis" of the biblical words has it that "two keys were bequeathed to St Peter, as the first pope, and to his successors in perpetuity ... the key of *ordo* (as exercised in priestly ministry) and the other, the key of jurisdiction."[121] In "Distinction 20," in the first part of the *Decretum*, Gratian adduced the same biblical lines to substantiate the apostolic basis for the church power to bind and loose people.[122] And canonists such as Raymond of Peñafort and Hostiensis elaborated on the two keys in the context of the priest's "knowledge of discerning between sins" (scientia discernendi peccatum et peccatum) and

121 Minnis, *Translations of Authority*, 70. Minnis clarifies the medieval distinction between the two keys: the key of *ordo* authorized the priest to free sinners from "the *culpa*, or moral guilt"; the key of jurisdiction "constituted the authority for the issue of indulgence, this being an extra-sacramental means of liberating the sinner from a part or all of his 'temporal' punishment or *pena*" (70).

122 See *Decretum* D. 20, d.a.c. 1, cols 113–14; Friedberg, *CIC*, 1: 65: "Vnde Christus dicturus Petro: 'Quodcumque ligaueris super terram erit ligatum et in caelis, etc' prius dedit sibi claues regni caelorum: in altera dans ei scientiam discernendi inter lepram & lepram, in altera dans sibi potestatem eijciendi aliquos ab Ecclesia vel recipiendi. Cum ergo quaelibet negotia finem accipiant vel in absolutione innocentium vel in condemnatione delinquentium, absolutio vero uel condemnatio non scientiam tantum, sed etiam potestatem praesidentium desideret: apparet quod divinarum tractatores scripturarum, etsi scientia Pontificibus praemineant, tamen, quia dignitatis eorum apicem non sunt adepti, in sacrarum quidem scripturarum expositionibus eis praeponuntur, in causis vero diffiniendis secundum post eos locum merentur." [Whence Christ would say to Peter: "Whatsoever you shall bind on earth shall be bound in heaven," and so on ... first he gave him the keys of the kingdom of heaven; with one [key], he gave him the knowledge of discerning between leper and leper, and with the other key, he gave him the power of casting some out of the church or of receiving them. Therefore, in whatever business is to be settled – either in the absolution of the innocent or in the condemnation of the delinquent – absolution or damnation requires not only knowledge alone but also the power of those in authority; it is clear that those

the "power of binding and loosing" (potestas ligandi et solvendi).[123] Thus far in the articulation of his view on pardons, the poem's narrator reflects a canonistic – one might even say, common – viewpoint of late medieval orthodoxy.

The narrator in the passage above, however, goes on to reciprocally revise that initial view in what appears to be a dialectical "contra" or counter-move. With the contrastive conjunction "ac," the narrator articulates a complementary, if not contradictory, view. The narrator affirms that "to truste vp this trionales" is "nat so syker" for the "soule" as the performance of "Dowel." And then, addressing an extra-textual audience in the second-person form ("ȝow renkes þat riche ben on this erthe"), the narrator admonishes them about the uncertainty of the papal instruments of grace. In considering papal indulgences (from the "pena" of sin) less certain for any merit than performing the penances mandated by canon law as well as keeping the commandments, the narrator qualifies the regnant canonist view that the papacy and salvation were inextricably intertwined, as made explicit in Boniface VIII's papal bull. The narrator's final juxtaposition of "Dowel" against "a pouheful of pardon" or "prouinciales lettres," raising questions about

---

treating divine scriptures (i.e., theologians), being above pontiffs (including bishops and popes) in knowledge, are certainly preferred with regard to the expositions of scriptures; however, with regard to cases to be settled, they deserve a second place because they have not attained to the apex of pontifical dignity.] Discussing the hypothetical case of a bishop lapsed into heresy, Gratian summarizes such a bishop's lack of power to excommunicate others; Gratian, *Decretum II*. C. 24, q. 1, c. 6, cols 1833–4; see also Friedberg, his editor, *CIC*, 1: 968: [Rubric in italics] "*In persona Petri, ligandi & soluendi ecclesia potestatem accepit*. Quodcumque ligaueris super terram, erit ligatum et in celo. Si hoc Petro tantum dictum est, non hoc facit ecclesia. Si autem in ecclesia fit (vti que quae in terra ligantur, in caelo ligentur, & quae soluuntur in terra, soluantur in caelo, quia, cum excommunicat ecclesia, in caelo ligatur excommuncatus; cum reconciliat ecclesia in caelo soluitur reconciliatus), si ergo hoc in ecclesia fit, Petrus, quando claues accepit, ecclesiam sanctam significauit." [*In the person of Peter, the church received the power of binding and loosing*: "Whatsoever you shall bind on earth will be bound even in heaven." If this was said to Peter alone, the church does not do this. If, however, it takes place in the church (so that what is bound on earth is bound even in heaven, and what is released on earth is also released in heaven, because when the church excommunicates, the excommunicated person is bound in heaven; when the church reconciles, the reconciled person is released in heaven) – if, therefore, this happens in the church, Peter, who received the keys, signified the holy church].

123 Raymond 63.867; for the corresponding passage in Hostiensis, see *Summa aurea*, 5, *De poenitentiis et remissionibus*, 1, col. 1658–9.

the efficacy of papal or episcopal documents to enable one to "passe into ioye" or to "saue soules," revisits and reinforces Repentaunce's concern (in Covetise's confession) with the enforcement of the law irrespective of the papal power to dispense with it.

Several passus later in both B and C in a scene dealing with the posthumous redemption of a pagan, we encounter once again, albeit much less explicitly, the prioritization of penitential "werkes" or "truth" over and above the pope's power as expressed in the "preiere of a pope." Trajan, the pagan in question, "took witnesse at a pope / How he was ded and dampned to dwellen in pyne / For an vncristene creature."[124] Trajan makes clear the powerlessness of the institutional church as he claims that "al þe clergie vnder Crist" could not rescue him "fro helle" / "But oonliche loue and leautee of my laweful domes"[125] but adds that "[the pope] Gregorie wiste þis wel, and wilned to my soule / Sauacion for þe sooþnesse þat he seiȝ in my werkes."[126] Trajan's "oonliche loue and leautee of [his] laweful domes," and "sooþnesse" "in werkes" clearly played a role over and above any papal prayer in securing for him release from perpetual "pyne" or "helle" in the afterlife. To move across several passus, from Repentaunce's to the narrator's views on the "power" of the pope, is to encounter an increasingly sharp emphasis on maintaining the rigour of the law over and above any dispensatory grace that earthly lawmakers have.

And, even more pertinent, Repentaunce's law-making foreshadows Conscience's ultimate discussion of "redde quod debes" and the limits Dobest and Piers place upon the clerical "power" to bind and loose souls. Towards the end of the poem in both B and C, Conscience tells the narrator that Christ "yaf Piers power, and pardon he grauntede: / To alle maner men, mercy and forȝifnesse; / [To] hym might men to assoille of alle manere synnes, / In couenaunt þat þei come and kneweliche to paye / To Piers pardon þe Plowman – *Redde quod debes*."[127] But, crucially, the narrator in both B and C hastens to clarify that this pope-like "power" of binding and loosing souls covers all sins "saue of dette one": "Thus haþ Piers power, be his pardon paied, / To bynde and vnbynde boþe here and ellis / And assoille men of alle synnes saue of dette one."[128]

124 B 11.141–3; the corresponding lines in C are at C 12.77–9.
125 B 11.144–5; the corresponding lines in C are at C 12.80–1.
126 B 11.146–7; the corresponding lines in C are at C 12.82–3.
127 B 19.184–8; the corresponding lines in C are at C 21.184–8.
128 B 19.189–91; the corresponding lines in C are at C 21.189–91.

The stipulation that the pardon can "assoille men of alle synnes saue of dette one" recalls and reinforces Repentaunce's reading of the regulative maxim that absolution is conditional upon restitution or the settling of any debts owed by the penitent to his creditors. Sinners like Covetise cannot be in "dette" to their neighbour(s) in order to be eligible for their confessor's remission of their sins.

In C, Repentaunce's invention of a law out of a regulative maxim can thus be read as the construction of a legal frame of reference for the poem's preoccupation with the "relacioun rect" between members of the Christian community. At the same time, given the "projective horizontality" of this invention across the poem, Repentaunce intervenes in a question that is as current as it is medieval: should the supreme lawmaker be subject to the law or be allowed to override it – especially in matters concerning restitutive justice?[129] The poem's answer in C, as I have suggested, tends towards the view that no one is above the law pertaining to restitution. It is in this sense alone that C can be seen as proposing or promulgating, albeit in a poetic mode, a solution from within the linguistic framework of the Latin maxim formulated as a rule by canonists and authorized by Pope Boniface VIII.[130] Such a solution or, shall we say, answer to the maxim's papal promulgator embodies the poem's striving after a socio-political ideal of justice "on this erthe" – a striving that proceeds from the transformation of a rule into a law and then making it binding on all those entrusted with its interpretation or implementation in the local parish as well as at the papal curia.

129 The expression is Ralph Hanna's; see his "The Versions and Revisions of *Piers Plowman*," 49.

130 Here, I borrow and adapt Fiona Somerset's insights into Langland's innovative use of Latin; see her "Expanding the Langlandian Canon," 86–7.

4 *Satisfactio Operis*: Maxim and Metaphor in Wrong's Trial[1]

Again and again we encounter in *Piers Plowman* penitent and confessor engaged in the perpetuation of sin. Mede laughs, Contricion forgets to weep, and Covetise fails to make restitution. Their fraternal confessors seek and receive gifts from them in return for their sacramental services. An unnamed fraternal confessor receives a "noble"[2] from Mede and Frere Flatrere gropes Contrition for a "pryue payement"[3] whereas Covetise's own parish priest is suspected of granting him absolution without insisting on restitution of the gains made by usury. The confessors parodied thus in the poem hardly touch on, much less require from their penitents, satisfaction ("satisfactio operis") – the final stage of the penitential process.

As with the clerical neglect of restitution discussed in the previous chapter, so with that of satisfaction: from illicit gifts grasped by fraternal confessors to licit indulgences granted by popes or bishops, penitential satisfaction is conspicuous by its avoidance by penitents or commutation by confessors in both B and C. Released not only from the *culpa* but also from the penances due to the *pena* of sin, the penitents nevertheless find themselves vulnerable to penalties in purgatory.[4] Under the friars, the

---

1 I thank Stephen A. Barney for his feedback on this chapter and, especially, on the Latin passages and their translations. I take responsibility for all errors.

2 C 3.47.

3 C 22.365.

4 Within *Piers Plowman* itself, the treatment of "pena" and "culpa" is complex and not necessarily the object of parody, given that Truth famously purchases an indulgence "a pena et a culpa" (B.7/C.9); see Minnis, "'Piers' Protean Pardon." Within the context of late medieval sacramental confession, the penalty ("pena") due to sin was generally settled by works of satisfaction whereas the guilt ("culpa") due to the

penitential forum serves as a site not for computing spiritually satisfactory penances but for commuting them for materially satisfying profits.

Not surprisingly, the tension between penance and pardon has attracted much critical attention since the time of Skeat's edition of *Piers Plowman*. But because most scholars have concentrated on the learned external contexts for the poem's representation of pardons, the treatment of satisfactory penances within the poem has largely been assumed rather than argued. Critiquing our tendency to read a concept or problem in Langland's versions by sole reference to extra-textual sources, Jill Mann has recommended that we focus on its usage within the internal context of the poem.[5] Following Mann's suggestion will help us correct our tendency to read the poem's penitential passages solely within the external contexts that scholars have identified as the poet's sources. Not only that, by attending to what Mann calls the poem's "dynamic" or its "linear development," we shall be able to witness the reciprocal action upon the sources themselves by the poem's allegorical characters – one that engenders novel poetic perspectives on satisfaction in B and C.[6]

---

same sin was absolved sacramentally in the penitential forum or forgiven simply by the penitent's contrition: whether contrition alone without sacramental confession remitted the culpa of sin was a matter of debate, as is evident in Gratian's discussion of the question at, for instance, *Decretum*, II. C. 33 Dist.1 d.a.c. 1, cols 2183–6; Friedberg, *CIC*, 1: 1159: "Vtrum sola cordis contritione & secreta satisfactione absque oris confessione quisque possit Deo satisfacere"; for a general survey of the theology on "pena" and "culpa" in the context of indulgences in late medieval England, see Swanson, *Indulgences*. In his *Summa de paenitentia*, Robert Courçon, however, treats satisfaction as the penance due to the *culpa*, not the *pena*, of sin; see Kennedy, "Robert Courçon on Penance."

5 Mann addresses the same section on Wrong's trial that I examine in this chapter; she highlights the emergence of "the problem of justice versus mercy" as a function of the poem's internal logic; see "Some Observations on 'Structural Annotation,'" 6.

6 Mann recommends attention to the poem's "dynamic" and "linear development" in her discussion of the trial of Wrong: "In the dispute between Pees and Wrong … when Meed's attempt to divert justice is firmly rejected by Conscience … this scene creates a *problem*: if the earthly king is not to be 'bought off' by Meed but is to insist on strict justice, then how can Christ, the heavenly king, be justified in 'redeeming,' buying back, humankind? ... At moments like these I wonder if the constant referral to topoi and discourses outside the poem has distracted attention from its linear development. The alignment of Langland's thought with discourses outside the poem (the Wheel of Fortune, or justice and mercy as appropriate kingly virtues) can blur the sense of the poem's *dynamic*, muffling the questions that drive it forward"; see "Some Observations on 'Structural Annotation,'" 6.

To what extent, then, do characters in B and C dynamically and internally develop notions of penitential satisfaction? How significantly do the two versions differ from each other in their reinventions on this subject? Nowhere are such questions more fruitfully pursued than in Reason's prosecution of Wrong in the "parlement" in passus 4. In the parliamentary proceedings against Wrong, I first uncover a gradual shift in perspective from the secular to the spiritual with regard to the punishment due to him. In Reason's justification of punishing Wrong with penances rather than with secular penalties, I call attention to an increasingly sharp focus on penitential satisfaction. As in the previous chapter, my effort here is to render visible the poem's reinvention of canon law in its interpretation of another normative Latin maxim on satisfaction: "Nullum malum inpunitum ... nullum bonum irremuneratum." This is the maxim that Reason has confessors interpret to determine the punishment for Wrong. Considered by John Alford "a common maxim, especially in the penitential tradition," it frames the complex and conflictual perspectives on the issue of punishment.[7]

When we compare the diverse usages of the Latin quotation in the passus with those commonly found across various penitential texts, we shall discover a novel theory of satisfaction generated from within the poem but with materials drawn from without. This is a theory shaped from chronologically different stages of the late medieval penitential tradition and approached from the dual perspective of penitent and confessor. From the viewpoint of the penitent, the poem shapes a notion of satisfaction as socially productive manual labour to be undertaken for the punishment due to sin. Such a notion was widespread in the period before the high medieval shift in emphasis in the penitential tradition from satisfaction to confession and contrition. This was a shift that Joseph Goering and, more recently, Atria A. Larson consider "the single most important change distinguishing the new directions in penitential teaching and practice in the twelfth and thirteenth centuries."[8]

From the viewpoint of the confessor, the poem also constructs satisfaction as a form of hermeneutic labour, namely, the confessor's task of interpreting the penitential canons for specific sins. In this, the poem moves away from a literalist reading of canonical penances to a

7 Alford, *A Guide to the Quotations*, 42.

8 Goering, "The Summa of Master Serlo," 296. See also the acknowledgement of Goering's position in Larson, *Master of Penance*, 494.

discretionary interpretation of them. In other words, the poem shifts the emphasis from imposing the penances required by the letter of the penitential canons to determining them by attending to their spirit – that is, according to the remorse of the penitent and her/his ability to perform them. This shift becomes increasingly apparent in the penitential treatises that arose with the emergence of the classical canon law and, as we have seen in chapter 1, is prominent in Raymond's treatment of confession and contrition. By 1215, the canons of Lateran IV had placed "a new emphasis" on the "actual confession of sins and contrition of heart rather than on the extent of the penance imposed."[9] By attending to the divergences between the confessors' interpretation of the same Latin maxim in B and C, we can see the poem's intervention in the administration of the penitential forum that canonists such as Raymond of Peñafort sought to regulate. Not unlike the confessors' manuals, the C version both reflects and shapes the answers to the interpretive challenges that confessors in fourteenth century England would have faced when computing penitential satisfaction. Such answers, I contend, comprise a site for the poetic shaping of the received canonist thought on satisfaction.

The Trial of Wrong in the B and C Versions of Passus 4

Passus 4 opens with Reason presiding over secular legal proceedings brought against Mede, but Wrong soon takes her place as defendant.[10] Personifying the "social world of Mede," Wrong faces accusations of sundry crimes against the plaintiff Pees who, by contrast, represents a private individual or, as Galloway suggests, the King's Peace.[11] In his diatribe against Wrong, Reason recalls and reinforces Conscience's critique of Mede's gift-giving (in passus 3, as already discussed in chapter 2) but now in terms of the broader conflict between justice and mercy.

9 Larson, *Master of Penance*, 494.

10 Unless otherwise stated, my analysis of passus 4 applies to both the B and C versions as they are for the most part almost identical with regard to Reason's trial of Wrong. In his "Commentary," Schmidt points to lines 40–107 of passus 4 as the space in which "Mede's Trial modulates into a *Trial of Wrong*, who has injured PEACE and represents the same principle as her vanished would-be groom False." See *Piers Plowman: A Parallel-Text Edition of the A, B, C and Z versions*, 2: 512.

11 Galloway sees Peace as both an individual plaintiff and as the allegorical representative of the King's Peace. See *The Penn Commentary*, 387.

To Reason, mercy obtained at the price of gifts compromises justice – even if such gifts are intended as restitution for the wronged party. Reason's polarization of justice and mercy points to or, to put it polemically, produces the grounds for the innovative thinking about penitential satisfaction that emerges in the course of Wrong's trial.

To be sure, the opposition between justice and mercy opens in a secular space inhabited by litigants, not by penitents. At the outset of passus 4, not the penitential forum but the "parlement" in any of its diverse senses that scholars have identified is the site of the trial of Wrong.[12] On the one side, Reason as royally appointed prosecutor demands that the defendant Wrong suffer the penalty already imposed by the king for his violation of Pees. On the other, "summe men radden Resoun" to "haue reuthe" towards Wrong.[13] Pleading for "mercy" on behalf of the defendant, Mede "profrede Pees a present al of puyre golde."[14] Although Pees inclines to accept the offer, Reason remains insistent that the defendant be punished. In C, Reason assumes the office of "cheef Chaunceller in Cheker and in Parlement," and reinforces his punitive ruthlessness towards Wrong by enumerating in the subjunctive mood several "impossible" conditions for mercy.[15] Deploring the commutation of penalties for mede-based compromises, Reason "emerges as the comprehensive antagonist and opposite of Wrong, embodying the self-sufficient principle of right and law."[16]

At one extended moment, Reason's language changes the frame of reference for prosecuting Wrong. Not only the meaning of Reason's words but also the grammatical moods in which they are delivered reframe justice increasingly from a penitential perspective rather than

12 A.V.C Schmidt glosses the word "parlement" as "a 'prerogative court' meeting under the king to hear complaints from private individuals, particularly against the administration of the law." See *Piers Plowman: Commentary*, 2: 512. Galloway's gloss to the same word notes that "Peace's petition is made in the first instance before clerks, earls, lawyers, and the King's Privy Council, comprised of Conscience and Reason." *The Penn Commentary*, 390.

13 C 4.105; see corresponding B 4.110.

14 C 4.91; see corresponding B 4.95.

15 C 4.185. Schmidt views Reason's conditions for mercy in lines B 4.108–17: "impossibilia … implicitly a programme for reform at all levels of society, if idealistic, are not in themselves incapable of being implemented"; see *Piers Plowman: Commentary*, 2: 513. Galloway, by contrast, is more optimistic and sees the same "impossibilia" as utopian and realizable; see *The Penn Commentary*, 376.

16 Galloway, *The Penn Commentary*, 402.

from a secular one, and, hence implicitly treat Wrong less as a criminal than as a penitent. The interplay of the subjunctive, indicative, and imperative moods orients attention away from a parliamentary to a penitential approach to Wrong's misdeeds – an approach that has been entirely absent from what has thus far (in the passus) been a secular legal process – whether at common law or in a royal prerogative court. Specifically in B 4.113–33/C 4.108–30, Reason resorts at first to the subjunctive mood to list the conditions to be fulfilled in order for him to grant mercy. And, in B 4.134–6/C 4.131–3, he switches to the indicative mood to state a conditional possibility for mercy. But, as if he hadn't made his point clear, Reason in B 4.137–44/ C 4.134–41 reverts to the subjunctive to reinforce the necessity of punishing Wrong, and, finally, in B 4.145–8/C 4.142–5, to a combination of the subjunctive and imperative moods to enjoin only confessors among the audience to interpret the previously subjunctively expressed rigour of royal justice. The last two modal shifts in Reason's language, in particular, cast Wrong's punishment under a penitential rather than a secular penal dispensation.

Here is the passage in which the modal variations gradually orient attention to penitential satisfaction:

"And yet," quod Reson, "by þe Rode! I shal no ruþe haue
While Mede haþ þe maistrie in þis moot-halle.
Ac I may shewe ensamples as I se ouþer.
I seye it by myself," quod he, "and it so were
That I were kyng with coroune to kepen a reaume,
Sholde neuere Wrong in þis world þat I wite myȝte
Ben vnpunysshed in my power, for peril of my soule,
Ne gete my grace þoruȝ giftes, so me God saue!
Ne for no mede haue mercy, but mekenesse it made;
For '*Nullum malum* þe man mette wiþ *inpunitum*
And bad *Nullum bonum* be *irremuneratum*.'
Late þi confessour, sire Kyng, construe þis [on] Englissh,
And if ye werchen it in werk, I wedde myne eris
That Lawe shal ben a laborer and lede afeld donge,
And Loue shal lede þi lond as þe leef likeþ" (B 4.134–48)[17]

17 I quote only the passage in B as it is similar to that in C, which can be found at C 4.131–45.

At first, Reason asserts, in the indicative mood, his refusal to have "ruþe" for Wrong as long as Mede dominates the moot-hall. But, then, after switching to the subjunctive mood in a conditional form, he justifies his lack of "ruþe" by reference not to a secular political factor but to a penitential one. As if admonishing the king and parliament about their possible leniency towards the defendant, Reason uses the subjunctive expression "That I were kyng" to envision an alternative form of royal justice in an alternative "reaume." In his introduction to Middle English grammar, R.D. Fulk observes that this kind of modally marked expression is "timeless but not tenseless: ...the preterite subjunctive is often used in constructions in which the present or future would be used if the mood were indicative."[18] The linguist Fredericus Visser regards such a hypothetical expression in early English as indicating the "modality" rather than the "meaning" of the utterance: the expression points to a mood of "non-fact" unbounded by any time ("wish, imagination, contingency, doubt, diffidence, uncertainty, supposition, potentiality, non-reality, etc").[19]

The shift from the immediate to the imagined, from the temporal indicative to the timeless subjunctive and conditional accompanies (if not causes) a shift in context: from that of royal power to that of penance, marked by the "nullum malum" quotation.[20] In imagining himself to be a king, Reason no doubt takes on a secular role. But, within this role, Reason mobilizes the discourse around the penitential forum and thereby invents a timeless parallel to the temporal court of secular law.

Within, as it were, such an imagined court, Reason petitions for the enforcement of Wrong's punishment in the language of the *cura animarum*. Not just because of Mede's dominance in the moot-hall but "for peril of my [Reason's own] soule," Reason refuses to moderate the penalty due to Wrong. To different degrees in both B and C, Reason underscores personal grounds for favouring justice over mercy. In B, Reason says "I sey it by myself."[21] In the corresponding lines in C, by contrast, Reason changes the preposition "by" to "for" ("Y sey it for mysulf") and thereby expresses a sharper focus on his (Reason's) care

18 Fulk, *An Introduction to Middle English*, 103.

19 Visser, *An Historical Syntax*, 786.

20 For my exploration of the implications of the subjunctive mood in medieval literature, I have both profited from and adapted words from Strohm, "The Subjunctive Grammar of Utopia," 2, 7.

21 B 4.137.

for his own soul (or the personified king's care for his own soul) as the justification for his ruthless prosecution of Wrong.[22] C's replacement of the indefinite article "a" with the determiner "any" to designate the hypothetical "reume" accentuates the universality of Reason's justice. Reason offers, however, one ground for mitigating the rigour of justice: "but mekenesse it made." In offering to grant Wrong "grace" in return for "mekenesse," Reason approaches Wrong more in a penitential than in a prosecutorial manner. Although "mekenesse" in Late Middle English carries the general meaning of gentleness, the same word within penitential usage is linked to contrition. Denise Baker calls attention to a similar collocation of grace and meekness in a passage in the *Shewings* in which Julian of Norwich describes how "afterward god reysed John [the Baptist] to manyfolde more grace and by the contricoun and the mekenesse that he had in hys lyuyng."[23] Just as, for the penitent Julian, "manyfolde more grace" is obtained by means of "the contricoun and the mekenesse," so, for the penitentially inclined Reason, "mekenesse" alone, not "giftes," will obtain his "grace" for the defendant.

In both the B and C versions of Reason's imagined kingdom ("reume"), justice originates as royal (issuing from the crowned king that he personifies) but acquires a spiritual character for the king or the royally appointed prosecutor. That is, Reason now sees the punishment of Wrong less as a secular penalty impacting only the defendant or his body (one may recall the king's sentence to confine Wrong's body in "irens" for seven years)[24] than as a penalty of spiritual import necessary for both the defendant and the prosecuting judge's spiritual wellbeing. Under the juridical dispensation of his subjunctively imagined realm, as Reason emphasizes, Wrong "[s]holde neuere" be "vnpunysshed in [Reason's] power," and "in þis world." Not to punish the wrongdoer in the here and now would entail spiritual peril to the king. Reason also offers in the same subjunctive vein a less subjective justification based on a Latin maxim that he "fragments and introduces macaronically into his verse":[25] "For *Nullum malum* þe man mette wiþ *inpunitum* / And bad *Nullum bonum* be *irremuneratum*." Articulating the consequences of evil and good, this Latin quotation, as Alford's entry on it notes, enjoys a

22 C 4.134.

23 Baker, *Julian of Norwich's "Showings,"* 72.

24 B 4.85–6: "And comaundede a constable to casten hym in irens / 'And [suffre] hym noȝt þise seuen yeer seen his feet ones.'" See also the corresponding C 4.81–2.

25 Gray, "Langland's Quotations," 55.

range of extra-textual usages that, I argue, provide the larger framework for the poem's reinvention of the canon law on satisfaction.[26]

To begin with, the Latin quotation has long elicited comment from scholars from Skeat to Schmidt: they have commented on the allegorical effects of the bilingual structure in which it occurs in the poem. Focusing on its macaronic form, Chambers, Knott, Galloway, and Schmidt underscore the allegory that results from Reason's integration of the Latin words with his own words in English.[27] Despite acknowledging the novelty of such an integration, they have sought to understand the quotation itself by reference to its origins outside the passus. Consequently, scholars have attended to the quotation's extra-textual meanings over and above those engendered by its usages within the poem: its initial usage by Reason, its subsequent usage within the exchanges between Reason and his intended internal audiences, and, finally, its divergent usages by the confessors across the B and C versions of the passus. By attending to these usages we shall uncover an innovative thinking about satisfaction worked out from within the poem – a thinking that at once invokes and differs from the meaning(s) of the quotation in Langland's sources, and thereby makes a contribution to the canonist thought on satisfaction.

The "Nullum malum ..." Maxim within the Passus

First we shall look at the sources to which scholars have traced the quotation. Editors of *Piers Plowman* have been unanimous in singling out Pope Innocent III's *De contemptu mundi* as the principal source for understanding Reason's Latin quotation.[28] Their identification of

26 For Alford's entry on the maxim, see *A Guide to the Quotations*, 42–3.

27 Chambers, "The Authorship of 'Piers Plowman'"; Knott, "Observations on the Authorship of 'Piers the Plowman' – (Concluded)"; Galloway, *The Penn Commentary*, 411–12; Schmidt, *Piers Plowman: Commentary*, 515.

28 Skeat, *The Vision of William*; in his gloss to line 140, Skeat writes: "The quotation is repeated in Pass. xxi., at l. 435. It is taken from the following: 'Ipse est iudex iustus ... qui nullum malum praeterit impunitum, nullum bonum irremuneratum,' Pope Innocent, *De contemptu mundi*, lib. iii. cap. 15." (83) Derek Pearsall writes: "An allusion to a frequently quoted passage (cf. XX 433) from *De contemptu mundi* (iii.15, in PL 217: 746) of Innocent III: '(It is a just judge who leaves) no evil unpunished, no good unrewarded,'" in *Piers Plowman by William Langland*, 94. In his *Commentary*, Schmidt glosses the quotation as "from the definition of the just judge in *De contemptu mundi*, iii 15 of Pope Innocent III (1160–1216)," but adds that "the present use of negative personifications entails a witty transposition of the original predicates: 'The man *No-ill* encountered *unpunished* / And urged that *No-good* go *unrewarded*'" (515).

Innocent III's text, however, appears to be dictated less by the quotation's role in passus 4 than by its recurrence in passus 18 where, spoken by Christ, it encapsulates the divine judgment of good and evil, and, as Stephen A. Barney notes, "measures the distance between human and divine justice."[29] Having already offered a detailed account of the eternal tortures awaiting the damned and the uselessness of penances for them, Innocent III uses the maxim to underscore the rigour of the divine judge:

> Ipse est judex, fortis et longanimis, qui nec prece, nec pretio, nec amore, nec odio declinat a semita rectitudinis, sed via regia semper incedens, nullum malum praeterit impunitum, nullum bonum irremuneratum relinquit. Hunc ergo nemo potest corrumpere, juxta quod dicit Psalmus: "Tu reddes singulis secundum opera sua" Psal. LXI. (*De contemptu mundi*, liber 3, caput 15)[30]

> He himself is the judge, strong and long-suffering, who neither by prayer, nor by gift, nor by love, nor by hatred departs from the path of rectitude but always advances on the royal way; he passes over no evil unpunished and leaves behind no good unrewarded. No one can corrupt him, just as the Psalm puts it: "you will render to each according to his deeds." Psalm 61:13

From a lexical perspective, both Innocent III and Reason share more or less the same words to characterize the just judge. Furthermore, both deploy the maxim in a juridical context. But these lexical and contextual correspondences between Reason and Innocent III's versions of the maxim do not necessarily indicate that the two versions mean the same thing, for meaning is also dependent upon usage. Mobilized by diverse agents and for diverse ends, versions of a maxim, despite containing the same words and being situated in similar contexts, can and, as discussed below, do vary divergently in meaning.

---

29 As Barney notes, the context of the maxim's appearance as personification in passus 4 is "distinctly secular" but its later use (in B 18.390–3/C 20.432–6) "measures the distance between human and divine justice"; he further adds that "C omits the lines from B (391–2) that supply rational grounds for Jesus's mercy, the cleansing of Purgatory, and the prayers for the dead ... that satisfy sin," *The Penn Commentary V*, 90–1.

30 All quotations from *De contemptu mundi* in this book are from the online version of Jacques-Paul Migne's *Patrologia Latina* (http://pld.chadwyck.com) and are cited by the title, the volume number, and the column, as here: *Patrologia Latina*, vol. 217, col. 0744D.

From the perspective of usage, then, both Innocent III and Reason deploy the same maxim but to signify two different kinds of judgment. Occurring at the end of chapter 15 ("De potentia, sapientia et justitia judicis"), the quotation as used by Innocent III encapsulates the divine judgment in the afterlife, not, as in Reason's case, human or royal judgment in the here and now.[31] Although Innocent III's characterization of the "just judge" (iudex iustus) and of his judgment resembles Reason's ideal of royal justice, the judge invoked in Innocent III's chapter is no earthly king but God himself, and the judgment no human sentence but the particular judgment of each man at his death and the Last Judgment. Despite the apparent similarity between the judicial contexts of the maxim's iteration in passus 4, the spatio-temporal referents of its words are, in Innocent III's case, the other world such as hell and heaven but, in Reason's case, as he puts it affirmatively, "in þis world." To be sure, Innocent III's usage of the quotation has more in common with Christ's usage of the same quotation in passus 18 where he speaks about justice and mercy in the afterlife. It is, therefore, likely that *Piers Plowman's* editors have attempted to understand Reason's usage of the quotation in terms of its verbal concordance with Christ's usage, and, given the latter's context of the Last Judgment, found Innocent's treatise to be a suitable intertext for understanding Reason's words.

Reason's quotation from the perspective of its usage outside passus 4 – whether in passus 18 or in *De contemptu mundi* – eclipses his own markedly different usages of it and, above all, the resultant implications for a poetically internal and canonistically productive understanding of penitential satisfaction. To grasp the innovative work the quotation is made to do within the B and C versions of the passus, we may do

31 "O quantus tunc erit timor et tremor, quantus erit fletus et gemitus; nam si 'columnae coeli contremiscunt et pavent ad nutum eius (Job XXVI), et angeli pacis amare flebunt (Isa. XXXIII)': peccatores autem quid facient? 'Si justus vix salvabitur, impius et peccatores ubi parebunt? (I Petr. IV).' Propterea clamat Propheta: 'Ne intres in judicium cum servo tuo, Domine, quia non justificabitur in conspectu tuo omnis vivens (Psal. CXLII).' – 'Si enim iniquitates observaveris, Domine, quis sustinebit? (Psal. CXX).' Quis enim non timeat judicem potentissimum, sapientissimum et justissimum? Potentissimum, quem nemo potest effugere, sapientissimum, quem nemo potest latere; justissimum, quem nemo potest corrumpere. 'Si fortitudo quaeritur, robustissimus est, sapiens corde, et fortis robore; si aequitas iudicii, nemo audebit pro me testimonium reddere; si justificare me voluero, os meum condemnabit me; si innocentem ostendero, pravum me comprobabit, etiam si simplex fuero (Job IX).'" See Innocent III, *De contemptu mundi*, liber 3, caput 15 (*PL* 217).

well to apply the lesson that Conscience teaches Mede in the previous passus about reading quotations in their linear entirety. In passus 3, Conscience critiques Mede for reading only a part of a quotation and ignoring the whole of it: Mede isolates a clause that "plesed hire herte" for "hadde she loked þat oþer half and þe leef torned / She sholde haue founden fel[l]e wordes folwynge þerafter."[32]

Schooled by Conscience, I shall now examine the usages of the "*Nullum malum*" quotation along the linear trajectory of Reason's trial to determine what they signify collectively. And, just as Conscience addresses properties of syntax to clarify the relations between Mede and Mercede in that passus, so I too will attend to the features of grammar that mark the usages of the quotation by Reason and the confessors addressed by him. By following and furthering Conscience's reading pedagogy, we can grasp, on the poem's own terms, the semantically diverse work the maxim does or is made to do. This is the work of having us think through satisfaction within the passus, for only then can we witness the poem's creative participation outside in the penitential discourse that embeds the same quotation to frame satisfaction albeit differently. Taken together, both the quotation's intra-textual usages in the passus and extra-textual usages that they invoke bear witness to the poem's simultaneous invocation of and intervention in the canonist thinking about satisfactory penances.

Let us return to Reason's initial usage of the quotation. The Latin words that Reason quotes stand out as borrowed, as comprising the speech of an authority or authorities other than his or, for that matter, the poem's own. Reason's integration of the Latin words into his own English and his silence about their authorship result in the kind of "derivative text" that Matthew Fisher has associated with "a particular model of English history writing common after the early thirteenth century."[33] Just as late medieval English history writing, in Fisher's reading, "at once lays claim to the authority derived from its textual antecedents while also standing as a distinct work," so, I claim, Reason's speech too engages in a similar activity. To adapt Fisher's words, Langland "translate[s] linguistically, textually, and temporally" an authoritative maxim for authorizing new ends.[34] By quoting the words in Latin, Reason invokes the authority associated with the learned tradition behind

32 B 3.339–42; see corresponding C 3.489–92.

33 Fisher, *Scribal Authorship*, 60.

34 Ibid.

the maxim but by casting them in a relative clause, Reason does something novel: he grammatically subordinates them to his own English words (foregrounded in the main clause) about retributive justice. One mode of apprehending the novelty of Reason's usage of the quotation is to pay attention to its clausal location and follow the rhetorical implications of such a placement.

By locating the quotation in an evidential clause subordinate to the main clause, Reason orients attention away from the authorship or original sources of the quoted text. This is because Reason's choice of the conjunction "for" (in "For *Nullum malum*") has the rhetorical effect of inducing the audience to think of the quoted words that follow as evidence for his main clause, which contains the words about his utopian vision of justice. In Middle English, the conjunction "for" is a "clause connector occupying an intermediate stage between parataxis and hypotaxis."[35] This conjunction is found in medieval texts not by itself but "in a clause which amplifies or explains another clause by giving an example, citing an authority, making a comparison."[36] Nested within a subordinating clause, the quotation thus functions as a self-evident explanation or amplification of Reason's vision of retributive justice. The structural position of the quotation precludes Reason's intended audience in the parliament from wondering about the semantic complexity or learned textual tradition of the Latin maxim: the "for" connector conveys the impression that the Latin words that follow are neither ambiguous nor unauthoritative. Put in another way, rather than situating the quotation within "a line of descent" from anterior Latin source to vernacular poem, Reason's usage of it places it alongside the temporal present of its iteration in the passus.[37]

The absence of citational reference to Innocent III in Reason's usage frees the quotation from its many authoritative moorings outside the poem. Citationally unmarked, the quotation is ready for mobilization in the

35 Kohnen, "'Connective Profiles' in the History of English Texts," 292, quoting Andreas H. Jucker in "Between Hypotaxis and Parataxis."

36 *Middle English Dictionary*, s.v. "for" (conj.).

37 I am drawing on Sarah Kay's adaptation of Edward Said's words about the incipital quotation as "a specifically secular form of innovation." See Kay, *Parrots and Nightingales*, 20. In the chapter "Beginning Ideas," Said writes: "Beginnings inaugurate a deliberately *other* production of meaning – a gentile (as opposed to a sacred) one. It is 'other' because, in writing, this gentile writing claims a status *alongside* other works: it is *another* work, rather than one in a line of descent from X to Y (*Beginnings*, 13).

here and now of the trial of Wrong. Sarah Kay has recently drawn a useful distinction between medieval "citation" and "quotation": the former signifies "referencing an author, work, or an opinion" whereas the latter stands for "something much more textually precise: the verbatim repetition, in its original form, of a passage that can be anything in length from a complete line of verse to a sequence of several stanzas."[38] Quotations without citations derive their authority on their own terms rather than on account of the status of their unnamed specific source(s) or author(s). This is particularly so for uncited quotations that happen to be maxims, whose truth-claims an audience would be expected to take for granted.

In light of Kay's differentiation between citations and quotations, Reason's Latin words appear as quoted without being cited. Unlike another category of Langland's Latin quotations whose authorship is either cited (by attributions to authorities such as Cato, Augustine, Seneca, and Christ) or self-evidently scriptural, Reason's quoted words belong to the category of "parable-like maxim[s]" that bear no specific reference to any extra-textual usage or authorial ownership.[39] Reason's "quotational" rather than "citational" usage of the maxim is no different than Peter the Chanter's own deployment of the same maxim in the entry on "Devs, Ivdex Districtvs" (God, the severe judge) in his alphabetical *Summa Abel*. (It is worth noting that Peter wrote his entry well before Innocent III wrote *De contemptu mundi* and that Innocent was a member of Peter's circle at Paris).[40] Presenting God as a punisher of sins rather than of sinners, Peter uses the connective "vnde" to underscore the self-evident nature of the quotation:

> Propter omnium peccatorum punitionem, idest quia omnia peccata punit. Vnde: Nullum malum inpunitum, sicut nullum bonum irremuneratum. Et Apostolus: "Reuelatur ira Dei de celo super omnem inpietatem, et iniusticiam hominum," idest uindicta "Dei" uenientis "de celo" ad iudicium, "super omnem impietatem" quantum ad Deum, "et iniusticiam" quantum ad proximum. Non dicit, "Super omnes impios et iniustos," ad ostendendum quod nullum peccatum remanebit impunitum.[41]

---

38 Kay, *Parrots and Nightingales*, 2.

39 Galloway characterizes Reason's Latin quotation as a "parable-like maxim." *The Penn Commentary*, 411.

40 I thank Stephen A. Barney for this observation.

41 Stephen A. Barney, who is currently editing Peter the Chanter's *Summa Abel* for the series *Corpus Christianorum, Continuatio Medievalis*, has generously provided this passage as quoted from Reims, Municipal Library manuscript 508, and corrected by him from other manuscripts.

> On account of the punishment of all sins, that is, he punished all sins. Whence: No evil unpunished, just as no good unrewarded. And the Apostle [Romans 1:18]: "the wrath of God is revealed from heaven over every impiety and injustice of human beings," that is the vengeance of God coming from "heaven" to judgment "over all impiety" insofar as God is concerned, "and injustice" insofar as the neighbour is concerned. He does not say, "over all the impious and the unjust" to show that no sin will remain unpunished.

By using the word "vnde" and omitting any mention of a source, Peter introduces the Latin words as a familiar lexical commonplace. At the same time, however, Peter treats it as semantically in need of clarification or interpretation: whence, he goes on to read the words of the maxim as pertaining to God's punishment of the sins of impiety and injustice (and not of the impious and the unjust sinners themselves).

In like fashion, Reason introduces the maxim as both "familiar and strange, empty and saturated."[42] For, just as it is referentially free from specific authorial ownership or extra-textual source, so it is free to refer to multiple authors or sources. Both these freedoms enable the maxim to authorize Reason's innovative albeit subjunctive vision of royal justice – a vision that, as we shall see, mobilizes a more realistic or, modally speaking, "indicative" innovation about, or even intervention in, two strands of the penitential thought about satisfaction.

The matter of Reason's prosecutorial mercilessness towards Wrong would in all likelihood rest settled or remain speculatively enclosed in the subjunctive were the Latin quotation not abruptly recast in a different modality and redirected to an audience singled out from the, as it were, *real* parliamentary space of Wrong's trial. Reason's choice of a dual modality of expression alone changes the context for understanding the quoted words and shifts the emphasis from his initial usage within the subjunctive confines of his vision to his subsequent usage within the grammatically indicative confines of Wrong's trial. To move across the two usages is to move from subjunctive vision to indicative realization, from a justification of punishing Wrong on personal grounds to a broader ecclesiastical reflection on penances to be interpreted and imposed by confessors: a reflection that, as we shall see, finds expression in a discursively marked vocabulary of satisfaction found in a penitential strand dominant well before Langland's day.

42 I adapt Paul Strohm's words from *Theory and the Premodern Text*, 167–8.

In both B and C, with Reason's redirection of the Latin maxim, the change from the purely subjunctive to a mood that hovers between the subjunctive and imperative, engenders something new: the introduction or irruption of a penitential frame of reference into the indicatively "real" parliamentary trial. Put differently, Reason's reformed vision of royal justice breaches its subjunctive clausal boundaries to impact the indicative world of Wrong's trial. Here is how it happens. With the third-person present subjunctive "Late þi confessour," Reason indirectly addresses the king's personal confessor, whom he then enjoins to "construe"[43] the same Latin maxim in English. With the vocative exclamation "Sire Kyng" that follows, Reason momentarily breaks out of his subjunctive mode into an imperative mode to exhort the king present before him to follow his injunction. Together, the third person subjunctive and the second person vocative would have the force of the imperative mood for Reason's audience and, presumably, for Langland's initial readers, especially those trained in Latin. This is because, as Olga Fischer observes, "[i]n Middle English the forms of the imperative singular and the subjunctive present singular coalesced."[44] From a rhetorical perspective then Middle English would recall Latin's use of second person singular for the imperative and the jussive subjunctive – a grammatical analogy borne out by Reason's bilingualism at this point of his speech. In any case, the twofold aspect of Reason's modality of address alone (irrespective of the quotation's meaning) indicates the new work that the quotation is now made to do.

Seen from its imperative aspect, Reason's address appears as a second person injunction to the king to allow ("Late") his confessor to put the maxim into practice. Seen from its subjunctive aspect, the same address appears to be a third person exhortation to the confessor. In either case, the maxim is no longer anchored in the non-factual context of an alternative royal justice where it functioned as a rationale for Reason's ideal of retributive justice. In redirecting the quoted words to "þi confessour" and enjoining him to interpret them, Reason takes the maxim out of its initial location within the king's prerogative or parliamentary court and places it within a forum administered by confessors. In doing so, Reason moves the context for the maxim from the domain of generalized secular law to that of the canon law of penance.[45]

43 B 4.145.

44 Fischer, "Syntax," 249.

45 The secular texts in which the quotation occurs include Walter Map's *De Nugis Curialium*.

The shift in context for the maxim is accompanied by a corresponding shift in audience-response within the passus. When multiple confessors ("Clerkes þat were confessours coupled hem togideres") translate the Latin maxim, they in turn underscore the change in the setting for and, hence, in the significance of, its meaning.[46] In a recent essay on Langland's learning, Christopher Cannon has remarked that school-room pedagogy – especially medieval texts of elementary Latin grammar used by school boys – has left its mark throughout *Piers Plowman*.[47] Reason's magisterial assignment of the Latin maxim to the royal confessor for its English translation illustrates the application of such a pedagogy in the interests of the king and his fraternal confessor. Like the canonists Raymond of Peñafort and Paul of Hungary, who directed their penitential texts to Dominican friars entrusted with the *cura animarum*, Reason directs the much shorter text of the quotation to the king's fraternal confessor to dramatize a teaching moment about satisfaction – namely, to demonstrate how the king's confessor should construe the normative words on good and evil to impose penances upon offenders like Wrong in the penitential forum.

Anne Middleton has made the case for *Piers Plowman* as a public poem in the sense that even as characters address each other internally, they should be read as speaking to an external audience.[48] And, more recently, Mary Clemente Davlin has furthered Middleton's claim about the poem's publicness by arguing that "Langland causes readers to perceive themselves as part of the community rather than as readers or audience."[49] Middleton's and Davlin's argument about *Piers Plowman*'s implication of a textually external audience within its poetic world reveals the quotation's appeal to interpreters beyond the king's confessor(s) – to contemporary confessors such as those among the monastic and fraternal readers that, as Morton Bloomfield and Lawrence Clopper have respectively argued, were likely to have been the intended audience for the poem.[50] With the movement of the quotation

46 B 4.149; see corresponding C 4.146.

47 Cannon, "Langland's *Ars Grammatica*." See also Cannon, "From Literacy to Literature." See also Lawler's response to Cannon in "Langland Versificator."

48 Middleton, "The Audience and Public of *Piers Plowman*," 113.

49 Davlin, "Chaucer and Langland as Religious Writers," 130.

50 Bloomfield's claim about monks comprising the intended audience for the poem is based on the structure of "the commentary or gloss" unique to the poem; see *Piers Plowman as a Fourteenth Century Apocalypse*, 31–2; Clopper claims that "Langland is deeply influenced by Franciscan thought," and "believe[s] that he directs his text to a special audience – the Franciscans – in order to call them to reform." See *Songes of Rechelesnesse*, 19.

from Reason to the confessors, the poem's "dynamic" can be said to turn inter-textual. This is because the usages that the king's confessor (or the other confessors) would most likely be familiar with would be found in confessors' manuals such as those that mention the quotation, where, as we shall see, it encapsulates the necessity of penitential satisfaction. When viewed simultaneously from the multiple perspective of its usages within and without the passus, the quotation, as we shall also see, emerges not merely as derivative of past usages but also, more significantly, as co-productive of thought about satisfaction.

The Outward Dynamic – From Intra-Textual Usage to Inter-Textual Usage

In his exhaustive study of Langland's Latin borrowings, Nicholas Gray identifies an assortment of canonically trained authors as the primary users of Reason's Latin quotation in their penitential writings.[51] Among them Gray singles out the Dominican professor of law Paul of Hungary and the canonist Hostiensis (whose *Summa aurea* Walter de Brugge, we may recall, mentions in his bequest) as offering the version of the quotation lexically closest to what Langland assigns to Reason.[52] As he puts it, "Langland's wording is exactly paralleled in Paul of Hungary's *De confessione*, and Hostiensis's *Summa aurea* (Liber 5, "De remissionibus," sec. 7, fol. 489r)."[53] Winfried Trusen, writes that Paul of Hungary was among three canonists who were granted the task of producing manuals that would enable confessors "to the find the right judgment" (das richtige Urteil zu finden).[54] From the start, the manuals were to exhibit a pronounced emphasis on the transmission of juridical knowledge.[55] Among

51 Gray, "Langland's Quotations," 55–6.

52 In his "*Forum internum*," Trusen notes that Paul of Hungary was a "jurist in Bologna" before he took up holy orders ("der vor seinem Eintritt in den Orden Rechtsgelehrter in Bologna war" (92–3).

53 Gray, "Langland's Quotations," 55–6.

54 Trusen, "*Forum internum*," 92: "Zunächst wurde an drei bekannte Kanonisten, die in Bologna gelehrt hatten, der Auftrag erteilt, möglichst rasch die lehrmässigen Grundlagen für eine Instruktion der Konfessoren, die der Orden in die Seelsorge schicken wollte, zu schaffen. Sie sollten Handbücher herstellen, die die Beichtväter in die Lage versetzen konnten, das richtige Urteil zu finden."

55 "Da die theologische Ausbildung anderweitig sichergestellt war, schien man von Anfang an das Schwergewicht auf die Kenntnisvermittlung der rechtlichen Materie gelegt zu haben." See Trusen, "*Forum internum*," 92.

the many places where Paul of Hungary underscores such knowledge is in the section on the impediments to confessions ("De impendimentis confexionum") where he deploys the quotation to warn against the sinner's desperation of, or over-confident belief in, divine mercy:

> Item nimia misericordia divina: qui credunt de[um] adeo misericordem quod neminem puniat et omnes salvos faciat in qua opinione dicitur oregenes fuisse propter illam auctoritatem: nichil eorum que fecisti domine. Set isti male attendunt prophetam dicentem misericordiam et iudicium cantabo tibi domine et regulam gregorii et augustini: nullum malum impunitum. nullum bonum irremuneratum, ut colligitur *De penit.* dis.1 cap. *Si peccatum* et consequentia. (201)[56]
>
> Another impediment is excessive divine mercy: those who believe God merciful to the extent that he would punish no one and would render all saved, of which opinion Origen is said to have been, on the basis of the authority [Wisdom 11.25: "O Lord, thou hatest nothing of what thou hast made"]. But these people listen poorly to the prophet saying, "I will sing of thy mercy and judgment, O Lord" (Ps. 100.1), and the rule of Gregory and Augustine, "No evil unpunished; no good unrewarded," which can be gathered from the canon *Si peccatum*, from Gratian's *De penitentia*, D. 1, canon 82, and the next canon *Sicut primi*, from Augustine's *De peccatorum meritis*.

From a lexical perspective, Paul of Hungary's quotation parallels Reason's. From the perspective of usage, however, Paul's and Reason's versions of the quotation differ significantly. In Paul's hands, the quotation serves to admonish the overconfident sinner about the necessity of confession: the sinner must go to confession or else face divine punishment in the afterlife.

In stimulating contrast to Paul's usage of the quotation is that of Hostiensis. Unlike Paul, Hostiensis places the quotation within the context of indulgences that relieve or reduce the penances enjoined by the confessor. Considering the case of the commutation of a seven-year long penance for the alms of seven *denarii*, Hostiensis first summarizes Raymond's view about the uncertainty of knowing whether the recipient is completely freed from the imposed penances. Hostiensis then offers his own view that Christ remitted all our sins and that his bloody

---

56 Paul of Hungary, *De confessione*, 201.

crucifixion and the blood of the martyrs and saints are sufficient for the expiation of the human sinner:

> Tu dicas credendum esse quod omnino liberatus est, quod dubium non est, quo ad ecclesiam militantem, unde nec tenetur ulterius jejunare: nam per indulgentiam injunctae poenitentiae remittuntur, vt patet *infra eodem cum ex eo* § *ad hoc*, ibi intra 40. dies de injunctis penitentiis, & c. sed dicas sic: Peccatum remanet impunitum, quod est contra August. dicentem, Nullum malum impunitum, nullum bonum irremuneratum, respondeo: nullum est impunitum, quia Christus peccata nostra tulit: & pro peccatis nostris mortuus est: & pro nobis omnibus passus est. Sed minima gutta sanguinis Christi sufficeret ad expiationem omnium peccatorum & redemptionem omnium hominum qui vnquam fuerint, vel esse possent, cum respectu Dei totus mundus nihil sit ... & filius Dei non solum guttam, sed totum sanguinem fuderit pro peccatoribus, & praeterea Martyres pro fide & ecclesia sanguinem suum fuderunt, & ultra quam peccassent puniti fuerunt: restat quod in dicta effusione omne peccatum punitum est: & haec sanguinis effusio est thesaurus in scrinio ecclesiae repositus, cujus claves habet ecclesia: vnde quando vult, potest scrinium aperire, & thesaurum suum cui voluerit communicare, remissiones & indulgentias fidelibus faciendo: & sic peccatum non remanet impunitum: quia punitum fuit in filio Dei & Martyribus sanctis suis, secundum dominum Hugo. Cardi. Nec obstat illud August. quia aut homo punit peccatum temporaliter, aut Deus puniet aeternaliter, vt innuitur *de poen. distinctio. sext. paragrapho fin.* Quia punitur in confessione propter verecundiam, vt patet in his, quae notatur *supra eodem sub rubri. de poen.* § *qualis, sub paragrapho amara.* [*Summa aurea*, 5, *De poenitentiis et remissionibus*, cols 1663–4][57]

> You should say that it should be believed that he [the person receiving indulgences] is completely freed [and] that there is no doubt regarding this for the militant church, whence he is not bound to fast any further: for by means of the indulgence the imposed penances are remitted, as is evident within the same chapter *cum ex eo*, paragraph *ad hoc*, there within 40 days concerning the imposed penance etc but you should say thus: sin remains unpunished, which is the opposite of what Augustine says: "No evil unpunished, no good unrewarded." I respond [to this maxim]: Nothing

57 I have not mentioned the section number in which this extract is found as the numbering is inconsistent but the passage cited above is to be found under the section beginning with "Ad quid valeant."

> is unpunished because Christ remitted our sins, and died for our sins, and suffered for all of us. But the least drop of Christ's blood would be sufficient for the expiation of all sinners and redemption of all human beings who ever existed or can exist, with respect to God, the whole world is nothing ... and the Son of God poured out not only a drop but all his blood for sinners and furthermore the martyrs shed their blood for faith and the church, and they were punished more than they had sinned. It remains that in the abovementioned effusion [of blood] every sin is punished, and this effusion of blood is the treasure reposed in the chest of the church, whose keys the church holds: whence, when the church wants, she can open the chest and convey the treasure to whomever she wants, by granting remissions and indulgences to the faithful: and thus sin does not remain unpunished, because it was punished in the Son of God and in his saintly martyrs, according to the Lord Cardinal Hugh of Saint-Cher. What Augustine says is no counter-argument, because either man punishes sin temporally or God punishes eternally, as is inferred from *De poenitentiis*, sixth distinction, in the last paragraph. Because [sin] is punished in confession on account of shame, as is evident in these words which are noted above in the same [section] under the rubric *De poenitentiis*, section *qualis*, in the paragraph *amara*.

Unlike Paul of Hungary, Hostiensis reads the maxim as an expression of Christ's remission of sins and redemption of sinners, and thereby orients it away from any penalty due to the sinner and his confessor.

The penitential sources to which Gray traces Reason's Latin quotation include those that contain the clause on punishment that also speaks to purgatorial penances. One such source is the *Summa de paenitentia* by Cardinal Robert Courçon – "perhaps the most influential in continuing and developing the unique blend of canon law and theology that characterized the practical 'theology' of many Parisian masters in the late twelfth and early thirteenth century."[58] Robert introduces the quotation in a "questio" that warns confessors about the penances they would have to suffer in purgatory should they impose less satisfaction on the penitent than is required by the penitent's guilt ("culpa"):

> [Rubric] "b. De sacerdote qui minorem vel maiorem iniungat penitentiam." Questio. Sequitur de secunda questione. Ecce aliquis sacerdos minorem iniungat satisfactionem penitenti quam exigat culpa eius uel

58 Goering, "The Internal Forum," 415.

canon penitentialis. Sed nullum malum inpunitum; ergo cum his non plene puniatur residuum illius penitentie supplebit in purgatorio; ergo pena quam iste sufferet in purgatorio imputabitur sacerdoti quia si eum hic sufficienter puniret statim volaret. (325)[59]

[Rubric] "b. Concerning a priest who should impose less or more penance." This question follows from the second question. Say that a certain priest should impose less satisfaction on the penitent than his guilt or the penitential canon requires. But no evil goes unpunished; therefore, when he [the penitent] is not fully punished by them [imposed penances], he will fulfill the remainder of his penance in purgatory; therefore, the penalty which he would suffer in purgatory will be imputed to the priest, because if he [the priest] were to punish him sufficiently, then he would fly up at once [from purgatory to heaven].

In keeping with the dialectical method of reasoning, Robert goes on to cite an "objection" (obiectio) that justifies reducing the penances otherwise required by the penitent's guilt, and then offers his own "solution" (solutio) that advises the confessor to exercise discretion when calculating satisfaction.[60] In Robert Courçon's "questio," the quotation

59 All quotations from Robert Courçon's *Summa de paenitentia* are taken from V.L. Kennedy's edition.

60 Here is the "obiectio" that Robert Courçon presents as saying that every priest should lessen rather than increase the penances for the penalty of sin: "Sed videtur quod omnis sacerdos debeat potius subtrahere de pena iniungenda quam augmentare penitentias quia dicit auctoritas, quod emolliende sunt pene et non exasperande, et misericordia superexaltat iudicium. Et Gregorius dicit: Culpa est totam persequi culpam. Preterea melius est ut penitens suppleat in purgatorio quam in gehennali supplicio; ne ergo austeritate penitentie redeat ad vomitum potius est mollienda pena quam exasperanda." Robert Courçon's own "solutio" of the contrary positions laid out in the "questio" and "obiectio" underscores the care the priest should take to examine every circumstance of the penitent diligently, and to remove all the roots and actions of sinning, and to see if the penitent is prone to returning to sin and, accordingly, diminish the "pena" lest the austerity of the "pena" should cause him as if to despair and to descend completely into hell: "Quod concedimus omnis circumstancia penitentis diligenter est attenda, scilicet utrum lubricus uel delicatus, utrum spiritualibus nequitiis infectus quia semper contraria contrariis sunt curanda … sacerdos in confessione debet precidere omnes radices et actiones peccandi et tandem si videat pronum et lubricum ad recidiuandum temperet et diminuat penam penitentie ne austeritate pene quasi desperando redeat in idipsum culpe et ita descendat in idipsum gehenne iuxta euangeli: *Nolite mittere uinum nouum in utres ueteres, alioquin rumpentur et uinum effundetur*" (325–6).

"nullum malum" is deployed to underscore the obligation to complete the full amount of satisfaction required by the "culpa" of the penitent. As the two conclusive conjunctions "therefore" (ergo) indicate, the "questio" applies the quotation also to the confessor, who will be responsible for the remainder ("residuum") of the penitent's satisfaction that will be supplied in purgatory and, significantly, imputed to him as well.

Unike Paul of Hungary but like Robert Courçon, Reason mobilizes the quotation to stress the confessor's culpability should the penitent receive less penance than is proportionate to his guilt. In Reason's hands, the quotation stands neither for the eternal punishment due to the impenitent nor for the purgatorial penance due to the penitent that has not completed all the imposed penances. Rather it stands for the confessor's work of translating the quotation into satisfactory penances. In this, Reason's usage parallels Alain de Lille's in his penitential treatise *Liber poenitentialis*. "Combining the traditional canons with the latest teachings of the schools of law and theology," Alain wrote the *Liber* for practical use by confessors.[61] Under the section on satisfaction, Alain deploys a version of the same quotation to justify the confessor's duty to calculate and impose satisfactory penances:

> [Rubric] "Quod sacerdos debet variare poenitentiam, si reus non potest sustinere, et quae virtutes contra quae vitia sint opponendae."
>
> ... Ergo quia contrariis contraria curantur qui rapuit aliena jam pauperibus distribuat sua. Ubi oculorum sequebatur lascivia, sacra inspiciatur pagina. Et his exemplis malum semper mutetur in contrarium, adhibita satisfactione peccatorum quia sicut nullum bonum irremuneratum ita nullum malum impunitum. Puniatur ergo malum temporali satisfactione, ne puniatur aeterna damnatione. Si autem peccator jejunare non potest, saltem oret, orationes etiam condiat eleemosynis.[62]

> [Rubric] "That the priest should vary penance, if the penitent is not able to sustain [it], and what virtues ought to be opposed to what vices."
>
> ... Because contraries are cured by contraries, anyone who pillages another's goods should distribute his goods to the poor. One who pursues things lustful to the eyes should examine the sacred page. And, in these

61 Goering, "The Internal Forum," 416; Goering notes on the same page that Alain dedicated his penitential treatise to Henry, Archbishop of Bourges (1119–99).

62 Alain de Lille, *Liber poenitentialis* 2: 7, 49–50.

> examples, evil should always be changed into its contrary, and satisfaction for sins be made because just as no good is unrewarded, so no evil is unpunished. Therefore, evil should be punished with temporal satisfaction, lest it be punished with eternal damnation. But if the sinner cannot fast, at least he should pray; also he should season prayers with almsgiving.

For Alain, the quotation frames his discussion of the satisfaction that the confessor ought to impose for the penitent's sins ("adhibita satisfactione peccatorum"). Both Paul of Hungary's and Alain's usages warn of the posthumous punishment that the sinner would suffer if s/he did not perform the appropriate penances due to the penalty for sin. However, for Alain, unlike for Paul of Hungary, the quotation is used to enjoin the confessor, not the penitent, to attend to the requirement of temporal satisfaction and thereby enable the penitent to avoid eternal damnation. In recommending specific penances (such as alms-giving, praying, and fasting), Alain further emphasizes the confessor's responsibility for imposing them upon the penitent in the interests of the latter's salvation.

While the parallel between Alain's and Reason's usages of the quotation helps us see the poem's reflection of a widespread concern with educating confessors about penitential satisfaction, it barely sheds light on the poem's innovation around the received thinking about satisfactory penances. To witness the poem's reinvention of satisfaction, as it were, we need to get to the point where Reason exhorts confessors to translate the quotation into "werk":

> And if ye werchen it in werk, I wedde myne eris
> That Lawe shal ben a laborer and lede afeld donge,
> And Loue shal lede þi lond as þe leef likeþ. (B 4.146–8)

The diction of labour and the figure of the labourer together evoke an idea of satisfaction as corporal work.[63] This idea is found not so much in Alain as in his contemporary Thomas of Chobham and, more generally, in the penitential tradition predating both writers. In his *Summa confessorum*, a treatise written for an audience of confessors in England on the eve of Lateran IV, Thomas characterizes satisfaction as the

63 In his "Study of *Piers Plowman*," Gray notes that "[o]f the three kinds of satisfaction, it is corporal penance, fasting and the like, which is most in evidence in *Piers Plowman*" (187).

performance of physical penances in the interests of the community at large:

> Ad quod dicendum est quod satisfactio non dicitur nisi quando aliquid datur ab uno et recipitur ab alio pro iniuria sibi illata ...
>
> Vel alia ratio potest esse quod omnis satisfactio debet esse penalis. Sed per fidem qua deus videtur, et per caritatem qua deus diligitur, potius est delectatio quam pena, et ideo non est ibi satisfactio.
>
> Per ieiunium autem hic accipitur omnis labor corporis, quia bene ieiunat qui fatigat corpus suum in servitio dei. Per eleemosynam autem intelligitur omne beneficium impensum proximo, sicut dicitur super illum locum: *omni ... petenti te tribue*, scilicet *rem vel increpationem* vel orationem. Per *rem* intelligis manualem eleemosynam vel consilium/vel protectionem, quia magnam eleemosynam facit qui bonum consilium dat pauperi vel alium defendit.[64]

> It must be said that it is not called satisfaction except when something is given by one and received by another for injury done to that person ...
>
> Or, another reason can be that every satisfaction must be painful. But, in light of the faith by which God is seen and the love by which God is loved, pleasure is more powerful than pain/penalty and there is no satisfaction there. However, as used here, "fasting" includes every labour of the body, because the one who fasts well fatigues his body in the service of God. By "alms" is understood every good thing undertaken for the neighbour, as mentioned in the commentary on that passage: "Give to everyone asking of you," whether some object or advocacy or prayer. By "object" understand physical alms-giving or advice or protection, because the one who gives good counsel to the poor or defends another offers great alms.

Here Thomas enumerates the actions that Alain associates with satisfaction but, unlike him, goes on to elaborate on its nature. To Thomas, an act of satisfaction should not be a "pleasure" (delectatio) but rather a "pain" (pena): it must be "painful" (penalis). Satisfaction entails what "fatigues the body" (fatigat corpus) "in the service of God" (in servitio dei). One such action is "fasting" (ieiunium), which is understood as the "labour of the body" (labor corporis). Another such action is "alms-giving" (eleemosyna), which too involves labour in that it is the "corporal" (manualem) work of offering advice or protection. In another

64 Thomas, *Summa confessorum*, art. 1, q. iiia, *De speciebus satisfactionis*, 9–10.

passage, Thomas explains what the sinner must undergo in order to make satisfaction:

> Sed quia pena est materia patientie, nec sine pena posset opus patientie exerceri, nec homo mereri per patientiam, ideo sine pena penitentia esse non potest.[65]
>
> But because pain is the matter ("materia") of suffering, and because, without pain, the work of suffering cannot be exerted nor can a human being merit through suffering; therefore, without pain ("pena"), penance is not possible.

What emerges into relief from these descriptions of satisfaction is a linguistic register of corporeal punishment. Lexically speaking, Thomas's diction of satisfaction – the "matter of suffering" and "the work of suffering to be exerted" – resonates with Reason's own diction of penance ("werchen" or "werk") in his advice to the confessors on translating the quotation.

Penitential literature pre-dating Thomas is even more explicit about corporeal labour as the primary means of experiencing or expressing satisfaction for sin. Writing in the twelfth century in his fourth sermon for Lent on "De poenitentia," the bishop Hildebertus characterizes "satisfaction by works" (operis satisfactio) in a language replete with verbs and nouns evocative of physical exertion:

> De operis satisfactione ipse idem alibi ait: "Laboravi in gemitu meo (Psal. VI, 7)." Memorans enim gemitum, et laboris plenitudinem per gemitum, operis satisfactionem nomine laboris significavit. Satisfactio autem maxime in tribus consistit, scilicet, jejunio, oratione et eleemosyna. Jejunium vero duplex est, corporale et spirituale. Corporale est, quo nos contemperamus a cibis; spirituale, quo abstinemus a vitiis. Non sufficit, nec valet carnem macerare corporali parsimonia, nisi intus castificet mentem spirituali abstinentia, quia vitia caveamus, delicta vitemus. Similiter est et oratio oris, et oratio cordis. Non valet clamor labiorum sine labore animorum ... Eleemosyna quoque gemina est, corporalis et spiritualis. Corporalis manum aperit, egentibus subvenit; spiritualis autem errantem corrigit, et delinquentem absolvit ... Omnis igitur eleemosyna duobus expletur modis, dando scilicet aliis bona nostra, et dimittendo eis mala sua.[66]

---

65 Thomas, *Summa confessorum*, art.1, q. ia, *De etymologia et de descriptio penitentie*, 6.

66 Hildebertus Cenomanensis, "Sermones de tempore, xxiii. In quadragesima sermo quartus. De poenitentia" in *Patrologia Latina*, vol. 171, cols 447B–48A.

> Concerning the satisfaction of work he [the Psalmist] said the same thing elsewhere: "I laboured in my grief (Psalm 6:7)" Remembering the lamentation and the fullness of labour through the lamentation, he referred to satisfaction by works as "labour." Satisfaction consists above all in three things: namely, fasting, prayer, and alms-giving. Fasting, however, is twofold: corporal and spiritual. Corporal fasting is when we are moderate with regard to food; spiritual fasting is when we abstain from vices. To macerate the flesh with corporal fasting neither suffices nor has value unless one chastizes the mind within with spiritual abstinence, bewaring vices and avoiding sins. In like manner, there is oral prayer and prayer of the heart. A cry coming from the lips has no value without mental labor ... Alms-giving too is twofold: corporal and spiritual. The corporal alms-giving opens the hand [letting the silver out] and helps the needy; the spiritual alms-giving, however, corrects the errant and absolves the offender. Therefore, any alms-giving is fulfilled in two ways: namely, by giving our goods to others, and forgiving their wrongdoing.

Both early and late medieval strands of the penitential tradition no doubt treated satisfaction under the spiritual and corporal aspects identified by Hildebertus. But, as medievalists have argued, from the mid-twelfth century, the penitential tradition became increasingly centred on the inner or, to use Hildebertus's expression, "spiritual" (spiritualis) rather than the "corporal" (corporalis) mode of atonement.[67] In the early medieval period, penitential literature stressed the necessity of the physical enactment of contrition. External penances such as charity and fasting were required for the expiation of the *pena* of sin.

With the rise of canon law as an academic discipline, however, penitential treatises such as Gratian's *De penitentia* (in the *Decretum*) held in balance both internal and external forms of penance. Others, especially works written around or after Lateran IV, such as Raymond's treatise for confessors (contained in his *Summa de paenitentia*, and discussed in chapter 1) stressed contrition as the central moment of penance and regarded satisfaction as an exterior expression of inner contrition. This is, of course, not to say that verbal or material expressions of contrition ("confessio oris" or "satisfactio operis") were set aside in favour of inner remorse ("contritio cordis"): rather the penitential tradition

67 Muzarelli, *Penitenze nel Medioevo*, 66–7. Muzzarelli singles out a treatise on penance called *Homo quidam* (1155–65) as the *cerniera* (link) between Penitentials focusing exclusively on external penalties and those increasingly concerned with examining the contrition of sinners.

became increasingly oriented towards the penitent's inner experience of contrition.[68]

Given the documented shift in emphasis from exterior to interior forms of penance in the penitential tradition by Langland's day, Reason's image of the law as a labourer working in a field stands out as atypical, as a throwback to an earlier phase in the history of sacramental penance. It recalls and foregrounds what Hildbertus called the "corporal" aspect of penance. Reason's labourer-figure can, of course, be related to such referents within the poem as Piers the Plowman and his pardon (given its promise of salvation to those who perform good deeds). At the same time, it can also be related to the ambivalent figure of the plowman in the Bible. Contextualizing a range of valences attributed to the labourer in Langland's own day, Paul Freedman sees the figure in the poem as an object of both reprobation and praise: associated with the "meritorious labour" of Abel as well as with the spiritually fruitless labour of Cain.[69] Uncovering in the early medieval tradition the association of priesthood and preaching with the figure of the plowman, Stephen A. Barney identifies Gregory the Great's *Moralia in Job* as the main source for the tropes supporting the figure of Piers the Plowman.[70] More recently, Katherine C. Little has explored Langland's labourer-figure from the perspective of its afterlife in the Protestant responses to it. In particular, she sees mid-sixteenth century responses to the labourer personified by Piers as exemplifying the means by which "authors can explore the changed relationship of work and 'works.'"[71]

In their variations, these scholarly insights attest to the ambivalence in the medieval figure of the labourer. Looking in at least two opposed directions, the figure has a certain hybrid status: "conceptually indeterminate," it "wavers between vocabularies" of sin and redemption, of work and works.[72] Although Reason does not explicitly confer on the figure either a sinful or redemptive significance, his location of it in the context of the confessor's construal of the quotation associates

68 In fact, elsewhere even in *Piers Plowman* we encounter the view that contrition alone without satisfaction (and confession) could in and of itself remit sin; see, for instance, the line "sola contritio delet peccatum" in B 11.81.

69 Freedman, *Images of the Medieval Peasant*, 34–5.

70 Stephen A. Barney, "The Ploughshare of the Tongue."

71 Little, "Transforming Work," 500; such authors, Little notes, offer "a religious resistance" to the separation of work or rural labour from works.

72 What Homi Bhabha says about the hybrid or ambivalent figure of the nation in narration can be said about the labourer in medieval narratives; see his *Nation and Narration*, 2.

agricultural work not just with preaching, as has been well documented by Barney, Friedman, and Little, but also, as I argue, with penitential labour. Evidence for Reason's characterization of the labourer and his work as penitential is found in a sermon of Peter Comestor. In a Lenten sermon ("In capite jejunii vel in die cinerum") written in the mid-twelfth century, around the time when the penitential tradition was becoming more expressly contrition-centred, Peter Comestor, who is credited with elaborating the tripartite penances and inventing purgatorial fire[73] analogizes the satisfaction undertaken by the penitent with the corporal work undertaken by the agricultural labourer:

> *Cum jejunaveris, faciem tuam lava, unge caput tuum oleo, ne videaris hominibus jejunans* (Matth. 6:17).[74] Si verba, quae audistis ex ore meo nostra putarentur, ridiculosus viderer: ludicrum est enim et detestabile jejunanti esse lotum facie, et delibutum unguento. Jejunantis autem est sordes quaerere, in cinere et cilicio sedere, sordidas vestes habere, esse in carnis maceratione, in victus attenuatione, in vultus tristitia et pallore, faciem non lavare, nec ad mensas opulenti capite delibuto sedere. Unde ille agricola in Evangelio (Luc. XVIII), cum praeciperetur ei, ut arborem succideret, ait: Sine hoc anno, ut fodiam, et stercora ponam, ut fructificet, non dicit: Ponam unguentum, sed stercora et sordes.[75]
>
> "When you fast, wash your face, anoint your head with oil so that you are not seen by men to be fasting" (Matthew 6:17). If the words, which you hear from my mouth, were taken to be mine, I would seem ridiculous: for it is ludicrous and despicable for the one fasting to be washed of face and anointed with oil. For it is appropriate for the one fasting to seek filth, to sit in ashes and sackcloth, to have filthy clothes, to macerate the flesh, to be emaciated, to be sad and pale in face, not to wash the face, nor to sit at the table with one's head richly anointed. Whence that farmer in the Gospel (Luke 18), when he was commanded to cut the tree, said: "Let it be this year so that I may dig, and I will place the dung, so that it may bear fruit"; he does not say: "I will apply ointment," but rather dung and offal.

---

73 Le Goff, *The Birth of Purgatory*, 156–7. Ian P. Wei notes that throughout *De sacramentis*, Peter "referred to purgatorial fire rather than purgatory." See Ian P. Wei, *Intellectual Culture in Medieval Paris*, 198.

74 I have supplied the correct biblical reference in parenthesis.

75 Peter Comestor, "Sermo X. In capite jejunii vel in die cinerum" in *Patrologia Latina*, vol. 198, cols 1749A.

In this sermon on the theme of fasting, Peter's characterization of satisfaction as corporal punishment is typical of its time, for it is found, as we have already seen, in near-contemporary treatises such as Thomas of Chobham's *Summa confessorum*. But what makes this passage relevant to Langland's poem is Peter's association of the penitent performing satisfaction with the biblical farmer digging and placing dung. Both Peter and Reason invoke the arduous activity of working in the field within the discursive context of penitential satisfaction. In effect, Reason and Peter are together thinking about satisfaction under the aspect of agricultural labour that is at once individually corporal and collectively beneficial: in exerting himself, the penitent as labourer brings fruit ("fructificet") to the community at large.

Tracing the poem's vivid image of agricultural labour to a certain moment in the penitential tradition may suggest that Reason retrieves or revives a corporal form of punishment that by Langland's day, according to the church, had to be undertaken with spiritual intention as well. But, reviewing the same image in Reason's subsequent use of it in his address to confessors will reveal a process that is productive of thinking about satisfaction rather than merely derivative from it. Specifically, Reason shifts the focus from the content of satisfaction per se to its calculation by confessors. In approaching satisfaction thus, Reason thinks innovatively about penances but now not from the perspective of what the penitent must endure but from the perspective of what the confessor must impose. The poem, as we shall see, draws upon and at the same time redescribes the prevailing method of computing satisfaction in the penitential forum.

Metaphor's Work of Invention in the Passus

Such a re-description or invention with regard to computing satisfaction proceeds less from the visual image of the labourer per se than from Reason's usage of the image within a metaphor to clarify how he wants the confessors to construe the Latin quotation. The metaphor does not inhere in any individual word or clause of the speech that Reason directs to the confessors: "'And if ye werchen it in werk, I wedde myne eris / That Lawe shal ben a laborer and lede afeld donge, / And Loue shal lede þi lond as þe leef likeþ.'"[76] Rather, the metaphor encompasses

76 B 4.146–8.

the totality of the three lines that bring together different senses of labour ranging from hermeneutic exercise (of "werchen" the quotation in "werk") to agricultural activity (of "led[ing] a feld donge"). Articulated across two clauses, the metaphor is conditional: it effects a change to the grammatical subject ("Lawe"), only if the condition stated in the subordinate clause is fulfilled according to the hermeneutic advice that Reason gives the confessors. That is, only if the confessor(s) and/or king "werchen" the quotation into "werk," "Lawe shal ben a laborer." At a literal level, then, the metaphor forecasts an unusual relationship between two familiar terms: "Lawe" signifying a legal system or discourse and "laborer" signifying a human being of a particular profession. What links or unites the two disparate referents is the "to be" form of the verb ("shal ben") – a verb establishing identity or sameness between what are, in medieval parlance, two semantically different words.

Of course, to approach the metaphor solely at its literal level – i.e., to equate "Lawe" semantically with "laborer" – is to ignore the transformative potential of the metaphor: the potential to re-define the received senses of "Lawe" and "laborer" in Middle English – senses that would not be seen as synonymous by medieval confessors or Langland's audience. At the same time, to read the metaphor solely figuratively is to ignore its potential to re-describe the extra-textual referents indicated by the redefined senses of the words "Lawe" and "laborer." To appreciate the metaphor's potential to redefine "Lawe" and "laborer," on the one hand, and to re-describe their empirically real referents, on the other, we need to view the metaphor as establishing a tension of non-identity between the two terms. This is the kind of tension that Langland frequently generates between objects yoked together by means of subjunctive forms such as "were I" (as in Reason's equating himself to a king in our discussion above) and "as it were," which is memorably used to introduce the dreamer in the Prologue, and clerics elsewhere in the poem.[77] Understood thus, the metaphor invites us to see someone as if it were someone else.

Helpful, perhaps, to clarify the metaphoric principle of "seeing as if" is the terminology used by Paul Ricoeur. I turn to him only because his theory of metaphor can enable us to grasp more fully the subtle but sustained

77 The most obvious example of this tension is found in the second line of the Prologue: "I shoop me into shroudes as I a sheep were" (Prologue, B 2); see also: "Ther preched a pardoner as he a preest were" (Prologue, B 68) and "Carpen as þei clerkes were of Crist and of hise myȝtes" (B 10.104).

work of reinvention around satisfaction that the metaphor performs in the passus. Seen through the lens and language of Ricoeur's metaphoric theory, Reason's metaphor initiates a tension of difference and identity in the relationship between the two terms: "the former classification" [of law,] "linked to the previous use of words, resists and creates a sort of stereoscopic vision in which the new situation [of law as labourer] is perceived in only the depths of the situation disrupted by the category mistake" [of relating the two disparate terms together].[78] In less abstruse language, Reason's metaphor foresees law as if it were a labourer: even as we know that law is semantically different from the labourer in common medieval parlance, we are invited to visualize what law would look like if it took on the properties that belong to the labourer: i.e., law as imagined or identified under the image of the labourer.

To adapt Ricoeur's words again, Reason's metaphor "does not just connect the predicate 'laborer' to the subject 'Lawe'" relationally but "implies besides, by means of the predicative relationship, that *what* is, is redescribed: it says *that* things really are this way."[79] Ordinarily speaking, the "to be" verb that links "Lawe" and "laborer" creates, rather than merely expresses, a resemblance between the two objects where there was previously none in the real world of Langland's day.[80] Ricoeur explains how the resemblance created by the metaphor involves a conceptual transferal across the terms that it links:

> Metaphor does not cover just what we have called "figure," that is, ultimately, transference of an isolated predicate operating in opposition to another (the alternative "red" or "orange"). It also covers what must be called "schema," which stands for a group of labels with the characteristic that a corresponding group of objects, "a realm," is picked out by it (for example, colour). Metaphor's power of reorganizing our perception of things develops from transposition of an entire "realm."[81]

More than merely endowing the figure of the labourer with penitential meaning, Reason's metaphor can be seen as transferring the entire

78 Ricoeur, "Metaphor and Reference," 272–3.

79 Ricoeur, "Metaphor and Reference," 292; emphasis mine.

80 Here, again, I am adapting Ricoeur's words about metaphor's capacity to create rather than to express an already existing resemblance between the terms that it relates; see his *Rule of Metaphor*, 292.

81 Ibid., 278.

discursive system or "schema" behind one term ("lawe") onto that of another ("labourer"). The transferal at the level of discourse or schema testifies to the passus's entry into the extra-textual world, into a re-envisioning of the penitential forum where confessors were entrusted with the task of translating the "Lawe" inherent in the Latin quotation into labour-intensive penances for their penitents. In relating law to a labourer, Reason's metaphor thus directs the confessors towards the interpretation of the quotation as the kind of satisfactory work that the labourer exemplifies. Such work, as we have already established, looks back to the fructifying labour undertaken by the plowman in an earlier medieval penitential tradition.

At the same time, the metaphor looks forward to a more contemporary penitential tradition (represented by the *Memoriale*) in which satisfaction was explicitly theorized as a result of clerical discretion and interpretation. Trained in the post-Gratian canonical principles for harmonizing justice and mercy, the confessor had to use his discretion to interpret the penitential canons to determine the satisfaction appropriate for the penitent. In sum, Reason's call to confessors to "werchen" the quotation into "werk" denotes satisfaction in the two senses of its composition and computation: not only as agricultural labour exemplifying the hard penances to be undertaken by the penitent but also as hermeneutic labour exemplifying the canonical principles of interpretation to be followed by the confessor. In drawing together both these senses, the metaphor "organizes" the administration of the penitential forum in a way different from how it was administered by errant confessors. The metaphor renders "manifest a way of being of things, which is brought to language thanks to semantic innovation [.] It would seem that the enigma of metaphoric discourse is that it 'invents' in both senses of the word: what it creates, it discovers; and what it finds, it invents."[82]

In the B and C versions of the same passus, the confessors' handling of satisfaction can be gleaned from their mutually exclusive interpretations of the Latin quotation. In B, the narrator affords us insight into the confessors' simoniacal reading of the quotation – one that results in the commutation of any penances into profits for the confessor. The corresponding report in C, by contrast, affords us insight into a non-simoniacal solution to the same crisis: the construal of the quotation in keeping with the penitential canons.

82 Ibid., 282–3.

In B, the narrator records the confessors' construal of the quotation thus:

> Clerkes þat were confessours coupled hem togideres
> Al to construe þis clause, and for þe Kynges profit,
> Ac noȝt for confort of þe commune, ne for þe Kynges soule;
> For I seiȝ Mede in þe moot-halle on men of lawe wynke,
> And þei lauȝynge lope to hire and lefte Reson manye. (B 4.149–53)

Here, the narrator spells out the principle of "þe Kynges profit" that governs the interpretation of the Latin quotation by the "confessours." The materialist reading of the Latin words, the narrator notes, favours neither "þe commune" nor "þe Kynges soule." The confessors' interpretation is diametrically opposed to the vision of penitential correction that Reason has thus far vigorously defended. Their interpretation is also at variance with that found in the penitential writings already considered above. (We may recall, for instance, that Alain de Lille construes the quotation to mean penances to be undertaken by the penitent for her/his spiritual welfare and for the sake of the neighbour or community whom s/he has injured. For Alain, the penitent should ideally perform acts of satisfaction in hopes of being reconciled to and reintegrated into her/his community). In the confessors' construal in B, however, we hear nothing about penances but everything about profits. What the confessors offer would materially enrich ("profit") the king to the detriment of both his subjects ("commune") and his own "soule."

The confessors' construal is greeted with Mede's approval: she winks at the audience and wins over from Reason "men of lawe." Both the construal and its effects on the audience exemplify the widespread neglect of satisfaction voiced in the section entitled "On false penance" (De falsa penitencia) in the *Memoriale presbiterorum*:

> Peccant igitur graviter et multorum animas decipiunt confessores moderni tam regulares et maxime mendicantes quam eciam seculares qui intromittunt se de confessionibus audiendis et ignorant quales penitencias secundum canones debent iniungere, et sic dicuntur ceci et duces cecorum. Item si pro favore alicuius persone vel eciam pro timore, omittunt veram peccatori iniungere penitenciam. Item si pro donis quibuscunque a peccatore receptis vel spe recipiendi levem iniungunt penitenciam, tacendo penitenciam a canone statutam, prout supra scribitur; quo casu confessor ceca

> cupiditate ductus, symoniam committere dicitur, sacramentum penitencie vendendo illicite.[83]
>
> Both regular, especially mendicant, as well as secular confessors, who put themselves in the business of hearing confessions and do not know what penances they should impose according to the canons, sin gravely and deceive the souls of many, and thus they are said to be blind, and leaders of the blind, again, if on account of a favour of some person or also on account of fear, they omit to impose the true penance; or if they impose a light penance by being silent about the penance established by the canon on account of gifts received from the sinner or in the hope of receiving [them]. In which case, the confessor, led by blind cupidity, is said to commit simony, by illicitly selling the sacrament of penance.

In these lines, the *Memoriale* provides an extra-poetic parallel to the scene of clerical interpretation in the B version of the passus.[84] Whether or not one considers this excerpt an influence on Langland's passage, what is noteworthy is that both writers identify a common concern or culprit in the penitential forum: Mede's impact upon the confessor's determination of satisfactory penances. Lamenting the confessor's blind desire ("ceca cupiditate") for gifts ("donis") or for a favour ("favore") – items personified by Mede in *Piers Plowman* – the *Memoriale* author deplores the commutation of the penances "according to the [penitential] canons" (secundum canones). Just as the confessors denounced in the *Memoriale* disregard canon law for the sake of material gifts and, hence, "deceive many souls" (multorum animas decipiunt), so Reason's confessors interpret the similarly normative quotation in a way that is detrimental to the king's own soul as well as to the commons. What I want to suggest is a confluence between poetic and penitential diagnosis of the confessor's neglect of satisfaction – neglect that stems from the commutation, rather than computation, of satisfactory penances.

---

83 *Memoriale presbiterorum*, vol. 2, 192; for rest of the section ("b.xxvii. De falsa penitencia"), see pages189–95 of vol. 2.

84 Stressing the *Memoriale's* castigation of errant confessors, Haren notes that the *Memoriale* insists that even indulgences "do not remove the necessity of performing the enjoined penance [which] is in keeping with his rigorous regard for the canonical sanctions and is less equivocal than the doctrine of Raymond and Hostiensis" (Haren, "A Study of the *Memoriale presbiterorum*," 1: 81).

"Kyndeliche What It Meneth" and the Manner of Interpretation in Canon Law

Whereas the B version of the passus, as I have just argued, presents the problem of commutation denounced at length in the *Memoriale*, the corresponding lines in C present a solution to it. In the C version of the narrator's report, the confessors are said to have interpreted the same Latin quotation according to a principle strikingly different from the one they follow in B but conceptually aligned with the one expressed by Reason and by the penitential writers:

> Clerkes þat were confessours couplede hem togederes
> To construe this clause, kyndeliche what it meneth.
> Mede in the mot-halle tho on men of lawe gan wynke
> In signe þat thei sholde with som sotil speche
> Reherce ther anon ryhte þat myhte Resoun stoppe. (C 4.146–50)

Although we do not learn exactly "what it [the Latin quotation] meneth" in English, we do know how the confessors translate the Latin words. In the passage, the presence of the adverb "kyndeliche" orients attention exclusively to the manner in which the confessors translate the Latin quotation rather than, as in B, to the matter of their construal.

To move from the B to C versions of the narrator's report, then, is to move from the matter to the manner of the quotation's construal. But, what does it mean for confessors to construe or translate the Latin clause "kyndeliche"? There is little in the immediate context to reveal its precise sense but looking at its usages elsewhere in the poem might help us understand how to interpret it here.

In passus 9, Witte deploys the adverb in its negative form ("vnkyndely") to deplore marriages motivated by greed for material property: "For some, as I se now sooþ for to telle, / For couetise of catel vnkyndely ben wedded."[85] Glossing "vnkyndeliche" as acting solely for material profit, Gerald O'Grady suggests that to act "kyndeliche" would be doing the opposite: not acting solely for profit.[86] In his

85 B 9.156–7.

86 O'Grady explains the word thus: "fourteenth century people marrying 'vnkyndeliche,' that is marrying for money." See "*Piers Plowman* and the Medieval Tradition of Penance," 362.

study of "kynde," Hugh White reads "kyndeliche" as "accurately" or "correctly" but notes that the nominal form "kynde" itself includes the modern sense of kindness or love or charity.[87] Hence, for instance, the expression "kynde knowynge," White explains, "brings with it the power of love" and "[w]hen Piers speaks of Truth dwelling in the heart in a chain of charity, we could understand him to be speaking of the presence of *kynde knowyinge* that teaches charity."[88]

If we read "kyndeliche" as denoting a charitable mode of action, then the confessors' manner of interpretation can be said to participate in the spirit of the classical canon law that Ivo of Chartres and Gratian were instrumental in advancing. One of the things that set their law and later canon law compilations apart from their earlier medieval predecessors was a hermeneutic methodology marked by the principle of charity. In the justly famous "Prologue" to his *Decretum* and *Panormia*, Ivo of Chartres foregrounds the centrality of charity to the implementation or interpretation of canonical norms:

> Si corripis, corripe cum caritate. Si parcis, parce cum caritate. Set in his adhibenda est summa diligencia, et mundandus oculus cordis, quatenus in puniendo vel parcendo sanandis morbis caritas sincera subveniat ... "Mortificabant animas que non moriebantur, et vivificabant animas que non vivabant," (Ezechiele 13:19). Sicut enim racio corporalis medicine vel depellere morbos vel curare vulnera, salutem servare vel augere intendit, nec medicus contrarius sibi esse videtur cum pro qualitate vel quantitate egritudinis vel egrotantis nunc mordencia nunc molliencia egrotanti medicamina apponit et nunc ferro secat cui fomento subvenire non poterat et e converso ei nunc subvenit fomento quem ferro secare non audebat; ita spirituales medici, doctores videlicet sancte ecclesie, nec a se nec inter se dissenciunt, cum illicita prohibent, necessaria iubent, summa suadent, venalia indulgent, cum secundum duriciam cordis delinquencium, pro correctione eorum vel cautela ceterorum severas penitencie leges imponunt, vel cum secundum devotionem dolencium et resurgere volencium considerata fragilitate vasis quod portant indulgencie malagma superponunt.[89]

---

87 Addressing the usage of the adverb in a similar context of clerical construal in the C text, Hugh White notes: "We might gloss *kyndelyche* 'accurately,' 'correctly,' when we hear that 'þise newe clerkes' cannot 'construe kyndelyche þat poetes made' (C.XVII 108–10)." See his *Nature and Salvation*, 43.

88 White, *Nature and Salvation*, 53.

89 The Latin quotation is drawn from Brasington's edition of Ivo's "Prologue" in *Ways of Mercy*, 117.

If you correct, then correct with charity. If you forgive, then forgive with charity. But in these things the greatest diligence should be employed. The eye of the heart should be cleansed insofar as sincere charity should assist in punishing or sparing the illnesses to be cured ... "They were destroying the souls that were not dying, and bringing to life the souls that were not living" (Ezekiel 13:19). Just as the principle of medicine intends to preserve or increase health, either to drive out illnesses or to cure wounds, the physician does not seem to contradict himself when, in light of the quality or quantity of the illness or the ill person, he sometimes applies gentle medicines and sometimes sharp ones, and at one time makes an incision with a knife, for whom a plaster could not be of help, or, conversely, at another time, a plaster helps him, whom he would not dare to cut with a knife; in the same way, spiritual physicians, namely doctors of the holy church, do not disagree among or between themselves when they prohibit illicit things, command necessary things, recommend the best, forgive venial matters, when they implement the severe laws of penance in accordance with the hardness of the heart of the delinquent for their correction or as a warning for others; or they place emollients of indulgence according to the devotion of the remorseful and of those willing to change, having considered the fragility of the vessel they carry.

The hermeneutical principle of charity expounded in Ivo's "Prologue" informed not just the administration of the church's external forum such as the inquisitorial courts but also, as Joseph Goering has argued, the forum of penance, or, more specifically, the interpretation of the penitential canons.

Traditionally scholars had distinguished between two phases of the penitential tradition on the basis of their differing approaches to the penitential canons. In the time before the rise of the classical canon law, the confessor treated the penitential canons as tariffs that had to be followed more according to their letter than according to their spirit: he had to impose whatever penances were prescribed by the canons for the confessed sins, and used discretion only when determining the penances for sins that were not indicated on the canonical list of tariffs. With the teaching of canon law at the schools, however, there emerged a shift in emphasis from the mere adherence to the penitential tariffs to the charitable interpretation of them in light of the penitent's inner contrition and the circumstances of his sinful actions. In the new historiography of penance (embodied in the suggestive *New History of Penance*), Joseph Goering and Rob Meens have recently nuanced the difference between the two penitential phases less in terms of the latitude of the confessor's discretion per se than in terms of the new legal education that informed his discretionary reading of the penitential canons.[90] With the adoption of Gratian's *Decretum* as a school text at the newly founded universities, as Goering explains, the penitential tradition reflected "the developments in juridical culture of the twelfth century."[91] Post-Gratian and especially post-Lateran IV penitential texts equipped the confessor with the "knowledge of the new skills of the ecclesiastical judge and of the canonical consultant."[92]

Like the confessors in C interpreting the quotation "kyndeliche," the canonically trained cleric was now expected to compute satisfaction not by mechanically selecting the penances recommended by the penitential canons but by exercising discretion diligently to temper justice with mercy, i.e., by increasing or decreasing the quality and quantity of satisfaction according to the sinner's ability to bear them. In *De paenitentiis et remissionibus*, Raymond of Peñafort singles out the diligence necessary for the computation of discretionary penances:

> Ex diligenti inspectione praedictae regulae, cum exceptionibus suis, poterit studiosus et diligens indagator invenire processum ad satisfactionem pro diversis criminibus secundum paenitentiales canones imponendam ... Et in hoc consistit eius arbitrium, scilicet, pro qua vel quibus circumstantiis, et quantum, et quando possit augeri vel minui poena canonica. (Raymond 48.848)
>
> From a diligent inspection of the above-mentioned rule, with their exceptions, the zealous and diligent inquirer can arrive at a procedure for imposing satisfaction for diverse crimes according to the penitential canons ... And in this consists his discretion, namely: because of what or which circumstances, and how much and when, the canonical penalty can be increased or decreased.

Other later medieval confessional manuals elaborate on Raymond's advice on exercising discretion about *satisfactio operis*. In his *Pars oculi*, William of Pagula (whom, as we may recall, Walter de Brugge mentions

90 Rob Meens, *Penance in Medieval Europe*, 190–225; see also Meens's "The Historiography of Early Medieval Penance," 73–95.

91 Goering, "The Internal Forum," *Traditio* 59 (2004): 199 n. 76.

92 Ibid., 199.

in his bequest) names the circumstances that the confessor must consult in order to moderate the satisfactory penances recommended by the penitential canons:

> Et sciendum est quod sacerdos potest pro suo arbitrio iniungere penitencias et moderare canones penitentiales et considerare debet omnes circumstancias, scilicet, persone, temporis, loci, et criminis.[93]

> And it should be understood that the priest is able to impose penances according to his discretion and to moderate the penitential canons, and he ought to consider all circumstances, namely of the person, time, place, and crime.

While the expression "according to his discretion" (pro suo arbitrio) underlines the confessor's freedom "to moderate" (moderare) the penitential canons, this discretion must occur in light of "all the circumstances" (omnes circumstancias) of the confessed sins.

The discretionary freedom that Raymond and William advise the confessor to exercise for calculating satisfaction privileges the manner of interpreting a canonical norm over the matter of penance recommended by that norm. Viewed in light of such a discretionary hermeneutics, the adverb "kyndeliche" in C takes on the sense of an equitable mode of reading a norm. Specifically, for the confessors to read "kyndeliche" is to interpret a penitential canon in ways that would ensure a balance between justice and mercy, between the letter of the law and its spirit.

To recapitulate our argument, the B and C versions of Wrong's trial shape a model of satisfaction that impacts both penitent and confessor. The versions are alike insofar as they revive and reinforce the model of corporal satisfaction to be undertaken by the penitent. Where the versions differ, however, is with regard to their representation of the confessors' manner of approaching a normative text on satisfaction. To discern the twofold sense of satisfaction as both matter and manner, as both the hard penances to be experienced by the penitent and the dialectical approach to be followed by the confessor is to sharpen our perspective not only on the differences between B and C with regard to a single passus but also on those between the two versions with regard to other passus addressing satisfaction.

---

93 *An Edition of the "Judica Me Deus,"* 58.

If Ralph Hanna is right that each so-called revision (or what I would call version) "represents a constructive intervention that creates poetic meaning anew, and this is a new poetic meaning that extends across the full text of this particular revised version," then the changes that mark C as distinct from B that I have examined in this chapter should have an impact on the rest of C, or, at the very least, on subsequent passages handling penitential satisfaction.[94] I want to conclude by briefly indicating evidence for such a "projective horizontality" in the banquet-centred discussion of penances in B passus 13 / C passus 15.[95]

In the B and C versions of the banquet scene, the narrator wrangles with a friar over the interpretation of "penaunce" and, when the friar defines it, censures him for not practising it.[96] In both versions, the narrator treats satisfaction as a bodily practice that even the friar who expounds it correctly must himself undertake personally. Such a view recalls and reinforces the corporal ideal of satisfaction that, as we have seen, is already foregrounded much earlier in passus 4, but now (in B passus 13 / C passus 15) extended to apply not just to penitents but also to the friar, whose characteristically corporeal sin – gluttony – the narrator deems culpable for depriving the poor of sustenance.

Where the two versions of the narrator's antifraternal critique in the same passus depart is in the characterization of the friar. The C version contains additional details about the friar's clerical education absent from B: the narrator tells us that the friar is a "doctour and dyvynour" and a "decretistre of canoen."[97] The narrator's identification of the friar as a "decretistre" (decretist) renders explicit Langland's recourse to the classical canon law (a decretist is a canonist schooled in Gratian's *Decretum*) to think through satisfaction. Hence, looking back on Wrong's trial in passus 4 from our location at the banquet in passus 15 in C (or passus 13 in B), we see that the canonist thinking that framed the prior dissension over the satisfactory punishment for Wrong is now explicitly identified in another debate over penances between a friar and the narrator. Whereas in passus 4 the narrator attends to the confessors' mode of interpreting a penitential text on satisfaction, here, in the later

94 Hanna, "The Versions and Revisions of *Piers Plowman*," 48–9.

95 Ibid., 49.

96 C 15.93–5: "Y schal iangle to þis iurdan, with his iuyste wombe, / And apose hym what penaunce is and purgatorie on erthe, / And why a lyueth nat as a lereth!" See corresponding B 13.84–5.

97 C 15.86.

passus, the narrator goes beyond that to admonish the confessor about not performing the penances themselves that he preaches. By assailing the friar for feasting upon expensive foods and admonishing him about penances, the narrator implies that the friar himself should have practised the abstinence he enjoins other sinners to undertake. Moving, then, from the narrator's revised report on the confessors in passus 4 to his revised critique of the friar in passus 15, we see, in C, a shift in emphasis in the representation of canon law as a frame of reference for thinking about satisfaction: the canonist framework implicit in the earlier passus is rendered explicit in the later passus. In the next chapter, we continue to address the representation of canon law in the two versions but with regard to their use of allegory. In doing so, we shall also see the extent to which the difference between B and C involves a difference in the poetics of fashioning and figuring forth canon law.

5 *Contritio Cordis, Confessio Oris, et Satisfactio Operis*: From Symbol to Sign in Patience's Sermon[1]

In its introduction to *Piers Plowman*, the online forum *Poetry Foundation* deems B to be "the most poetic of the three versions" and C "more prosaic" [in comparison to B].[2] Graduate students appear to endorse this verdict not least because they are more likely to access *Piers Plowman* in its B version. I have heard them praise B and justify their distaste for C on grounds of verbosity: "C rambles, B cuts to the chase."[3] Nearly a century ago, Mabel Day expressed a similar sentiment about B and C, albeit in a less colloquial vein. At one point in her article on the A, B, and C versions of the poem, she asserts that C "carefully removes so many obvious inconsistencies in B" and at another that "[a]t all times, C loves to paraphrase, often apparently with no object except to weaken his original, often by substituting a generality for some graphic detail."[4] In the intervening decades, Day's view has received corroboration in our recognition of the poetics underlying the C version's treatment of penance.[5] In a number of places where C differs from B, scholars have noted in C a

1 This chapter is a revised version of my article "From Covenantal Symbol to Institutional Sign: The C-Revisions in Passus 16 of *Piers Plowman*," *Exemplaria* 23.2 (summer 2011): 147–70.

2 See http://www.poetryfoundation.org/bio/william-langland: "The B-text is the most poetic of the three versions, and the majority of criticism (including this book) is based upon it. In comparison, the C-text is more prosaic. C is almost a total revision of B, except for the last two *passus* which are untouched."

3 I have heard this consensus expressed more or less in this form at informal discussions of the B and C texts at Yale, Fordham, UCLA, and, more recently, at the International *Piers Plowman* Conference at Washington University in 2015.

4 Day, "The Revisions of *Piers Plowman*," 2, 6.

5 For an early but substantial discussion of the poetics of Langland's revisions, see Donaldson, *"Piers Plowman": The C-text and Its Poet*.

less critical attitude towards the clergy and its administration of the *cura animarum* than is found in the corresponding places in B. In his synoptic view of what some scholars have seen as authorial changes from B to C, Schmidt, for instance, underscores the tendency in C towards verbal rather than visual clarification about institutional penance: "[C] generally is marked by a tendency to push what is memorably *seen* ever closer to what can be meaningfully *said* [emphasis by Schmidt]."[6] Arguing that Langland made "several apparent attempts ... to protect his poem from the suspicion of Wycliffitism," Pearsall claims that they are "part of the endeavor in C to clarify the argument of the poem."[7]

In comparing passages from B and C, I, however, neither argue nor assume that one version revises the other. Nor, for that matter, do I claim that C registers a single poet's attempts to distance himself from the perceived reception of B by Wycliffites or other anticlerical radicals in the latter quarter of the fourteenth century. Nevertheless, my running claim has been that when we read certain passages from B and C in parallel format, then C emerges as more co-productive of canon law than B, and as far more innovatively invested in the church's institution of penance than scholars such as Aers would grant.[8] By mobilizing the discourse around contrition, restitution, and satisfaction, the poem's allegorical figures from Repentaunce to Reason improvise within the literal and conceptual register of canon law – improvisations that are more evident in C than in B, regardless of any convictions about the poem's versional evolution or a single poet's process of continual revision. And, given that personified principles and not just personalized individuals do much of the talking and thinking about law, C's reinvention of canon law, as I have been arguing, pertains as much to the legal as to the literary.

Less foregrounded in my examination so far, however, has been a particular form of such a poetics: allegory. That is, if I am right that C does indeed engage canon law more co-productively than does B, then it remains for us to refine our existing knowledge about the allegorical poetics chosen to effect such an engagement. Are there crucial differences between B and C in their allegorical modes of representing and reshaping the received canonist thought and practice? And, if so, to what extent do such differences shed light on the poem's range of

6 Schmidt, "Langland's Visions and Revisions," 9.
7 Pearsall, "Langland and Lollardy," 22.
8 Aers, *Beyond Reformation?* 170–1.

approaches to the discourse of canon law, and offer further evidence for C's more innovative poetics at the level of allegory?

To answer these questions is to acquire a sharper sense of C's shaping of the canonist thought on penance at the levels of both institutional doctrine and allegory. To answer these questions is also to address Larry Scanlon's twofold observation about medieval scholarship's inadequate understanding of the "penitential tradition," and medievalists' neglect of Paul de Man's theory of allegory.[9] That is, I seek to advance Scanlon's theoretical inquiry into the convergence in *Piers Plowman* of institutional penance and allegorical representation but in the context of the C text and in light of Emily Steiner's influential work on the B text's "documentary poetics."[10] This twofold sense will help us discover in certain C passages a doctrinally and allegorically precise means by which the poem not only courts but also challenges the discourse of penance produced by canonists and theologians. Specifically, this chapter addresses a barely studied cluster of C lines that Steiner astutely singles out as "shifting the [B text's allegorical] terms of documentary culture."[11] My method of inquiry is a close reading of a B passage on a penitential document designated as a "patente" against the comparable C passage, which introduces a "chartre" as the analogous document. Scholarship on the B and C passages dealing with the "patente" and "chartre" has long been disproportionate. Whereas the "patente" has received sustained and favourable scholarly scrutiny, the "chartre" has attracted cursory and sometimes disparaging attention.[12] The

9 Scanlon, "Personification and Penance," 1 and 6.

10 Steiner, *Documentary Culture*, 10.

11 Steiner's study of Langland's "documentary poetics" focuses on the B text, with occasional remarks on its representation in C. Having closely examined the "patente" in the B text, Steiner briefly considers the "chartre" that replaces it in the C text, remarking perceptively that C "make[s] more explicit statements about the role of the church and the sacraments in salvation" and that "one consequence of this rewriting is to reassert ecclesiastical authority by shifting the terms of documentary culture" (*Documentary Culture*, 217).

12 Steiner's analysis of the B passage on the "patente" suggests the need for closer attention to Langland's handling of the "chartre" in the corresponding C passage (*Documentary Culture*, 217). Steiner sees the charter as a reduction of the original patent of Christ "to one line, very awkwardly attached to the lines around it, and subordinated to a larger discussion about the three stages of penance. Langland has also replaced the impassioned lines about Christ comforting 'alle maner peple' which precede Hawkyn's pardon in the B-text with a pedantic explanation of penance as the source of Dowel for both the ignorant and the learned" (*Documentary Culture*, 217).

C passages that frame the "chartre" have been dismissed as "ambiguous" and "pedantic" and, in general, so neglected that Bryan P. Davis has called for closer attention to the poetic modes in which the document is constructed in C.[13]

Both doctrinally and allegorically, the "chartre," in C, represents the institutional (rather than the Christological) means by which penance is to be administered. The substitution of the "patente" with the "chartre" marks a shift in emphasis from a penitential strand grounded in Christ's covenantal words (the context for the "patente" in the B passage) to one grounded in the church's confessional process (the context for the "chartre" in the corresponding passage in C). The "patente" is represented in a mode that evokes a medieval tradition in which covenants, even if recorded in writing, were primarily oral agreements articulated through material and visually expressive symbols – a tradition that historians such as Michael Clanchy have characterized as oral, memorial, reciprocal, and feudal.[14] By contrast, the "chartre" is represented in a mode that evokes a later medieval tradition in which documents relied increasingly on verbal signs rather than on visual symbols. Alford glosses the "chartre" as "a written document, signed and sealed, which grants certain rights and privileges, or conveys landed property."[15] This is the tradition that Clanchy has characterized as written, documentary,

13 Ibid., 216–17. Noting that "Hawkyn's patent has been entirely excised from C," Davis asks, "could this [the excision] be to remove any similar ambiguity between secular vehicle and religious tenor that it might have created?" Davis, "A Response to Steiner's 'Langland's Documents,'" 109.

14 The title of Clanchy's book *From Memory to Written Record: England 1066–1307* captures the transition from memorial symbolism to scriptorial verbalism: "[b]efore documents were used, the truth of an event or transaction had been established by personal statements, often made on oath, by principals or witnesses" (232). Commenting on the oral character of legal documents such as grants, Clanchy writes that "[b]efore conveyances were made with documents, the witnesses 'heard' the donor utter the words of the grant and 'saw' him make the transfer by a symbolic object, such as a knife or a turf from the land" (203; see also ibid., 220). In a recent essay on the semiotic basis of medieval seals, Miriam Bedos-Rezak speaks of "an irreversible movement [that] had already commenced during the eleventh century that was to shift preeminence from personal to textual presence"; see Bedos-Rezak's "Medieval Identity," 1490. For a classic discussion of the relations between orality and literacy in the Middle Ages, see Brian Stock, "Medieval Literacy, Linguistic Theory, and Social Organization," 13–29, and Jesse Gellrich, "Orality, Literacy, and Crisis in the Later Middle Ages," 461–73.

15 Alford, *A Glossary*, 25–6.

unilateral, and institutional.[16] Dispensing with the descriptive mode in which the "patente" is presented in B, the comparable passage in C adopts a definitional mode to characterize the "chartre."

To move from the passage in B to the corresponding one in C is, as I argue in Part I of this chapter, to move from Christ's penitential "patente" described as materially visual, reciprocal, and feudal, to the church's penitential "chartre" defined as verbal, unilateral, and institutional. In Part II of the chapter, I contend that the C version of Patience's sermon both courts and challenges the penitential semiotics that, as already argued in chapter 1, frames Mede's and Contricion's confessions. In C, Patience's sermon on the "chartre" draws upon the canonistic conception of penance as a semiotic process of mediation between the penitent's inner contrition and divine remission – a process introduced and described in light of the confessors' manuals discussed in chapter 1. At the same time, Patience's manner of expounding the "chartre" challenges such a conception by presenting the penitential process as more temporal than semiotic, as more processual than terminal, and as more individual than institutional. When we move from the "patente" in B to the "chartre" in C, we witness the transformation of the semiotic register of the canon law into a temporal one. This transformation, I argue, contains evidence for C's most innovative contribution to the canonist thought on penance: the C passages cast the "chartre" – and thereby the received canonistic thought that authorizes it – as less certain about salvation than the "patente" issued by the non-institutional Christ. Together both parts of the chapter claim that the C passages under discussion offer a more radical re-envisioning of the institution of private sacramental penance than found elsewhere in either version of the poem and than argued in the preceding chapters.

---

16 Clanchy argues that "the English experience of literacy … presents itself as a relatively coherent whole in the period 1066–1307 because the country was dominated by a centralizing royal bureaucracy" (5–6). As Clanchy, Pettitt, and other scholars writing on the differences between orality and literacy in the later Middle Ages make clear, oral elements such as gesture and tone of voice found written forms of expression via diction, punctuation, register, and syntax. For instance, Pettitt notes, "[t]he differences between post-textual and pre-textual tradition, meanwhile, need not be exaggerated. Once it loses touch with the original, post-textual transmission is as oral and aural as pre-textual." See his "Textual to Oral," 20; see also Clanchy, *From Memory to Written Record*, 205.

Part I

The "Patente" as Covenantal Symbol in the B Passage (passus 14, lines 174–95)

Occurring at the end of Patience's sermon to the penitent Haukyn, the "patente" in B documents the covenant between Christ and fallen humanity. Exhorting Haukyn not to despair at his inability to keep his sin-stained coat clean, Patience explains Christ's covenant in terms of a feudal analogy:

"Ac poore peple, þi prisoners, Lord, in þe put of meschief –
Conforte þo creatures þat muche care suffren
Thoruȝ derþe, þoruȝ droghte, alle hir dayes here,
Wo in wynter tyme for wantynge of cloþes,
And in somer tyme selde soupen to þe fulle;
Conforte þi carefulle, Crist, in þi riche –
For how þow confortest alle creatures clerkes bereþ witnesse:
Conuertimini ad me et salui eritis.
Thus *in genere* of his gentries Iesu Crist seide
To robberis, to reueris, to riche and to poore,
To hores, to harlotes, to alle maner peple.
Thou tauȝtest hem in þe Trinitie to taken bapteme
And be clene þoruȝ þat cristnyng of alle kynnes synnes,
And if vs fille þoruȝ folie to falle in synne after,
Confession and knowlichynge and crauynge þi mercy
Shulde amenden vs as manye siþes as man wolde desire.
Ac if þe pouke wolde plede herayein, and punysshe vs in conscience,
He sholde take þe acquitaunce as quyk and to þe queed shewen it –
Pateat, &c: Per passionem Domini –
And putten of so þe pouke, and preuen vs vnder borwe.
Ac þe parchemyn of þis patente of pouerte be moste,
And of pure pacience and parfit bileue.
Of pompe and of pride þe parchemyn decourreþ,
And principalliche of alle peple, but þei be poore of herte." (B 14.174–95)

In this sermon, Patience locates the "patente" within a context of reciprocal obligations that bind the divine "Lord" and his human "prisoners." Identifying the "Lord" with Christ, Patience calls upon him to care for the "poore peple, þi prisoners" or "þo creatures þat muche care suffren." In his invocation, Patience underlines Christ's role as a comforter of people who are likened to "prisoners" under his care and are variously identified as "robberis," "reueris," "riche," "poore," "hores," and "harlotes." As comforter, Christ educates them about the means to salvation. Patience not only reports Christ's teachings to his people on topics such as baptism and the Trinity, but also has Christ speak in his own words. As the "clerkes" bear witness, Christ articulates in his own voice the reciprocal terms of salvation: "*Conuertimini ad me et salui eritis* (convert to me and you will be saved) / Thus *in genere* of his gentries Iesu Crist seide..."[17] In presenting Christ's covenantal offer in the second person narrative, Patience renders him audibly and immediately present to his people.

To reinforce the intimate relation between the divine and the human embodied by Christ's covenant, Patience invokes "þe acquitaunce" or the "patente."As Steiner has persuasively argued, Patience locates the "patente" within the late medieval lyrical tradition comprising poems called the *Charters of Christ*, which "are allegories of salvation by means of two elaborate conceits: Christ's crucified body as a legal document, and salvation history as the issuing and completion of a land grant."[18] As a contract between the divine and the human, Christ's charter derives its legal force from the principle of mutual agreement integral to the feudal trothplight. The "immanent power of the various texts of *The Charter of Christ*," as Richard Firth Green explains, "resides not merely in the preeminence of the grantor but in the momentous nature of the trothplight to which they attest."[19] In his discussion of medieval trothplights, Green argues that such texts construct the Christological charters as "symbolizing, rather than merely recording, the legal facts to which they attested."[20] The *Charter of Christ* texts present Christ's documents not as signs indicating the message of his covenant but as symbols in which the message and

17 B 14.181.

18 In the *Long Charter*, as Steiner notes, Christ follows the proper legal procedure of the "livery of seisin," and the resultant charter is "the crucified body of Christ and the contract of the Atonement: the stretching of the parchment is the nailing of his body to the cross; the pen is the scourge; and the ink the spit of his tormenters" (*Documentary Culture*, 50).

19 Green, *A Crisis of Truth*, 276.

20 Ibid., 275. For a comprehensive discussion of Langland's "patente" as a symbolic trothplight, see the chapters "Charter and Wed" and "Bargains with God" in Green's *A Crisis of Truth*.

medium are one and the same.[21] In Steiner's words, the document "*is* the crucified body of Christ."[22] This concept of ontological identity underlying a material document and Christ is by no means a postmedieval anachronism but rather, as Miriam Bedos-Rezak has shown in her study of seals, dates back to the eleventh and twelfth centuries.[23]

Given the underlying logic of identity between material document and authorizing subject in the poetic tradition of the *Charter of Christ*, the "patente" in B is a symbol: the "chirographum dei" (handwriting of God) "drawn up on the cross" and "roughly synonymous with Christ's body."[24] The "patente" exemplifies the medieval symbol that, as János Bak explains, is an object of sense-experience that calls up a person, group, or action.[25] Briefly stated, the "patente" appeals to the sense of sight. As Steiner explains, from an etymological perspective, the word "patente" calls attention to its Latin verb-form "patere" (to lay bare) and thus foregrounds the visible dimension of Christ's covenant.[26] Likewise, as John Alford's gloss to the historical sense of the "patente" suggests, the poem's use of the word "patente" to designate Christ's covenant appears to be motivated by the openness or public visibility integral to the historically real patents that the Crown issued: the "patente" is "not sealed up but exposed to open view and usually addressed to all subjects of the realm."[27]

---

21 For a detailed reading of *Piers Plowman* in light of the texts of the *Charter of Christ*, see Jill Averil Keen, *The Charters of Christ and Piers Plowman* (New York: Lang, 1999).

22 Steiner, *Documentary Culture*, 50 (emphasis mine).

23 Miriam Bedos-Rezak argues that seals "participated in this same logic [of sameness whereby] conceptions of the sign and the human subject appear to be closely related [and] … operated on the basis of a newly elaborated premise of a dialogic connection between semiotics, theology, ontology, and anthropology." See her "Medieval Identity," 1492.

24 Steiner, *Documentary Culture*, 104.

25 Bak's explanation of the medieval symbol is as follows: "die Rede von verhältnismässig naheliegenden Symbolen, nämlich von Zeichen und Gesten, von Objekten und Handlungen, die als solche sichtbar und unter Umständen auch hörbar oder tastbar sind. Auch der grösste Kreis symbolischer Kommunikation gehört zur bildlichen Form solcher Mitteilungen, in denen das objektiv Vorhandene (das gemalte, gezeichnete, gestickte oder gewebte Bild oder das Bildwerk aus Stein, Holz usw.) grundsätzlich über sich hinausweist und eine (im Regelfall von den Betrachtern gar nie real wahrgenommen) Person, Persongruppe oder Handlung heraufbeschwört." See "Symbolik und Kommunikation," 42–3.

26 Steiner, "Medieval Documentary Poetics," 100.

27 Alford, *A Glossary*, 111.

In its etymological and historical senses, the "patente" evokes a document that is as immediately visible and available to the people as Christ himself has been shown to be in the B passage. Writing about similar late medieval documents pertaining to gifts or land-transfers, Jesse Gellrich remarks that the "document itself is not considered for what it 'signifies,' but for what it actually embodies – the gratuity of a donor conveyed physically by the document recording the transfer."[28] All this is to say that the "patente" in B does not merely point to Christ but is coextensive or identical with Christ himself. It is Christ in the form of a visible document recording the covenant of salvation – a covenant whose terms are visible and, hence, credible to every believer.

The "Chartre" as Institutional Sign in the C Passage (passus 16, lines 22–36)

To turn from the "patente" in B to the comparable "chartre" in C is to leave behind a discourse centred on human-divine relations conveyed through the language of visual symbols. In the C passage on the "chartre," one encounters a penitential strand in which the relationship between the human and the divine is no longer immediate or personal but mediated and institutional. Expressed through the language of verbal signs and encapsulated by the "chartre," this penitential strand originates from "Holy Churche" and presents the ecclesiastical institution as the intermediary between Christ and the sinner. Specifically, in C, Patience presents the "chartre" as interposing the institutional stages of penance between the divine and the human:

"Riht so haue reuthe on vs alle, þat on þe rode deydest,
And amende vs of thy mercy and make vs alle meke,
Lowe and lele and louynge, and of herte pore.
And sende vs contricion to clanse with oure soules,
And confessioun to kulle alle kyne synnes
And satisfaccioun þe whiche folfilleth þe Fader wille of heuene.
And these ben Dowel and Dobet and Dobest of alle.
Cordis contricio cometh of sorowe of herte,
And *Oris confessio*, þat cometh of shrifte of mouthe,
And *Satisfaccio*, þat for soules paieth and for alle synnes quyteth:

28 Gellrich, "Orality, Literacy, and Crisis," 467.

Cordis contricio, Oris confessio, Operis satisfaccio –
Thise thre withoute doute tholieth alle pouerte
And lereth lewed and lered, hey and lowe to knowe
Ho doth wel oþer bet, or beste aboue alle;
And Holy Churche and charite herof a chartre made.
And bote these thre þat Y spak of at domesday vs defende,
Elles is al an ydel, al oure lyuynge here –
Oure preyeres and oure penances and pilgrimages to Rome,
Bote oure spensis and oure spendyng sprynge of a trewe welle."
(C 16.22–39)

In this analogous passage in C, the "chartre" expresses a relationship between the divine and human, but no longer within the context of the immediately personal reciprocal ties between divine saviour and human sinner – the context of the B passage in which the "patente" is located. In the lines in C, Patience evokes a new context for the "chartre" – one in which the church's institution of penance mediates between the divine and the human. To foreground the institutional means by which the divine relates to the human, Patience shifts the emphasis from Christ and his people (an emphasis found in B) to the tripartite penitential process mandated by the church.

From the outset, the C version of Patience's sermon indicates a distance or even departure from the world of the corresponding sermon in B: a world marked by a "tremendous sense of the intimacy and adjacency of the holy."[29] In the passage in C, we enter a world where Patience enacts the impersonality, inaccessibility, and silence of the divine to the human. No longer does Patience portray the divine under the human aspect of "Crist," much less under that of the more personal and salvation-promising name "Iesu." In referring to him, Patience uses terms that rhetorically underscore his distance from the "vs" on whose behalf he is invoked. Patience speaks of the one "þat on þe rode deydest." Such recourse to periphrasis not only depersonalizes Christ but also accounts for the excision of Christ's own words from the passage in C.

Just as Christ is not directly named, so the human beneficiaries of divine help are left nameless, un-individuated and unidentified. Absent from the passage in C are the names of professions under which Christ's

29 Green, *Crisis of Truth*, 340, quoting Peter Brown, "Society and the Supernatural: A Medieval Change," *Daedalus* 104 (spring 1975): 141.

people are distinguished: the "robberis," "reueris," "riche," "poore," "hores," and "harlotes" to whom Christ, in the passage in B, immediately conveys his Covenant. In C, Patience subsumes B's profession or class-based addressees of Christ under the collective but undifferentiated plural "vs." In so doing, Patience de-personalizes, or, properly speaking, de-classes the human in the same way as he has already dehumanized the divine.[30] In leaving out the B passage's focus on the interpersonal relationship between Christ and his people, the corresponding C passage prepares the grounds for a new object of attention: institutional penance.

In C, Patience deepens the focus on institutional penance by narrowing the conspectus of the theological means to salvation found in the corresponding passage in B. The Trinity, baptism, confession, and divine mercy comprise the varied topics concerning salvation mentioned in the passage in B. In the passage in C, by contrast, we find no such variety but rather a concentrated focus on just one topic encapsulated by the "chartre."

Issued by "Holy Churche" and "charite," the "chartre" signifies the church's sacrament of penance, which, as we have seen, is conventionally divided into three stages: contrition, confession, and satisfaction. Unlike the "patente" which, as the "clerkes" of the passage in B claim, promises salvation to all those who follow Christ, the "chartre" neither receives any mention by clerics nor signifies any promise of salvation. The "chartre" will, to cite a key verb denoting its function, "defende" those penitents who have followed the three stages of the church's confessional process. As an institutional sign, the "chartre" will legally represent such penitents before their divine judge on Judgment Day. From a penitential perspective, the three stages of the confessional process signified by the "chartre" interpose between the penitent and the divine judge, between, in light of the B passage, the poor sinning vassals and Christ their feudal lord.

The "chartre's" ratification of the three stages of the confessional process and its role as an instrument of advocacy (rather than as a covenant of salvation) articulate a relationship between the divine and the human founded not on personal covenantal ties but on impersonal institutional ones such as those existing between a lawyer and a judge. In light of Paul Strohm's influential work on late medieval feudalism,

30 I thank Jay Gundacker for suggesting this insight.

one may understand the "chartre" as signifying less an older, land-based and oath-bound tie between lord and vassal than a more recent fiscal and "contractual" bond between "lord and retainer."[31] In having the "chartre" invoke the abstract church, not the individualized Christ, as the mediator between the penitent and God, Patience, in C, renders the legal institution integral to the spiritual outcome for the penitents on Judgment Day.

In the C passage, Patience elaborates the interposition of the "chartre" between the penitent and God by redefining the role assigned to Christ in the corresponding passage in B. In C, Patience assigns to the divine the role of enabling penitents to follow the church's penitential process: God is not a comforter or an exemplar for all penitents to emulate (as in the comparable lines in B) but an enabler of the three penitential stages stipulated by the "chartre." In C, Patience invokes divine "reuthe" not in the wider sense of "comfort" for all (as in B) but in the narrower sense of enabling "vs" penitents to acquire the appropriate disposition to participate in the sacrament of penance. Located within the context of sacramental confession, "reuthe" takes on the sense of the divine action of rendering each penitent's heart poor, loyal, meek – i.e., contrite and, hence, internally primed for the church's sacrament. Such "reuthe" amends by "send[ing]" or initiating the three actions of institutional penance: "contricion to clanse with oure soules," "confessioun to kulle alle kyne synnes" and "satisfaccioun þe whiche folfilleth þe Fader wille of heuene."[32] Both theologically and allegorically, Patience, in C, orients attention away from the interpersonal relationship between Christ and his "prisoners" towards an institutionally regulated relationship between a non-personified divinity and a non-specified group ("vs"), towards canon law.

Theologically speaking, to move from B to C is to move from the Christocentric "patente's" offer of redemption from original sin to the church-centred "chartre's" defence against actual sin. Whereas B foregrounds Christ's promise to redeem penitents from the debt of the original sin inherited from Adam and Eve, C concerns itself with the church's legal means of defence against sins that penitents commit in the here and now. As Steiner explains, "if Patience calls this patent an acquittance or pardon from debt, it is one only in the sense that it

31 Strohm, *Social Chaucer*, 16–17.

32 C 16.22–7.

pardons the debt of original, not actual sin."[33] By invoking the "patente," Patience urges Haukyn to look back in time and repose faith in Christ's word on the cross that promised to deliver mankind from the debt of original sin. Indeed, earlier on in the same sermon in both B and C,[34] Patience foreshadows the covenant in speaking of "mesure" as a principle of living righteously as well as invoking "Cristes wordes." But while the C passage stops short of elaborating upon either, the passage in B goes on to dwell at length on "feiþ," asserting that such "feiþ" is the very basis of sacramental penance itself: "Forþi mesure we vs wel and make oure feiþ oure sheltrom; / And þoruȝ feiþ comeþ contricion ... And þouȝ a man myȝte noȝt speke, contricion myȝte hym saue, / And brynge his soule to blisse, by so þat feiþ bere witnesse ... *Ergo* contricion, feiþ and conscience is kyndeliche Dowel."[35] The comparable C passage does not have lines mandating "feiþ" in Christ's word on the cross. By invoking the "chartre" in C, Patience urges Activa Vita to look forward in historical time to the sacrament of penance available to all sinners. Ratified by the church, the "chartre" or, specifically, its three parts will "defende" all those penitents who have confessed against "alle kyne synnes" – i.e., the actual sins that they have committed in their lives. What, in B, is the Christocentric covenant about original sin is, in C, a church-centric document about actual sin. By drawing not upon the biblically grounded visual symbol of the *chirographum dei* but upon the historically grounded verbal sign of the "chartre," the C passage aligns itself with the church and its mechanisms for administering penance.

Allegorically speaking, the shift in emphasis from the individual Christ's covenant (in B) to the institutional church's penitential system (in C) is made manifest by a movement away from the visual details that characterize the passage in B and the inclusion, in the corresponding C passage, of verbal details. The absence of visual symbolism from the C passage is all the more evident when it is seen not just alongside the B passage on Patience's sermon discussed so far, but also alongside an

33 Steiner, "Langland's Documents," 101. Augustine and later exegetes, as Steiner observes, "continued to explain the chirograph as the debt of original sin owed to the devil. In the mid-thirteenth century, Jacobus de Voragine explained that 'this sort of debt the apostle calls a chirograph, which Christ took and nailed to the cross'" (ibid., 96).

34 B 14.82–7; C 15.273–5.

35 B 14.81–7.

earlier B passage (in the same passus) where Haukyn is introduced and Conscience expounds to the narrator the three stages of sacramental penance. Expressing the visual symbolism shared by the tradition of the *Charter of Christ*, this earlier B passage (as well as the one on Patience's sermon discussed so far) serves to foreground the added non-visual aspects of the passage on the "chartre" in C. Considering the visual symbolism of both B passages will throw into relief the C passage's verbal mode of representation and at the same time provide evidence for C's alignment with canon law at the level of allegory.

In B, both Haukyn's self-presentation and Conscience's exposition of the penitential sacrament immediately precede Patience's sermon on the "patente." Haukyn appears in the visual figure of the coat that he wears. As Alford notes, "[t]he chief device by which Haukyn's character is revealed to us is his sin-besmirched coat; [s]o closely identified is it with Haukyn himself that one is tempted to assume that in describing the coat, Langland is describing the man."[36] Reading Conscience's description of the coat within the context of the Sermon on the Mount, Alford argues that the meaning of the coat is "not constant but multifarious and shifting" and that the coat "has become identified with treasure in heaven, where rust and moth do not corrupt and thieves do not break through and steal."[37] Commenting on the visual aspects of Haukyn's self-characterization, Maura Nolan points out that "in a tricky poetic maneuver, Langland stops readers and forces us [*sic*] to *see*, rather than simply *hear*, the figure of Hawkyn."[38] On Haukyn's own terms, the coat ("hater") functions as a visually constructed symbol that makes manifest his sins.[39] He "haue but oon hater" and he "slepe[s] þerinnne o nyȝtes" and "[i]t haþ be laued in Lente and out of Lente boþe"; likewise, he confesses that he "kouþe ... neuere ... kepen [the coat] clene an houre, [and] [t]hat [he] ne soiled it wiþ siȝte or som ydel speche, / Or þoruȝ werk or þoruȝ word, or wille of [his] herte."[40] The coat is no different from its bearer, for its stains are the sins that Haukyn

36 Alford, "Haukyn's Coat," 133.

37 Ibid., 136.

38 Nolan, "The Fortunes of *Piers Plowman*," 619.

39 Reinforcing the location of the visual image of the "cote" within "the parable of the wedding guest [from the New Testament] whose lack of an appropriate garment condemns him to outer darkness," Green points to the opening section of the Middle English poem *Cleanness* as a contemporary poetic source in which another dirt-infested "cote" is "emblematic of its wearer's spiritual state" (*Crisis of Truth*, 365).

40 B 14.1–14.

committed by word and deed, and the coat's cleansing is associated with Lent, when penitents purge themselves via confession. In short, the coat appears as a material vestimentary symbol that is allegorically part of Haukyn's sinning self.

In B again, Conscience's exposition of the penitential sacrament is as visually and materially symbolic as Haukyn's self-presentation. To describe the three stages of penance, Conscience too draws upon the same tradition of the *Charter of Christ* that Patience, as Steiner has argued, engages to describe the "patente." In pointing out that, in B, even the sacrament of penance finds expression in the same symbolic lexicon used to express the "patente," I wish to suggest that Conscience aligns the penitential sacrament allegorically closer to Christ and his covenant than to the institutional church and the canon law of penance.

The following excerpt from the A text of *The Charter of Christ* draws upon images that vividly describe the conversion of Christ's body into a parchment to be inscribed with his covenant:

Ffrend & foe þat with me metton
In my nede alle me for-letton
To a pyler I was ply3t
I tugged and tawed al a ny3t
And waschon in myn ovne blod
And streyte y-streyned vpon þe rod
Streyned to drye vp-on a tre
As parchemyn oveth for to be. (A 73–80; 26b)[41]

It is precisely such tropes of visual symbolism (of tugging, tanning, washing, stretching, and drying) that Conscience (in B) employs to vivify to Haukyn the action of institutional penance. Advising Haukyn on cleaning the coat, Conscience says:

"And I shal kenne þee," quod Conscience, "of Contricion to make
That shal clawe þi cote of alle kynnes filþe –
Cordis contricio ...

41 Spalding, *The Middle English Charters of Christ*. All quotations from the A-text of *The Charter of Christ* are from Spalding's edition and are cited parenthetically by version, line, and page.

Dowel shal wasshen it and wryngen it þoruȝ a wis confessour –
Oris confessio ...
Dobet shal beten it and bouken it as bright as any scarlet,
And engreynen it wiþ good wille and Goddes grace to amende þe;
And siþen sende þee to Satisfaccion for to sonnen it after:
Satisfaccio – Dobest." (B 14.16–22)

Although Conscience does not describe any charter of Christ in this passage, his visually symbolic lexicon is just as material as that found in the passage cited from the A text of *The Charter of Christ*. By speaking in such a symbolic mode, Conscience treats the penitential sacrament as more covenantal than institutional, closer to the material action of Christ than to that of the historical church. Put differently, Conscience locates the penitential sacrament within the symbolic context of Christ's charter and thereby focuses on his covenant rather than on the procedures of penance themselves.

Adopting and reinforcing Conscience's symbolic mode of exposition, Patience, in the sermon that follows, describes the "patente" to Haukyn. Patience's identification of the "patente" with the word "parchemyn," as Steiner has established, not only highlights its material and visual form but also invokes the literary tradition of the *Charter of Christ* where Christ's body is identified and described as a "parchment" in the material language of symbols that Conscience, as I have just discussed, uses to describe the sacrament of penance. In sum, both B passages – Conscience's elaborate description of the penitential sacrament and Patience's telegraphically brief description of the "patente" – share the same symbolic lexicon used to identify and describe Christ's covenant.

Seen now in light of the concrete material and visual symbolism that pervades the B passages discussed above, the C passage leading up to the "chartre" stands out as symbolically impoverished. Activa Vita's appearance, Patience's definition of the penitential sacrament expounded by Conscience, and the imagining of the "patente" in terms of the "chartre" lack the precise, visually material features that distinguish their respective counterparts in B. In the C passage, what emerges into relief is a non-visual, non-material verbal mode of characterization, which, as I shall attempt to demonstrate in Part II of this chapter, is how canonists talk about the institution of private sacramental penance. In adopting such a mode of talking about penance, the C version allegorically enacts its alignment with the church's mediatory function of regulating the relationship between the penitent and God, between sin and its remission.

To move from B's Haukyn to C's Activa Vita is to move from visual allegory to verbal allegory, from a concrete individualized entity to an abstract general category of which such an entity might be a member. As a proper name that can refer to any person, Haukyn, in B, is at first semantically empty but goes on to acquire a specific penitential meaning in light of its bearer's visually rich self-characterization. With regard to Barney's distinction between concrete and abstract names in *Piers Plowman* and other medieval literary works, the name Haukyn exemplifies "the extreme of concreteness" that proper names in general have.[42] By contrast, the name Activa Vita in the C text stands for an abstraction. Adapting Barney's words on allegorical names, Activa Vita "*pretends to name, not things, but whatever lies under things* – substances, relations, intentions, faculties, categories, powers, ideas."[43]

As with Activa Vita, so with the "chartre." Patience conveys no visual or material impressions of the "chartre." We do not see what the document looks like or get a sense of what it is made of. Langland's choice of the word "chartre" may well have been dictated by its historically grounded sense of a legal document that, as Alford explains in his gloss to the word, is "signed and sealed."[44] Unlike the "patente" which is "not sealed up but exposed to view," the "chartre's" visually closed character enables it to function solely as a verbal sign.[45] As presented by Patience, the "chartre" functions as a verbal sign complementing the visual and material signs (such as tears and shame) theorized by Raymond and discussed in our reading of Mede's and Contricion's confessions in chapter 1. There my focus was on the visible signs of heart-felt remorse (or their absence). Here, I shift the emphasis from visual to verbal signs, and, in doing so, broaden the focus onto the entire tripartite penitential process that, as we shall see, was understood by Peter Lombard, Gratian, Thomas of Chobham, and Raymond as a system of

42 Barney explains the distinction between concrete and abstract names thus: "We speak of a name as 'concrete' when it urges our consciousness to nestle close to the thing (milk), and 'abstract' when it urges us to think of classes or aspects of things, perhaps no longer of physical things at all ('nutriment') … Allegorical names are not concrete, but abstract" (*Allegories of History*, 23).

43 Ibid., 22 (emphasis in original).

44 Alford, *A Glossary*, 25.

45 Ibid., 111.

signs that mediate the penitent's access to God and his divine gifts. Read in light of the theological and canonistic thought on the semiotic character of contrition, confession, and satisfaction, Patience's manner of defining the "chartre" in C demonstrates the penitential institution's mediatory role between the penitent and God.

Part II

The "Chartre" as Verbal Sign and Penitential Discourse

Foremost among the medieval thinkers on the semiotic character of the penitential sacrament is Peter Lombard. In a recent essay on the relationship between penitential theology and canon law, Joseph Goering argues that Peter "builds upon and transmits to students a tradition shared by both theologians and jurists."[46] Identifying Book 4 of Peter Lombard's *Sententiarum Libri Quatuor* as "dedicated entirely to a study of 'signs,'" Goering notes that Peter's distinction between "things" (Books 1–3) and "signs" (Book 4) "won the day in the schools, and, as a result, his way of presenting the tradition to his students shaped the way it was to be treated in the schools for centuries to come."[47] Based on Gratian's *Tractatus de Penitentia,* and couched in the terminology of signification and reference central to the medieval discourse on signs, Peter's reflections on sacramental penance will help us appreciate the extent to which the C version's treatment of the "chartre" at once courts, extends, and challenges the semiotics informing the discourse of canon law.

In "Distinction 22" of Book 4, Peter Lombard sheds light on such a semiotics. Clarifying the distinction between sign and referent, Peter uncovers the semiotic character of the relationship between the penitent's contrition for sins and the remission from them that God grants. Peter begins by defining the sacrament as "the sign of the sacred referent" (Sacramentum enim signum est sacrae rei).[48] Distinguishing

46 Peter Lombard's *Sententiarum Libri Quatuor*, as Goering notes, "predominate in the faculties and schools of theology" in the same way "as Gratian's *Decretum* became a touchstone for juridical education throughout the rest of the Middle Ages" ("Penitential Theology," 228). For Peter's indebtedness to Gratian's *Tractatus de Penitentia*, see Larson, *Master of Penance*.

47 Goering, "Penitential Theology," 229.

48 Peter Lombard, *Sententiarum Libri Quatuor* (Paris: Louis Vives, Libraire-Editeur, 1892), 639; all quotations from Peter's text refer to this edition and are cited by reference to the abbreviated title, the distinction, and the page number, as here: *Sent*. 4. d.22, 639.

between exterior and interior penance in terms of the distinction between sign and referent, Peter first surveys various views on the character of the sacrament. He then notes that some regard the sacrament as "exterior penance" or "the sign of interior penance, namely [the sign of] contrition of heart, and of humility" (Quidam dicunt sacramentum hic esse, quod exterius tantum geritur, scilicet exterior poenitentia: quae est signum interioris poenitentiae, scilicet, contritionis cordis, et humilitatis).[49] Some others, however, Peter goes on to point out, consider the sacrament to be "exterior and interior penance, not two sacraments but one, as the species of bread and wine are not two sacraments but one" (exteriorem poenitentiam et interiorem esse sacramentum, nec duo sacramenta, sed unum ut species panis et vini non duo sunt sacramenta, sed unum).[50] Peter goes on to distinguish between the two kinds of penance in terms of sign and referent:

> aliud rem et non sacramentum, scilicet, remissionem peccatorum. Interior enim poenitentia, et res est sacramenti, id est, exterioris poenitentiae: et sacramentum remissionis peccati, quam signat et facit. Exterior quoque poenitentia et interioris signum est, et remissionis peccatorum. (*Sent*. 4. d. 22, 639)

> [they call] another the referent and not the sacrament, namely, the remission of sins. For interior penance is the referent of the sacrament, that is, [the referent] of exterior penance. And exterior penance is the sign of interior penance, and [the sign] of the remission of sins.

In this passage, the word "signum" signifies the external or expressive aspect of penance whereas the word "res" indicates the internal or non-expressive penitential aspect: the "remission" from sins.

In his *Decretum*, Gratian, Peter Lombard's intellectual *magister*,[51] draws upon the language of signs to report a common view on the distinction between outward and inner penitence in his tract on penance ("De Penitentia"). In summing up the so-called contritionist position – that contrition of the heart alone remits sin – Gratian uses the analogy

49 Ibid.

50 *Sent*. 4. d. 22, 639.

51 As Larson argues, Gratian to his contemporaries was neither a theologian nor a canonist but a "magister" – a term that captures the complex pedagogical role he played for theologians and canonists alike; see her *Master of Penance*, 366.

with signs to explain that oral confession plays a declarative rather than causative role:

> Fit itaque confessio ad ostensionem paenitenciae, non ad impetrationem ueniae, sicut circumcisio data est Abrahae in signum iustitiae, non ita causam iustificationis, sic confessio sacerdoti offertur in signum veniae acceptae, non in causam remissionis accipiendae. (*Decretum, II*, C33, q. 3, d.p.c. 37, col. 2205–6; *CIC*, 1: 1167)
>
> Therefore, confession is made for the demonstration of penitence, not for the procurement of pardon; just as circumcision was given to Abraham as a sign of justice/righteousness, not as the cause of justification, so confession is offered to the priest as a sign of the pardon that has already been received, not as the cause of remission yet to be received.[52]

The penitent's verbal account of sins narrated before the confessor is a sign insofar as it only points to the referent that has already been granted. That is, as a sign, oral confession declares rather than generates the pardon or mercy that, as Gratian explains earlier in the tract, is obtained solely by the inner contrition of the heart.

The difference between sign and referent occupied later canonists and theologians including, as we have already mentioned in chapter 1, Raymond of Peñafort and Thomas of Chobham (*Summa confessorum*), who popularized the penitential orthodoxy in late medieval England.[53] Thomas of Chobham recalls but also reinterprets the semiotic and mediatory role that Gratian assigns to confession. In a "questio" on "the power of the keys" (de potestate clavium), Thomas characterizes the confessor's role more as institutional than as sacramental:

> Et dicunt quidam / quod hic est sensus: sacerdos absolvit aliquem a peccato, id est ostendit eum absolutum. Sed videtur hoc esse falsum, quia sacerdos nec in ecclesia nec alibi ostendit populo quis venerit ad confessionem.

---

52 I have modified my translation in light of Atria Larson's in *Master of Penance*, 58.

53 Underscoring the popularity of Thomas's *Summa* in England and on the Continent north of the Alps, F. Broomfield notes that "[i]t was in the possession of the lower ranks of the clergy … [and that] [o]n the evidence available, we may conclude that it must have been one of the most influential *summae confessorum*, and so it may be presumed that it was one of the best guides for confessors produced during the medieval period" (Thomas of Chobham, *Thomae de Chobham summa confessorum*, ed. Broomfield, lxxiv–lxxv).

> Ideo melius dicendum est quod sacerdos absolvit penitentem ab obligatione fori penitentialis et ab impetitione diaboli. Et est simile in foro iudiciali. Aliquis enim petit debitum ab aliquo coram iudice, et ipse in rei veritate nihil ei debet. Actor producit falsos testes et cadit a probatione. Iudex absolvit reum non a debito, quia nihil debuit, sed absolvit eum ab observatione fori iudicialis ne oporteat eum iterum ire ad iudicium propter hoc, et absolvit eum ab impetitione actoris, ut actor de cetero ab eo tale debitum non possit petere. Similiter sacerdos non absolvit penitentem a peccato, quia prius dimissum est ei in contritione, sed absolvit eum / quantum ad hoc ne iterum oporteat eum venire ad confessionem propter hoc peccatum. (*Summa confessorum*, q. viiia. *De potestate clavium*, 207–8)
>
> And some say that this is the sense: the priest absolves someone from sin, that is, he signifies to him that he is absolved. But this seems to be false, because the priest neither in the church nor anywhere signifies [absolution] to the people who come to confession.
>
> Therefore, it is better to say that the priest absolves the penitent from the obligation of penitential forum and from the accusation of the devil. And, likewise, in the judicial forum, one [a plaintiff] demands from someone a thing owed in front of a judge, and [that accused person] himself, in point of truth, owes nothing to him. The plaintiff produces false witnesses and fails. The judge absolves the accused not from the thing owed because he owed nothing but he absolves him from the observation of the judicial forum so that he [the accused] should not come again to judgment on account of this case, and the judge absolves him from the accusation of the plaintiff so that the plaintiff would not be able to demand from him [the accused] the same thing owed. Likewise, the priest does not absolve a penitent from sin, because the sin was earlier on remitted in contrition, but the priest absolves him inasmuch as he does not require him to come again to confession on account of that sin.

Recalling Gratian's position about confession not causing the remission of sin, Thomas regards the "absolution" that the confessor grants as indicative of the release of the penitent from an institutional obligation: namely, the requirement (expressed by canon 21) to confess once and, hence, not to confess the same sin again. The analogy that Thomas draws between the confessor's office and that of a judge foregrounds the confessor's role as an institutional intermediary with little or no direct access to the ultimate "referent" (res) of remission that

God alone grants. The confessor, in Thomas's conception of private sacramental penance, behaves like a judge insofar as he determines and pronounces on institutional obligations rather than on their ultimate non-institutional or divine ends. To recapitulate, for Thomas, the confessor deals with signs that serve as a semiotic means of mediating the relationship between the penitent's contrition and God's gift of remission. The divine referent (the remission of sins that God grants), mediated by such signs, is at no point created by or made available to the confessor.

Like Thomas, Raymond also treats the sacrament of penance within a similar semiotic framework. In chapter 1, I focused on Raymond's characterization of the confessor as a judge attentive to visual signs of contrition or of its absence. Here, I want to return to a passage in which Raymond envisions the entire penitential process as unfolding in a semiotic mode:

> Item circa ista nota quare confessio sive paenitentia dicitur sacramentum. Sunt enim ibi tria notanda, scilicet, confessio, contritio, et mundatio. Confessio est signum tantum, scilicet, contritionis. Contritio est res et signum: res signi confessionis, signum mundationis. Mundatio est res signi tantum, scilicet, contritionis. (*Summa de paenitentia*, 3, *De paenitentiis et remissionibus*, 13.811)

> Note why confession or penance is called a sacrament. There are here three things to be noted, confession, contrition, and purification. Confession is the sign only, namely of contrition. Contrition is the referent and sign: the referent of the sign of confession, the sign of purification. Purification is the referent of the sign only, namely of contrition.

In this passage, Raymond treats not just visual but also verbal signs in the penitential forum as a means of mediation between the penitent and God. That is, not only contrition but also confession are the intermediary means to the end "purification" (mundatio), the word Raymond uses for remission. Although Raymond regards "contrition" (contritio) as being both sign and referent, he makes it clear that contrition is a referent with regard only to "confession" (confessio) and not to "purification" (mundatio) – the ultimate referent that does not and cannot function as a sign. In his *Glossa* to Raymond's *Summa de paenitentia*, William of Rennes clarifies the two signs of confession and contrition and their relationship to the referent purification:

> *Confessio est signum*: Scilicet propter dolorem, & planctum enormem, quae apparent in verbis confitentis, & se accusantis; contritio vero est signum mundationis propter hanc similtudinem, quia sicut illud, quod conteritur, annihilatur, ita macula peccati per contritionem omnino tollitur, & sic anima mundatur. (Gloss ad v. *Confessio est signum*, 12.447)

> *Confession is a sign*: namely on account of grief, and great lamentation, which manifest themselves in the words of the one confessing, and accusing himself; contrition, however, is the sign of purification on account of this similarity, because just as that which is ground is destroyed, so is the mark of sin completely removed by contrition, and the soul is thus purged.

Thomas's, Raymond's, and William's expositions of confession, contrition, and purification unfold as a movement from signs of confession and of contrition to the non-signifying referent purification/remission. All three thinkers treat the penitential process as an institutional means by which the confessor elicits and evaluates signs that mediate between human contrition and divine remission.

Patience, however, takes a different approach to the same process in C. In deploying the "chartre" rather than the "patente" as central to penance, Patience, in C, has a dramatically different effect from that of Thomas, Raymond, and William. In the imitation of the semiotic process, Patience enacts the uncertainty about the penitent's remission of sins and thereby contests the correlation between sign and referent theorized by the penitential theorists. In continually deferring the meaning of the "charter," Patience calls into question the viability of the referent "remission" in Thomas's and Raymond's expositions of the working of the penitential sacrament. To begin with, Patience's exposition initiates the process of deferral by desisting from naming the "chartre" until after its constituent parts have been identified, renamed, translated, and repeated. First, Patience prenames the "chartre" by identifying its three parts as "contricioun," "confessioun," and "satisfaccioun."[54] Then, he renames the three parts respectively as "Dowel," "Dobet," and "Dobest." At the same time, he translates the three Dos by identifying them respectively with the three conventional penitential terms in Latin: "Cordis contricio," "Oris confessio," and "Satisfaccio." And, finally, he repeats the three Latin terms (with a slight variation

54 I owe this point about pre-naming to Frank Grady, who commented on an early version of this chapter.

on "Satisfaccio"). Such an expository mode of pre-naming, renaming, translating, and repeating results in a chain of nominatives in which each member of the chain refers to or is displaced by another synonymous one, and no single member is identified with a final meaning.

Patience's scheme of expounding the "chartre" invites comparison with one that Barney identifies as common to allegorical works such as the *Distinctiones Abel*, a composition that offers "an especially useful entrée into the methods and ideals of medieval allegoresis."[55] As Barney explains:

> A well-formed article in the *Distinctiones Abel* may be compared with a rewrite rule in modern linguistics: a token on the left (the title) is "rewritten" on the right in an expanded "realization" of the token, often with optional arbitrary choices included in the expansion ... The right-hand, expanded material does not replace, but rather explicates, unfolds, divides the left-hand token.[56]

Having repeatedly named the three penitential parts of the "chartre" in English and Latin, Patience glosses them in two distinct registers. Patience first glosses the three parts of the "chartre" in a register that can best be described as dramatic and non-formal, for it avoids the dogmatic prose of penitential discourse. Contrition serves to "cleanse with oure soules," confession to "kulle alle kyne synnes," and satisfaction to "folfilleth þe Fader wille of heuene." The notion of contrition as killing sins, and the role of satisfaction as fulfilling the Father's will of heaven have nothing technical in diction but they dramatize the action of penance in vivid demotic language. In his subsequent glosses of the Latin terms for the three parts of the same "chartre," Patience adopts a more arid or formal register than the dramatic or colloquial one he used at first. He explains that "Cordis contricio" proceeds from "sorowe of herte," "Oris confessio" from "shrift of mouth," and "Satisfaccio" from "alle synnes quyteth." Compared with the non-formal terms deployed previously to gloss confession and satisfaction ("kulle alle kyne synnes," and "folfilleth þe Fader wille of heuene"), the expressions "shrift" and "quyteth" are not only more literal translations of their Latin penitential equivalents but more technical or canonistic in diction.

55 Barney, "Visible Allegory," 88.
56 Ibid., 93–4.

Patience's mode of pre-naming, renaming, and glossing the institutional "chartre" courts and contests the mode in which sacramental penance unfolds in the penitential forum. Whereas Patience recalls the difference between sign and referent that Thomas and Raymond distinguish, he redefines the difference in terms of temporal deferral.[57] That is, even as Patience expounds the "chartre" within a semiotic frame of reference regulated by theologians and canonists, he reciprocally adapts that frame to present uncertainty at the end of the penitential process. Whereas for Thomas or Raymond, the confessor typically resolves the difference between the penitent's signs of contrition and the referent remission at the conclusion of every confession, for Patience, the "chartre" offers no such resolution until "domesday." Specifically, the "chartre" holds out no hope of the referent ("res") of remission in the here and the now. As Holy Churche and Charite remark, the "chartre" looks forward eschatologically, as it will "defende" penitents only at "domesday." In other words, in C's handling of the "chartre," the difference between sign and referent is characterized not so much as semiotic but as historical or temporal.

The poem's transformation of the semiotic difference between sign and referent into a temporal one qualifies as a canonistic reinvention and can best be grasped in light of Paul de Man's theory of allegory as a verbal mode of signification. Distinguishing allegory from symbol, de Man regards the former as expressive of "a relationship between signs in which reference to their respective meanings has become of secondary importance."[58] For de Man, allegory exists on the condition that a sign "refer to another sign that precedes it."[59] The meaning of an allegorical sign consists of a temporally previous sign with which "it can never coincide, since it is of the essence of the previous sign to be pure anteriority."[60] By contrast, the symbol, for de Man, "postulates the possibility of an identity or identification": the meaning of a symbol does not consist of a previous symbol as the symbol embodies what it expresses.[61] To recapitulate de Man's difference between allegory and symbol, allegory "designates primarily a distance in relation to its own origin, and, renouncing the nostalgia and the desire to coincide,

57 I am grateful to Frank Grady for suggesting this formulation.
58 de Man, "The Rhetoric of Temporality," 207.
59 Ibid.
60 Ibid.
61 Ibid.

it establishes its language in the void of this temporal difference," whereas the symbol designates a unity of sign and referent.[62]

In naming, renaming, and repeating the three parts of the "chartre," Patience produces triadic sets of penitential names or signs, where the sets, while no doubt referring to each other in a continuum, are non-identical with regard to both language and register. In light of de Man's distinction between symbol and allegory, the "patente" postulates an identity or identification of document and Christ himself whereas the "chartre" "consists only in the repetition (in the Kierkegaardian sense of the term) of a previous sign with which it can never coincide."[63] That is, each triadic set of names that Patience assigns to the three parts of the "chartre" underscores the "distance" from its penitential meaning: the distance between name and meaning, between the immediate "signa" or "indicia" (associated with contrition, confession, and satisfaction) and the ultimate "res" of remission, between the human penitent and the divine judge. This distance is not only semiotic but also temporal. Whereas de Man indicates the temporal dimension of the allegorical sign by characterizing its "essence" as "pure anteriority," the poem indicates the temporal dimension of his equally allegorical sign by characterizing its essence as futurity: the "chartre" looks forward to "domesday."

In C, Patience has recourse to grammar in order to foreground the semiotic distance (between the "signa" and "res") as temporal. In so doing, he lends a radical quality to his invention, for he extends and challenges the difference (between sign and referent) theorized by canonistic writings on sacramental penance. Patience equates the "chartre's" three parts of sacramental penance with Dowel, Dobet, and Dobest. Considering Dowel, Dobet, and Dobest "a device for labeling divisions," Robert Frank long ago recognized them (the three Dos) as non-referential or formal figures.[64] More recently, D. Vance Smith has regarded the three Dos as denoting the verb-like motive "activity of change itself":

> [T]he difficulty that characters in *Piers Plowman* and the poem's later readers encounter when they try to establish boundaries of Dowel, Dobet, and Dobest is the inevitable consequence of the fundamentally verbal nature

62 Ibid.

63 Ibid.

64 Frank, *Piers Plowman and the Scheme of Salvation*, 43.

> of the three modes. Each mode signifies more than a changed life; it signifies the activity of change itself. Their processual nature effaces distinctions between them. Each shades imperceptibly into the next, a series of accidents in a single continuum.[65]

The verb-like "processual nature" of the three Dos or their "shading imperceptibly into the next" in a "single continuum" allegorically enacts the movement of the stages of the official penitential process – a process in which contrition, confession, and satisfaction function as signs temporally distant from but inclining towards the divine referent of remission.

In identifying the parts of the "chartre" with the three Dos, Patience offers a grammatical enactment of the "distance" between the sign of the "chartre" and the *res* of divine remission, for, as Anne Middleton and Smith have demonstrated, the three Dos are identified with verbs in a number of places in the poem.[66] In her justly famous essay on Dowel, Dobet, and Dobest, Middleton comments on their "processual nature" by arguing that the three Dos exemplify Priscian's grammatical theory of the verb: "the three words, which share the substantive form of the essential transitive verb 'do' modified in three progressive degrees, 'stand for' action considered *per se*, rather than as a set of finite acts or completed predications in time ... [they], then, are occurrence without occasion, the essence of Christian action rather than exemplary instances of it."[67]

Sharpening Middleton's insight into the verbal character of Dowel, Dobet, and Dobest, Smith has more recently argued that Langland constructs the three Dos from infinitives and thus "they signify the passage of time, the 'flux,' of the verb."[68] Among the medieval grammarians whom Smith draws on to substantiate his claim, Albertus Magnus may be singled out for his definition of the infinitive verb – a definition that may shed further light on the status of the "chartre" as a verbal sign expressive of a distance from but inclination towards a referent:

65 Smith, *The Book of the Incipit*, 204.

66 As Smith has noted, Langland treats the three Dos as infinitives in a number of passages in the B and C texts; in B 13.128–30, two of the Dos are named infinitives ("Dowel and Dobet are two infinites") whereas in C 15.126–8, the three Dos are indirectly spoken of in terms of the infinitive verb; for a comprehensive discussion of the three Dos as infinitive verbs, see Smith, *The Book of the Incipit*, 202–11.

67 Middleton, "Two Infinites," 175.

68 Smith, *The Book of the Incipit*, 207.

> [opp.1] sed verbum infinitivi modi significat per modum fluentis et dependentis, et non per modum per se stantis cum sit verbum, quia omne verbum significat per modum fluxus et fieri (126) ... [Resp. alia] Sed verbum infinitivi modi significat per modum inclinabilis ad aliud cui repugnat modus per se stantis, quia modus inclinabilis ad aliud est illud quo conceptus verbi significatur secundum quod verbum est pars orationis ... Cum ergo verbum infinitivi modi manet verbum, oportet quod significet sub modo inclinationis aliud ... [Nota Bene] Sed infinitivo est duas naturas considerare: unam per quam egreditur ab alio, et se habet in ratione distantis ... Bene potest apponere, sicut et alia verba, quia significat per modum distantis. (*Quaestiones Alberti de Modis Significandi*, 126, 130, 134)

> But the infinitive verb signifies through the mode of flowing and depending, and not through the mode of being still because every verb signifies through the mode of flux and of being ... But the infinitive verb signifies through the mode of inclination to something to which the mode of standing still [i.e., of independence] is repugnant because the mode of inclination to another thing is that by which the concept of the verb is signified, according to which the verb is a part of speech ... therefore for infinitive verb to remain a verb, it is necessary for it to signify by means of inclining to something ... [Take note] but there is a twofold nature in the infinitive verb: one through which it proceeds from another thing, and contains within itself the concept of distance ... It can well be a predicate, like other verbs, because it signifies through the mode of distance.

To return to the C passage, Patience's exposition of the three Dos comprising the terms of the "chartre" enacts grammatically the penitential action as "a mode of flowing" or "inclination" towards the referent remission. Now, the action of penance, as expounded by Peter Lombard, Thomas, and Raymond, among other orthodox penitential thinkers of the late Middle Ages, finds a conclusion in the here and now whenever the confessor pronounces absolution to the penitent. The same action, as allegorically enacted in the C passage on the "chartre," however, finds no end in the present but in the future. As I have already discussed above, the "chartre" comes into effect only at "domesday" – when the relationship between sign and referent will be matched once and for all.[69] Shifting the emphasis from the visual to the verbal, from

69 I thank Frank Grady for suggesting this crucial distinction and helping me craft this entire section.

Christ to the church, and from original sin to actual sin, the C text's handling of the penitential document results in a vision of penance that inclines forward to "domesday." Such an eschatological vision of penance, despite proceeding from stable allegorical figures representing the institutional church, is provisional with regard to the penitent's attainment of remission. Unlike the "patente" (in B) that looks back towards original sin and promises salvation to those that convert and follow Christ's word, the "chartre" (in C) functions as a sign that points ahead in time towards a referent whose availability to penitents is not certain. Not just the "chartre's" location in a process of deferrals of its meaning but also its eschatological role as that of an advocate at Judgment Day suggests that the revised document will merely stand for – plead for – the remission of penitents.

In a recent study of penance and remission in *Piers Plowman*, David Aers persuasively argues that Langland's eschatology is Christocentric, drawing the general conclusion that Langland defers the resolution of an eschatological issue to the future:

> Langland allows the hope for universal reconciliation through cross and resurrection to coexist with counterpossibilities. He does not seek to harmonize or resolve an eschatological question now. He waits, in hope, in a theological vision of salvation and sin that is thoroughly Christocentric.[70]

Although I agree with Aers's thesis about Langland's general tendency to desist from settling eschatological questions in the "now," I am less sure about the extent to which Christology informs the vision of penance articulated in the revised passage on the "chartre" – especially given that Christ and his "patente" are marginalized in C. However, as Aers astutely indicates, Langland allows for "counterpossibilities." As possibilities, they belong not to the "now" but to the hereafter, to Judgment Day. These are possibilities not of any certain "universal reconciliation" between sign and referent, between penitent and God, but only of advocacy, of institutional representation, of the kind of limited defence that the "chartre" as synecdoche for canon law promises to offer.

The C version's treatment of the "chartre" as a means of institutional advocacy rather than a means to any certain outcome (say, salvation) has much in common with the handling of other instruments of canon

70 Aers, *Salvation and Sin*, 119.

law elsewhere in both versions of the poem. Like pardons and prayers, charters too, although presented as canonically valid, are nevertheless not regarded as sufficient to secure for their recipients salvation. More specifically, C treats the instruments of canon law as legitimate even as it raises questions about their efficacy or, more precisely speaking, about the degree to which they are "syker."[71] In this, C's handling of the "chartre" recalls and reinforces a critical poetics that we have seen in the previous chapters: a poetics of shaping the law by courting and contesting the received canonist thought. As we may recall, in his reflections on the pardon in both B and C, the narrator too deems canonically valid instruments such as indulgences and masses for the soul in purgatory as "nat so syker for þe soule, certes, as ys Dowel."[72] As in the pardon-scene, the narrator uses the contrastive marker "Yet" to express his uncertainty about canon law, so here, in the "chartre" scene, by means of the comparative structure "not so ... as," C holds in tension the institutional means of canon law, on the one hand, and the sacramental ends pertaining to God's judgment alone, on the other. And, to a greater degree than B, C is generated by canonistic thought and at the same time generative of limits upon it.

71 C 9.331.
72 C 9.331.

Epilogue

I opened this study with witnesses to the co-presence and co-preservation of a copy of *Piers Plowman* together with books of canon law. The earliest extant codicological and manuscript evidence of the poem's production and reception, I suggested, also registered clues to an absent presence: the conceptual grounds shared by *Piers Plowman* and canonistic treatises including those itemized by readers such as Walter de Brugge. I argued that the textual community of the literary and legal thus intimated sheds light on the reinvention of canon law within *Piers Plowman* but also with implications for understanding how non-canonists could have mobilized the discourse of canon law in a world in which the poem's versions and canon law books circulated. I conclude now with another witness to yet another book-event recorded also in the Middle Ages, but at what we would now retrospectively regard as their close. It is an epistolary account not of preservation but of destruction. I do so to gesture towards the eventual – perhaps even inevitable – sundering of the ways shared by *Piers Plowman* and the legal treatises examined in this study, and to the implications of that separation for postmedieval literary reinventions of and interventions in the discourse of canon law.

Sometime in the 1520s, Martin Luther wrote George Spalatin a letter in which he itemized the books of canon law that he bequeathed to a wintry fire one December morning. Quite a number of them are among those we have just read alongside *Piers Plowman*:

> Anno 1520 decima Decembris hora nona exusti sunt Wittenbergae ad orientalem portam iuxta s. crucem omnes libri Papae: *Decretum, Decretales* [*Decretales Gregorii IX* or the *Liber extra*], [*Liber*] *Sextus, Clementinae,*

> *Extravagantes*, et bulla novissima Leonis X, item *Summa Angelica, Chrysopassus* Eckii, et alia eiusdem auctoris, Emseri et quaedam alia, quae adiecta per alios sunt: ut videant incendiarii Papistae, non esse magnarum virium libros exurere, quos confutare non possunt ...
>
> On December 10, 1520, at nine o'clock in the morning, [these] papal books were burned in Wittenberg at the eastern gate near the Church of the Holy Cross: the *Decretum*, the *Decretals* [the *Decretals of Gregory IX*], the [*Liber*] *Sextus*, the *Clementines*, the *Extravagantes*, and the most recent bull of Leo X [the bull pronouncing Luther's conditional excommunication for heresy]; also, the *Summa Angelica*, Eck's *Chrysopassus* and other books by this author, the writings of Emser, and certain other books that were added by other people. This was done so that the incendiary papists may see that it doesn't take much to burn books that they cannot refute.[1]

This epistolary account of book-burning has long been infamous for Luther's flagrant reaction to the papal bull (*Exsurge Domine*) that threatened his excommunication. But these fiery words also capture a more general historical moment when canon law had already become a comprehensive and coherent body of texts wedded to and wielded by a powerful elite. The *Corpus iuris canonici*, whose limbs Luther dismembered and cast onto the pyre, now belonged exclusively to the "incendiary papists" (incendiarii papistae) and not to their reformers or to "the Kyng and þe Commune and Kynde Wit þe þridde"[2] that the narrator in the Prologue to *Piers Plowman B* sees as shaping the law. No longer was the *Corpus* regarded as the open book that the distinguished historian Stephan Kuttner considered it to be in the time of Gratian and his late medieval disciples. Already by the 1520s, Luther and his followers viewed it as a closed canon – impervious to the kinds of "commune" invention that have been the subject of my study. Simply put, Luther's letter registers a paradigm-shift from a world in which canon law was for reformers and revolutionaries – real and allegorical – capable of revision and renewal to a world in which they saw it as closed to any kind

---

1 This passage comprises the opening paragraph of a letter that Luther wrote to George Spalatin, whom he characterizes as "the learned and devout man … court chaplain and my friend in the Lord." See Martin Luther, "To George Spalatin," in *Luther's Works*, trans. and ed. Gottfried G. Krodel, vol. 48 (Philadelphia: Fortress Press, 1963), 186–7. (I have edited the translation slightly).

2 Prologue B 121.

of reinvention. After all, invention in the twofold sense understood in this book cannot but proceed from a continuous interaction with and improvisation around traditions that have already been handed down. Not unlike the modernist work, *Piers Plowman* reinvents canon law by unfolding in "what is not merely the present but the present moment of the past," for its poet is conscious, "not of what is dead, but of what is already living."[3]

Writing about sixteenth-century Protestant receptions of the poem, James Simpson argues that "a particular configuration of theology, ecclesiology, and politics" that we see in *Piers Plowman* "had become impossible after the 1530s."[4] To Simpson's list of items that constitute such a configuration, I would add such books of canon law as bequeathed by Walter de Brugge, burned by Luther, and brought to bear upon the B and C versions of *Piers Plowman* in this study. In the wake of Luther's wholesale repudiation of the canonists and their writings, "influential Protestant[s]" and the "Tudors" read *Piers Plowman* no longer as turning towards canon law but as looking away from it towards "an enlightened age to come" – one that they now inhabited.[5]

I would go even further to claim that the poem's innovations within the terms of canon law become increasingly strange and unintelligible to readers to whom the church's legal institution no longer represented an open dialectical process but a closed dogmatic system of jurisprudence. It is precisely the recovery of such a process for twenty-first century readers of *Piers Plowman* that this book has attempted. More particularly, my intention has been to restore the B and C versions of *Piers Plowman* to the immediacy of a moment: a moment of reinvention of and, hence, intervention in the canon law that Luther sought to extirpate by consigning its *Corpus* to the flames one dark cold day.

3 These words have been adapted from T.S. Eliot's "Tradition and Individual Talent," in his collected essays *The Sacred Wood*, 47–59.

4 Simpson, "Edifying the Church," 343–4.

5 Here, I borrow Simpson's words to make my point. Ibid., 344.

Bibliography

Primary Sources

Ad C. Herennium: De ratione dicendi (Rhetorica ad Herennium). Translated by Harry Caplan. Cambridge, MA, and London: Harvard University Press/ Heinemann, 1968.

Aegidius Romanus (Giles of Rome). *De Ecclesiastica Potestate.* Edited by R.W. Dyson. Woodbridge: Boydell Press, 1986.

Alain de Lille. *Liber poenitentialis.* Edited by Jean Longere. 2 vols. Louvain: Editions Nauwelaerts, 1965.

Albertus Magnus. *Quaestiones Alberti de Modis Significandi.* Translated and edited by L.G. Kelly. Studies in the History of the Language Sciences 15. Amsterdam: John Benjamins, 1977.

Augustine. Epistola 153.6.20. In *Patrologia Latina,* vol. 33, cols 0653–66. Accessed online at http://pld.chadwyck.com. The online version is based on Patrologia Latina, ed. J.P. Migne. Paris, *1844–65.*

Bartholemew of Brescia. *Glossa ordinaria in Decretum Gratiani;* see *Corpus juris canonici (CJC).* 3 vols. Rome, 1582. Also available online at http://digital.library.ucla.edu/canonlaw/index.html.

Bernard of Parma. *Glossa ordinaria in Librum extra;* see *Corpus juris canonici (CJC).* 3 vols. Rome, 1582. Also available online at http://digital.library.ucla.edu/canonlaw/index.html.

Bernard of Pavia. *Summa decretalium.* Edited by Ernst Adolph Theodor Laspeyres. Regensburg: Josef Manz, 1860; reprint Graz: Akademische Druck-u. Verlagsanstalt, 1956.

The Book of Vices and Virtues. Edited by W. Nelson Francis. EETS os 217. London: Humphrey Milford, Oxford University Press, 1942.

Chaucer, Geoffrey. *The Riverside Chaucer.* 3rd ed. Edited by Larry D. Benson. Boston: Houghton Mifflin, 1987.

Constitutiones Concilii quarti Lateranensis una cum commentariis glossatorum. Edited by Antonio García y García. Monumenta Iuris Canonici, A: Corpus Glossatorum, 2. Vatican City: Biblioteca Apostolica Vaticana, 1981.

Corpus iuris canonici (CIC). Edited by Emil Friedberg. 2 vols. Leipzig: Akademische Druck- u. Verlagsanstalt, 1879–81; reprint Graz, 1959.

Corpus juris canonici (*CJC*). 3 vols. Rome, 1582. Also available online at http://digital.library.ucla.edu/canonlaw/index.html.

Corpus iuris civilis. Edited by P. Krüger, Th. Mommsen, R. Schöll, and G. Kroll. 3 vols. Berlin, 1872–95.

Dan Michel's Ayenbite of Inwyt. Edited by Richard Morris. EETS os 23. London: Trübner, 1866.

Decrees of the Ecumenical Councils. Vol. 1: *Nicea I to Lateran V*. Edited by Norman P. Tanner. Washington, DC: Georgetown University Press, 1990.

Durandus de Saint-Pourçain. *Durandi a sancto porciano in sententias theologicas Petri Lombardi commentariorum, libri quatuor*. Lyons, 1587.

Dynus Muxellanus. *Commentarius mirabilis super titulo de regulis iuris*. Lyons, 1540.

Gottofredo da Trani. *Summa super titulis decretalium*. Lyons, 1519; reprint Aalen: Scientia Verlag, 1968.

Gratian. *Decretum Magistri Gratiani*. In vol. 1 of *Corpus iuris canonici (CIC)*, edited by Emil Friedberg. Leipzig: Akademische Druck-u. Verlagsanstalt, 1879–81; reprint Graz, 1959.

– *Corpus juris canonici* (*CJC*). 3 vols. Rome, 1582. Also available online at http://digital.library.ucla.edu/canonlaw/index.html.

Gregory IX. *Decretales Gregorii IX* (*Liber extra*). In vol. 2 of *Corpus iuris canonici (CIC)*, edited by Emil Friedberg. Leipzig: Akademische Druck-u. Verlagsanstalt, 1879–81; reprint Graz, 1959.

– *Corpus juris canonici* (*CJC*). 3 vols. Rome, 1582. Also available online at http://digital.library.ucla.edu/canonlaw/index.html.

Haren, Michael. "A Study of the *Memoriale presbiterorum*, a Fourteenth-Century Confessional Manual for Parish Priests." Vols 1 (Commentary) and 2 (Text). PhD diss., Oxford University, 1975.

Higden, Ranulph. *Speculum Curatorum: A Mirror for Curates*. Book I, *The Commandments*. Edited and translated by Eugene Crook and Margaret Jennings. Dallas Medieval Texts and Translations 13. Leuven: Peeters, 2012.

Hildebertus Cenomanensis. "Sermones de tempore, xxiii. In quadragesima sermo quartus. De poenitentia." In *Patrologia Latina*, vol. 171, cols 447B–48A. Accessed online at http://pld.chadwyck.com. The online version is based on Patrologia Latina, ed. J.P. Migne. Paris, 1844–65.

Hostiensis. *Summa aurea*. Cologne: Zetzner, 1612.

Huguccio. *Summa decretorum: Tom. I, Distinctiones I–XX*. Monumenta Iuris Canonici, Series A. Corpus Glossatorum. Vol. 6. Edited by Oldrich Prerovsky. Vatican City: Biblioteca Apostolica Vaticana, 2006.

Innocent III. *De Contemptu Mundi*. In *Patrologia Latina*, vol. 217, cols 701–46. Accessed online at http://pld.chadwyck.com. The online version is based on Patrologia Latina, ed. J.P. Migne. Paris, 1844–65.

Johannes Andreae. *Apparatus in Librum Sextum* (c. 1304) = *Glossa Ordinaria* to *Liber Sextus, Corpus Juris Canonici (CJC)*. 3 vols. Rome, 1582. http://digital.library.ucla.edu/canonlaw/index.html.

– *In titulum de regulis iuris novella commentaria, vulgo mercuriales*. Facsimile edition Johannes Andreae [1581]. Turin: Bottega d'Erasmo, 1966.

Johannes Teutonicus. *Glossa ordinaria in Decretum Gratiani*; see *Corpus juris canonici (CJC)*. 3 vols. Rome, 1582. Also available online at http://digital.library.ucla.edu/canonlaw/index.html.

John Burgh. *Pupilla Oculi*. Paris, 1527.

John of Freiburg. *Summa confessorum* 2.7 *De usuris*. In "John of Freiburg and the Usury Prohibition in the Late Middle Ages: A Study in the Popularization of Medieval Canon Law 273–327," by John A. Lorenc. PhD diss., University of Toronto, 2013.

Langland, William. *Piers Plowman: A Parallel-Text Edition of the A, B, C and Z versions*. 2 vols. Edited by A.V.C. Schmidt. London and New York: Longman, 1995 (vol. 1) and 2011 (vol. 2).

Lombard, Peter. *Sententiarum Libri Quatuor*. Paris: Louis Vives, Libraire-Editeur, 1892.

Lyndwood, William. *Provinciale*. 1432. Oxford 1679; reprint Farnborough, 1968.

Mandeville, John. *Mandeville's Travels, from MS. Cotton Titus C.xvi, I*. Edited by P. Hamel. EETS os 153. London: Oxford University Press, 1919.

Middle English Dictionary. Ann Arbor: University of Michigan Press. Last updated 2013. http://quod.lib.umich.edu/m/med/.

Paul of Hungary. *De Confessione*. Bibliotheca Casinensis. Vol. 4, 191–215. Monte Cassino, 1880.

Peter Comestor. "Sermo X. In capite jejunii vel in die cinerum." In *Patrologia Latina*, vol. 198, cols 1749A–52B. Accessed online at http://pld.chadwyck.com.The online version is based on *Patrologia Latina*, ed. J.P. Migne. Paris, 1844–65.

Piers Plowman: Concordance, Will's Visions of Piers Plowman, Do-Well, Do-Better and Do-Best. Edited by Joseph S. Wittig. London and New York: Athlone Press, 2001.

Raymond of Peñafort. *Summa de iure canonico; Summa de paenitentia; Summa de matrimonio*. Edited by Xaviero Ochoa Sanz and Aloisio Diez. 3 vols. Rome: Commentarium pro religiosi, 1975–8.

– *Summa sancti Raymundi de Peniafort Barcinonensis, ordinis praedicatorum, de poenitentia, et matrimonio cum glossis Ioannis de Friburgo*. Rome: Giovanni Tallini, 1603; reprint Farnborough, 1967.

Robert Courçon. *De Usura*. Edited by Georges Lefèvre. Lille: Au siège de l'Université, 1902.

– *Summa de paenitentia*. Edited by V.L. Kennedy. *Mediaeval Studies* 7 (1945): 291–336.

Robert Grosseteste. *Templum dei*. Edited by Joseph Goering and F.A.C. Mantello. Toronto: Pontifical Institute of Mediaeval Studies, 1984.

– [falsely attributed.] *Tractatus de Grammatica*. Edited by Karl Reichl. Munich: Verlag Ferdinand Schöningh, 1976.

Rolle, Richard. *Judica Me Deus*. Edited by J.P. Daly. Salzburg: Institut für Anglistik und Amerikanistik Universität Salzburg, 1984.

Shelley, Percy Bysshe. "A Defence of Poetry." In *English Essays: Sidney to Macaulay*. Vol. XXVII. The Harvard Classics. New York: P.F. Collier & Son, 1909–14.

Simon of Tournai. *Les Disputationes de Simon* de *Tournai*. Edited by Joseph Warichez. Spicilegium Sacrum Lovaniense, Études et Documents 12. Louvain: 1932.

"Statutes of Exeter II" and "Statutes of Salisbury I." In *Councils & Synods, with Other Documents Relating to the English Church*. Vol. 2, *A.D. 1205–1313*, edited by F.M. Powicke and C.R. Cheney. Oxford: Oxford University Press, 1964.

Summa "cum ad sacerdotem." In "*Summa penitentie fratrum praedicatorum*: A Thirteenth-Century Confessional Formulary," edited by Joseph Goering and P.J. Payer. *Mediaeval Studies* 55 (1993): 1–50.

Testamenta Eboracensia: A Selection of Wills from the Registry of York (1300–1551). Edited by James Raine Sr., James Raine Jr., and John W. Clay. 6 vols. Surtees Society. London: J.B. Nichols and Son, 1836–1902.

Ulrich of Strasbourg. *Summa de summo bono*. Erlangen; Universitätsbibliothek MS 530, II.

William of Pagula. *Pars Oculi*. In *Judica Me Deus*, by Richard Rolle, edited by J.P. Daly. Salzburg: Institut fuer Anglistik und Amerikanistik Universitaet Salzburg, 1984.

William of Rennes. *Glossa*. In *Summa sancti Raymundi de Peniafort Barcinonensis, ordinis praedicatorum, de poenitentia, et matrimonio cum glossis Ioannis de Friburgo*. Rome: Giovanni Tallini, 1603; reprint Farnborough, 1967.

Wyclif, John. *The English Works of Wyclif Hitherto Unprinted*. Edited by F.D. Matthew. EETS os 74. London: Kegan Paul, Trench, Trübner, 1880.

Secondary Sources

Adams, Robert, and Thorlac Turville-Petre. "The London Book-Trade and the Lost History of *Piers Plowman*." *RES* 65 (2014): 219–35.

Aers, David. *Beyond Reformation? An Essay on William Langland's Piers Plowman and the End of Constantinian Christianity*. Notre Dame, IN: University of Notre Dame Press, 2015.
– *Faith, Ethics and Church: Writing in England, 1360–1409*. New York: D.S. Brewer, 2000.
– *Salvation and Sin: Augustine, Langland, and Fourteenth-Century Theology*. Notre Dame, IN: University of Notre Dame Press, 2009.
– *Sanctifying Signs: Making Christian Tradition in Late Medieval England*. Notre Dame, IN: University of Notre Dame Press, 2004.
Alford, John A. *Piers Plowman: A Glossary of Legal Diction*. Cambridge: D.S. Brewer, 1988.
– "Haukyn's Coat: Some Observations on *Piers Plowman* B XIV. 22–7." *Medium Aevum* 43 (1974): 133–8.
– "Langland's Learning." *The Yearbook of Langland Studies* 9 (1995): 1–17.
– "Literature and Law in Medieval England." *PMLA* 92 (1977): 941–51.
– "More Unidentified Quotations in *Piers Plowman*." *Modern Philology* 81 (1983–4): 278–85.
– *Piers Plowman: A Guide to the Quotations*. Medieval & Renaissance Texts & Studies 77. Binghamton, NY: Center for Medieval and Early Renaissance Studies, 1992.
– "Some Unidentified Quotations in *Piers Plowman*." *Modern Philology* 72 (1974–5): 390–9.
Amassian, Margaret, and James Sadowsky. "MEDE and MERCEDE: A Study of the Grammatical Metaphor in *Piers Plowman* C: IV 335–409." *Neuphilologische Mitteilungen* 72 (1971): 457–76.
Austin, Greta. *Shaping Church Law around the Year 1000: The Decretum of Burchard of Worms*. Farnham, Surrey: Ashgate, 2009.
Bak, János. "Symbolik und Kommunikation im Mittelalter. Ein *Rohbericht*." In *Kommunikation und Alltag in Spätmittelalter und früher Neuzeit*, edited by Helmut Hundsbichler, 39–46. Vienna: Verlag der Österreichischen Akademie der Wissenschaften, 1992.
Baker, Denise. *Julian of Norwich's "Showings": From Vision to Book*. Princeton, NJ: Princeton University Press, 1994.
Baldwin, Anna. *A Guidebook to Piers Plowman*. Basingstoke and New York: Palgrave Macmillan, 2007.
Baldwin, John. *Masters, Princes, and Merchants: The Social Views of Peter the Chanter and His Circle*. Princeton, NJ: Princeton University Press, 1970.
Barney, Stephen A. *Allegories of History, Allegories of Love*. Hamden, CT: Archon, 1979.
– *The Penn Commentary on Piers Plowman, V: C Passus 20–22; B Passus 18–20*. Philadelphia: University of Pennsylvania Press, 2006.

– "The Ploughshare of the Tongue: The Progress of a Symbol from the Bible to *Piers Plowman*." *Mediaeval Studies* 35 (1973): 261–93.

– "Visible Allegory: The *Distinctiones Abel* of Peter the Chanter." In *Allegory, Myth, and Symbol*, edited by Morton W. Bloomfield, 87–107. Cambridge, MA: Harvard University Press, 1981.

Barr, Helen. "Major Episodes and Moments in *Piers Plowman* B." In *The Cambridge Companion to Piers Plowman*, edited by Andrew Cole and Andrew Galloway, 15–32. Cambridge: Cambridge University Press, 2014.

– "*Piers Plowman* and Poetic Tradition." *Yearbook of Langland Studies* 9 (1995): 39–56.

– *Signes and Sothe: Language in the Piers Plowman Tradition*. Piers Plowman Studies 10. Cambridge: D.S. Brewer, 1994.

– "Wycliffite Representations of the Third Estate." In *Lollards and Their Influence in Late Medieval England*, edited by Fiona Somerset, Jill C. Havens, and Derrick G. Pitard, 197–216. Woodbridge: Boydell, 2003.

Bedos-Rezak, Brigitte Miriam. "Medieval Identity: A Sign and a Concept." *American Historical Review* 105 (2000): 1489–1533.

Bennett, J.A.W., ed. *Piers Plowman: The Prologue and Passus I–VII of the B Text as Found in Bodleian MS. Laud Misc. 581*. Oxford: Clarendon Press, 1972.

Benson, C. David. "Another Fine Manuscript Mess: Authors, Editors and Readers of *Piers Plowman*." In *New Directions in Later Medieval Manuscript Studies: Essays from the 1998 Harvard Conference*, edited by Derek Pearsall, 15–28. Woodbridge: York Medieval Press, in association with Boydell, 2000.

Bergfeld, Christoph. "Zur Jurisprudenz des *forum internum*." *Ius Commune* 16 (1989): 133–47.

Bhabha, Homi, ed. *Nation and Narration*. London: Routledge, 1990.

Biller, Peter. "Confession in the Middle Ages: Introduction." In *Handling Sin: Confession in the Middle Ages*, edited by Peter Biller and A.J. Minnis, 3–33. York Studies in Medieval Theology 2. York: York Medieval Press, 1998.

Blanco, Arturo. "Prassi sacramentale della riconciliazione ed uso del confessionale (I)." *Annales Theologici* 11 (1997): 3–66.

Bloomfield, Morton W. *Piers Plowman as a Fourteenth-Century Apocalypse*. New Brunswick, NJ: Rutgers University Press, 1962.

Bossy, John. "The Social History of Confession in the Age of the Reformation." *Transactions of the Royal Historical Society*, 5th ser. 25 (1975): 21–38.

Boyle, Leonard E. "The 'Oculus Sacerdotis' and Some Other Works of William of Pagula: The Alexander Prize Essay." *Transactions of the Royal Historical Society*, vol. 5 (1955): 81–110.

– *Pastoral Care, Clerical Education and Canon Law, 1200–1400*. London: Variorum, 1981.

– "A Study of the Works Attributed to William of Pagula: With Special Reference to the *Oculus sacerdotis* and *Summa summarum*." PhD diss., Oxford University, 1956.

– "The *Summa* for Confessors as a Genre, and Its Religious Intent." In *The Pursuit of Holiness in Late Medieval and Renaissance Religion*, edited by Charles Trinkaus with Heiko A. Oberman, 126–30. Leiden: Brill, 1974.

– "*Summae Confessorum*." In *Les genres littéraires dans les sources théologiques et philosophiques médiévales: Définition, critique et exploitation*, 227–37. Louvain-la-Neuve: Institut d'Études Médiévales de l'Université catholique de Louvain, 1982.

Brasington, Bruce C. *Ways of Mercy: The Prologue of Ivo of Chartres Edition and Analysis*. Muenster, Hamburg, and London: LIT Verlag, 2004.

Braswell, Mary Flowers. *Chaucer's "Legal Fiction": Reading the Records*. Madison, NJ: Fairleigh Dickinson University Press; London: Associated University Presses, 2001.

– *The Medieval Sinner: Characterization and Confession in the Literature of the Middle Ages*. Rutherford, NJ: Fairleigh Dickinson University Press; London: Associated University Presses, 1983.

Britnell, R.H. *The Closing of the Middle Ages? 1471–1529*. Oxford: Blackwell, 1997.

– "Forstall, Forestalling and the Statute of Forestallers." *English Historical Review* 102 (1987): 89–102.

– "Price-Setting in English Borough Markets, 1349–1500." *Canadian Journal of History* 31 (1996): 1–15.

Brundage, James. *Medieval Canon Law*. London: Longman, 1995.

– "The Rise of the Professional Jurist in the Thirteenth Century." *Syracuse Journal of International Law and Commerce* 20 (1994): 185–90.

– "The Teaching and Study of Canon Law in the Law Schools." In *The History of Medieval Canon Law in the Classical Period, 1140–1234: From Gratian to the Decretals of Pope Gregory IX*, edited by Wilfried Hartmann and Kenneth Pennington, 98–120. Washington DC: Catholic University of America Press, 2008.

Burden, John. "Between Crime and Sin: Episcopal Justice between Burchard and Gratian." Diss. in progress at Yale University, 2018.

Burrow, John A. "The Action of Langland's Second Vision." In *Essays on Medieval Literature*, 79–101. Oxford: Clarendon Press, 1984.

Calabrese, Michael. "Prostitutes in the C Text of *Piers Plowman*." *Journal of English and Germanic Philology* 105 (2006): 275–311.

Canning, Joseph. *Ideas of Power in the Late Middle Ages*. Cambridge: Cambridge University Press, 2011.

Cannon, Christopher. "From Literacy to Literature: Elementary Learning and the Middle English Poet." *PMLA* 129 (2014): 349–64.

– "Langland's *Ars Grammatica*." *The Yearbook of Langland Studies* 22 (2008): 1–25.

Capobianco, C. "De ambitu fori interni in iure ante Codicem." *Apollinaris* 8 (1935): 591–605; *Apollinaris* 9 (1936): 364–74.

Cargill, Oscar. "The Langland Myth." *PMLA* 50 (1935): 36–56.

Carlson, Paula J. "Lady Meed and God's Meed: The Grammar of 'Piers Plowman' B 3 and C 4." *Traditio* 46 (1991): 291–311.

Ceccarelli, Giovanni. "Risky Business: Theological and Canonical Thought on Insurance from the Thirteenth to the Seventeenth Century." *Journal of Medieval and Early Modern Studies* 31 (2001): 607–58.

Chambers, R.W. "The Authorship of 'Piers Plowman.'" *The Modern Language Review* 5 (1910): 1–32.

Chandler, Peleg W. "Recent French Works on Insurance." In *The Law Reporter*. Vol. 8., 49–66. Boston, 1846.

Clanchy, M.T. *From Memory to Written Record: England 1066–1307*. Cambridge, MA: Harvard University Press, 1979.

– "Introduction." In *New Approaches to Medieval Communication*, edited by Marco Mostert, 3–13. Turnhout, Belgium: Brepols, 1999.

Clopper, Lawrence M. *"Songes of Rechelesnesse": Langland and the Franciscans*. Ann Arbor, MI: University of Michigan Press, 1997.

Cole, Andrew. *The Birth of Theory*. Chicago: University of Chicago Press, 2014.

– *Literature and Heresy in the Age of Chaucer*. Cambridge: Cambridge University Press, 2008.

– "William Langland and the Invention of Lollardy." In *Lollards and Their Influence in Late Medieval England*, edited by Fiona Somerset, Jill C. Havens, and Derrick Pitard, 37–58. Woodbridge: Boydell, 2003.

Cole, Andrew, and Andrew Galloway, eds. *Cambridge Companion to Piers Plowman*. Cambridge: Cambridge University Press, 2014.

Cormack, Bradin. *A Power to Do Justice: Jurisdiction, English Literature, and the Rise of Common Law, 1509–1625*. Chicago: University of Chicago Press, 2008.

– Cormack, Bradin, Martha C. Nussbaum, and Richard Strier, eds. *Shakespeare and the Law: A Conversation among Disciplines and Professions*. Chicago: University of Chicago Press, 2013.

Costa, Pietro. *Iurisdictio: Semantica del potere politico nel pubblicistica medieval (1100–1433)*. Milan: Giuffrè, 2002.

Cowley, Robert, ed. *What If: The World's Foremost Military Historians Imagine What Might Have Been*. New York: Berkley, 2000.

Craun, Edwin D. "Ȝe, by Peter and by Poul! Lewte and the Practice of Fraternal Correction." *The Yearbook of Langland Studies* 15 (2001): 15–34.

Davies, Rees. "The Life, Travels, and Library of an Early Reader of *Piers Plowman*." *The Yearbook of Langland Studies* 13 (1999): 49–64.

Davis, Bryan. "A Response to Steiner's 'Langland's Documents.'" *The Yearbook of Langland Studies* 14 (2000): 108–9.

Davlin, Mary Clemente. "Chaucer and Langland as Religious Writers." In *William Langland's Piers Plowman: A Book of Essays*, ed. Kathleen Hewett-Smith, 119–44. New York: Routledge, 2001.

Day, Mabel. "The Revisions of *Piers Plowman*." *Modern Language Review* 23 (1928): 1–27.

De Man, Paul. "The Rhetoric of Temporality." In *Blindness and Insight: Essays in the Rhetoric of Contemporary Criticism*, 187–228. Minneapolis, MN: University of Minnesota Press, 1983.

Denery II, Dallas G. *Seeing and Being Seen in the Later Medieval World: Optics, Theology and Religious Life*. Cambridge: Cambridge University Press, 2005.

Derrida, Jacques. *Of Grammatology*. Translated and edited by Gayatri Chakravorty Spivak. Baltimore, MD: Johns Hopkins University Press, 1976.

Derrida, Jacques, and F.C.T. Moore. "White Mythology: Metaphor in the Text of Philosophy." *New Literary History* 6 (1974): 5–74.

Dijk, Conrad van. "Giving Each His Due: Langland, Gower and the Question of Equity." *The Journal of English and Germanic Philology* 108 (2009): 310–35.

– *John Gower and the Limits of the Law*. Publications of the John Gower Society 8. Cambridge, England; Rochester, NY: D.S. Brewer, 2013.

– "'Nede hath no law'": The State of Exception in Gower and Langland." *Accessus: A Journal of Premodern Literature and New Media* 2.2 (2015): 24–44.

Donaldson, E. Talbot. *Piers Plowman: The C-text and Its Poet*. Yale Studies in English 113. New Haven, CT: Yale University Press, 1949.

Eichbauer, Melodie H. "Gratian's *Decretum* and the Changing Historiographical Landscape." *History Compass* 11 (2013): 1111–25.

Eliot, T.S. *The Sacred Wood: Essays on Poetry and Criticism*. 7th ed. London: Methuen, 1960.

Epstein, Richard A. "Beyond Textualism: Why Originalist Theory Must Apply General Principles of Interpretation to Constitutional Law." *Harvard Journal of Law and Public Policy* 37 (2015): 705–20.

Fischer, Olga. "Syntax." In *The Cambridge History of the English Language*. Vol. 2, *1066–1476*, edited by Norman Blake, 207–408. Cambridge: Cambridge University Press, 1992.

Fisher, Matthew. *Scribal Authorship and the Writing of History in Medieval England*. Columbus: Ohio State University Press, 2012.

Fitzgerald, Christina M., and John T. Sebastian, eds. *The Broadview Anthology of Medieval Drama*. Peterborough, Ont.; Buffalo, NY: Broadview Press, 2012.

Fletcher, Alan J. "The Essential (Ephemeral) William Langland: Textual Revision as Ethical Process in *Piers Plowman*." *The Yearbook of Langland Studies*, 15 (2001): 61–98.

Frank, Robert. *Piers Plowman and the Scheme of Salvation: An Interpretation of Dowel, Dobet, and Dobest*. Yale Studies in English 136. New Haven, CT: Yale University Press, 1957.

Freedman, Paul. *Images of the Medieval Peasant*. Stanford, CA: Stanford University Press, 1999.

Fulk, R.D. *An Introduction to Middle English: Grammar: Texts*. Peterborough, ON: Broadview Press, 2012.

Galloway, Andrew. "The Account Book and the Treasure: Gilbert Maghfeld's Textual Economy and the Politics of Mercantile Accounting in Ricardian Literature." *Studies in the Age of Chaucer* 33 (2011): 65–124.

– "Non-literary Commentary and Its Literary Profits: The Road to Accounting-ville." *The Yearbook of Langland Studies* 25 (2011): 9–23.

– *The Penn Commentary on "Piers Plowman"* I: *C Prologue – Passus 4; B Prologue – Passus 4; A Prologue – Passus 4*. Philadelphia: University of Pennsylvania Press, 2006.

– "*Piers Plowman* and the Subject of the Law." *The Yearbook of Langland Studies* 15 (2001): 117–40.

Gellrich, Jesse. "Orality, Literacy, and Crisis in the Later Middle Ages." *Philological Quarterly* 67 (1988): 461–73.

Göller, Emil. *Die paepstliche Poenitentiarie von ihrem Ursprung bis zu ihrer Umgestaltung unter Pius V*. 4 vols. Rome: Loescher, 1907–11.

Goering, Joseph. "The Internal Forum and the Literature of Penance and Confession." In *The History of Medieval Canon Law in the Classical Period, 1140–1234: From Gratian to the Decretals of Pope Gregory IX*, edited by Wilfried Hartmann and Kenneth Pennington, 379–428. Washington DC: Catholic University of America Press, 2008.

– "The Internal Forum and the Literature of Penance and Confession." *Traditio* 59 (2004): 175–227.

– "The Scholastic Turn (1100–1500): Penitential Theology and Law in the Schools." In *A New History of Penance*, edited by Abigail Firey, 219–37. Leiden: Brill, 2008.

– "The Summa of Master Serlo and Thirteenth-Century Penitential Literature." *Mediaeval Studies* 40 (1978): 290–311.

– *William de Montibus (c. 1140–1213): The Schools and the Literature of Pastoral Care*. Toronto: Pontifical Institute of Mediaeval Studies, 1992.

Goering, Joseph, and Pierre J. Payer. "The *Summa penitentie fratrum predicatorum*: A Thirteenth-Century Confessional Formulary." *Mediaeval Studies* 55 (1993): 1–50.

Goetz, Werner. "Das Ringen um den gerechten Preis in Spätmittelalter und Reformationszeit." In *Beiträge zur Diskussion um das pretium iustum*. Erlanger Forschungen, Reihe A, Bd. 29, 21–32. Erlangen: Universitätsbund Erlangen-Nürnberg e.V., 1982.

Goldstein, R. James. "Ve Vobis qui ridetis (Lk. 6.25): Laughter in *Piers Plowman*." *The Yearbook of Langland Studies* 29 (2015): 25–60.

Gradon, Pamela. "Langland and the Ideology of Dissent." *Proceedings of the British Academy* 66 (1980): 179–205.

Gray, Nicholas. "Langland's Quotations from the Penitential Tradition." *Modern Philology* 84 (1986): 53–60.

– "A Study of *Piers Plowman* in Relation to the Medieval Penitential Tradition." PhD diss., University of Cambridge, 1984.

Green, Richard Firth. *A Crisis of Truth: Literature and Law in Ricardian England*. Philadelphia: University of Pennsylvania Press, 1999.

– "Medieval Literature and Law." In *The Cambridge History of Medieval English Literature*, edited by David Wallace, 407–31. Cambridge: Cambridge University Press, 1999.

Grossi, Paolo. *L'Ordine Giuridico Medievale*. Bari and Rome: Laterza, 1995

Gundacker, Jay. "Absolutions and Acts of Disobedience: Excommunication and Society in Fourteenth-Century Armagh." *Traditio* 64 (2009): 183–212.

Hanna, Ralph. "On the Versions of *Piers Plowman*." In *Pursuing History: Middle English Manuscripts and Their Texts*, 203–43. Stanford: Stanford University Press, 1996.

– "The Versions and Revisions of *Piers Plowman*." In *The Cambridge Companion to Piers Plowman*, edited by Andrew Cole and Andrew Galloway, 33–49. Cambridge: Cambridge University Press, 2014.

Haren, Michael. "Friars as Confessors: The Canonistic Background to the Fourteenth-Century Controversy." *Peritia* 3 (1984): 503–16.

– "Social Ideas in the Pastoral Literature of Fourteenth-Century England." In *Religious Belief and Ecclesiastical Careers in Late Medieval England: Proceedings of the Conference Held at Strawberry Hill, Easter 1989*, edited by Christopher Harper-Bill, 43–59. Woodbridge: Boydell and Brewer, 1991.

– "Confession, Social Ethics and Social Discipline in the *Memoriale Presbiterorum*," in *Handling Sin: Confession in the Middle Ages*. Edited by Peter Biller and A.J. Minnis. Woodbridge: York Medieval Press, 1998, 109–22.

– "The Interrogatories for Officials, Lawyers and Secular Estates of the *Memoriale Presbiterorum*," in *Handling Sin: Confession in the Middle Ages*. Edited by Peter Biller and A.J. Minnis. Woodbridge: York Medieval Press, 1998, 123–63.

– *Sin and Society in Fourteenth-Century England*. Oxford: Oxford University Press, 2000.

Harwood, Britton. *Piers Plowman and the Problem of Belief.* Toronto: University of Toronto Press, 1992.

Haskins, Charles Homer. *The Renaissance of the Twelfth Century.* Cambridge, MA: Harvard University Press, 1927.

Hazard, Harry W., and Norman P. Zacour, eds. *The Impact of the Crusades on the Near East.* Vol. 5 of *A History of the Crusades*, edited by Kenneth M. Setton. Madison, WI; University of Wisconsin Press, 1989.

Helmholz, R.H. "Notable Ecclesiastical Lawyers: X: John de Burgh (fl 1370–1398)." *Ecclesiastical Law Journal* 18 (2016): 67–72.

– *Oxford History of the Laws of England: The Canon Law and Ecclesiastical Jurisdiction from 597 to the 1640s.* Oxford: Oxford University Press, 2004.

– *The Spirit of Classical Canon Law.* Athens, GA: University of Georgia Press, 1996.

Hewett-Smith, Kathleen. "'Nede ne hath no lawe': Poverty and the Destabilization of Allegory in the Final Visions of *Piers Plowman.*" In *William Langland's 'Piers Plowman': A Book of Essays*, edited by Kathleen Hewett-Smith, 233–53. New York: Routledge, 2001.

Hoedl, L. "Die sacramentale Busse und ihre kirchliche Ordnung im beginnenden mittelalterlichen Streit um die Bussvollmacht der Ordenspriester." *Franziskanische Studien* 55 (1973): 330–74.

Holsinger, Bruce. "Vernacular Legality: The English Jurisdictions of *The Owl and the Nightingale.*" In *The Letter of the Law: Legal Practice and Literary Production in Medieval England*, edited by Emily Steiner and Candace Barrington, 154–84. Ithaca, NY: Cornell University Press, 2002.

Hort, Greta. *Piers Plowman and Contemporary Religious Thought.* London: London Society for Promoting Christian Knowledge, 1938.

Hudson, Anne. *Lollards and Their Books.* London: Hambledon, 1985.

– *The Premature Reformation: Wycliffite Texts and Lollard History.* Oxford: Oxford University Press, 1988.

Jasanoff, Sheila. "The Idiom of Co-Production." In *States of Knowledge: The Co-Production of Science and the Social Order*, edited by Sheila Jasanoff, 1–12. London: Routledge, 2004.

Jones, Mike Rodman. *Radical Pastoral, 1381–1594: Appropriation and the Writing of Religious Controversy.* Farnham, Surrey: Ashgate, 2011.

Jucker, Andreas H. "Between Hypotaxis and Parataxis: Clauses of Reason in *Ancrene Wisse.*" In *Historical English Syntax*, edited by Dieter Kastovsky, 203–20. Berlin: Mouton de Gruyter, 1991.

Kay, Sarah. *Parrots and Nightingales: Troubadour Quotations and the Development of European Poetry.* Philadelphia: University of Pennsylvania Press, 2013.

Kaye, Joel. *A History of Balance, 1250–1375: The Emergence of a New Model of Equilibrium and Its Impact on Thought*. Cambridge: Cambridge University Press, 2014.

Kean, P.M. "Love, Lawe and *Lewte* in *Piers Plowman*." *Review of English Studies* 15 (1964): 241–61.

Keller, Eve. *Generating Bodies and Gendered Selves: The Rhetoric of Reproduction in Early Modern England*. Seattle: University of Washington Press, 2007.

Kelly, Henry Ansgar. "Penitential Theology and Law at the Turn of the Fifteenth Century." In *A New History of Penance*, edited by Abigail Firey, 239–317. Leiden and Boston: Brill, 2008.

Kennedy, Kathleen E. "Retaining a Court of Chancery in *Piers Plowman*." *The Yearbook of Langland Studies* 17 (2003): 175–89.

Kennedy, V.L. "Robert Courçon on Penance." *Mediaeval Studies* 7 (1945): 291–336.

Kerby-Fulton, Kathryn. "*Piers Plowman*." In *The Cambridge History of Medieval English Literature*, edited by David Wallace, 513–38. Cambridge: Cambridge University Press, 1999.

– "Professional Readers of Langland at Home and Abroad: New Directions in the Political and Bureaucratic Codicology of *Piers Plowman*." In *New Directions in Later Medieval Manuscript Studies: Essays from the 1998 Harvard Conference*, edited by Derek Pearsall, 103–29. York: York Medieval Press, 2000.

– *Reformist Apocalypticism and Piers Plowman*. Cambridge: Cambridge University Press, 1990.

Kerby-Fulton, Kathryn, and Denise Louise Despres. *Iconography and the Professional Reader*. Minneapolis: University of Minnesota Press, 1999.

Kerff, Franz. "Libri Paenitentiales und kirchliche Strafgerichtsbarkeit bis zum Decretum Gratiani: Ein Diskussionsvorschlag." *Zeitschrift der Savigny-Stiftung für Rechtsgeschichte* 75 (1989): 23–57.

Knott, Thomas A. "Observations on the Authorship of 'Piers the Plowman' – (Concluded)." *Modern Philology* 15 (1917): 23–41.

Kohnen, Thomas. "'Connective profiles' in the History of English Texts." In *Connectives in the History of English*, edited by Ursula Lenker and Anneli Meurman-Solin, 289–308. Amsterdam: John Benjamins, 2007.

Körntgen, K. *Studien zu den Quellen der frühmittelalterlichen Bußbücher, Quellen und Forschungen zum Recht im Mittelalter* 7. Sigmaringen: Jan Thorbecke Verlag, 1993.

Kottje, Raymund. "'Buße oder Strafe?' Zur 'Iustitia' in den 'Libri Paenitentiales.'" In *La giustizia nell'alto medioevo (secoli V–VIII)* I, *Settimane di studio* 42, 443–74. Spoleto: Centro italiano di studi sull'alto Medioevo, 1996.

Kuttner, Stephan. *Harmony from Dissonance: An Interpretation of Medieval Canon Law*. Latrobe, PA: Archabbey Press, 1960.

– "The Revival of Jurisprudence." In *Renaissance and Renewal in the Twelfth Century*, edited by Robert L. Benson and Giles Constable with Carol D. Lanham, 299–323. University of Toronto Press, in association with the Medieval Academy of America, 1991.

Kuttner, Stephan, and Beryl Smalley. "The 'Glossa Ordinaria' to the Gregorian Decretals." *English Historical Review* 60 (1945): 97–105.

Ladd, Roger A. *Antimercantilism in Late Medieval Literature*. NY: Palgrave Macmillan, 2010.

Landau, Peter. "Die Bedeutung des kanonischen Rechts für die Entwicklung einheitlicher Rechtsprinzipien." In *Die Bedeutung des kanonischen Rechts für die Entwicklung einheitlicher Rechtsprinzipien*, edited by Heinrich Scholler, 23–47. Baden-Baden: Nomos, 1996.

Langer, Ullrich, "Invention." In *The Cambridge History of Literary Criticism*, edited Glyn P. Norton, vol. 3: 136–44. Cambridge: Cambridge University Press, 1999.

Larson, Atria A. *Master of Penance: Gratian and the Development of Penitential Thought and Law in the Twelfth Century*. Washington, DC: Catholic University of America Press, 2014.

– "The Reception of Gratian's *Tractatus de penitentia* and the Relationship between Canon Law and Theology in the Second Half of the Twelfth Century." *Journal of Religious History* 37 (2013): 457–73.

Lawler, Traugott. "Harlots' Holiness: The System of Absolution for Miswinning in the C version of *Piers Plowman*." *The Yearbook of Langland Studies* 20 (2006): 141–89.

– "Langland Versificator." *The Yearbook of Langland Studies* 25 (2011): 37–76.

– "The Pardon Formula in *Piers Plowman*: Its Ubiquity, Its Binary Shape, Its Silent Middle Term." *The Yearbook of Langland Studies* 14 (2000): 117–52.

– "The Secular Clergy in Piers Plowman." *The Yearbook of Langland Studies* 16 (2002): 85–129.

Lawton, David. "The Subject of Piers Plowman." *The Yearbook of Langland Studies* 1 (1987): 1–30.

Le Goff, Jacques. *The Birth of Purgatory*. Chicago: University of Chicago Press, 1986.

Little, Katherine. "Transforming Work: Protestantism and the *Piers Plowman* Tradition." *Journal of Medieval and Early Modern Studies* 40 (2010): 497–526.

Mann, Jill. "Some Observations on 'Structural Annotation.'" *The Yearbook of Langland Studies* 25 (2011): 1–8.

McLaughlin, T.P. "The Teaching of the Canonists on Usury (XII, XIII, and XIV Centuries)." *Mediaeval Studies* 1 (1939): 81–147.

– "The Teaching of the Canonists on Usury (XII, XIII, and XIV Centuries)." *Mediaeval Studies* 2 (1940): 1–22.

Meens, Rob. "The Historiography of Early Medieval Penance." In *The New History of Penance*, edited by Abigail Firey, 73–95. Leiden: Brill, 2008.

– *Penance in Medieval Europe, 600–1200*. Cambridge: Cambridge University Press, 2014.

Mezey, Naomi. "Out of the Ordinary: Law, Power, Culture and the Commonplace." *Law and Social Inquiry* 26 (2001): 145–67.

Michaud-Quantin, Pierre. *Sommes de casuistique et manuels de confession au Moyen Âge (XII–XVI siècles)*. Louvain: Éditions Nauwelaerts, 1962.

Middleton, Anne. "Acts of Vagrancy: The C Version 'Autobiography' and the Statute of 1388." In *Written Work: Langland, Labor, and Authorship*, edited by Steven Justice and Katheryn Kerby-Fulton, 208–317. Philadelphia: University of Pennsylvania Press, 1997.

– "The Audience and Public of *Piers Plowman*." In *Middle English Alliterative Poetry and Its Literary Background: Seven Essays*, edited by David Lawton, 101–23. Woodbridge, Suffolk: D.S. Brewer, 1982.

– "Two Infinites: Grammatical Metaphor in *Piers Plowman*." *ELH* 39 (1972): 169–88.

Minnis, Alastair. "'Piers' Protean Pardon: The Letter and Spirit of Langland's Theology of Indulgences." In *Studies in Late Medieval and Early Renaissance Texts in Honour of John Scattergood*, edited by Anne Marie D'Arcy and Alan J. Fletcher, 218–40. Dublin: Four Courts, 2005.

– *Translations of Authority in Medieval English Literature: Valuing the Vernacular*. Cambridge: Cambridge University Press, 2009.

Morozzo della Rocca, Raimondo, and Attilio Lombardio. *Documenti del commercio veneziano nei secoli XI–XIII*. Rome: Istituto italiano per il Medio Evo, 1940.

Morris, Richard, ed. *An Old English Miscellany*. EETS os 49. London: Trübner, 1872.

Mörsdorf, K. "Der Rechtscharakter der iurisdictio fori interni." *Münchener Theologische Zeitschrift* 8 (1957): 161–73.

Müller, Wolfgang P. "Pardons for Sexual Misconduct: Ordinary Routine and Papal Intervention in the Later Middle Ages." In *The Roman Curia, the Apostolic Penitentiary and the Partes in the Later Middle Ages*, edited by Kirsi Salonen and Christian Krötzl, 171–81. Acta Instituti Romani Finlandiae 28. Rome: Instituti Romanum Finlandiae, 2003.

– "The Price of Papal Pardon: Päpste, Pilger, Pönitentiarie." In *Festschrift für Ludwig Schmugge zum 65. Geburtstag*, edited by Andreas Meyer, Constanze Rendtel, and Maria Elisabeth Wittmer-Butsch, 457–81. Tübingen: Max Niemeyer Verlag, 2004.

Müller, Wolfgang P., and Mary E. Sommar, eds. *Medieval Church Law and the Origins of the Western Legal Tradition: A Tribute to Kenneth Pennington*. Washington, DC: Catholic University of America Press, 2006.

Musson, Anthony, ed., *Expectations of the Law in the Middle Ages*. Woodbridge, Suffolk: Boydell, 2001.

Muzzarelli, Maria Giuseppina. *Penitenze nel Medioevo: Uomini e modelli a confronto*. Bologna: Patron, 1994.

Newhauser, Richard. "The Parson's Tale." In *Sources and Analogues of the Canterbury Tales*, edited by Robert M. Correale and Mary Hamel, vol. 1: 529–613. Cambridge: D.S. Brewer, 2002.

Nielson, Jonathan M. *Paths Not Taken: Speculations on American Policy and Diplomatic History, Interests, Ideals, and Power*. Westport, CT: Praeger, 2000.

Nolan, Maura. "The Fortunes of *Piers Plowman* and Its Readers." *The Yearbook of Langland Studies* 20 (2006): 1–41.

Noonan, John T. *The Scholastic Analysis of Usury*. Cambridge, MA: Harvard University Press, 1957.

Novikoff, Alex J. *The Medieval Culture of Disputation: Pedagogy, Practice, and Performance*. Philadelphia: University of Pennsylvania Press, 2013.

O'Grady, Gerald. "*Piers Plowman* and the Medieval Tradition of Penance." PhD diss., University of Wisconsin, 1962.

Padovani, Andrea. "Birth of a Legal Category: Subjective Rights." *Divus Thomas* 116 (2013): 37–53.

Pantin, William A. *The English Church in the Fourteenth Century*. Cambridge: Cambridge University Press, 1955.

Payer, Pierre J. "The Humanism of the Penitentials and the Continuity of the Penitential Tradition." *Mediaeval Studies* 46 (1984): 340–54.

Pearsall, Derek. "Langland and Lollardy: From B to C." *The Yearbook of Langland Studies* 17 (2003): 7–23.

– *Piers Plowman: A New Annotated Edition of the C Text*. Exeter: University of Exeter Press, 2008.

– *Piers Plowman by William Langland: An Edition of the C-Text*. York Medieval Texts, Second Series. London: E. Arnold, 1978.

Pennington, Kenneth. *The Prince and the Law, 1200–1600: Sovereignty and Rights in the Western Legal Tradition*. Berkeley, CA: University of California Press, 1993.

– Pettitt, Thomas. "Textual to Oral: The Impact of Transmission on Narrative Word-Art" in *Oral History of the Middle Ages: The Spoken Word in Context*, edited by Gerhard Jaritz and Michael Richter. Krems: Medium Aevum Quotidianum, 2001.

Posner, Richard A. Law and Literature. Cambridge, MA: Harvard University Press, 2009.

– *Law and Literature: A Misunderstood Relation*. Cambridge, MA: Harvard University Press, 1988.

Quera, M. "De Contritionismo et Attritionismo in Scholis usque ad Tempus S. Thomae Traditio." Analecta Sacra Tarraconensia 4 (1928): 183–202.

Quick, Anne Wenley. "The Sources of the Quotations of *Piers Plowman*." PhD diss., University of Toronto, 1982.

Ricoeur, Paul. *The Rule of Metaphor: The Creation of Meaning in Language*. Toronto: University of Toronto Press, 1977.

Rusconi, Roberto. "'Confessio generalis.' Opuscoli per la practica penitenziale nei primi cinquanta anni della introduzione della stampa in Italia." In *I Frati Minori tra '400 e '500. Atti del XII Convegno Internazionale, Assisi, 18-19-20 Ottobre 1984*, 189–227. Assisi: Università di Perugia, Centro di studi Francescani 1984.

Said, Edward. *Beginnings: Intention and Method*. New York: Columbia University Press, 1985.

Salonen, Kirsi, and Ludwig Schmugge. *A Sip from the "Well of Grace": Medieval Texts from the Apostolic Penitentiary*. Washington DC: Catholic University of America Press, 2009.

Scanlon, Larry. "Personification and Penance." *The Yearbook of Langland Studies* 21 (2007): 1–29.

Scase, Wendy. *Piers Plowman and the New Anticlericalism*. Cambridge Studies in Medieval Literature 4. Cambridge and New York: Cambridge University Press, 1989.

Schlesinger, Arthur M. *The Cycles of American History*. Boston: Houghton Mifflin, 1986.

Schmidt, A.V.C. "Langland's Visions and Revisions." *The Yearbook of Langland Studies* 14 (2000): 5–27.

Schmitz, Hermann Josef. *Die Bussbücher und die Bussdisciplin der Kirche*. Mainz: F. Kirchheim, 1883.

Seabourne, Gwen. *Royal Regulation of Loans and Sales in Medieval England: Monkish Superstition and Civil Tyranny*. Woodbridge, Suffolk, and Rochester, NY: Boydell, 2003.

Seaton, James. "Law and Literature: Works, Criticism, and Theory." *Yale Journal of Law and the Humanities* 11 (1999): 479–507.

Silano, Giulio. "The *Regulae Iuris* and the Jurists: Reflections in Margin to *Liber Sextus* 5.13." In *Rule Makers and Rule Breakers: Proceedings of a St. Michael's College Symposium, 1–2 October, 2004*, edited by Joseph Goering, Francesco Guardiani, and Giulio Silano, 71–192. New York and Ottawa: Legas, 2006.

Simpson, James. "Edifying the Church." In *The Oxford English Literary History*. Vol. 2, *1350–1547. Reform and Cultural Revolution*, 322–82. Oxford: Oxford University Press, 2002.

– *"Piers Plowman": An Introduction to the B-Text*. 2nd revised ed. Exeter: Exeter University Press, 2007.

– *"Piers Plowman": An Introduction to the B-Text*. London: Longman, 1990.

– "Religious Forms and Institutions in *Piers Plowman*." In *The Cambridge Companion to Piers Plowman*, edited by Andrew Cole and Andrew Galloway. 97–114. Cambridge: Cambridge University Press, 2013.

– "Spirituality and Economics in Passus 1–7 of the B Text." *The Yearbook of Langland Studies* 1 (1987): 83–103.

Skeat, Walter. *The Vision of William Concerning Piers Plowman*, Part IV Section I, "Notes to the Texts A, B, and C." EETS os 67. Millwood, NJ: Kraus Reprint Co., 1987.

Smith, D. Vance. *The Book of the Incipit: Beginnings in the Fourteenth Century*. Minneapolis, MN: University of Minnesota Press, 2001.

– "*Piers Plowman* and the National Noetic of Edward III." In *Imagining a Medieval English Nation*, edited by Kathy Lavezzo, 234–60. Minneapolis, MN: University of Minnesota Press, 2003.

Somerset, Fiona. "'Al þe comonys with o voys atonys': Multilingual Latin and Vernacular Voice in *Piers Plowman*." *The Yearbook of Langland Studies* 19 (2005): 107–36.

– *Clerical Discourse and Lay Audience in Late Medieval England*. Cambridge: Cambridge University Press, 2005.

– "Expanding the Langlandian Canon: Radical Latin and the Stylistics of Reform." *The Yearbook of Langland Studies* 17 (2003): 73–92.

Somerville, Robert, and Bruce C. Brasington, trans. *Prefaces to Canon Law*. New Haven, CT: Yale University Press, 1998.

Spalding, Mary C., ed. *The Middle English Charters of Christ*. Bryn Mawr, PA: Bryn Mawr College, 1914.

Stein, Peter. *Regulae Juris: From Juristic Rules to Legal Maxims*. Edinburgh: Edinburgh University Press, 1966.

Steinberg, Theodore. *Piers Plowman and Prophecy: An Approach to the C-Text*. Garland Studies in Medieval Literature 5. New York: Garland Publishing, 1991.

Steiner, Emily. *Documentary Culture and the Making of Medieval English Literature*. Cambridge: Cambridge University Press, 2003.

– "Langland's Documents." *The Yearbook of Langland Studies* 14 (2000): 95–115.

– "Medieval Documentary Poetics and Langland's Authorial Identity." In *Crossing Boundaries: Issues in Cultural and Individual Identities in The Middle*

Ages and the Renaissance, edited by Sally McKee, 79–105. Arizona Studies in the Middle Ages and the Renaissance 3. Turnhout: Brepols, 1999.

– *Reading Piers Plowman*. Cambridge: Cambridge University Press, 2013.

Stock, Brian. *Listening for the Text: On the Uses of the Past*. Baltimore and London: Johns Hopkins University Press, 1990.

– "Medieval Literacy, Linguistic Theory, and Social Organization." *New Literary History* 16 (1984): 13–29.

Strohm, Paul. "Historicity without Historicism?" *Postmedieval: A Journal of Medieval Cultural Studies* 1 (2010): 380–91.

– *Hochon's Arrow: The Social Imagination of Fourteenth-Century Texts*. Princeton, NJ: Princeton University Press, 1992.

– *Social Chaucer*. Cambridge, MA: Harvard University Press, 1989.

– "Some Generic Distinctions in the *Canterbury Tales*." *Modern Philology* 68 (1971): 321–8.

– "*Storie, Spelle, Geste, Romaunce, Tragedie*: Generic Distinctions in the Middle English Troy Narratives." *Speculum* 46 (1971): 348–59.

– "The Subjunctive Grammar of Utopia." Unpublished plenary lecture delivered at the conference Histories of the Future. Rutgers University, 2010.

– *Theory and the Premodern Text*. Minneapolis, MN: University of Minnesota Press, 2000.

Sutton, Josephine D. "Hitherto Unprinted Manuscripts of the Middle English *Ipotis*." *PMLA* 31 (1916): 114–60.

Swanson, R.N. *Indulgences in Late Medieval England: Passports to Paradise?* Cambridge: Cambridge University Press, 2007.

Szittya, Penn R. *The Antifraternal Tradition in Medieval Literature*. Princeton, NJ: Princeton University Press, 1986.

Tentler, Thomas. *Sin and Confession on the Eve of the Reformation*. Princeton, NJ: Princeton University Press, 1977.

Thomas, Arvind. "Canon Law and Fraternal Subversions of the 'Silent Middle Term' in *Piers Plowman* B and C Texts." *Modern Philology* 110 (2012): 24–48.

– "From Covenantal Symbol to Institutional Sign: The C Revisions in Passus 16 of *Piers Plowman*." *Exemplaria* 23 (2011): 147–70.

– "The Subject of Canon Law: Confessing Covetise in *Piers Plowman* B and C and the *Memoriale presbiterorum*." *The Yearbook of Langland Studies* 24 (2010): 139–68.

Thomas of Chobham. *Thomae de Chobham Summa confessorum*. Edited by F. Broomfield. Analecta Mediaevalia Namurcensia 25. Louvain: Editions Nauwelaerts, 1968.

Trinkaus, Charles, and Heiko A. Oberman, eds. *The Pursuit of Holiness in Late Medieval and Renaissance Religion*. Leiden: Brill, 1974.

Trusen, Winfried. "*Forum internum* und gelehrtes Recht im Spätmittelalter: *Summae confessorum* und Traktate als Wegbereiter der Rezeption." *Zeitschrift der Savigny-Stiftung für Rechtsgeschichte, Kanonische Abteilung* 57 (1971): 83–126.

Visser, F. Th. *An Historical Syntax of the English Language, Part II*. Leiden: Brill, 1972.

Warner, Lawrence. "Impossible *Piers*." *RES* 66 (2015): 223–39.

– *The Lost History of "Piers Plowman": The Earliest Transmission of Langland's Work*. Philadelphia: University of Pennsylvania Press, 2011.

– *The Myth of Piers Plowman: Constructing a Medieval Literary Archive*. Cambridge: Cambridge University Press, 2014.

– "The Ur-B *Piers Plowman* and the Earliest Production of C and B." *The Yearbook of Langland Studies* 16 (2002): 3–39.

Watson, Nicholas. "Censorship and Cultural Change in Late-Medieval England: Vernacular Theology, the Oxford Translation Debate, and Arundel's Constitutions of 1409." *Speculum* 70 (1995): 822–64.

Wei, Ian P. *Intellectual Culture in Medieval Paris: Theologians and the University, c. 1100–1330*. Cambridge: Cambridge University Press, 2012.

Wei, John C. *Gratian the Theologian*. Studies in Medieval and Early Modern Canon Law 13. Washington, DC: Catholic University of America Press, 2016.

Weigand, Rudolf. "The Development of the *Glossa ordinaria* to Gratian's *Decretum*." In *The History of Medieval Canon Law in the Classical Period, 1140–1234: From Gratian to the Decretals of Pope Gregory IX*, edited by Wilfried Hartmann and Kenneth Pennington, 55–97. Washington, DC: Catholic University of America Press, 2008.

– "Versuch einer neuen differenzierten Liste der Paleae und Dubletten im Dekret Gratians." *Bulletin of Medieval Canon Law*, new ser. 23 (1999): 114–28.

Weimar, Peter. "Argumenta Brocardica." In *Zur Renaissance der Rechtswissenschaft im Mittelalter*, 45–80. Goldbach: Keip Verlag, 1997.

White, Hugh. *Nature and Salvation in Piers Plowman*. Cambridge: D.S. Brewer, 1988.

Winroth, Anders. *The Making of Gratian's Decretum*. Cambridge: Cambridge University Press, 2000.

Witte, John, Jr., and Frank S. Alexander, eds. *Christianity and Law: An Introduction*. Cambridge: Cambridge University Press, 2008.

Wogan-Browne, Jocelyn, Nicholas Watson, Andrew Taylor, and Ruth Evans, eds. *The Idea of the Vernacular: An Anthology of Middle English Literary Theory, 1280–1520*. University Park: Pennsylvania State University Press, 1999.

Wood, Diana. "'Lesyng of Tyme': Perceptions of Idleness and Usury in Late Medieval England." In *The Use and Abuse of Time in Christian History*, edited by R.N. Swanson, 107–16. Woodbridge, Suffolk: Boydell Press for the Ecclesiastical History Society, 2002.
– *Medieval Economic Thought*. Cambridge: Cambridge University Press, 2002.
Wood, Sarah. *Conscience and the Composition of Piers Plowman*. Oxford: Oxford University Press, 2012.
– "'Ecce Rex': *Piers Plowman* B.19.1–212 and Its Contexts." *The Yearbook of Langland Studies* 21 (2007): 31–56.
Yeager, Stephen. *From Lawmen to Plowmen: Anglo-Saxon Legal Tradition and the School of Langland*. Toronto: University of Toronto Press, 2014.
Yunck, John A. *The Lineage of Lady Meed: The Development of Mediaeval Venality Satire*. Notre Dame: University of Notre Dame Press, 1963.

Index

www.ingramcontent.com/pod-product-compliance
Lightning Source LLC
LaVergne TN
LVHW090154080826
844660LV00013B/803/J
* 9 7 8 1 4 8 7 5 0 2 4 6 1 *